REMEMBER THE DAYS
HISTORY FOR JUNIOR READERS

BOOK TWO:
MEDIEVAL DAYS

by Rob and Julia Nalle

"Remember the days of old; consider the generations long past. Ask your father and he will tell you; your elders, and they will explain to you."

— *Deuteronomy 32:7*

"I remember the days of long ago; I meditate on all your works and consider what your hands have done. I spread out my hands to you; I thirst for you like a parched land."

— *Psalm 143:5-6*

Copyright ©2016, Rob and Julia Nalle. All rights reserved.
Printed in the USA.

Published in Palmyra, Virginia by BiblioPlan Inc.

Hardback Version ISBN No. 978-1-942405-56-6

Copyright Policy

All of the content in these pages is copyrighted by BiblioPlan Incorporated! Therefore:

Please visit www.biblioplan.net to see how we may best serve your family, homeschool cooperative or Christian school. Or email contactus@biblioplan.net.

Welcome to BiblioPlan!

BiblioPlan is a classical history curriculum that covers World History, U.S. History, Church History, Geography and more, starting at Creation and continuing through modern times. Our program is divided into four years of study.

➤ **Year One, Ancients** covers Ancient and Biblical History from Creation to the Fall of Rome, with World Geography

➤ **Year Two, Medieval** covers World and Church History from the Fall of Rome to the Renaissance, with World Geography

➤ **Year Three, Early Modern** covers U.S., World and Church History from 1600 – 1850, with U.S. Geography

➤ **Year Four, Modern** covers U.S. and World History from 1850 – 2000, with Missionary Highlights and U.S. Geography

Remember the Days is BiblioPlan's four-volume textbook for grades K – 6. Each volume is divided into 34 weeks for a 34-week school year. The easiest way to follow our program is as follows:

1. Cover one chapter each week, spreading the material over three days.

    a. Grades K – 2: Read to your students, feeling free to paraphrase or skip whatever you choose.

    b. Grades 2 – 6: Younger students may need help reading; while older students may read independently. Either way, we recommend reading and discussing alongside your students to help them get the most out of every lesson.

2. Either throughout the week, or at week's end, work on your assignments. All assignments for grades K – 2 come from a supplement called **Cool History for Littles**. History assignments for grades 2 – 6 come from a supplement called **Cool History for Middles**. Geography assignments for grades 2 – 6 come from a supplement called **Hands-On Maps for Middles**. All supplements are sold separately. Use your judgment to decide how much help your students need on any assignment.

Textbooks, Cool Histories and Hands-On Maps are only part of all that BiblioPlan has to offer! Another key resource is the **Family Guide**, which provides outside reading resources to go with each week's lessons. The Family Guide also offers writing assignments, video options and more.
    Besides all these, BiblioPlan also offers:

❖ **Craft Books**: arts, crafts and activities to go with each week's lesson

❖ **Timelines**: flowcharts for students to assemble, filled with cutouts of important historical figures

❖ **Notebooking**: fun projects that help students research and record history and geography

❖ **Coloring Books**: simple sketches from history for younger students to color

To learn more, please visit our website: www.biblioplan.net. Or email: contactus@biblioplan.net.

We dedicate this book to Rob's mother, Sharon Fry Nalle.

The fear of the Lord is the beginning of knowledge,
    but fools despise wisdom and instruction.
Listen, my son, to your father's instruction
    and do not forsake your mother's teaching.
They are a garland to grace your head
    and a chain to adorn your neck.

                                 — Proverbs 1:7-9

Table of Contents

PROLOGUE: What Was the Medieval Era?

The **medieval era**, also called the **Middle Ages**, was a 1,000-year period between the **Fall of Rome** and the **Renaissance**. Medieval times started in the 400s, and lasted until the 1400s.

Historians who study Western Europe divide the medieval era into three shorter parts. The first part was the **Dark Ages**, which lasted from about 400 – 1000. There are two reasons for the name "dark." One is because in the Dark Ages, the bright light of Greek and Roman learning went out.

Most of the **barbarians** who conquered Rome could neither read nor write. Without reading and writing, higher learning was out of their reach! So when barbarians took over Western Europe, higher learning disappeared there. Doctors forgot how to heal; engineers forgot how to build great buildings; and sculptors forgot how to carve fine art.

The lack of learning also led to the second reason for the name "dark." Since most barbarians couldn't write, they couldn't record stories for historians to read. Without more stories, much of their history will always be unknown, or "dark."

The name **barbarian** comes from the Greek word *barbaros*, meaning "babbling." The ancient Greeks called anyone who didn't speak Greek a barbarian, or babbler. The Romans used the same word.

Thus "barbarian" wasn't a real name. Instead, it was an insulting nickname for outsiders— uncivilized people from outside the Greek and Roman empires.

Thanks to the Dark Ages, the word "medieval" actually has two meanings. "Medieval" usually means "belonging to the Middle Ages." But it can also mean "ignorant" or "backward." Some people of modern times see the people of medieval times as dim-wits— ignorant fools who were so blinded by old superstitions that they couldn't see the enlightened reason of the future.

One example of a backward medieval attitude was the strange practice of **trying animals in court**.

Most moderns believe that animals act mainly on instinct, and can't possibly make moral decisions like people can. Apparently, medieval judges believed otherwise. From time to time, medieval judges hauled animals into court, where they placed them on trial for moral crimes like theft, assault and even murder.

Medieval freemen and serfs working on their lord's castle

The strangest things about medieval animal trials were the punishments. Some courts hanged convicted pigs to death, just as if they were people! To punish a swarm of insects or rodents, some medieval judges announced that the swarm must have been possessed by a demon, and then asked God to smite the demon!

An accused pig on trial for its life in 1494

††††††††††††††††††††††††††

The second part of the medieval era was the High Middle Ages, which lasted from about 1000 – 1300. The High Middle Ages were the glorious days of castles, knights and knights' tournaments. They were also the ugly days of the Crusades— long, horrible wars between Christians and Muslims.

The third part of the medieval era was the Late Middle Ages, which lasted from about 1300 – 1500. The Late Middle Ages were some of the worst times in all of history— deadly days of war and crisis.

The worst war of the Late Middle Ages was the Hundred Years' War, a long struggle for the throne of France. Despite its name, the Hundred Years' War actually lasted well over 100 years— all the way from 1337 – 1453. Imagine being at war for more than a century! Around 1430, France came very close to falling under the Crown of England. The only thing that stopped it was the inspiring Christian faith of a teenaged peasant girl called Joan of Arc.

The Tower of London, started by William the Conqueror soon after he conquered England in 1066

The worst crisis of the Late Middle Ages was an epidemic called the Black Death. Early in the Hundred Years' War, a disease called bubonic plague killed astonishing numbers of people. When the plague had run its course, somewhere between one-third and six-tenths of all Europeans lay dead.

After reading all of this, you might be afraid that studying the medieval era will be too depressing. But take heart— for it can also be fascinating! So if you ever find yourself getting depressed, then just count your blessings, and thank the Lord that you weren't born in the Late Middle Ages.

The first known civilizations all grew up around one of four rivers. In the fertile valleys around these four rivers, mighty kings built the first great empires.

One was the Nile River, which flows through Egypt. The first great Egyptian king was **Menes**, who lived around 3,000 BC. The buildings and art left behind by the ancient Egyptians are some of the most amazing man-made objects in all the world. Historians may never discover all the mysteries hidden in that enormous tomb, the **Great Pyramid of Giza**. Nor may they ever fully understand the feelings that inspired incredible statues like the **Great Sphinx**!

A second river was the Tigris-Euphrates River, which flows through Iraq. The land between the Tigris and Euphrates was called *Mesopotamia*, which means "between the rivers." The first great Mesopotamian king, **Sargon**, lived around 2,300 BC. Like the Hebrew hero Moses, Sargon started as a baby in a reed basket floating down a river. From this humble beginning, Sargon somehow arose to become the mightiest king the world had yet seen!

The Great Sphinx of Giza, Egypt

A third river was the Yellow River, which flows through China. **King Yu** founded the first Chinese dynasty, the **Xia dynasty**, around 2,200 BC. Yu's greatest accomplishments were water projects— huge dams and canals to control the flooding that made life around the Yellow River so dangerous and unpredictable.

A fourth river was the Indus River, which flows through India, Pakistan and Afghanistan. The oldest known people of India were the **Harappan people**, who mysteriously vanished around 1750 BC!

✝✝✝

Among the cleverest of all ancient peoples were the Greeks. The first known Greek people, the **Minoans**, appeared on the island of Crete around 1800 BC. Other Greek peoples followed, building cities all around the Aegean Sea and beyond.

Bronze head believed to represent Sargon

The Parthenon standing on the Acropolis of Athens, Greece

At first, **tyrants** ruled the Greeks, just as tyrants ruled everyone else. Around 500 BC, though, a Greek leader called **Cleisthenes** rebuilt the government of Athens in a new way. Athens became the first known **democracy**— the first place on Earth where every free man had a voice and a vote in his government.

The worst threat to Greece came from the Persian Empire. Around 550 BC, a military genius called **Cyrus the Great** assembled the largest empire the world had yet seen. The Persian Empire stretched all the way from Egypt in the west, to Iran in the center, to part of India in the east.

> A **tyrant** is an absolute ruler who does just as he pleases, paying no attention at all to the rights of his people.

After conquering almost everything else, the Persians tried to conquer Greece as well. If they had succeeded, then the Persian language and culture might have spread all around the Mediterranean Sea.

Two key events kept that from happening.

The first key event was the **Greco-Persian Wars**. The Persians sent staggering numbers of troops to invade Greece— the largest armies the world had yet seen. Against such overwhelming odds, Greece seemed sure to fall. Yet somehow, the Greeks managed to win when they needed to, forcing the Persians to retreat.

The second key event was the rise of a Greek military genius called **Alexander the Great**. 150 years after the Persians retreated, the unstoppable Alexander conquered the whole Persian Empire. For a few short years, most of the known world belonged to the Greek Empire of Alexander the Great. This is why it was Greek language and culture, not Persian, that spread all around the Mediterranean Sea.

If Alexander the Great had survived, then who knows how long the Greek Empire might have stood? Of course, Alexander didn't survive. Instead, Alexander died young in 323 BC, leaving his generals to divide his huge empire into smaller kingdoms.

As the Greek Empire faded, an even greater empire arose to take its place.

Mosaic of Alexander the Great doing battle with the Persians

CHAPTER 1:

The Western World after the Fall of Rome

The Roman Empire

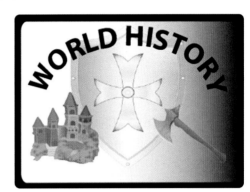

The Roman Empire was one of the biggest, most powerful empires of all time. The matchless might of Rome left deep marks on everything it touched, from language and culture to law and government. All Western countries, and even some Eastern ones, still bear those marks today.

Of course, Rome wasn't always an empire. Rome started out as a single city, founded on a hill beside the Tiber River in central Italy. The name "Rome" came from the man who founded this city: **Romulus**, who happened to have a twin brother named **Remus**.

According to legend, Romulus almost didn't survive long enough to found Rome.

The Founding of Rome (753 BC)

The story of Romulus starts with King Numitor, ruler of a small kingdom along the Tiber. Numitor had several sons, but only one daughter: a princess called Rhea. Unfortunately, Numitor also had a jealous brother called Amulius. One day, Amulius attacked Numitor and drove him off his throne. To save himself, Numitor had to run away fast— leaving Rhea and her brothers behind.

Amulius' first act as king was to kill all of Rhea's brothers. That way, he could be sure that none of them would ever claim his throne. Amulius' one act of mercy was to let Rhea live. For Rhea was only a girl; and in those days, no girl could ever rule an Italian kingdom.

However, there was still a chance that Rhea might hurt Amulius. If Rhea should ever have a son, then that son might claim his grandfather's throne. But Amulius knew an easy way to keep Rhea from having sons. He simply sent her to live in a women's temple, where she would never meet any men!

A little later, Amulius got a nasty surprise. Despite living in a temple, Rhea somehow had not one son, but two: the twin brothers Romulus and Remus.

The moment Amulius found out, he sent a servant to kill the twins. Fortunately for Rome, the servant couldn't bring himself to kill such beautiful children. So he set the twins in a basket, and then abandoned them on the banks of the Tiber.

Left in the wild to fend for themselves, most infants certainly would have died. But these were no ordinary infants. According to legend, the Tiber River rose, picked up the basket and carried it downstream, where it snagged on a gnarled root of a fig tree. Next, a wild she-wolf fed the twins milk, while a woodpecker carried them food. Finally, a shepherd called Faustulus found the twins, adopted them and raised them as his own.

Thus from the very beginning, the Romans were marked as a special people with a special destiny— according to legend.

Romulus and Remus drinking milk from a she-wolf

Over the centuries, the Romans lived under three main types of government. Rome was a **kingdom** from 753 – 509 BC; a **republic** from 509 – 27 BC; and an **empire** from 27 BC – 476 AD.

A **kingdom** is a country ruled by a **monarch**— that is, a king or queen. Rome had seven kings over the years, beginning with Romulus and ending with a tyrant called **Tarquin the Proud**.

A **republic** is a country governed by representatives who are elected by the people. After overthrowing Tarquin the Proud, the last thing free Romans wanted was another tyrant. So they built a government that left no room for tyrants: a republican government. The modern-day United States is a republic, and so are many other free countries around the world.

"The Shepherd Faustulus Bringing Romulus and Remus to His Wife" by artist Nicolas Mignard

An **empire** is a large country or group of countries, all ruled by one all-powerful emperor. Around 50 BC, a popular Roman called Julius Caesar made his people forget how bad tyrants could be. Under Caesar, Rome started its fall from the freedom of a republic to the tyranny of an empire.

Most tales of ancient Rome read more like legend than history. Any eyewitness records of the original tales were all burned by Rome's enemies long ago. The tales that remain are mostly half-remembered legends of men like Cincinnatus— mighty heroes whose deeds represent the highest ideals of the Roman republic.

The **consuls** headed Rome's government and commanded its armies, much like presidents do in the United States.

Cincinnatus was born into the wealthier class of Romans, the **patrician** class, around 519 BC. As a young man, Cincinnatus quickly became one of Rome's favorite soldier-politicians. His popularity pushed him steadily upward through the ranks of government— all the way to **consul** in 460 BC.

Unfortunately for Cincinnatus, one of his sons got into serious trouble with the law; and that trouble led to a costly fine. To raise the money for the fine, Cincinnatus had to sell almost everything he owned, keeping only a small plot of farmland. When his time as consul was over, Cincinnatus had to tend his small farm with his own hands, just like a peasant.

"Cincinnatus Leaves the Plow for the Roman Dictatorship" by Juan Antonio Ribera

Cincinnatus was doing just that— tending his farm— when some senators dropped by to make an unusual request.

Soon after Cincinnatus left office, Rome found itself in terrible danger: an enemy had trapped a Roman army in a mountain pass, and was threatening to destroy it. Not even the best Roman generals knew what to do— that is, until someone thought to call on Cincinnatus.

All agreed that Cincinnatus was the one man in all of Rome with enough skill and courage to rescue those trapped soldiers. But even Cincinnatus would have to act quickly— which meant that he would need a great deal of power, even more power than a consul.

Desperate to save Rome, the Senate offered Cincinnatus all the power Rome had to give. The senators who came calling at Cincinnatus' farm that day offered to make him **Dictator of Rome**— a supreme general with the power to command every Roman citizen. The only limit on Cincinnatus'

> A **dictator** was a supreme general with the power to command any Roman citizen to do anything at all.

power was time. Cincinnatus was to lay down his power after six months— for no Roman wanted another tyrant like Tarquin the Proud!

In his first act as dictator, Cincinnatus commanded every able-bodied man in Rome to be ready to march by the end of the next day. Equipped with this new army and a bold, clever strategy, Cincinnatus quickly crushed Rome's enemies and rescued that trapped Roman army.

But Cincinnatus was more than just a great soldier; he was also a great citizen. After the war, Cincinnatus could have used his powers as dictator to grow rich again— could have taken back all of the property he'd sold to pay his son's fine. But Cincinnatus was a strong believer in republican government. He knew that if a dictator ever seized power in Rome, then the Roman people might lose their freedom forever. And so, for the good of Rome, Cincinnatus humbly laid down his power and went back to his tiny farm— just sixteen days after the Senate had proclaimed him dictator!

It was in laying down his power that Cincinnatus became a Roman legend. Some men spend their whole lives fighting for power; and once they have it, they never want to lay it down. Unlike such power-hungry men, Cincinnatus wasn't seeking power when the crisis arose. Instead, power sought

Symbols of Roman Power

The **fasces** was a cylinder-shaped bundle of wooden rods, all bound around an ax with the head sticking out one side. From the beginning, Roman leaders used fasces as symbols of power. The bundled rods represented the strength that came from the unity of the Roman people; while the ax represented Rome's power over life and death.

A **toga** was a long woolen dress robe worn by Roman men, usually over a tunic. Togas were so bulky and inconvenient as to be utterly useless for physical labor— which meant that the only Romans who wore them were the ones who didn't need to labor. Thus the toga became a mark of wealth and status. For example, members of the Roman senate usually wore togas, but slaves almost never wore them.

Roman women wore a different type of dress robe called a **stola**.

Statue of a toga-wearing Cincinnatus handing over the fasces, an important symbol of Roman power

Cincinnatus— not because he was high-born, but because he was the best man for the job! Then when his task was over, Cincinnatus traded his dictator's toga for the garb of a humble farmer— proving that in his mind, the needs of Rome stood far above his own needs.

Sadly, few Romans cared very much for the needs of two kinds of people: women and slaves. Roman men treated their wives like property, not like free people. As for slaves, the Romans owned them by the hundreds of thousands, using them mercilessly for all sorts of hard labor. Slaves mined countless tons of copper, iron, silver and gold ores; quarried countless blocks of stone for buildings; raised countless crops to feed hungry Romans; and pulled oars on countless ships. Many did these things under the most miserable conditions imaginable— with no pay, and with little hope of ever being free again.

A Roman Warrior's Equipment

The **galea** was a Roman battle helmet designed to protect as much of the head and neck as possible. Galeae were made of cast bronze with iron trim, and often had colorful crests made of horse hair or feathers.

The **pugio** was a small dagger that served as both weapon and general-purpose knife. Wealthier warriors carried ornate pugios decorated with carvings and even gems; while poorer warriors carried plain ones.

The **gladius** was a short double-edged stabbing sword, about 18-22 inches long. A heavy round ball at the end of the handle helped balance the blade, making the gladius easier to handle.

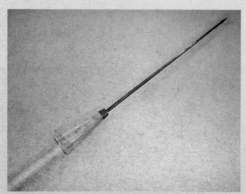

The **pilum** was a light javelin, or throwing spear, about seven feet long. Roman soldiers often threw their javelins just before they drew their swords, hoping to knock out as many enemies as possible before closing in for hand-to-hand combat.

The **scutum** was a rectangular shield that was curved to fit around a warrior's body, covering him from shoulder to knee. Warriors standing side by side could interlock their shields to create a strong protective wall.

As long as Rome produced selfless heroes like Cincinnatus, republican government stayed strong in Rome. It was only later, when greedy Romans began to care more for themselves than they did for Rome, that the republic gave way to an empire.

From Republic to Empire

Rome traced its sad path from free republic to tyrannical empire through three rulers: Julius Caesar, Caesar Augustus and Tiberius.

Julius Caesar was a clever soldier and politician who won the Roman people's admiration in two ways: through glorious victories on the battlefield, and through generous gifts to poor Romans.

Julius Caesar (100 BC - 44 BC)

In Caesar's day, mobs of idle Romans wandered the streets of Rome, depending on the government for their daily bread. Caesar took advantage of these greedy mobs, feeding their hunger with expensive public parties.

In 49 BC, a rival called Pompey tried to stand in Caesar's way. In the process of defeating Pompey, Caesar claimed the same title that the Senate had once given Cincinnatus: "Dictator of Rome."

Unlike Cincinnatus, though, Caesar had no intention of laying down his power. Caesar might even have become the first Emperor of Rome— if a group of senators hadn't assassinated him on the Ides of March, 44 BC.

Caesar Augustus (63 BC - 14 AD)

After the assassination, several ambitious men fought to take Caesar's place. One was **Octavius Caesar**, Julius Caesar's biological nephew and adopted son. Another was **Marc Antony**, one of Julius Caesar's most trusted generals. Antony hoped to defeat Octavius by joining forces with Queen Cleopatra of Egypt. Antony's hopes turned to ash, though, when Octavius defeated him at the famous **Battle of Actium**. Both Antony and Cleopatra finally committed suicide, leaving Octavius to conquer Egypt.

Octavius Caesar used the riches of Egypt to transform Rome— rebuilding it from sagging city of dirty brick into a proud city of gleaming marble. The more money he spent to benefit Rome, the more honors the Roman Senate heaped upon him. One of those honors was the title he carried into history: *Augustus*, meaning "Honored One."

Despite his lofty title, **Caesar Augustus** was always careful to avoid the title "emperor." He much preferred another title the Senate gave him: *Princeps*, meaning "First Citizen." By insisting that he was only a citizen, and not an emperor, Caesar Augustus fooled the Roman people into believing that their country was still a republic.

Model of ancient Rome with the Circus Maximus in the foreground and the Coliseum in the background

The **Circus Maximus** was a long public racetrack that stood near the Roman Coliseum. The Romans used their Coliseum for gladiator fights, executions and other big public events; but they used the Circus Maximus mainly for horse-drawn chariot races. The Circus Maximus may have held as many as 150,000 spectators on race days.

The Roman diet was heavy on three basic foods: grains, grapes and olives. Romans ate their beloved olives whole; used them in relishes and spices; and pressed them into olive oil, which they used to cook or dress other foods.

If the rise of Caesar Augustus didn't mark the end of the Roman Republic, then the rise of **Tiberius** certainly did. Just before Caesar Augustus died, he handed down the office of First Citizen to his step-son Tiberius. If Rome had still been a republic, then Tiberius would have had to win an election. Instead, power passed directly from father to son— which meant that the Roman people had forgotten the ideals of Cincinnatus, trading the freedom of a republic for the tyranny of an empire.

Which is not to say that the end of the republic meant the end of Roman prosperity— quite the opposite! The reign of Caesar Augustus was the beginning of the *Pax Romana*, a "Roman Peace" that lasted 200 years. The Roman Empire was never larger, nor its power and wealth ever greater, than during the *Pax Romana*.

Around 180 AD, the long *Pax Romana* finally drew to a close, and Rome's fortunes began to fade. After that, problems plagued Rome on all sides. One problem was that

The Fall of the Western Roman Empire (476 AD)

each time an emperor died, his former generals fought over his throne. These fights weakened Rome's defenses, leaving her more open to attack.

To better defend his vast empire, Emperor Diocletian tried splitting it in two— forming a **Western Roman Empire** and an **Eastern Roman Empire**. Diocletian hoped that two emperors would be stronger than one, since each would have less territory to defend. Unfortunately, splitting the empire created new problems— including high new taxes to pay for two expensive governments.

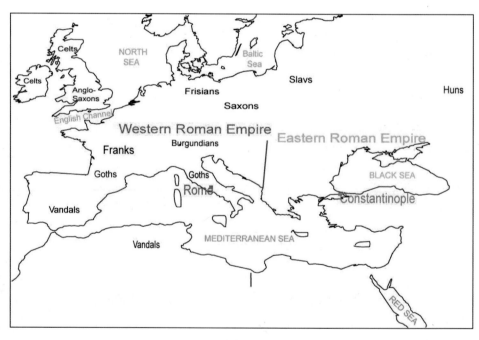

The worst problem of all came from outsiders called **barbarians**. Around 400 AD, huge numbers of barbarians started pouring across Rome's old boundaries, the Rhine and Danube Rivers. As mighty as the Romans were, even they couldn't fight off so many barbarians all at once!

The fall of the Western Roman Empire came in stages. A barbarian people called the **Visigoths** sacked Rome for the first time in 410 AD. The next big threat came from **Attila the Hun**, who nearly sacked Rome in 452. The **Vandals** succeeded where Attila had failed, sacking Rome in 455.

To **sack** a city is to ravage it— to attack its people, loot its treasure and destroy some of its buildings.

Finally in 476, the last Emperor of the Western Roman Empire fell. Oddly enough, this last emperor was named Romulus!

As for the Eastern Roman Empire, it survived for another 1,000 years— but under a different name. The capital of the Eastern Roman Empire lay far to the east, in a Greek-speaking city called Constantinople (now Istanbul, Turkey). The Greek culture of Constantinople was quite different from the Latin culture of Rome. Because of this, and because Constantinople had once been called *Byzantion*, the Eastern Roman Empire is called the **Byzantine Empire**.

The Early Christian Church

The whole history of the early church happened in Roman times. Jesus Christ was born to the Virgin Mary around 6 – 0 BC, when Caesar Augustus was emperor. Roman soldiers crucified Christ around 30 – 33 AD, when Tiberius was emperor. After Christ rose from the dead and ascended into heaven, His apostles set out to spread His gospel all over the known world— most of which was controlled by Rome.

The gospel could not have come at a better time. When Christ's apostles set out to "make disciples of all nations," as the Bible says in Matthew 28:19, the road-loving Romans had already built convenient roads all over their vast empire. Also, the law and order of the *Pax Romana* was just beginning— which made traveling those roads far safer. These two advantages, the *Pax Romana* and the Roman roads, were extremely helpful to the first Christian missionaries.

Of course, any help the Romans gave the early church was purely unintentional. The Roman Empire didn't want to help Christians— no, it wanted to destroy them! Christian-hating

Persecutions of Early Christians

emperors like **Nero**, **Trajan** and **Decius** tortured and murdered countless Christians.

One such tortured Christian was the bishop of Antioch, Syria: Ignatius of Antioch. Ignatius probably studied under the Apostle John, who of course was a close friend of Jesus. When John died, Ignatius was one of the last men alive who had studied under someone who had studied under Jesus Himself. Knowing how other Christians looked up to him, Ignatius felt a duty to speak out loudly about his faith.

"The Ascension" by Rembrandt

When Ignatius was about 70 years old, the Christian-hating Emperor Trajan decided to make an example of this loud-speaking Christian. The Romans loved to make examples of Christian leaders. They had learned that if they silenced one Christian leader, then the rest would usually fall silent as well. With this in mind, Trajan ordered Ignatius of Antioch arrested and hauled off to Rome for trial.

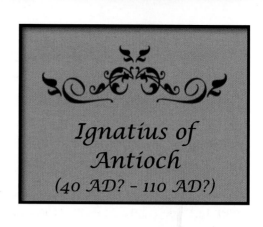

Ignatius of Antioch
(40 AD? - 110 AD?)

But Ignatius refused to fall silent. On his way to Rome, Ignatius wrote inspiring letters to churches all over the empire. Ignatius' letters show that he was not afraid to die— no, he welcomed death! Since Christ Himself had died, Ignatius was not surprised that Christ's followers should have to die as well. In fact, Ignatius considered it a high honor to die for Christ. For he cared about his future life in heaven far more than he did about his present life on Earth. To the struggling young church at Rome, Ignatius wrote:

"I would rather die and come to Jesus Christ than be king over the entire earth… Let me be food for the wild beasts, for they are my way to God."

The emperor was happy to grant Ignatius' wish. Around 110 AD, Trajan fed the old saint to hungry lions at the Roman Coliseum.

Ignatius of Antioch being attacked by lions in the Roman Coliseum

Just as the Bible predicted in James 1:3, the testing of Christians' faith produced endurance. Despite many such horrible persecutions as the one Ignatius suffered, the early church continued to grow.

〰〰〰

The more the early church grew, the more church officers it needed.

Bishops and Popes

The Book of Acts records that at first, the apostles directed everything themselves. Then, as the church started to grow, the apostles chose seven **deacons** to help them (Acts 6:1-6). Later, the Apostle Paul chose **elders**— also called **presbyters**— to manage the new churches he founded (Acts 14:23).

Later still, Paul set trusted disciples like Timothy and Titus in charge of several churches each. Timothy, Titus and Ignatius were all early **bishops**— overseers who managed all Christian churches in a large area.

In the beginning, no one bishop was more powerful than any other. Over time, though, the bishop of Rome grew more powerful than the rest— probably because Rome itself was so powerful.

As the most powerful bishop in the whole Christian world, the bishop of Rome took on a new title: *Papa*, or Father. English speakers know the Bishop of Rome as the **Pope.**

According to Catholic tradition, the **Apostle Peter** was the first pope. The special authority of Peter comes from these words of Christ in Matthew 16:18-19:

"And I tell you that you are Peter, and on this rock I will build my church, and the gates of Hades will not overcome it. I will give you the keys of the kingdom of heaven; whatever you bind on earth will be bound in heaven, and whatever you loose on earth will be loosed in heaven."

Tradition also says that when Peter died, he handed down his power to the next pope in line, who in turn handed it down to the next. Even today, each new pope inherits power from the pope before him, in an unbroken line that stretches all the way back to Peter. Catholics call this handing-down of power **Apostolic Succession**.

Symbols of the Pope

The popes of medieval times used **papal coats of arms** as symbols of authority. Each pope designed his own special coat of arms. Many papal coats of arms included the two keys from Matthew 16:18-19. One key represented the power to bind sin, while the other represented the power to loose sin.

Coat of arms of Leo X, the pope who reigned during the early years of the Protestant Reformation. Pope Leo's arms included both the Keys of St. Peter and the Papal Tiara.

On special occasions, medieval popes also wore the **Papal Tiara**— a fantastically expensive crown with three gem-studded tiers. However, later popes felt that such a rich ornament was too extravagant for a servant of Christ. After all, Christ had been the son of a poor carpenter. No pope has worn the papal tiara since 1965, when Pope Paul VI laid it down on the altar of St. Peter's Basilica in Rome.

Part of every bishop's job was to keep the Christian faith pure. From the beginning, false teachers called **heretics** tried to lead Christians astray. As defenders of Christ's church, bishops tried to stop **heresies** before they spread too far.

> A **heretic** is someone who spreads false teachings about Christ. Such teachings are called **heresies**.

The First Heresies

One of the first big heresies was **Gnosticism**. The word "Gnostic" comes from the Greek word *gnosis*, meaning "knowledge." The Gnostics taught that people could only be saved through certain special knowledge— mysterious secrets that only Gnostics knew. One Gnostic secret was that the spirit world was good, but the physical world was evil.

The trouble started when Gnostics tried to blend this secret with Christianity. Gnostic Christians asked, "How could a spirit as good as Christ's possibly live inside an evil physical body?" The answer, they replied, was that he couldn't. Since Christ was too good for the physical world, his body couldn't have been real. Instead, Gnostics said, Christ's body must have been an **illusion**.

The bishops of the early church answered these Gnostic heretics with one of the most important statements of faith ever written: the **Apostles' Creed**. In modern English, the Apostles' Creed reads:

> An **illusion** is something that appears to be real, but really isn't. The Gnostics believed that Christ's physical body was only an illusion.

"I believe in God the Father, Almighty Maker of Heaven and Earth.

"And in Jesus Christ His only begotten Son, our Lord, who was conceived by the Holy Spirit, born of the Virgin Mary, suffered under Pontius Pilate, was crucified, dead and buried. He descended into hell. On the third day, He arose from the dead. He ascended into heaven, and sits at the right hand of God the Father Almighty, from whence He will come to judge the quick [living] and the dead.

"I believe in the Holy Spirit, the holy catholic [universal] church, the communion of the saints, the forgiveness of sins, the resurrection of the body, and the life everlasting."

By insisting that Christ was born and died, the Apostles' Creed dismissed the idea that Christ's body wasn't real. Unlike the Gnostics, the bishops of the early church insisted that Christ was really a man— but also really God, both at the same time.

Constantine the Great

When the Apostles' Creed first appeared, probably around 150 AD, most Romans still hated Christians. Almost no one would have believed that Rome would have a Christian emperor one day!

Much to everyone's surprise, that day came in the early 300s, when a Christian called Constantine claimed the throne of the Roman Empire.

Before the 300s, Constantine stood with one foot in the Roman world, and the other in the Christian world. His father Constantius started as a Roman general, and ended as Emperor of Rome. His mother Helena may have started as a lowly Christian stable-maid. While Constantius raised his son to be an emperor, Helena raised him to be a Christian.

Constantine the Great (272 - 337)

"Apparition of the Cross to Constantine" by artist Jacopo Vignali

Constantine's moment of decision came in 312 AD, just before the most important battle of his life. One record says that on the night before the battle, Constantine received a strange vision telling him to mark all of his soldiers' shields with a special symbol. That symbol combined the first two letters in the Greek word for "Christ." When Constantine went on to beat an army twice the size of his, he gave credit to Christ.

The symbol from Constantine's vision

The following year, 313 AD, was a banner year for Christians— for that was the year when Constantine announced the famous **Edict of Milan**. For the first time, the Edict of Milan made it legal for all Romans to worship any god they chose— even Christ. After nearly three hundred years of persecution, Christians all over the Roman Empire were finally free to come out of hiding!

Even so, Constantine was on his deathbed before he finally allowed a priest to baptize him.

Saint Helena
(250? – 330?)

But before he died, Constantine sent his mother Helena to the Holy Land. Helena used Roman money to build two of the best-known churches in the world: the **Church of the Holy Sepulcher**, which stands on Calvary Hill in Jerusalem; and the **Church of the Nativity**, which stands in Bethlehem.

Legend says that in digging the foundations for the Church of the Holy Sepulcher, Helena discovered three wooden crosses— one belonging to Christ, and two belonging to the criminals who were crucified on either side of Christ (Luke 23:33). To find out which was the True Cross of Christ, Helena asked a deathly ill woman to touch all three. Nothing happened when the woman touched the first two. When she touched the third, though, the power of Christ miraculously healed her.

The Seven Continents

A **continent** is a vast body of land, far larger than an island. Planet Earth has seven continents: **Africa, Antarctica, Asia, Australia, Europe, North America** and **South America**. Together, these continents cover about three-tenths (30%) of Earth's total surface. The other seven-tenths (70%) is mostly covered with water.

The largest continent, Asia, is home to about six-tenths (60%) of the world's people. More than half of these live in one of the two most populated countries on Earth, **China** and **India**. China comes in first, with nearly 1.4 billion people. India comes in second, with nearly 1.3 billion. As of 2016, Earth is home to a total of about 7.1 billion people.

Antarctica is so unbearably cold that no one lives there full-time! However, as many as several hundred scientists may be living in science stations on Antarctica at any one time.

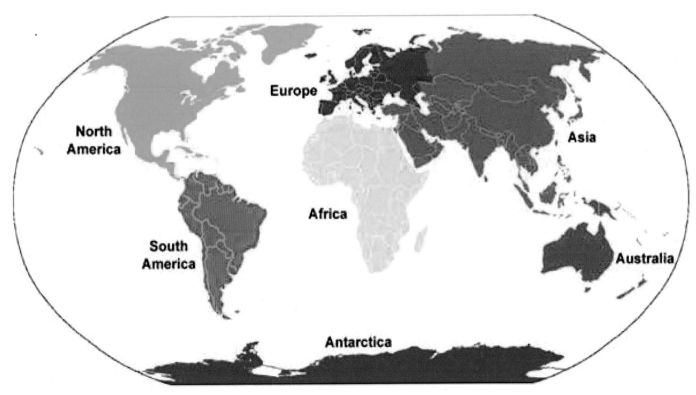

CHAPTER 2

The Five Oceans

An **ocean** is a vast body of water, far larger than a sea. By most people's count, Planet Earth has five oceans: the **Arctic** Ocean, the **Atlantic** Ocean, the **Indian** Ocean, the **Pacific** Ocean and the **Southern** Ocean.

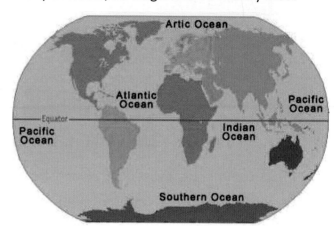

Together, these oceans cover about seven-tenths, or 70%, of Earth's total surface.

Since all five oceans blend together, some say that Earth really has only one ocean: the **World Ocean**.

The British Isles

The **British Isles** are a group of islands that lie just off the northwest coast of mainland Europe.

Two of the British Isles are far larger than all the rest. The largest is **Great Britain**, which is home to three countries: **England**, **Scotland** and **Wales**. Great Britain lies just across the English Channel from France, and just across the North Sea from Belgium and the Netherlands.

The second largest of the British Isles is **Ireland**, which is home to two countries: **Northern Ireland** and the **Republic of Ireland**. Ireland lies west of Great Britain, just across the Irish Sea.

The ancients used different names for different parts of the British Isles. For example, Britannia was the Roman name for southern Great Britain— the part the Roman Empire held for almost 400 years. Caledonia was the Roman name for northern Great Britain— the unconquered part that lay north of Britannia.

The Celtic People

Before the Romans conquered Britannia, the British Isles belonged to an ancient people called the Celts.

The Celts lived in many parts of Europe, not just the British Isles. Over the centuries, Celts brushed up against Greeks, Romans and many other ancient peoples.

A Celtic warrior in blue war paint

Unlike the Romans, the Celts never built an empire. Instead, the Celts remained divided into tribes, each led by a warrior chieftain or a petty king. Every Celtic tribe was unique, with a special name and story all its own. Every tribe was also independent— except when the tribes banded together against a common foe, such as the invading Roman Empire.

Because they were a tribal people, the Celts built no great cities or towering structures like the Romans'. However, they did fashion clever pottery, jewelry, tools and weapons. They even fashioned a kind of armor that was good enough for the Romans to borrow.

An ancient hauberk on display at a museum in France

Chain mail was an early armor made by weaving together rings of bronze or iron. Celtic blacksmiths probably fashioned their first chain mail sometime after 300 BC. Their Roman neighbors admired chain mail so much that they copied it, spreading this Celtic invention around the world.

Because chain mail was nearly as flexible as fabric, blacksmiths could weave it into armor for any part of the body. The most common mail piece was a long shirt called a **hauberk**. But there were also chain mail helmets, scarves, aprons, leggings, even socks and gloves. Even in the 1300s, when the first plate armor came along, chain mail was still popular. For chain mail was cheaper, lighter and far more flexible than any plate armor.

Celtic families often lived in circular, one-room buildings called roundhouses. The Celts probably built their roundhouse walls by mixing mud with straw, and then spreading thick layers of this mixture over a frame of sticks. Roundhouse roofs were cone-shaped, and probably covered with **thatch.**

With all of that thick mud and thatch, most families probably needed only small fires in the centers of their roundhouses to keep them warm. Unlike Native American tepees, roundhouses probably didn't have smoke holes in their roofs— because if they had, then any sudden draft might have drawn the flames up into the thatch, setting fire to the roof! Instead, the Celts probably just let smoke seep out of their smoky roundhouses through tiny gaps in the thatch.

Thatch is a roof covering made of bundled straw or reeds, all bound to the roof frame in thick layers.

Modern-day reconstruction of a Celtic roundhouse

The leaders of the **Celtic religion** were mysterious priests called **druids**. Much of what the druids believed and taught is now forgotten— for the Celts had no written language, which meant that the druids never wrote down their scriptures and rituals.

Two druids, one with a crown of mistletoe

Even so, historians know part of what the Celts believed. For example, they know that the Celts were **polytheists**. Celtic gods and goddesses often appeared in threes; for the number three was special to the Celts.

Historians also know that the Celts were tree-lovers— great admirers of the strength and long life found in trees. The druids taught that certain trees and plants were sacred, especially oak and mistletoe. Many druid rituals took place in sacred tree groves.

The Celts also believed in **reincarnation**. The idea of reincarnation inspired great courage in Celtic warriors. If a warrior truly believed in reincarnation, then he had no reason to fear dying in battle— for he felt sure that his soul would not die, but would simply move into a different body.

> **Polytheists** believe in many gods, not just one.

> **Reincarnation** is the belief that when people die, their souls move into new bodies and live on.

Some druids taught that if the Celts wanted their gods' help to win a battle, then they must offer sacrifices before that battle. Some evil druids even sacrificed live human beings to their gods.

The druids' fierce teachings about war and sacrifice are not surprising; for the Celts were a fierce people. **Celtic warriors** were legendary for their great height, strength and ferocity. They fought like madmen, holding nothing back, throwing their whole bodies into every blow.

Some Celtic warriors went into battle wearing only two items: a little bit of armor, and a lot of blue war paint. The Celts may have worn blue because they believed that it helped them channel power from their gods. On the other hand, they may have worn it for a simpler reason: because their gruesome blue faces terrified their enemies!

> The blue pigment for the Celts' war paint may have come from a flowering plant called **woad**.

"Girl with a Hoop" by Renoir

Since ancient times, children all over the world have played a game called **hoop rolling**. Players use sticks to roll large hoops along the ground, competing to see who can keep his hoop rolling the longest without letting it fall.

The Roman Empire in Britannia

As Rome grew, the Celts shrank. Each time the Romans conquered new territory in Europe, the beaten Celts had to retreat farther and farther from Rome. By about 50 BC, the only lands left to the Celts were the British Isles.

In time, the Romans set out to conquer the British Isles as well.

The first Roman general to attack the Celts on Great Britain was Julius Caesar. But Caesar wasn't trying to conquer Great Britain. Instead, he was trying to conquer **Gaul**, most of which is now France.

Unfortunately, war is never simple. Each time Caesar conquered new territory in Gaul, more Celts fled across the English Channel to Great Britain. But they didn't stay in Britain. Instead, they often sailed back to Gaul for revenge! When Caesar invaded Britain in 55 – 54 BC, he was mainly trying to stop the Celts' revenge attacks.

Almost 100 years passed before the Romans invaded Great Britain again. This time, though, the Romans came to stay. In 43 AD, Emperor Claudius sent four whole **legions** of Roman soldiers into Britain— as many as 40,000 troops! Although the Celts fought as fiercely as always, their simple tribes were no match for the mighty Roman Empire. In 50 AD, the Romans finally conquered southern Great Britain— the part they called **Britannia**.

> A **legion** was a large, well-organized Roman army unit that might contain anywhere from 5,000 to 10,000 troops.

—STOP—

Caratacus was a Celtic warrior chief who fought to drive the Romans off Great Britain. Caratacus tried **guerrilla tactics** against the Romans. In other words, he and his men would leap out of hiding, attack swiftly and then disappear before the Romans could strike back.

As long as Caratacus stuck to guerilla tactics, he did well. In 50 AD, though, Caratacus tried to tackle a big Roman army head-on. The result was a disaster. After losing the **Battle of Caer Caradoc**, the fleeing Caratacus was betrayed by a former friend and handed over to the Romans in chains.

As a proud Roman, Emperor Claudius thought he knew just what to do with a beaten **barbarian** like Caratacus. First he would haul Caratacus to the Roman Forum, where he would hold a crowd-pleasing victory parade to show off his beaten foe. Then he would execute Caratacus for daring to defy Rome. Roman hearts would swell with pride as Claudius proved, once again, that Rome was unstoppable.

> The Romans called any uncivilized person who came from outside the highly civilized Roman Empire a **"barbarian."**

But Caratacus turned out to be no ordinary barbarian. Unlike other so-called "barbarians" the Romans had conquered, Caratacus was well-educated and well-spoken. Instead of cowering before the emperor, Caratacus delivered a proud speech. "Why on Earth," Caratacus asked, "should it be a crime to defy Rome? For who on Earth would willingly become a slave?"

Much impressed by his thoughtful foe, Claudius decided to spare Caratacus' life— but not to send him home. Instead, Claudius gave Caratacus a house in Rome, where the great Celt lived out the rest of his days in peace.

Caratacus touring Rome after his release

Britannia was to remain in Roman hands for most of the next 400 years.

Even so, the Roman Empire wasn't quite as unstoppable as Emperor Claudius had believed. After conquering Britannia, the Romans tried to conquer northern Great Britain as well— the part they called **Caledonia**. Each time they tried, though, a fierce Celtic people called the **Picts** drove them back. Even worse, the Picts kept crossing into Britannia to raid outposts and steal supplies— making life miserable for the Romans.

After more than 70 years of trouble with the Picts, a new emperor called **Hadrian** proposed a new way to protect Britannia: by building an enormous wall. If Hadrian's Wall was to work, then it would need several virtues.

> First, it would need to stretch all the way across Great Britain. Even at its narrowest point, the big island was still about 75 miles wide— which meant that Hadrian's Wall would have to be about 75 miles long.

> Second, it would need to be high, thick and strong. The finished wall was built mostly of stone, and stood about 15 feet high and 8 feet thick.

> Third, it would need soldiers and forts to guard it— for without these, the Picts could simply climb the wall when no one was looking. The finished wall included at least one fort at every milepost. Most of these forts were small. But sixteen of them were quite large, complete with strong gates, barracks for troops and barns for horses.

A surviving section of Hadrian's Wall just south of Scotland

For most of the next 300 years, Hadrian's Wall marked the northernmost border of the whole Roman Empire. Try as they might, the Romans could never hold anything north of Hadrian's Wall for long.

Nor were the Picts the only people who gave the Romans trouble. Around 400 AD, barbarian tribes started invading the Western Roman Empire from all sides at once (Chapter 1). To fight off these barbarians, Rome called home some of its troops from far-off provinces like Britannia.

The Roman Retreat from Britannia (410 AD)

Despite these extra troops, the Goths managed to sack Rome itself in 410 AD (Chapter 1). In Roman eyes, this was an utter disaster. The whole empire was starting to collapse! Desperate to save itself, the dying Roman Empire called its last armies home from Britannia.

The British Dark Age

A lot can change in 400 years. When the Romans first invaded Britannia, the Celts fought like madmen to keep them out. But when the Romans retreated, the people of Britannia mourned to see them go.

They mourned because the Romans were not only great conquerors, but also great teachers. In four hundred years, the people of Britannia had learned much from the Romans. That learning had made them happier, healthier and more comfortable than ever before. By the time the Romans left, the people of Britannia admired the Romans far more than they admired their own ancestors, the Celts.

Thus the people of Britannia no longer saw themselves as Celts. Instead, they saw themselves as **Romanized Britons**— a new people who were proud of their Roman learning.

These new Britons longed to defend their civilized way of life against the uncivilized barbarians beyond Hadrian's Wall. Unfortunately, the barbarians outnumbered the Britons, just as they outnumbered Romans all over the empire! If the Britons were to fight off the barbarians, then they would need more troops.

To get those troops, British kings hired foreign **mercenaries.** Oddly enough, these mercenaries would turn out to be a bigger problem than the barbarians they were hired to fight!

> A **mercenary** is a soldier who will fight for anyone who can afford to pay him.

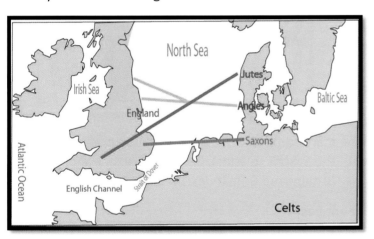

The first to hire mercenaries was probably a British king called **Vortigern**. When barbarians threatened his kingdom, Vortigern summoned a people called the **Saxons** for help. Vortigern's Saxons came from across the North Sea, probably near what is now Denmark.

In exchange for Saxon help, Vortigern paid both money and land. The first Saxon land in Britain was a southeastern region called **Kent**.

Soon, more British kings were inviting more mercenaries to other parts of Britannia. A people called the **Angles** came mainly to the east, north of Saxon territory. A people called the **Jutes** came mainly to the southwest, west of Saxon territory. Over time, the Jutes blended with the Saxons, leaving two main tribes of foreigners in Britain: Angles and Saxons.

The Angles and Saxons soon discovered that they liked Britain very much. More Angles and Saxons poured into Britain, demanding more and more money and land. If the Britons didn't pay, then the Angles and Saxons simply took what they wanted, driving the poor Britons out of their homes. In time, Angles and Saxons conquered most of southern Britain!

> The Angles grew so powerful in southern Britain that the country took on a new name: what had once been Roman Britannia now became "Angle-land," or simply "**England**."

Like the barbarians who conquered Rome, the Anglo-Saxons who conquered Britannia could neither read nor write. So of course, they left behind few written records.

Without written records, historians can only guess at what happened in Britannia after the Anglo-Saxons took over. In conquering Britannia, the Anglo-Saxons brought on a **British Dark Age**.

> The **British Dark Age** was a time when the bright light of Roman learning went dark in Britain. Few historical records survive from the British Dark Age.

Wherever history leaves a gap, legend rushes in to fill it. The gap of the British Dark Age is filled mostly with the **legend of King Arthur**.

If Arthur ever really lived at all, then he was probably a British king who lived in the early 500s. According to legend, Arthur led the Britons to a great victory over their worst enemies, the Saxons. With this victory, Arthur bought a short time of peace and prosperity— a golden age when the heroic Arthur and his beautiful wife Guinevere reigned from their new castle at Camelot, aided by virtuous knights like Lancelot, Gawain and Galahad.

The Angles and Saxons who took over Britannia divided their territory into seven kingdoms. Historians call these seven kingdoms the **Heptarchy**— a combination of "hepto," meaning "seven," and "archy," meaning "rule." The seven Anglo-Saxon kingdoms of the Heptarchy were (1) East Anglia, (2) Essex, (3) Kent, (4) Mercia, (5) Northumbria, (6) Wessex and (7) Sussex.

Like so many good things, the golden age of Arthur ended in treachery.

For years, Arthur never knew that he had a son named Mordred, born to a woman he had met before he married Guinevere. After Mordred grew up, he did the unthinkable: he turned traitor, joining forces with the Saxons to attack his father. Arthur and Mordred killed each other in battle; the Saxons took over Britain; and Britain descended into its Dark Age.

These basic ideas of Arthur's story are easy enough to believe. Unfortunately, the story also contains magical details which are impossible to believe! For example, Mordred's mother **Morgan le Fay** was said to be an enchantress who cast a magical spell on Arthur. Arthur's wise old helper, **Merlin**, was said to be a powerful wizard. Arthur's sword, **Excalibur**, was said to be sharp enough to cut through steel, and bright enough to blind Arthur's enemies. Excalibur's sheath was said to be more magical yet— blessed with the incredible power to save the one who wore it from being wounded.

With so much magic mixed into Arthur's story, it is hard to know how much of it is real— or even if Arthur himself was real. Serious historians see Arthur as an entertaining legend, rather than real history.

Another tale that mixed magic with history was the **legend of the Holy Grail**. The real Holy Grail was the cup that Jesus used to serve the wine of the Last Supper— in other words, the first Holy Communion (Matthew 26:27-28). What happened to the real Holy Grail, no one knows. But according to

Arthur of Britain woven into a tapestry

legend, the long-lost Holy Grail wound up in Britannia— perhaps because **Magnus Maximus** carried it there.

After defeating the Saxons, Arthur and his Knights of the Round Table needed a new mission to keep their hearts loyal and their fighting skills sharp. The quest to find the long-lost Holy Grail became that mission. The legends say that a few of Arthur's knights caught glimpses of the Holy Grail; but none ever managed to bring it back to Camelot.

Magnus Maximus was a soldier-turned-Roman-emperor who once commanded troops in Britannia. Maximus was also a devoted Christian, which may explain why legend has him carrying the Holy Grail to Britannia.

As junior emperor over part of the Western Roman Empire, Maximus ruled for just a few years before two senior emperors joined forces to crush him. These emperors hated Maximus so much that merely executing him wasn't enough to satisfy them. Instead, they added the ***damnatio memorae***— a dreaded punishment which made it a crime for any Roman even to speak Maximus' name, or to remember him in any way.

〰〰〰〰〰〰〰〰〰〰〰〰〰〰〰〰〰〰〰〰〰〰〰〰〰〰〰〰〰〰

If the Angles and Saxons had no written language when they conquered Britannia, then when did they learn to write? The answer may lie in a long poem titled *Beowulf*.

Beowulf is the oldest surviving long poem written in Old English, the language of the Angles. Exactly how old *Beowulf* is, no one knows for sure. Saxon storytellers may have recited *Beowulf* aloud for many years before someone finally wrote it down.

Like the tales of King Arthur, *Beowulf* mixes magic with legend. Beowulf is a mighty Anglo-Saxon warrior who tackles three monsters too terrible to be real. The first is a hideous man-eater called Grendel, who kills many warriors before Beowulf finally tears off his arm. Next comes Grendel's furious mother, bent on revenge. Fifty years after he kills Grendel's mother, a much older Beowulf tackles a huge, fire-breathing dragon. This last monster turns out to be Beowulf's undoing. Although Beowulf manages to kill the dragon, he soon dies of his battle wounds.

Beowulf fighting the dragon

What makes *Beowulf* so important is that it is the only surviving work of literature from the British Dark Age. Thus it gives the modern world a rare glimpse into the world of that time.

Celtic cross

The **Celtic knot** is a form of art that first appeared in the British Isles around 400 AD, when the Roman army was beginning to head back to Rome. The basic pattern of the Celtic knot is a woven cord that appears to have no beginning and no end. British artists used Celtic knots in all sorts of places— drawing them in books, weaving them into fabric and carving them onto monuments. Art scholars have identified eight basic Celtic knot patterns, along with several variations.

At first, the endless pattern of the Celtic knot may have represented the druids' teachings about endless reincarnation. Later, British Christians used Celtic knots to decorate beautiful books called **illuminated manuscripts**. One well-known example of the Celtic knot appears on the **Celtic cross**.

The Arian Controversy

The **Arian Controversy** was a bitter argument over this question: Was Jesus Christ really God, or was He only a special human being? Most Christians believed that Christ was really God. A priest called **Arius** believed otherwise.

Ever since Jesus Christ was born, people have found it hard to believe that He was really the Son of God. Even the people who knew Jesus best, His own disciples, needed time to understand who He was. One example of the disciples' confusion appears in Mark 4:41, after Jesus somehow calms a wild storm on a lake. In awe at what the Lord has done, the disciples turn to one another and ask:

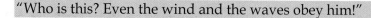

"Who is this? Even the wind and the waves obey him!"

Everything changed after Jesus rose from the dead. That very day, Jesus opened the Scriptures to his disciples on the road to Emmaus, explaining who He was and why He had had to die (Luke 24:13-32). After hearing from the risen Jesus, the disciples finally understood that He was the Son of God.

Centuries later, Arius offered a new way of thinking about Jesus. Arius was an Egyptian priest from Alexandria, a leading city of the early church. Around 315 AD, Arius started teaching that Christ was part of God's creation, not part of God Himself. Arius said that in the beginning, God created Christ first, and then Christ helped God create everything else. In other words, Arius said, "There was a time when the Son [Christ] was not."

Arius arguing about Christ

The big problem with Arius' words was that they denied these words from John 1:1-3:

"In the beginning was the Word [Christ], and the Word was with God, and the Word was God. He was with God in the beginning. Through him all things were made; without him nothing was made that has been made."

Arius went against a very important Christian belief: that Christ the Son is God, just as God the Father is God. If what Arius said was true, then Christ the Son would have been lower than God the Father— which would have meant that Christ wasn't fully God.

Arius' main opponent was another priest from Alexandria, a brilliant Bible scholar called **Athanasius**.

Athanasius
(296 - 373)

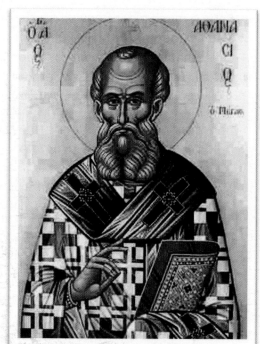

Icon of Athanasius

Unlike Arius, Athanasius was convinced that Christ was God— for God alone has the power to forgive sin. If Christ were not God, Athanasius wondered, then how would Christ's sacrifice on the cross save sinners from their sin? "Jesus that I know as my Redeemer," Athanasius said, "cannot be less than God."

The contest between Arius and Athanasius came to a head in 325 AD. That was the year when Emperor Constantine held an important church meeting called the **Council of Nicaea**. Basically, the Council of Nicaea declared that Athanasius was right, and Arius wrong. Christ the Son is not lower than God the Father, as Arius wrongly said. Instead, true Christians are to believe in a

> The **Council of Nicaea** was the first meeting of the whole Christian Church. In 325 AD, bishops from all over the Roman Empire gathered at Nicaea to discuss the Arian Controversy. This was the council that first wrote the **Nicene Creed**, an important statement of faith that many churches still recite today.

Holy Trinity of one God in

three persons— God the Father, God the Son and God the Holy Spirit. All three persons of the Holy Trinity are equally God.

This does not mean that Christians worship three gods! Instead, each person of the Trinity represents one of three ways in which God has revealed Himself to man. God the Father revealed Himself by creating everything we see. God the Son revealed Himself by being born as a man, by bearing the penalty for man's sin, and then by rising from the dead. God the Holy Spirit revealed Himself as the Lord and Giver of life, and by speaking through the prophets.

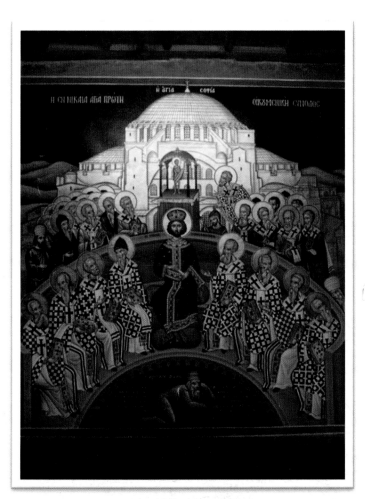

Emperor Constantine and his bishops at the Council of Nicaea, with the condemned Arius under their feet

The Arian Controversy didn't end at Nicaea. Poor Athanasius had to defend his ideas often, and sometimes lost. Over the years, Athanasius' enemies managed to kick him out of Alexandria no fewer than five times! No matter what happened, Athanasius never stopped insisting that Christ was both God and man— fully divine and fully human, both at the same time. The persistent Athanasius is now honored as a "doctor of the Catholic Church"— in other words, one of the greatest theologians of all time.

Athanasius is also remembered as a father of the **canon of Scripture**. Athanasius was among the first to collect the twenty-seven books of the New Testament, and to insist that only these twenty-seven were inspired by God.

> The **canon of Scripture** is the list of God-inspired books that make up the Holy Bible. Athanasius was a father of the New Testament canon.

CHAPTER 3:

The Christian Church in the Early Middle Ages

Europe

Europe is the sixth largest continent, smaller than all other continents except Australia.

Europe is also part of **Eurasia**—a huge land mass that includes both Europe and Asia. Because no ocean or sea divides Europe from Asia, mapmakers use two boundaries to divide them. The first boundary is the north-south line of the **Ural Mountains** and the **Ural River**. Europe lies west of this line, and Asia east. The other boundary is the east-west line of the **Caspian Sea**, the **Caucasus Mountains** and the **Black Sea**. Europe lies north of this line, and Asia south.

Three big peninsulas jut from the southern edge of Europe. To the west lies the **Iberian Peninsula**, home to Spain and Portugal. In the center lies the **Italian Peninsula**, home to the Republic of Italy. And to the east lies the **Balkan Peninsula**, home to Greece, Bulgaria and more.

The giant peninsula that juts off northern Europe is **Fenno-Scandia**. The Scandinavian nations of Norway and Sweden lie on Fenno-Scandia. So does Finland, as well as part of Russia.

Relics

A **relic** is a very old object that is connected to someone from Christian history, either Christ Himself or one of the saints. A relic might be something a saint owned, something a saint touched, or even the bones of a saint.

Some Christians believe that relics may still work miracles, even after all these years.

The Bible itself tells of miracles that happened when people touched relics. The first miraculous relics were the bones of the prophet Elisha. The Old Testament says in 2 Kings 13:21:

"Once while some Israelites were burying a man, suddenly they saw a band of raiders; so they threw the man's body into Elisha's tomb. When the body touched Elisha's bones, the man came to life and stood up on his feet."

The New Testament tells of more such miracles, including these from Acts 19:11-12:

"God did extraordinary miracles through Paul, so that even handkerchiefs and aprons that had touched him were taken to the sick, and their illnesses were cured and the evil spirits left them."

With miracles like these, it isn't hard to understand why early Christians were fascinated with relics. Some would travel any distance, and pay any price, for their chance to see a miracle.

In modern times, though, most Christians are more doubtful about relics. Most relics have changed hands so many times that it is hard to know for sure if they ever truly belonged to a saint. Who can say for sure that at some unguarded moment over the centuries, some greedy soul didn't steal the real relics, leaving false ones in their places?

Even so, the Catholic Church still preserves many relics. Some are supposed to be pieces of wood from the True Cross, the cross upon which Roman soldiers crucified Jesus. Others are supposed to be iron from the spikes that held Jesus on the cross. Besides these, there are also the sword of St. Peter, which the Apostle Peter used to slice off the ear of the high priest's servant in John 18:10; the Spear of Longinus, which a Roman soldier used to pierce Jesus' side in John 19:34; and many others.

Well-known Relics

The **Shroud of Turin** is a linen burial cloth that is supposed to bear an image of Jesus' face. Some people believe that the face was burned onto the shroud by the same mighty power that raised Jesus from the dead. Others believe that some medieval artist painted the face as part of a clever hoax.

An altered photo of the Shroud of Turin

Reliquaries are special containers made to show and preserve relics. A reliquary may be a glass-sided display case like the one at left, which is supposed to hold the chains Roman soldiers used to bind St. Peter. A reliquary may also be a church-shaped casket like the one at right, which is supposed to hold remains of St. Thomas Becket (Chapter 13).

The Monastic Movement

The first Christians almost never worshiped in church buildings. Instead, most worshiped in **house churches**. These were small groups that met quietly in believers' homes, where it was easier to hide from the prying eyes of the Christian-hating Romans.

Some early Christians also dug secret chambers called **catacombs**, hidden in and around cities like Rome and Naples. Most

House churches were small groups of Christians who met in believers' homes.
Catacombs were secret underground chambers built by early Christians, mainly to bury their dead.

catacombs began as burial places for Christian dead. For the Romans usually burned their dead; while Christians preferred to bury their dead, in hope of the resurrection. A few catacombs also held special rooms for church services.

All of that changed when **Constantine** came along. As we read in Chapter 1, Constantine was the first Christian Emperor of Rome.

Under the approving nod of Constantine, Christianity moved from forbidden to fashionable. Constantine donated public lands to churches, and even spent public

Grave niches in the walls of a catacomb beneath Rome, photo courtesy Dnalor 01

money to build the first Christian cathedrals. No longer did Roman Christians have to hide in catacombs!

But Constantine's help came with a price. Before Constantine, most churches were poor. The few churches that did have extra money rarely spent it on buildings— for they had no buildings. Instead, they used extra money to help hurting church members, or to benefit the poor.

After Constantine, though, churches found all kinds of new uses for money. For the first time, churches could spend money on big buildings and rich possessions. Now some churches paid more attention to worldly treasures than they did to their people.

Not all Christians were comfortable with riches. Some felt that the richer Christians grew, the less they followed Christ. After all, Christ was never rich in worldly treasures. Instead, Christ taught his disciples to be "rich toward God"— to store up treasures in heaven, as He said in Matthew 6:19-21:

"Do not store up for yourselves treasures on earth, where moths and vermin destroy, and where thieves break in and steal. But store up for yourselves treasures in heaven, where moths and vermin do not destroy, and where thieves do not break in and steal. For where your treasure is, there your heart will be also."

Saint Anthony of Thebes
(251? – 356?)

One of the first Christians who felt this way was **Anthony of Thebes**.

The future Saint Anthony was born into a rich Christian family from Thebes, Egypt— near the famous Valley of the Kings, where the ancient Egyptians buried so many pharaohs. Anthony's father died when his son was only 18, leaving him enough money to stay rich all his life.

But Anthony was one of those rare Christians who really took Christ's words to heart. So instead of keeping his family fortune, Anthony followed the advice Jesus gave to the rich young man in Mark 10:21-22:

"Jesus looked at him and loved him. 'One thing you lack,' he said. 'Go, sell everything you have and give to the poor, and you will have treasure in heaven. Then come, follow me.' At this the man's face fell. He went away sad, because he had great wealth."

Unlike the rich young man from Mark, Anthony really did sell all of his father's property and give to the poor— holding back only enough to care for his sister. He then moved out to the deserts of Egypt, where he lived one of the hardest lifestyles any Christian has ever lived.

Anthony's reason for moving to the desert was simple: he wanted to put the material world out of his mind so that he could focus on the spiritual world. Anything that reminded Anthony of his old life was a distraction, something that might come between him and God. So Anthony gave up women— for fear that if he married, then he might love his wife more than he loved God. And Anthony ate no more than he absolutely needed to— for fear that if his stomach was too full, then he might forget to thank God for daily bread. Anthony sometimes ate only once every 3 – 4 days!

Anthony of Thebes being tempted by demons

> St. Anthony was an **ascetic**— someone who denies himself all worldly pleasures so that he can devote himself entirely to God.

Denying oneself isn't easy, especially if one has once been rich. Many times over the years, Anthony was tempted to leave his harsh desert and go back to the comfort of city life. Medieval artists painted several pictures of Anthony in his desert home, steadfastly battling the demons of temptation.

Anthony never gave in to temptation, no matter what demons he faced. True to his promises, Anthony remained in his desert home for the rest of his life— which lasted an incredible 105 years! In resisting temptation so long and so well, Anthony won a reputation as one of the holiest Christians who ever lived.

〰〰

Anthony of Thebes was one of the first **monks**. Monks and nuns are devoted believers who withdraw from the world they can see to focus on the world they can't see— the invisible spiritual world of God. Monks are men, and nuns are women. Both use **spiritual disciplines**— things like prayer, fasting, studying the Bible and serving others— to draw closer to God.

> Monks, Nuns and Monasteries

As Anthony's reputation grew, more and more monks followed him into the desert, trying to live lives as holy as his.

Some of these monks formed the first **monasteries**. These were communities of monks who lived together, worked together, and helped each other fight off the temptations of the outside world.

Every monk who joined a monastery vowed to live by that monastery's rules. Most monasteries lived by their own special rules, which their leaders wrote to help monks stay true to their faith. Although some rules were stricter than others, nearly all monasteries required at least three common vows.

The first common vow was the **Vow of Poverty**. The monk promised to give up all of his worldly

> A **monastery** is a community of monks who live and work together.

possessions, holding back little or nothing for himself. Some monasteries allowed their monks to own absolutely nothing, except maybe a bowl to hold their food.

The second common vow was the **Vow of Chastity**, in which the monk promised never to marry. And the third was the **Vow of Obedience**— in which the monk promised to do whatever his monastery's leader, the **abbot**, ordered him to do.

Early monks worked hard to support themselves. Most monasteries sewed all of their own clothes, and grew as much of their own food as they could. Most also made trade goods— valuable items to sell, so that they could buy things they couldn't make for themselves. Some monasteries made wine, beer or baked goods; others cloth or shoes; still others furniture.

St. Catherine's Monastery at the foot of Mount Sinai, Egypt, built in the 500s

Older monasteries often had several buildings, all arranged around a central court. Of course, each monastery had its church or chapel. Each also had a dormitory filled with **cells**— tiny bedrooms for the monks. Many also had schools and/or hospitals. There might also be a library for the monastery's precious books, as well as a **scriptorium** for copying books.

A **scriptorium** was a room in which special monks called **scribes** copied out books by hand.

Some monasteries surrounded themselves with walls, which served two purposes. First, they protected the monks' bodies. Second, they shielded the monks' minds from the temptations of the outside world.

To set themselves apart from other men, some monks cut their hair in a special style called the **tonsure**. Tonsured monks shaved the tops of their heads, but kept a ring of unshaven hair around the top.

In addition to their habits, some nuns wore a white headdress called a **wimple**.

Part of every abbot's job was making sure that his monks kept their vows. Some abbots allowed their monks to eat only once per day in winter, and twice in summer. Monks ate in silence, not talking and laughing like schoolboys. Eating too much, talking too much and laughing too much were all signs that monks no longer felt sorry for their sins— which meant that they were no longer grateful for Christ's sacrifice.

Early monks never let themselves get too comfortable. For example, they often wore **hair shirts** beneath their **habits**, or outer robes. They wove their hair shirts from the scratchiest goat hair, deliberately making them as rough and itchy as possible. The constant discomfort of hair shirts served as a constant reminder of Christ's sufferings.

Early monks slept as little as possible; for sleep was also too comfortable. Such luxuries as soft beds and comfortable chairs were unthinkable. Many slept on the hard floor in their hair shirts and habits, ready to rise for prayer at a moment's notice.

Medieval monasteries often followed the **canonical hours**, a daily schedule that set aside certain times for prayer and worship. Such monasteries called all monks to prayer seven times each day. The idea for the canonical hours may have come from King David, who wrote in Psalm 119:164:

"Seven times a day I praise you for your righteous laws."

More Giants of the Early Church

The future **Saint Jerome** was born into a wealthy family from a part of the Roman Empire called Dalmatia, just across the Adriatic Sea from Italy. Wanting the best education for his son, Jerome's father sent him to school in Rome.

Young Jerome was an excellent student— when he wasn't wasting time at theaters and parties, as most rich young men did. Although Jerome called himself a Christian, he rarely studied the Bible. Instead, he learned what most Roman schools taught: the classics of Greek literature, great works by Homer, Plato and many others.

Saint Jerome
(340? – 420)

Years later, while suffering through a serious illness, Jerome had a life-changing vision. Just what Jerome saw, no one now knows for sure. Some say that he saw himself in the afterlife, being punished for wasting his life reading Greek classics when he should have been studying the Bible.

Whatever Jerome saw, this vision marked the end of his classical studies. As soon as he recovered, Jerome focused his whole attention on his new life's work— becoming a great Christian scholar.

A **scholar** is someone who studies a subject deeply, learning all there is to know about it.

Jerome went on to become one of the best Christian scholars of all time. Jerome's friend Augustine of Hippo paid him this highest of compliments: "What Jerome is ignorant of, no mortal has ever known."

The Vulgate

Before Jerome's time, there was no complete translation of the Bible in Latin. Instead, there were several incomplete translations, all in different styles of Latin from different times.

Jerome changed all that. In 382, the pope asked Jerome to translate the four gospels into good Latin. Now Jerome understood why he had spent all those years studying Greek! Since Matthew, Mark, Luke and John all wrote their books mostly in Greek, the Greek expert Jerome was the perfect choice to translate their work.

After finishing this first assignment, Jerome went on to translate the rest of the Greek New Testament into Latin.

Translating the Old Testament would turn out to be much harder. For the Old Testament authors wrote in

"St. Jerome in his Study" by Domenico Ghirlandaio

Hebrew, which Jerome didn't know as well as he knew Greek. So Jerome spent years learning Hebrew from a Jewish-born man who was now a Christian. Then Jerome spent more years finishing an enormous task: translating all 39 books of the Hebrew Old Testament into Latin.

The result of Jerome's long years of work was one of the most important books of all time: a complete Latin Bible called the **Vulgate**. Its name comes from *versio vulgata*, Latin for "the version commonly used."

Actually, to say that Jerome's Vulgate was "commonly used" would be a huge understatement! From the next 1,000 years, the Vulgate was the only version of the Bible that most people in the West ever saw or heard. No matter what their native language, Western priests always read the Bible in the Latin of the Vulgate.

₪₪₪₪₪₪₪₪₪₪₪₪₪₪₪₪₪₪₪₪₪₪₪₪₪₪₪₪₪₪₪₪₪

Saint Monica
(331 – 387)

The future **Saint Monica** started as a Christian mother from Hippo, a port in North Africa (now Annaba, Algeria). Like all Christian mothers, Monica wanted all of her children safe in the arms of Christ.

So Monica grieved to see her eldest son resisting Christ. The worst day of Monica's life came when her eldest son rejected Christ altogether, and instead took up a strange religion called Manichaeism.

In fear for her son's life, Monica cried to her bishop— begging him to do something, anything, to save her son. Touched to the heart by Monica's tears, the bishop told her that she must never stop praying for her son. For he promised her, "the child of those tears shall never perish."

At the time, Monica had no idea that she was praying for a future saint.

Early in life, **Saint Augustine of Hippo** was anything but a saint. Despite all of Monica's pleading, young Augustine drank too much, gambled too much and partied too much. Worst of all, Augustine had a child with a woman who wasn't his wife. Although it pained Augustine to disappoint his mother, he loved his wicked lifestyle too much to give it up.

Saint Augustine
of Hippo
(354 – 430)

One day when Augustine was 32 years old, a devoted Christian named Alypius stopped by to share some scriptures from Paul's letter to the Romans. In his head, Augustine knew that everything Paul said was right; but in his heart, he still didn't feel ready to give his life to Christ. Anguished to the point of tears, Augustine walked away so that Alypius wouldn't see him crying.

As Augustine walked along his tortured way, he heard a childish voice coming from a nearby house— or at least, he thought he heard a childish voice. The child seemed to be chanting, "Take up and read, take up and read." Augustine searched his memory for some childhood song or game that used these words, but couldn't think of one.

Augustine of Hippo with his beloved mother Monica

Finally, Augustine understood what he was supposed to "take up and read": the Bible! Running back to Alypius, Augustine seized the Book of Romans, opened it and read the first words that met his eyes.

Just as Anthony of Thebes found his life verses in Mark 10:21-22, so Augustine found his life verses in Romans 13:13-14. From the moment he read those verses, Augustine knew that the Lord had called him to give up his life of sin and serve the Church. Other than Alypius, the first person to hear the good news of Augustine's conversion was his faithful mother Monica, who had never stopped praying for her son.

Augustine went on to become one of the best servants the Church ever had. He is best remembered for two important Christian ideas: (1) original sin and (2) total depravity.

According to Augustine, the original sin happened when Adam and Eve deliberately disobeyed God in the Garden of Eden (Genesis 3). As parents of the whole human race, Adam and Eve handed down sin to all of their children. This means that everyone is born "totally depraved"— completely sinful, and completely unable to turn toward God without Christ's help.

> **Original sin** means that all human beings are born under the sin of Adam and Eve.
> **Total depravity** means that all human beings are completely sinful, and completely unable to turn toward God without Christ's help.

Original sin helps explain why God the Father had to send His Son Jesus Christ. Out of all people who ever lived on earth, only Christ wasn't born into original sin— for Christ was born of God, not of Adam. Christ went on to live the only perfect, sinless life ever. So only Christ can help people who are born in sin turn away from their sin, and turn toward God.

The Pelagian Controversy

A preacher called **Pelagius** disagreed with Augustine. Like Anthony of Thebes, Pelagius was a monk who denied himself every day, turning away from sin every day. "If I can turn away from sin," Pelagius thought, "then why can't others do the same?" Pelagius taught that people aren't born into original sin. Instead, Pelagius said, people choose to sin— which means that if they try hard enough, then they can also choose not to sin.

The problem was that if Pelagius was right, then Augustine was wrong about original sin— which meant that people could turn toward God on their own, without Christ's help.

Just as the Council of Nicaea met to answer Arius (Chapter 2), so the Council of Carthage met to answer Pelagius. In 418, the Council of Carthage decided that Augustine was right, and Pelagius wrong. True Christians were to believe what Augustine taught: that all people are born into original sin, and need Jesus Christ to save them from their sin. As for Pelagius, the Council declared him a heretic.

Christian Missionaries in the British Isles

When the Roman army left the British Isles, it left behind many Christians there— including, if the legend is true, King Arthur and his knights (Chapter 2). However, there were also other religions there. The Celtic religion of the druids had not yet died out; and the invading Anglo-Saxons brought in pagan religions of their own.

Three hundred years later, almost everyone in the British Isles called himself a Christian. Many missionaries spent their whole lives carrying the gospel to the British Isles. This section describes three such missionaries: Saint Patrick, Saint Columba and Saint Augustine of Canterbury.

Saint Patrick
(? – 493)

The future **Saint Patrick** was born to Christian parents in a Christian part of Scotland. Patrick was still a teenager when Celtic raiders kidnapped him and carried him off to Ireland. There Patrick became what no Christian boy ever dreamed of being: a slave to a druid, a priest of the Celtic religion.

At first, young Patrick hated his master's savage religion. Later, though, his hatred turned to pity for the Irish people. Patrick understood now why the Irish lived like savages. It was because they had never heard of the mercy and salvation that God offered in Jesus Christ!

After about 6 years in Ireland, Patrick received a vision. Somehow, he just knew that a ship was waiting somewhere to take him back to Scotland. So Patrick slipped away from his druid master and headed for a port on the east coast. The fact that this port lay 200 miles away, all of it on foot, didn't stop him. Upon reaching the coast, the tired Patrick boarded his waiting ship and sailed home to Scotland.

After all he'd been through, Patrick expected to find peace and safety in Scotland. Instead, he received another vision. This time, poor Irishmen appeared to Patrick, begging him to come and "walk among us once more." And so, ignoring the dangers that all Christians faced in Celtic Ireland, Patrick sailed back to share the gospel with the Irish people he had grown to love.

Patrick spent the rest of his life in Ireland— arguing with druids, sharing the gospel and baptizing new Christians. As the one missionary who did more to bring Christianity to Ireland than any other, Saint Patrick became the patron saint of Ireland.

The name of Patrick is also tied to three well-known Irish legends. The first says that one day as Patrick sat on a hilltop, trying to fast and pray, some snakes attacked him. So Patrick asked God to banish all snakes from Ireland— which explains why there are no wild snakes in Ireland, even now.

A second legend says that Patrick used the **shamrock** to represent the Holy Trinity. The shamrock is a three-leafed clover found all over Ireland. Patrick said that just as the shamrock is one plant with three leaves, so God is one God in three persons: God the Father, God the Son and God the Holy Spirit.

Yet another legend says that Patrick drew the first **Celtic cross** (Chapter 2). One day as Patrick was preaching to some Celts, they showed him a standing stone engraved with a circle— probably a monument to a Celtic moon goddess. Patrick answered by drawing a cross through the circle, and then filling his cross with a Celtic knot. To Patrick, the endless Celtic knot represented the endless love of God.

Stained glass of Saint Patrick holding a shamrock

Saint Columba
(521 - 597)

Saint Columba did what Patrick did, only in reverse: instead of being born in Scotland and ministering in Ireland, Columba was born in Ireland and ministered in Scotland.

In 563, Columba moved from Ireland to the island of **Iona**. Iona is one of the Inner Hebrides, which lie just off Scotland's northeast coast. There Columba built a new monastery, which he used to train Scottish ministers. From his base at Iona, Columba sent ministers all over Scotland, planting churches wherever they went.

Columba making the sign of the cross at the gates of Inverness

However, there was one city where Columba's ministers weren't welcome. This was **Inverness**, which lay near the northern end of the famous **Loch Ness**.

Inverness was the home of **Brude**, a stubborn Pictish king who wanted nothing to do with Christianity. When Brude heard that Columba was on his way to Inverness, he barred his gates. But Columba drew the sign of the cross in the air; and as he did so, the bars flew back, and the gates swung wide. In awe of Columba's miracle, Brude changed his mind about Christianity. Columba went on to baptize all of Inverness.

～～～～～～～～～～～～～～～～～～～～～～～～～～～～～～～～～

Around 595 AD, a powerful pope called Gregory the Great decided to send a missionary to Great Britain. Sharing the gospel was only part of this missionary's task. The other part was to establish the Church of Rome's authority over Britain. Gregory wanted all British Christians to know that he was their holy father, and that they must obey him.

The pope's love of authority led him to choose an older man, a monastery leader who already knew all about authority. The man Pope Gregory chose was another Augustine— not Augustine of Hippo, but the future **Saint Augustine of Canterbury**.

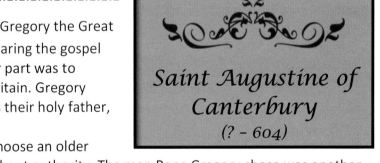

Saint Augustine of Canterbury
(? - 604)

At first, Augustine was most unhappy to be the pope's choice. After all, Augustine was a monk, not a missionary. He had expected to serve out his life in a safe monastery, not risk his neck in a barbarian backwater like Britain. For Augustine had heard how savage the Anglo-Saxons were, and how many ships had sunk while crossing the treacherous English Channel.

Halfway to Britain, a frightened Augustine announced that the savage Anglo-Saxons simply weren't ready for civilization, and started to turn back! Before he did, though, Pope Gregory wrote another letter ordering him on to Britain.

Canterbury Cathedral, seat of the Archbishop of Canterbury

After landing in southeastern England, Augustine set up his church capital at a place called **Canterbury**, Kent. Pope Gregory appointed Augustine as the first **Archbishop of Canterbury**— the overseer of all churches in the large **see**, or church territory, around Canterbury.

Ever since then, the Archbishop of Canterbury has been the official leader of all English churches.

Augustine of Canterbury went on to convert many Saxons to Christianity— including the first Christian Anglo-Saxon king ever, Ethelbert of Kent.

Christ on His throne in an illustration from the Book of Kells

ꛯꛯꛯꛯꛯꛯꛯꛯꛯꛯꛯꛯꛯꛯꛯꛯꛯꛯꛯꛯꛯꛯꛯꛯꛯꛯꛯꛯꛯ

The Book of Kells

Before about 1450, when Johannes Gutenberg invented the printing press, all books had to be copied by hand. Some monks spent their whole lives in dreary scriptoriums, copying out books word-for-word.

Not all books were plain words, though. To make their books more pleasing to the eye, some monks added fancy initials to start every page, or even every paragraph. The best books also had hand-painted illustrations by the monastery's best artists. Any hand-copied, hand-illustrated book from medieval times is called an **illuminated manuscript**.

> *"Writing is excessive drudgery. It crooks your back, it dims your sight, it twists your stomach and your sides."*
>
> *"As the harbor is welcome to the sailor, so is the last line to the scribe."*
>
> — Scribes' comments found in the margins of two medieval manuscripts

One of the best illuminated manuscripts ever made is the **Book of Kells**. This is a copy of the four gospels created by the monks of Iona around 700 – 800 AD, probably in honor of Saint Columba. Stunning art marks almost every page of the Book of Kells, making it a precious treasure.

Around 800 AD, a band of fierce Vikings raided Iona, scattering frightened monks in all directions. One of those monks probably carried the precious Book of Kells to the monastery at Kells, Ireland, which is how the book got its name.

Unfortunately, Kells turned out to be no safer than Iona had been. Around 1,000 AD, some unknown thief stole the book, no doubt for the gold and gems on its cover. After ripping off the valuable cover, the thief hid the rest under some damp sod, where monks later found it. The Book of Kells is still missing its cover, and still bears water damage from its time under the sod.

A hand-drawn initial letter from the Book of Kells, complete with Celtic knot

The Black Sea

The Black Sea is a big sea on the border between Europe and Asia. Like the Mediterranean, the Black Sea is an **inland sea**— one that is almost completely surrounded by land.

To reach the Black Sea from the Mediterranean, ships must first sail through the **Aegean Sea**. The Aegean is the "duck's wing" of the Mediterranean that reaches up between Greece and Turkey. From there, ships must sail on through three narrow bodies of water: (1) the **Dardanelles** strait, (2) the **Sea of Marmara** and (3) the **Bosporus** strait.

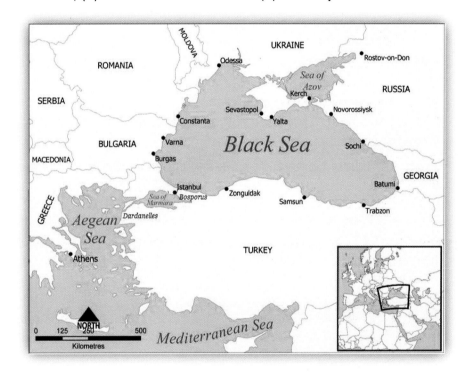

At the southern end of the Bosporus stands a very old, very important city. Over the centuries, different peoples have called this city by different names. The ancient Greeks called it **Byzantion**, or **Byzantium** in Latin. The Romans renamed it **Constantinople** after Constantine, their first Christian emperor. And in the 1900s, the people of Turkey renamed it **Istanbul**.

The main thing that made Constantinople so important was its location. Since the Bosporus was so narrow, Constantinople acted like a gatehouse between the Black Sea and the Mediterranean Sea. Whoever controlled Constantinople had the power to decide who could trade in the Black Sea, and who could not.

Besides its great location, Constantinople was also blessed with a great natural harbor called the **Golden Horn**. The calm, deep waters of the Golden Horn made Constantinople the perfect place to load and unload trade ships.

Just west of the Black Sea lies a large section of Europe called the **Balkan Peninsula**, or simply the **Balkans**. The Balkan Peninsula is the largest of the three peninsulas that jut off Europe's southern edge; the other two are the Iberian and the Italian. One of the oldest countries in the world, Greece, covers the southern end of the Balkans.

In medieval times, Constantinople and the Balkans were the heart of the Byzantine Empire.

The Byzantine Empire

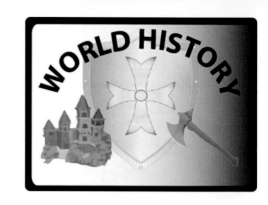

WORLD HISTORY

"**B**yzantine Empire" was a new name for the **Eastern Roman Empire**. This was the part of the Roman Empire that lived on after the fall of Rome in 476 AD (Chapter 1).

Back in 285 AD, Emperor Diocletian split his struggling Roman Empire in two. After that, the Roman Empire was really two empires, one in the west and another in the east. The Western Roman Empire usually had its capital at Rome; while the Eastern Roman Empire always had its capital at Constantinople.

It was only the Western Roman Empire that fell in 476. As for the Eastern Roman Empire, it lived on for nearly 1,000 years— all the way to 1453, when the Ottoman Empire finally captured Constantinople (Chapter 20).

So why the new name? The answer is that the East was different from the West. One difference was that most easterners spoke Greek, not Latin as the Romans did. More differences lay in the church. Over time, the Greek churches of the East grew far apart from the Latin churches of the West.

In light of all of these differences, historians gave the Eastern Roman Empire a different name: "Byzantine Empire." The word "Byzantine" comes from *Byzantion*, the original Greek name of Constantinople.

> **Emperor Justinian I (483? - 565)**

Of course, the people of the Byzantine Empire didn't know about this name change— because it hadn't happened yet! In their minds, the Byzantine Empire was still just the Roman Empire. Byzantine emperors like **Justinian I** didn't see the fall of Rome as a historic milestone. Instead, they saw it as a setback— a bump along the road toward rebuilding the great Roman Empire.

For someone who wound up so powerful, Emperor Justinian I came from rather humble beginnings. The future emperor was born a **commoner** by the name of Flavius. However, Flavius had two advantages which most commoners didn't. One was that his uncle, whose name was Justin, happened to be the best general in the Byzantine army. The other was that General Justin had no sons.

> A **commoner** is someone born into a family with no royal or noble blood.

Justin's big chance came in 518, when an elderly emperor died. Since this emperor also had no sons, the empire held an election to decide who would take his place. As the empire's favorite general, Justin easily won this election.

Like most royals, Emperor Justin I needed an heir to take his place when he was gone. So he decided to adopt his nephew Flavius. Along with adoption came a new adoptive name: "Justinian," meaning "son of Justin."

Mosaic of Justinian I from the Basilica of San Vitale in Ravenna, Italy

Empress Theodora (500 - 548)

Justinian's wife, **Empress Theodora**, also started out as a commoner. Her father was a lowly animal trainer, teaching tame bears to entertain crowds between chariot races. Young Theodora followed her father into the entertainment business, becoming an actress in naughty plays. Since the Byzantines looked down on entertainers, it seemed unlikely that Theodora would ever be anything but an actress.

A trip to Egypt changed all that. When Theodora was about 16, she moved from Constantinople to Alexandria, Egypt, where she became a Christian. As an upstanding young Christian woman, Theodora couldn't possibly earn her living as an actress in naughty plays! So instead, the future empress took up an even humbler profession: she became a wool-spinner.

Years before he became emperor, Justinian somehow crossed paths with the lowly Theodora. He longed to marry her; but unfortunately, an old law forbade nobles to marry entertainers— even if they weren't entertainers anymore.

In desperation, Justinian begged his uncle Justin to repeal that old law. Justin finally did, allowing Justinian and Theodora to marry in 525. When Justin died two years later, the once-lowly Theodora took on one of the loftiest titles in the world: Empress of the Byzantine Empire!

The first thing Justinian did as emperor was to repair his empire's legal system. Before Justinian, the Byzantine Empire was a confusing collection of conquered peoples, each with its own laws. Justinian wanted to unite all of his people under the same law— one righteous set of laws that would be the same all over his vast empire. Historians call this law the **Justinian Code**.

Empress Theodora

The **Justinian Code** consisted of four main parts. First came the **Codex**, which contained the laws themselves. Next came the **Digests**, which explained the thinking behind the laws. The **Institutes** were textbooks for law students; and the **Novels** presented new laws written after the Codex.

One important purpose of the Justinian Code was to make the Byzantine Empire more Christian. The very first law insisted that all good citizens must be faithful Christians!

The Justinian Code (written 529 - 534)

Thus under Justinian I, Roman law came full circle. Earlier emperors had made it illegal to be a Christian. But Justinian made it illegal to be anything but a Christian.

Justinian's strong opinions about law and order almost ruined him. In January 532, riots in Constantinople almost drove Justinian off his throne.

The Nika Riots started over a chariot race, of all things. Fast, dangerous chariot racing was as popular in Constantinople as it had been Rome. The city's main racing arena, the **Hippodrome**, held up to 100,000 fans, all screaming for one of four teams: the Greens, the Blues, the Whites and the Reds. Justinian and Theodora were Blues fans, but the Greens were also popular.

The Nika Riots were named for the cries of the rioters, who shouted "Nika"— Greek for "Conquer!"

Mosaic of a chariot race winner

After an especially important chariot race, a fight broke out between Blues fans and Greens fans. When the fight was over, several people lay dead.

Most racing fans saw these deaths as accidents— unfortunate, but forgivable under the circumstances. But Justinian saw them differently. As a strong believer in law and order, Justinian insisted on arresting the killers, both Blue and Green, and sentencing them to death.

The next big racing event at the Hippodrome fell on January 13, 532. From the start of the first race, both Greens and Blues chanted at Justinian, warning him not to execute his prisoners. The longer Justinian didn't answer, the angrier the chanters grew.

At race's end, the chanters demanded that Justinian release his prisoners. When Justinian refused, they started to riot! That very night, rioters burned part of the Great Palace of Constantinople. The next few days saw more fires, destroying more of Constantinople's best buildings.

As the week wore on, Justinian learned that his enemies in the Hippodrome had elected a new emperor to take his place. At this, Justinian decided that his reign was probably over— and that he had better get out of Constantinople while he still could!

Theodora chose this moment to prove her courage. When the Empress heard that Justinian was planning to run away, she stopped him with these famous words:

"Those who have worn the crown should never survive its loss. Never will I see the day when I am not saluted as empress. Royalty makes a fine burial shroud."

In other words, Theodora would rather die young as an empress than live on forever as a disgraced commoner. Taking courage from Theodora, Justinian decided to either save his throne or die trying.

Justinian's plan took advantage of the hatred between Greens fans and Blues fans. Six days after the Nika Riots began, Justinian sent a loyal supporter called Narses into the Hippodrome. At Narses' belt hung a purse bulging with gold. Heading straight for the Blues, Narses reminded Blue leaders that Justinian had always been a Blue. He also reminded them that the man they had elected to replace Justinian was as Green as Green could be. And each time Narses spoke, a bit of gold passed from his purse to a Blue leader's purse.

Whether it was the reminders or the gold, Justinian's plan worked. After considering the situation, the Blues decided to walk out of the Hippodrome— much to the astonishment of the Greens. With the Blues out of the way, Justinian's best troops descended on the rioters who remained, killing them by the thousands.

Justinian I Coin

Instead of weakening Justinian, the Nika Riots ended up strengthening him.

One of the buildings destroyed by the Nika Riots was an old cathedral called the **Hagia Sophia**. Actually, this was the second Hagia Sophia to be destroyed. Another riot had destroyed the first Hagia Sophia long ago, in the time of John Chrysostom (below).

The Hagia Sophia

Outside the Hagia Sophia

Once again, the empire had to rebuild the Hagia Sophia. Justinian vowed to make his new Hagia Sophia the grandest church ever built—grander, even, than Solomon's Temple in Jerusalem.

Five years later, Justinian delivered on his vow. The third Hagia Sophia is without a doubt one of the grandest buildings ever built!

The most fantastic detail of the Hagia Sophia was its domed roof. This immense dome measured 102 feet across the base, and soared to an incredible 180 feet high at its peak. Forty arched windows ringed the base of the dome, filling the church with warm, glowing light. The effect was so stunning that the human eye could hardly take it all in.

Another fine detail of the Hagia Sophia was the **mosaic** art inside. The Byzantines were expert mosaic artists, and the mosaics inside the Hagia Sophia were some of their best. They filled whole fields of their mosaics with *tesserae* cut from real

> A **mosaic** is a work of art made of many small tiles, all cemented onto a wall, floor or ceiling. Mosaic tiles are called **tesserae.**

gold, silver and precious stones. The warm glow from the Hagia Sophia's high windows made the sight of these mosaics even more stunning.

As the finest cathedral in the East, the Hagia Sophia became a symbol of Eastern Christianity. The **Patriarch of Constantinople**, leader of all Eastern churches, made his headquarters inside the Hagia Sophia.

〰〰〰〰〰〰〰〰〰〰〰〰〰〰〰〰〰〰〰〰〰〰〰〰〰〰〰〰〰〰

After putting down the Nika Riots, Justinian turned to the greatest task of his life: taking back the lost territories of the Western Roman Empire. Justinian owed most of his victories to the expert skills of his favorite general, a Byzantine hero called **Belisarius**.

The first place Belisarius took back was North Africa. His enemies there were the **Vandals**— the same Vandals who had sacked Rome back in 455. Since then, the Vandals had moved over to North Africa. The

Inside the Hagia Sophia, looking up at the dome

Vandals' capital, Carthage, is now part of Tunis, Tunisia.

The big showdown between Belisarius and the Vandals came at the **Battle of Ad Decimum**. *Ad Decimum* was nothing but a milepost on the road to Carthage, ten miles south of the city.

At first, Belisarius seemed doomed to defeat— for the Vandals brought 15,000 troops to the Battle of Ad Decimum, twice as many as Belisarius brought. Early in the battle, the Vandals' numbers forced Belisarius to retreat.

Mosaic featuring Mary and Jesus at center, with Emperor Constantine on the right and Emperor Justinian on the left. Constantine offers Jesus the walled city of Constantinople, while Justinian offers the Hagia Sophia.

As the Vandals advanced, though, the Vandal King Hilderic learned that his brother had just been killed in battle. At the sight of his beloved brother's body, Hilderic collapsed in grief— forgetting all about his army! Without Hilderic to lead it, the Vandal army collapsed, leaving Belisarius to snatch victory from the jaws of defeat.

Thus Justinian took back the part of North Africa that had been lost at the fall of Rome.

The next place Belisarius took back was his most important: Italy. His

Restoring the Roman Empire

enemies there were the Ostrogoths— the same Ostrogoths who had collapsed the Western Roman Empire back in 476. If Justinian could recapture Italy from the Ostrogoths, then he truly would have restored the lost glory of the Roman Empire!

Belisarius' work in Italy was slow, but steady. He took back Sicily, the big island off the toe of the Italian Peninsula, in 535. The next year saw Belisarius moving up the peninsula, taking back Naples and Rome. By 540, Belisarius held the whole Italian Peninsula!

Thus Justinian took back much of what the Roman Empire had lost— although he never took back far-off provinces like Britannia and Gaul.

卐卐卐卐卐卐卐卐卐卐卐卐卐

All of Belisarius' greatest victories came before a tragedy called the **Plague of Justinian**.

In the middle years of Justinian's reign, a killer disease swept through the Byzantine Empire. The

The Byzantine Empire under Justinian. Red marks the empire at the beginning of Justinian's reign. Red and orange together mark the empire at the height of Justinian's reign.

Italy
Rome
Black Sea
Spain
Constantinople
Greece
Mediterranean Sea
AFRICA
Egypt
Red Sea

Plague of Justinian reached Egypt in 541. From there, Egyptian grain carried the plague around the Mediterranean world, all the way to Constantinople in 542 – 543.

The Plague of Justinian was probably an outbreak of **bubonic plague**. The germs that cause

The Plague of Justininan (541 - 543)

bubonic plague live in fleas, which in turn live in the coats of rats

and mice. Each time a flea-bitten rat took a bite of Egyptian grain, it left behind plague germs. Since Egyptian merchants sold their grain all over the Byzantine Empire, catching the plague was easy: all one had to do was carry home a sack of flour.

Unfortunately, Byzantine doctors knew nothing of germs— which meant that they had no way to fight the deadly plague. On its worst days in Constantinople, the Plague of Justinian may have killed an astonishing 5,000 people per day— or even twice that many!

Nor was Constantinople the only city that suffered. The terrible Plague of Justinian may have killed about one-third of everyone alive in the empire when it struck— as many as 100

Plague victims receiving a blessing

million people! Young or old, rich or poor made no difference to the cruel plague; it killed all alike. With so many people dying at once, a sadder time is hard to imagine.

Yet another victim of the plague was the Byzantine army. After the Plague of Justinian, the army was too weak to defend all the ground Belisarius had taken back.

〰〰〰〰〰〰〰〰〰〰〰〰〰〰〰〰〰〰〰〰〰〰〰〰〰〰〰〰〰

The year 565 was a terrible year for the Byzantines— for that was the year when both Belisarius and Justinian died. Between the Plague of Justinian and the loss of these two heroes, the Byzantine Empire was sure to be in serious trouble the next time an enemy attacked.

The attack in Italy came from the **Lombards**. The Lombards were yet another barbarian tribe from the north,

The Lombards

much like the Vandals and the Ostrogoths. Three years after Justinian died, the Lombards swept down into northern Italy. Now that the Plague of Justinian

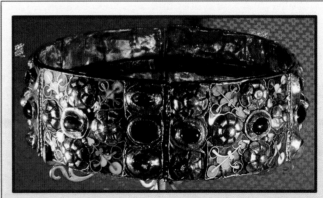

For centuries, any man who wanted to call himself "King of Italy" had to wear a symbolic crown called the **Iron Crown of Lombardy**. Although this crown is made mostly of gold and gems, it also has an iron ring inside. Legend says that the iron for this ring came from one of the spikes Roman soldiers used to nail Jesus to the cross.

had weakened the Byzantine army, the Lombards had little trouble beating it. The Byzantines retreated, leaving the Lombards to settle into their new home in northern Italy.

The Lombards would hold northern Italy for the next few hundred years. Part of northern Italy is still called "**Lombardy**" after the Lombards.

The Lombards weren't the only threat the Byzantines faced after Justinian died. Over on the Balkan Peninsula, a people called the **Slavs** swept down from the north. The **Persians** were always a threat in the east. Then came the worst threat of all: the **Islamic Empire**, founded by the prophet Muhammad on the Arabian Peninsula. See Chapter 5 for more on the Islamic Empire.

Like the Roman Empire before it, the Byzantine Empire struggled to survive against so many threats. One advantage that helped the Byzantines survive was a terrible weapon called **Greek Fire**.

Greek Fire was a sticky, hot-burning fuel that Byzantine troops hurled at all sorts of enemy targets, from ships

Greek Fire

to chariots and supply wagons. Wherever it struck, Greek Fire blazed hotter than a torch. Hot fires like these spread quickly, and are very hard to put out.

Greek Fire was especially deadly to enemy ships. Besides the fuel itself, the Byzantines invented a ship-mounted flamethrower

Byzantine marines hurling Greek Fire at their enemies

that could spray Greek Fire from a distance. Fires that hot were impossible to ignore— for any ship that burned near the water line was sure to sink. Once a ship was burning with Greek Fire, its crew was too busy fighting the fire to fight the Byzantines!

As powerful as Greek Fire was, though, it wasn't powerful enough to save the empire forever. The Byzantine Empire grew and shrank many times after Justinian; but it shrank more than it grew.

Heroes of the Eastern Church

The Christians of the West sometimes forget that Christianity started in the East. Some of the greatest heroes of the early church came from the Eastern Roman Empire.

The original **Saint Nicholas** was the Bishop of **Myra**, a town in the Eastern Roman Empire. Myra stood near what is now Demre, Turkey. Although Nicholas was a real person with a real history, most stories from his life read more like legend than history.

Saint Nicholas
(270? - 343?)

According to legend, Nicholas loved to give secret gifts to the poor— coins, small purses or other treasures, all given when no one was looking. Nicholas was particularly anxious about one poor family he knew, a father with three daughters. This father was so poor that he couldn't afford to pay his daughters' **dowries**. Without dowries, his daughters would never find husbands. And in those days, women without husbands had little hope of leading happy lives.

A **dowry** was the money and property a bride brought into her marriage, given to the groom by the same father or brother who gave away the bride.

As for Nicholas, he had plenty of money to pay the girls' small dowries. Unfortunately, their father was too proud to take money. So instead of paying the dowries in public, Nicholas paid them in secret. The night before the eldest daughter was old enough to marry, Nicholas quietly tossed a purse through her window. He did the same for the second daughter when she grew old enough.

By the time the third daughter grew old enough to marry, her proud father had caught on, and was waiting at the window. So instead of tossing the purse through the window, Nicholas tossed it into the open top of the chimney! It so happened that the third daughter had just hung her freshly-washed stockings over the fire to dry— so that instead of falling into the fire, Nicholas' purse fell into her stocking.

Over the centuries, the story of Nicholas spread around the world, changing a bit with each new telling. The name "Saint Nicholas" changed to "Sinterklaas," which eventually became "Santa Claus." The round-bellied, white-bearded Santa Claus that everyone now knows was created by a cartoonist called Thomas Nast, who first drew Santa that way in 1863.

St. Nicholas passing money through a window

ꀀꀀꀀ

One of the greatest heroes of the early church in the East was a preacher named John Chrysostom. Actually, "Chrysostom" was more an honorary title than a name. The Greek-speakers of the East called John *chrysostom*, Greek for "golden-mouthed," because he was one of the greatest preachers who ever lived.

Before he was a preacher, John was a brilliant young student from Antioch, Syria. Like the young St. Jerome, the young John Chrysostom couldn't decide: should he study Greek classics, or the Bible?

John was about 25 years old when he finally decided to study the Bible. To aid his studies, John became a monk, setting aside all worldly comforts so that he could focus on God alone (Chapter 3).

But John was no ordinary monk. Most monks allowed themselves a few small comforts— enough to stay healthy. John, on the other hand, was so strict with himself that he refused even to sit down. He

John Chrysostom

spent week after week, month after month on his feet, studying Scripture constantly. He slept only rarely, and ate as little as he possibly could.

This hard lifestyle turned out to be more than John's poor body could stand. A few years as a monk wrecked John's health, forcing him to move back to Antioch and become a preacher.

Even so, John never forgot his time as a monk. Back in Antioch, John preached about his life as a monk. He warned his people that true Christians cared nothing for riches, but instead gave away everything to help the poor. John based his sermons on Bible verses like Matthew 25:44-45:

> "They also will answer, 'Lord, when did we see you hungry or thirsty or a stranger or needing clothes or sick or in prison, and did not help you?' He will reply, 'Truly I tell you, whatever you did not do for one of the least of these, you did not do for me.'"

The more John preached, the greater his reputation grew. By 397, John's reputation was so great that the Eastern church offered him its highest office: **Archbishop of Constantinople**.

Unfortunately, the people who called John to Constantinople had no idea what he preached in his sermons. They only knew that John Chrysostom was supposed to be the best preacher in the East. And they felt that as the capital of the Eastern Roman Empire, Constantinople deserved the best preacher.

So when John showed up in Constantinople, preaching about Christians sacrificing themselves for the poor, he was headed for trouble. The poor loved John; but the rich hated him. Even John's fellow preachers didn't want to sacrifice themselves for the poor. The rich wanted to even less— for Constantinople was one of the richest cities in the world. John was especially hard on the emperor's wife, Empress Eudoxia. He blasted the empress for spending fortunes on clothes and jewelry for herself, while spending not a penny to help the poor.

To **banish** someone is to send him or her out of the country, into **exile**.

The empress would turn out to be John's worst enemy. In 403, Eudoxia ordered John's fellow church officers to **banish** him from Constantinople. But the poor wouldn't hear of it. The poor people of Constantinople loved John Chrysostom so much that when they heard of his banishment, they started to riot! This was the riot that destroyed the first Hagia Sophia cathedral. The second Hagia Sophia, of course, was destroyed by the Nika Riots (above).

To calm the rioting, Eudoxia ordered John back for a second chance. Most preachers would have taken this second chance— but not John Chrysostom! Instead, John only criticized Eudoxia more harshly. So Eudoxia banished John again, this time farther away.

On his way to his second exile, John's weak health finally failed. This great champion of the poor died in 407.

John Chrysostom on his way to exile

The Monophysite Controversy

Over time, the churches of the East, West and South grew apart from one another. One of the first big arguments between the three was over an Egyptian teaching called monophysitism.

Most Christians believe that Jesus Christ has two natures: the divine nature of God, and the human nature of a man.

Around 400 AD, some Egyptian Christians decided that Christ couldn't have a human nature. They felt that no sinful human nature could possibly be holy enough for God. And so, the Egyptians said, Christ must have only one nature: His divine nature. When the Son of God came down to Earth as a man, His divine nature must have absorbed His human nature— much like a sponge absorbs water. This is what the word **monophysite** means: "one nature."

Just as the Council of Nicaea met to answer Arius (Chapter 2), and the Council of Carthage met to answer Pelagius (Chapter 3), so the Council of Chalcedon met to answer the monophysite Christians of Egypt. Basically, the Council of Chalcedon

> ### The Council of Chalcedon (451)

decided that the monophysites were wrong. Just as Athanasius said to Arius, Christ must be both divine and human— fully God and fully man, both at the same time. If the Egyptians were right, then Christ couldn't be fully man. And if Christ wasn't fully man, then He never could have suffered the same temptations as man— which meant that He never could have conquered sin.

Nothing the Council of Chalcedon said or wrote could change the Egyptians' minds. Instead of agreeing with the Council, the Christians of Egypt decided to split off from all others.

Thus began a new church in Egypt: the Coptic Orthodox Church. The name "Coptic" comes from a Greek name for the Egyptian people.

The split between Coptic Christians and others has never healed. Even today, the Coptic Orthodox Church of Egypt is still separate from both the Roman Catholic Church and the Eastern Orthodox Church.

Empress Theodora, wife to Emperor Justinian I, became a monophysite Christian as a youth, during her fateful trip from Constantinople to Egypt.

The symbol of the Coptic Orthodox Church is a special cross called the **Coptic Cross**. The Copts may have developed this special cross from the **ankh**, an ancient Egyptian hieroglyph that represented eternal life.

Tabula was a favorite Byzantine board game that was much like modern-day backgammon. One difference is that tabula players rolled three dice, while backgammon players roll only two.

The Arabian and Sinai Peninsulas

The **Arabian Peninsula** is a big, boot-shaped peninsula in West Asia. If the Italian Peninsula looks like a ladies' dress boot, then the Arabian Peninsula looks more like a men's work boot.

Arabia lies just across the **Red Sea** from Africa. Southeast of Arabia lies the **Arabian Sea**, which opens into the Indian Ocean. Northeast of Arabia lie the **Persian Gulf** and the **Gulf of Oman**.

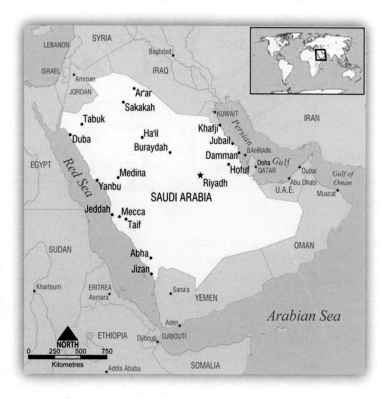

Just west of the Arabian Peninsula lies a much smaller peninsula called the Sinai. The Sinai is a triangle with bodies of water on all three legs. The **Mediterranean Sea** forms the northern leg; the **Gulf of Suez** forms the southwest leg; and the **Gulf of Aqaba** forms the southeast leg.

The distance between the Mediterranean Sea and the Gulf of Suez is only about 100 miles. Yet for most of human history, ships had no way to cross that 100 miles. Instead, they had to sail all the way around Africa— a voyage thousands of miles long!

All of that changed in 1869, when French and Egyptian builders finished a fantastic engineering project called the Suez Canal. Beginning at **Port Said** on the Mediterranean Sea, laborers dug out countless tons of sand and rock, carving a broad channel all the way to **Port Suez** on the Gulf of Suez. Before the Suez Canal, any voyage from the Mediterranean Sea to the Arabian Sea was a dangerous journey of many weeks. That same journey now takes less than one day!

Both Arabia and the Sinai are mostly desert wilderness. For most of human history, the only people who lived in these deserts were wandering nomads— including **Moses**, who led the children of Israel through the Sinai wilderness on their long Exodus from Egypt.

However, the side of Arabia that lies along the Red Sea receives more rainfall than the rest. This greener part of Arabia is where the prophet **Muhammad** founded one of the world's largest religions: Islam.

The Rise of Islam

Both Muhammad and Moses could trace back their roots to the same ancestor: Father Abraham.

The Book of Genesis tells that Abraham had two sons. The younger son, **Isaac**, was born to Abraham's wife **Sarah**. The older son, **Ishmael**, was born to Sarah's handmaiden— a slave woman called **Hagar**. Isaac would become the father of all Jews; while Ishmael would become the father of all Arabs.

The Book of Genesis also tells how Jews and Arabs split.

From the moment she became pregnant with Ishmael, Hagar mocked Sarah. For Hagar had a son; while Sarah couldn't seem to have one. Sarah longed to send Hagar away, but couldn't— for she knew that Abraham would never send away the mother of his only son.

Ishmael was about 13 years old when Abraham's people got the surprise of their lives: the 90-year-old Sarah was pregnant with Isaac!

Ishmael versus Isaac

The birth of Isaac set up a contest between him and Ishmael. Both mothers wanted to know: would Isaac inherit Abraham's great wealth, or would Ishmael? On the one hand, Ishmael was the older son. On the other hand, Ishmael had been born to a lowly slave woman— while Isaac was born to Abraham's true wife.

The moment of decision came when Isaac was **weaned**. In ancient times, a lot of children died as babies, before they were weaned.

> A **weaned** child is one who is old enough to eat solid food instead of his mother's milk.

The fact that Isaac didn't die before weaning meant that he would probably live a long life. To celebrate that life, a grateful Abraham threw a weaning feast.

At this feast, Sarah saw Ishmael making fun of Isaac. The sight brought years of rage against Hagar flooding into Sarah's heart. So Sarah went to Abraham, angrily telling him to "get rid of that slave woman and her son, for that woman's son will never share in the inheritance with my son Isaac" (Genesis 21:10).

As a good father who loved both of his sons, Abraham hated to send Ishmael away. But when Abraham prayed, God told him to do as Sarah asked. God promised to make Ishmael the father of a nation, just as He would make Isaac the father of a nation. Trusting God to protect Ishmael, Abraham gave Hagar some food and a skin of water, and then sent her and Ishmael off into the desert alone.

Hagar and Ishmael waiting in the wilderness

When the water in the skin ran out, Hagar felt sure that Ishmael would die. Just when all seemed lost, though, an angel appeared to Hagar, reminding her of God's promise to Ishmael. The next moment, God opened Hagar's eyes to something she had missed before: a well right beside her, filled with sweet water! Instead of dying in the desert that day, Ishmael lived on to become the father of the Arab people— just as God had promised.

The location of Hagar's well is very important. Arabs call it the **Zamzam Well**, and believe that it is the same well that still stands in **Mecca**, Arabia.

The miracle of Hagar, Ishmael and the Zamzam Well is the oldest reason why Mecca is holy to Arabs. But it is not the only reason.

Arab traditions tell many more stories about Ishmael. One tradition tells that Abraham didn't just abandon Ishmael in the wilderness, never to see him again. Instead, Abraham and Ishmael worked together on an important task.

The Kaaba and the Black Stone

Long ago, tradition says, God showed Adam and Eve how and where to worship Him. To mark the spot for the very first **altar**, God sent down a special stone from heaven. Arabs call this holy stone the **Black Stone**.

> An **altar** is a special place for worship.

Later, both the first altar and the Black Stone were lost— for the Great Flood of Noah washed everything away (Genesis 6-8).

Many centuries later, Abraham showed up at Ishmael's tent with a strange story. God had appeared to Abraham in a vision, telling him to rebuild the first altar. The new altar, which Arabs call the **Kaaba**, was to stand in Mecca, just a few yards from the Zamzam Well.

As father and son labored together, an angel brought the long-lost Black Stone to lay in the eastern corner of the Kaaba. The Black Stone is still part of the Kaaba today.

These three holy items— the Black Stone, the Kaaba and the Zamzam Well— mark Mecca as the holiest city in the Arab world.

The Kaaba as it appears today, covered with a tapestry called the *kiswah*. This Kaaba is only a copy of the first Kaaba, which collapsed long ago.

Muhammad (570 - 632)

Mecca is also holy to Arabs for another reason: because the prophet **Muhammad**, founder of Islam, was born there. Muhammad's father died before he was born; and his mother died when he was six years old. The uncle who raised Muhammad taught him to earn a living the way many Arabs did: as a traveling trader.

Most of the Arabs Muhammad met were **polytheists**— people who believed in many gods. Before Muhammad, the Kaaba was filled with idols, each carved to represent a different god.

> **Polytheists** believe in many gods. **Monotheists** believe in just one god.

Cave of Hira

Besides these many gods, some Arabs also believed in one mighty god who ruled all other gods. They called this god **Allah**.

When Muhammad was in his 30s, he started spending most of his time alone, **meditating** on this Allah. To avoid distractions while he was meditating, Muhammad holed up in a private place called the Cave of Hira, about two miles outside Mecca.

To **meditate** is to think deeply about something.

One day while Muhammad was meditating, something unexpected happened. Tradition says that in 610, the archangel Gabriel suddenly appeared to Muhammad in the Cave of Hira, bringing him a vision straight from Allah! This was the first of many visions Muhammad received, telling him all about who Allah was and how Allah wanted to be worshipped.

At first, these visions seemed so strange that even Muhammad himself didn't believe them. He feared that this Gabriel might really be a demon, not an angel. In time, though, Muhammad started sharing his visions with the Arabs of Mecca.

The first thing Muhammad shared was that the Arabs' old way of worship was all wrong. The many gods whom most Arabs worshipped were all false gods. Instead, Muhammad said, all must worship the one true god— almighty Allah. Furthermore, Allah hates all those who worship false gods. In other words, Muhammad was not a polytheist like most Arabs of his day. Instead, he was a strict **monotheist**!

Muhammad called his new religion Islam, and his followers Muslims. Both words came from the Arabic *salema*, which means "surrender," "submission" or "peace." What both names mean is that Muslims must surrender to the will of Allah in order to make peace with him.

Few Meccans believed Muhammad at first. The city leaders treated Muhammad and his few followers horribly, trying to stamp out his new religion before it could take hold.

Muhammad himself laid the first stones for this oldest mosque in the world: the Quba Mosque, built at Medina just after the Hegira. The high towers, called *minarets*, are for calling faithful Muslims to prayer five times each day.

The Hegira (622)

After several years of cruel mistreatment in Mecca, Muhammad took his message to a new city. In 622, Muhammad led his followers from Mecca to Yathrib, a city about 200 miles to the north. Yathrib— which would later change its name to **Medina**— became Islam's new home.

Muhammad's life-changing trip from Mecca to Medina is called the **Hegira**. In the future, Muslims would look back on the Hegira as the most important beginning in all of history: the beginning of the world-conquering Islamic Empire.

The Hegira is so important to Muslims that they base their calendar on it. The Islamic Calendar marks its years not as "BC" or "AD," but as "BH" or "AH"— "Before Hegira" or "After Hegira."

Medina turned out to be a far more welcoming home than Mecca had been. Muhammad won followers so quickly that he soon ruled Medina. Soon after that, Muhammad ruled all of the Arab tribes around Medina.

As Islam spread beyond Medina, Muhammad's followers had more trouble back in Mecca. The Meccans who had driven out the Muslims back in 622 had also taken over the Muslims' property; and the Muslims wanted it back.

Since Muhammad wasn't ready to attack Mecca, his followers settled for the next best thing: robbing traders on their way to and from Mecca. Muhammad himself led more than two dozen raids against Meccan traders. And with each raid, Muhammad brought home more wealth and power.

Eight years after the Hegira, Muhammad finally felt wealthy and powerful enough to take Mecca itself. In January 630, Muhammad led a big army down to Mecca and captured the city. Thus Mecca, the holy birthplace of Muhammad, joined the Islamic Empire.

One of the first things Muhammad did as master of Mecca was to destroy every old idol in the Kaaba. From then on, the Kaaba was a shrine to no other god but Allah.

From Medina to Mecca and beyond, Islam spread like wildfire. By the time Muhammad died in 632, his Islamic Empire ruled the whole Arabian Peninsula!

> The new government Muhammad set up in Medina was a **theocracy**— a government in which religious leaders control not only religion, but also the military, the police and everything else.
>
> The **Islamic Empire** was a theocracy that ruled the whole Muslim world.

ᄂᄃ

The Islamic faith rests on the **five pillars**, or five basic beliefs.

The first pillar of Islam is *Shahada*, Arabic for "faith" or "creed." All good Muslims know this creed well, and repeat it often: "There is no god but Allah, and Muhammad is his prophet."

Islamic Beliefs

The second pillar of Islam is *Salah*, Arabic for "prayer." Five times each day, Muslims must drop whatever else they may be doing, turn toward Mecca and pray.

Muslim tradition says that just before the Hegira, the archangel Gabriel set Muhammad on a winged horse and flew him off to a holy place— probably the Temple Mount in Jerusalem, where Solomon's Temple had once stood.

From there, Muhammad flew up to heaven, where Allah explained to him how Muslims should worship. Muhammad's trip to heaven is called the Night Journey, and it is one of the most important stories in Islam.

Tradition says that at first, Allah expected Muslims to pray fifty times each day! But Muhammad begged Allah to change his mind, protesting that fifty was too many. So Allah mercifully reduced it from fifty to five. From that day until this, **muezzins** have called Muslims to prayer five times each day.

The **Dome of the Rock** is a shrine that Muslims built to mark the spot Muhammad visited on his Night Journey. The shrine stands on the Temple Mount in Jerusalem, the same place where King Solomon built the Hebrew Temple.

— Start —

A **muezzin** is a Muslim prayer caller who stands in a special tower called a **minaret**.

Another story explains why Muslims turn toward Mecca when they pray. Early in his reign, Muhammad followed some Jewish traditions, in hopes that the Jews might accept Islam someday. After all, both Jews and Muslims believed in one God! One Jewish custom Muhammad followed was turning toward Jerusalem when he prayed.

Later, Muhammad realized that the Jews would never follow any king from the family of Ishmael. For the Jews insisted that their promised Messiah must come from the family of King David. So Muhammad stopped turning toward Jerusalem, and turned toward Mecca instead.

The third pillar of Islam is *Zakat*, Arabic for "giving." Muslims must give freely to the poor, never hoarding their wealth.

The fourth pillar of Islam is *Sawm*, Arabic for "fasting." Most Muslim fasting happens during a special month called **Ramadan**.

Muslims honor Ramadan, the ninth month of the Islamic calendar, as the holy month when Allah sent his first visions to Muhammad. Faithful Muslims celebrate Ramadan in several ways. One way is to read or listen to the entire Quran (below). Another way, especially in Egypt, is to hang special **Ramadan lanterns**.

The most important way to celebrate Ramadan, though, is by fasting. Good Muslims fast every day from sunup to sundown, all through Ramadan. In the strictest Islamic countries, no one except small children, pregnant women, nursing mothers and the sick may eat anything at all during the day. Relief comes after sundown, when all are allowed to break their fast with a meal.

The fifth pillar of Islam is *Hajj*, Arabic for "pilgrimage." At least once in their lifetimes, all able-bodied Muslims must take a **pilgrimage** to Mecca. The point of this pilgrimage is to remember and honor the origins of their faith.

A **pilgrimage** is a religious journey.

A **hajji** is a Muslim pilgrim on the **Hajj** to Mecca.

In the last month of the Islamic year, Muslims from all over the world gather at Mecca for the great

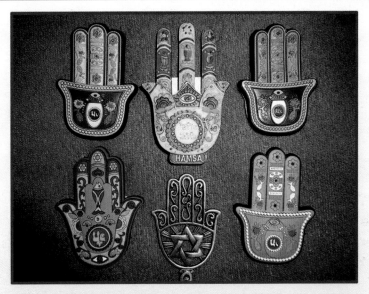

Khamsa amulets are hand-shaped good-luck tokens used all over the Middle East and North Africa, especially in Morocco. Their name comes from the Arabic word for "five," meaning the five fingers of the hand.

Both Muslims and Jews use khamsa amulets. Muslim khamsa may represent the hand of Fatima, daughter to the prophet Muhammad; and the five fingers may represent the Five Pillars of Islam. Jewish khamsa may represent the hand of Miriam, sister to Moses; and the five fingers may represent the five books of the Torah: Genesis, Exodus, Leviticus, Numbers and Deuteronomy.

pilgrimage called the Hajj. The five days of the *Hajj* are filled with rituals to remind **Hajjis** how their faith began. One ritual has all *Hajjis* walking around the Kaaba counterclockwise seven times. If they can come close enough through the surging crowd, then they may touch or kiss the Black Stone on each pass. If not, then they may simply point to the stone with their right hands as they pass.

Muslims believe that their holy book, the Quran, contains a perfect record of every

The Quran

vision Muhammad ever received. According to tradition, Muhammad's visions were so powerful that he could always recite them word-for-word, exactly as he had received them from Gabriel. Muhammad often recited from his visions when he preached; but he never wrote them down.

When Muhammad died in 632, his devoted followers were anxious to write down his visions quickly, lest any be forgotten. So they wrote down his sermons from memory, and then collected them in the *Quran*— which is Arabic for "he recited."

According to tradition, Muhammad's followers remembered his sermons so well that the Quran recites his visions word-for-word, exactly as Allah spoke them to Muhammad through Gabriel.

More Muslim Beliefs

➢ Muslims believe that if they want to go to paradise when they die, then they must first please Allah on earth. One way to please Allah is to show constant devotion to him. Another way is to lead a righteous life under Islamic law.

➢ Anything that is forbidden under Islamic law is called **haram**; while anything approved is called **halal**. Among many other things, pork, alcohol and gambling are all **haram**.

➢ **Jihad** is an Arabic word for "struggle." A Muslim *jihad* may be a spiritual struggle; or it may be an armed struggle against the unbelieving enemies of Islam, whom Muslims call **infidels**.

A very old Quran on display in a museum

One Thousand and One Nights, also called *The Arabian Nights*, is a wonderful collection of old folk tales from Arabia, Persia and other Middle Eastern countries. Some of the best-known stories in the world come from *The Arabian Nights*— including "Sinbad the Sailor," "Aladdin and the Wonderful Lamp" and "Ali Baba and the Forty Thieves."

One Thousand and One Nights

All of these stories come wrapped inside a special story called a **frame story**. The frame story of *The Arabian Nights* tells of an Arabian kingdom with a terrible problem. Its king, whose name is **Shahryar**, no longer trusts any woman!

The story begins with Shahryar getting married for the first time. Soon after the wedding, Shahryar is horrified to learn that his wife has been carrying on with another man. Naturally, Shahryar executes his wife for her terrible crime.

Then he goes a step farther. Wounded by his wife's faithlessness, Shahryar bitterly declares that no woman on Earth can ever be faithful to her husband!

Despite his bitterness, Shahryar still wants a new wife. So he asks his top adviser, his **vizier**, to find him one.

After spending a single night with this new wife, Shahryar takes a simple step to make sure that she can never be unfaithful to him: he kills her. This happens again and again: Shahryar marries a new bride one night, and then kills her the next morning. Before long, the vizier has real trouble finding new brides!

"Scheherazade and Sultan Shahryar" by artist Ferdinand Keller

The answer to the vizier's trouble turns out to be his clever daughter, whose name is **Scheherazade**. With permission from her father, Scheherazade herself becomes Shahryar's next bride.

After the wedding, Scheherazade offers to tell Shahryar a bedtime story. When Shahryar agrees, Scheherazade starts telling him the first tale of *The Arabian Nights*. But Scherezade doesn't finish her tale. Instead, just when her tale reaches its climax— its most exciting moment, when Shahryar is dying to know what happens next— Scheherazade suddenly refuses to say another word! If the king wants to hear the end of her story, Scheherazade says, then he will just have to let her live until tomorrow night.

Fighting his distrust of women, Shahryar agrees to let Scheherazade live— just until tomorrow night, when he can hear the end of her fascinating tale. The next night, Scheherazade finishes her story as promised; but she doesn't stop there. Instead, she moves on to the second tale of *The Arabian Nights*, which Shahryar finds just as fascinating as the first! Night after night, Scheherazade finishes her tale from the night before, and then starts a fresh new tale that leaves the king in agonized suspense.

After 1,001 nights, or nearly three years, Scheherazade finally runs out of tales to fascinate her husband. By this time, though, the two have been married long enough to have children together, and Shahryar has learned to trust women again. —STOP—

The Iconoclastic Controversy

Islamic law forbids Muslims to use **idols** in worship. The law is so strict that Muslim artists almost never make images of people or animals. For in Muslim eyes, all such images look too much like idols. Most of all, Muslim artists never make images of Muhammad— for fear that if they did, then misguided Muslims might worship Muhammad instead of Allah.

The Muslims' hatred of images may have helped spark trouble between Christians in the East.

Unlike Muslims, some Eastern Christians worshipped with special images called **icons**. Some icons pictured Jesus or a saint; while others pictured scenes from the Bible or the lives of saints. Some Eastern Christians filled their whole churches with icons, covering them from floor to ceiling with these inspiring images.

> An **idol** is an image of a false god.
> An **icon** is any image that Eastern Christians use for worship and prayer. Icons come in many types, from painted pictures to carven sculptures, tiled mosaics and more.

A mosaic icon of Jesus from the Hagia Sophia in Constantinople

A painted icon of Jesus from St. Catherine's
Monastery on Mt. Sinai, Egypt

An *iconostasis*, or wall of icons, from the front of an Eastern church

Around 700 AD, a major argument arose between two kinds of Eastern Christians. One kind loved icons, and the other hated icons.

Those who loved icons were called **iconophiles**. To an iconophile, icons were a good way to remember people from the Bible— much like mourners gaze at pictures to remember lost loved ones. Over time, gazing at icons became a beloved tradition, much like singing hymns or reading Scripture in church.

Those who hated icons were called **iconoclasts**. The iconoclasts saw icons the same way Muslims saw them: as idols. Iconoclasts accused iconophiles of worshipping idols, instead of worshipping Christ as they should.

> An **iconophile** is someone who loves to use icons in worship. An **iconoclast** is someone wants to tear down all icons.

Iconophiles denied this. For in their eyes, icons and idols were two very different things. An idol was an image of a false god, something that wasn't real. An icon, on the other hand, was an image of a real person from church history— someone whom all Christians should honor. The iconophiles found it unfair to accuse them of worshipping idols, when what they were really doing was gazing at icons.

The bitter argument between iconoclasts and iconophiles dragged on for about 120 years, off and on. Every so often, a band of iconoclasts would attack an iconophile church, fighting to tear down or plaster over its icons. The iconophiles would fight back, trying to defend their icons.

The end of the argument came at an important church meeting called the **Synod of Constantinople**. The iconophiles won! In 843, the Synod of Constantinople declared that it was perfectly alright for Christians to use icons in worship.

However, the synod also offered an important bit of advice. Christians should only **venerate** icons, not worship them. To venerate an icon is to honor the holy person pictured in that icon, which is fine. To worship an icon is wrong— for true Christians are to worship Christ alone.

೮೮

Pope Gregory the Great
(540? - 604)

Long before the iconoclastic controversy, a strong pope called **Gregory the Great** brought great change to the churches of the West.

The future Pope Gregory was born to wealthy Roman parents around 540 AD. The years of Gregory's youth were the same years when Belisarius took back Italy for Emperor Justinian I of the Byzantine Empire (Chapter 4).

Soon after Justinian and Belisarius died, the Lombards took over northern Italy (Chapter 4). Dealing with the Lombards would turn out to be the biggest problem of Gregory's career. Gregory spent six years in Constantinople, begging the Byzantine Empire to send armies against the Lombards. When that failed, Gregory returned to Rome, where the church elected him pope in 590.

The new Pope Gregory claimed more authority than any other pope before him. In fact, Gregory even claimed military authority!

Since the government of fallen Rome was too weak to deal with the Lombards, Gregory dealt with them himself. Gregory acted as if he were the Governor of Rome, and not just the head bishop of the Church of Rome. Gregory even raised armies to defend Rome against the Lombards—something no pope before him had ever done. The idea of governing states and leading armies was unthinkable to some churchmen, but not to Gregory!

Years later, when other popes started doubling as military leaders, they took Gregory as their model.

Besides all this, Gregory also changed the church itself in important ways. For example, Gregory taught that one of the three main monastic vows, the vow of chastity, should not apply only to monks. Instead, it should apply to all priests. It is partly because of Gregory that Catholic priests never marry, even today!

Gregory also worked to improve his churches' worship services. He started a school for church musicians, and may have inspired a new style of church music called the **Gregorian Chant**. And Gregory was the missionary pope who sent Augustine of Canterbury to minister to the Anglo-Saxons of Britannia (Chapter 3).

Pope Gregory I

CHAPTER 6:   France

F rance is the largest nation in Western Europe. Strong natural barriers protect France on most sides:

➢ To the northwest lies the stormy **English Channel**, which divides France from **England**.

➢ To the west lies the huge **Bay of Biscay**, which opens onto the Atlantic Ocean.

➢ To the southwest lie the **Pyrenees Mountains**, which divide France from **Spain**.

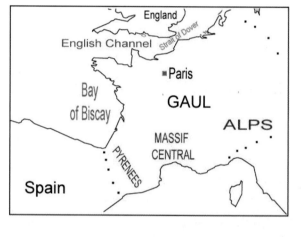

➢ To the south lies the **Mediterranean Sea**. The French enjoy a long, lovely coastline on the Mediterranean.

➢ To the southeast and east lies the biggest mountain range in all of Europe: the **Alps**, which divide France from **Italy**, **Switzerland** and **Germany**.

France's barriers to the northeast are not as strong. Between the Alps and the North Sea, the land descends from high mountains to low, marshy plains dotted with rivers.

T he biggest river in this region is also one of the most beautiful rivers in the world: the famous **Rhine River**. The name "Rhine" comes from the Celtic word *renos,* which means "raging flow." Rising in the Swiss Alps, the Rhine rages mostly northward before draining into the North Sea.

A view of Katz Castle on the Rhine River, with the Lorelei in the background

The Rhine River has always been an important waterway for shipping. In medieval times, nobles who lived along the Rhine liked to charge tolls for the use of their river. To enforce those tolls, they built strong, beautiful castles.

O ne such castle stands near a famous rock called the **Lorelei**.

The Lorelei is a huge arm of rock that juts out into the Rhine not far from Koblenz, Germany. This big rock is named for a poor girl who went mad when the man she loved chose to marry someone else. In a fit of grief, Lorelei hurled herself from the top of the great rock, dashing herself to pieces on the hidden rocks below.

According to legend, the power of Lorelei's grief changed her into a **siren**— much like the Sirens of Greek mythology. As the siren Lorelei sings her mournful song, she lures sailors onto the hidden rocks near the Lorelei's base— where they shipwreck on the same rocks that killed poor Lorelei!

The Roman name for what is now France was **Gaul.**

Roman Gaul

The story of Roman Gaul is a lot like the story of Roman Britannia (Chapter 2). Like Britannia, Gaul belonged mainly to the Celts before the Romans came. Like Britannia, Gaul was swallowed up as the Roman Empire grew northward. And like Britannia, Gaul fell to the barbarians as the dying Roman Empire shrank back to the south.

Yet another thing Gaul and Britannia had in common was **Julius Caesar**. It was Julius Caesar who finally conquered all of Gaul for Rome.

The Gallic Wars (58 – 51 BC)

The wars Caesar fought in Gaul are called the **Gallic Wars**. These wars weren't easy for the Romans— for as always, the Celts fought like wild men. In fact, a Celt by the odd name of **Vercingetorix** came close to killing Julius Caesar.

Vercingetorix was a skilled general from a Celtic tribe in south central Gaul. His strategy was to unite all Celtic tribes against the Romans. Like Caratacus, Vercingetorix sometimes beat the Romans— but only when he stuck to small battles (Chapter 2).

The big showdown between Vercingetorix and the Romans came in 52 BC. In that year, Caesar finally trapped Vercingetorix inside a hilltop fort at a place called **Alesia**. With the Roman army completely surrounding the fort, Vercingetorix's only hope was his Celtic friends outside. If those friends could strike Caesar from behind, then Vercingetorix might be able to break through and escape.

This plan almost worked. One of the darkest days in Caesar's life came during the **Battle of Alesia**, when Vercingetorix and his friends both struck the Romans at once— Vercingetorix from inside Alesia, and his friends from outside.

To save his army, Caesar had to divide it. While the rest of the Roman army dealt with Vercingetorix, Caesar personally led about 6,000 cavalrymen in a bold

Vercingetorix surrendering to Julius Caesar

charge against Vercingetorix's friends. The sight of so many Roman cavalry terrified Vercingetorix's friends. So they scattered, leaving Vercingetorix all alone inside Alesia. He surrendered to Caesar the next day.

In beating Vercingetorix, Caesar also beat the last organized Celtic army in Gaul. After the Battle of Alesia, most Gallic Celts no longer resisted the Romans.

A **province** was a section of the Roman Empire governed by a **provincial** governor.

With the Gallic Wars at an end, mighty Rome finally took over all of Gaul. The Roman government divided Gaul into **provinces**, each with a provincial governor.

Along with Roman government came Roman law, Roman learning and the Roman way of life. Over time, the Celts' descendants in Gaul became "Romanized," just as the Celts' descendants in Britain became Romanized (Chapter 2).

〰〰〰

The Persecution at Lyon (177 AD)

Like other Romans of their day, the Romans of Gaul tended to despise Christians. One of the worst Roman persecutions of Christians ever happened at the city of Lyon, Gaul in 177 AD.

A total of 48 innocent Christians died at Lyon that year. One was a poor girl whose sufferings are too painful too imagine.

Blandina was a slave girl whom the Romans arrested for **cannibalism**, of all crimes. Romans often accused Christians of cannibalism, for a strange reason: because

Cannibalism is the terrible crime of eating human flesh.

Blandina
Died 177 AD

when Jesus led the first Holy Communion, He spoke of eating His flesh and drinking His blood (Matthew 26:26-28).

Knowing what terrible tortures awaited them, the Christians of Lyon tried their best to encourage each other. They warned each other never to deny Christ, no matter what the Romans might do to them. For one thing, to deny Christ was to discourage one's brothers and sisters in Christ. There was also the warning in Matthew 10:32-33, where Jesus says:

"Whoever acknowledges me before others, I will also acknowledge before my Father in heaven. But whoever disowns me before others, I will disown before my Father in heaven."

Since Blandina was only a poor slave girl, and also rather frail, her friends feared that she might deny Christ at the first sign of torture. Instead, Blandina held up as long as anyone. Despite the worst the Romans could do, Blandina never denied her faith in Christ!

When they couldn't destroy Blandina's faith, the Romans finally destroyed Blandina herself. In the end, Blandina's frustrated torturers wrapped her in a net and tossed her under the feet of raging bulls.

Blandina netted and thrown before raging bulls

The terrible persecution at Lyon fell near the end of the *Pax Romana*, the 200-year-long "Roman Peace." After the *Pax Romana*, the once-mighty Roman Empire started to weaken. The growing weakness of the Romans left openings for their enemies— the outsiders whom they liked to call "barbarians."

> The *Pax Romana*, or "Roman Peace," lasted from about 27 BC – 180 AD. After 180, the mighty Roman Empire began to slip toward its fall, which finally came in 476.

Barbarians in Gaul

The strongest outsiders in Gaul were the **Franks**. The Franks were a group of tribes who had lived east of the Rhine River, in what are now the Netherlands and northwestern Germany. Although the meaning of the Franks' name is uncertain, it may have come from a word that meant "fierce."

Sensing Roman weakness, the fierce Franks started moving west of the Rhine in 275 AD. The first Frankish homes in Gaul stood in what is now Belgium.

A second set of strong outsiders were the **Alemanni**, who came from what are now Switzerland and southwestern Germany. The name *Alemanni* may mean "all men"— which may mean that the Alemanni were made up of many different tribes. When the Romans grew weak, the Alemanni started seizing territory in eastern Gaul.

A third set of strong outsiders were the **Burgundians**, who moved all the way from Scandinavia to find new homes along the Rhine River. A Burgundian king called **Gundahar** moved west of the Rhine in 411 AD, setting up the **Burgundian Empire** just south of the Alemanni. Gundahar's empire lasted just 27 years, until a Roman general called **Flavius Aetius** defeated him in 437. Even so, the Burgundians were still a dangerous force in Gaul.

> Besides being king of the Burgundians, Gundahar is also famous for another reason: because he is a character in the **Ring Cycle**, a famous set of operas by the German composer Richard Wagner.

The most dangerous outsiders of all, though, were a people called the **Huns**.

The Huns were a tribe of fierce warriors from somewhere in East Asia. Almost everything the Huns did, they did on horseback. Hunnic warriors fought on horseback; held meetings on horseback; ate on horseback; and sometimes even slept on horseback. According to one Roman historian, the Huns were so used to horses that they seemed to feel a bit dizzy when they stepped down. One reason why historians know so little about the Huns is because they were always on the move, never settling in one place for very long.

This unusual way of life was part of what made the Huns so dangerous. Unlike the Franks, the Huns didn't come to Gaul looking for new homes. Instead, they came looking for new people to conquer! The Huns were a lot like a plague of locusts. They flooded into an area, swallowed up everything in sight and then moved on.

Huns in battle

Whenever the Huns invaded a new area, their first step was to attack a few cities and towns— killing men, women and children alike. When everyone in the area was thoroughly terrified, the Huns rode from city to town, demanding **tribute payments** from the survivors. Faced with a choice between paying tribute or fighting the Huns, most cities chose to pay!

> A **tribute payment** was a set amount of money or goods that a conquered people had to pay their conquerors every month or every year.

Demanding tribute was a way of life for the most dangerous Hun of all:

Attila the Hun

Attila the Hun. Attila and his elder brother Bleda inherited the Hunnic Empire when their uncle died in 434. Thirteen years later, Bleda died as well— maybe of natural causes, or maybe because Attila killed him.

At the time, the Huns lived mainly in the East, just north of the Eastern Roman Empire. In 450, though, an unusual letter drew Attila's attention from East to West. That letter came from **Honoria**, the troubled older sister of a Western Roman Emperor called **Valentinian III**.

Honoria suffered from two big troubles. The first was that Honoria flirted with too many men— a fault which deeply embarrassed her emperor brother. To stop all the embarrassment, Valentinian locked Honoria in a nunnery while he tried to find a husband for her.

Honoria's second trouble was the husband her brother found. To keep Honoria out of trouble, Valentinian arranged for her to marry a rather dull member of the Roman senate. The fun-loving Honoria wanted nothing to do with a dull senator; but her brother insisted.

With nowhere else to turn, Honoria turned to someone with the power to frighten her emperor brother. In 450, Honoria wrote a pleading letter to Attila the Hun, of all people— more or less asking him to marry her! As a token that her letter was sincere, Honoria sent her engagement ring along with it.

To Valentinian's horror, Attila took Honoria's foolish offer seriously— or at least, he pretended to take it seriously. Pretending that Honoria really wanted to marry him, Attila demanded a huge **dowry** from her brother. Atilla wanted half of the Western Roman Empire!

"Attila and his Hordes Overrun Italy" by artist Eugene Delacroix

> A **dowry** was the money and property a bride brought into her marriage, given to the groom by the father or brother who gave away the bride.

Naturally, Valentinian refused to pay such a ridiculously large dowry.

The emperor's refusal was all the excuse Attila needed. In 451, Attila led a huge Hun army into the Western Roman Empire. His first target was Roman Gaul, where he immediately started burning cities and killing innocents.

Huns versus Romans, Franks and others
at the Battle of the Catalaunian Plains

Gaul's defenses were in the hands of Flavius Aetius— the same Roman general who had defeated the Burgundians back in 437. In need of troops to fight Attila, Flavius called on the only ones he could find: the so-called "barbarians" who were living in Gaul. Many of the barbarians who came to Flavius' aid were Franks.

The big showdown between Flavius and Attila came at the Battle of the Catalaunian Plains, fought in 451. To the amazement of all, Flavius won! Just why Attila lost this battle, when he had never lost before, no one knows. It may be that Attila's long trip from the east had worn out too many horses— forcing the horse-loving Huns to fight as slightly-dizzy foot soldiers. Whatever the reason, this stunning defeat sent Attila retreating to the east.

Attila returned west the following year, 452. This time, his target was Rome itself.

Although Attila didn't capture Rome, he did lay waste of northern Italy— just as he had laid waste of eastern Gaul the year before. Attila's merciless attacks in Italy and Gaul mark him as the most terrifying barbarian in Roman memory.

The attacks of Attila the Hun continued until his mysterious death in 453. Some say that one of Attila's own wives stuck a knife between his ribs.

The Rise of the Franks

Besides the big defeat of Attila the Hun, the Battle of the Catalaunian Plains produced one other big result: it helped the Franks become the most powerful people in Gaul.

Before the 500s, there was no one great king of all the Franks. Instead, there were several kings, each with his own small territory. Because the Franks had no written language as yet, historians know very little about these early Frankish kings.

One of the first known Frankish kings was Merovius. Judging from the dates when he lived, Merovius may have been the Frankish general who helped Flavius Aetius beat Attila the Hun at the Battle of the Catalaunian Plains.

Merovius went on to become the Frankish version of King Arthur— an honored king who was part history, and part legend. The first great dynasty of Frankish kings, the Merovingian dynasty, is named for Merovius.

The first great dynasty of Frankish kings, the **Merovingian dynasty**, takes its name from Merovius. The kings of the Merovingian Dynasty are also called the **"long-haired kings"** because none of them ever cut their hair or beards.

The story of the Merovingian kings becomes a bit clearer after Merovius. Merovius' grandson, whose name was **Clovis**, was the first great king of all the Franks.

Like his Frankish ancestors before him, Clovis was a **pagan** when he started his reign. But Clovis had something his ancestors didn't have: a Christian wife called **Clotilda**, who was a Burgundian princess before she married Clovis.

> A **pagan** is a non-Christian who worships idols.

The Conversion of Clovis

As a Christian, Clotilda hated her husband's false gods. She often reminded Clovis that his so-called "gods" were really only idols. They were all carved from random chunks of wood or stone, making them no more god-like than a rock (Isaiah 44:9-20). The God whom Clovis ought to worship, Clotilda said, was the One who had created all things by the power of His Word. As a believing pagan, Clovis replied that it was his gods who had created all things, not Clotilda's.

What changed Clovis' mind was an important battle between the Franks and the Alemanni in 496. Midway through the **Battle of Tolbiac**, Clovis began to fear that his gods had abandoned him, and that the Alemanni might win. So Clovis prayed this promise to Jesus Christ: that if Christ would give Clovis the victory, then Clovis would believe in Christ and be baptized.

According to a medieval historian called Gregory of Tours, Clovis' prayer had hardly left his lips when the Alemanni suddenly turned and fled the battlefield!

Clovis calling upon Christ for aid at the Battle of Tolbiac

True to his word, Clovis became a Christian soon after his miraculous victory at Tolbiac. The **baptism of Clovis** was one of the most memorable scenes in all of French history. Legend says that during the baptism, a white dove delivered a bottle of holy oil straight from heaven. This sign from heaven marked Clovis as the special king God had chosen to lead all the Franks.

Since the King of the Franks was becoming a Christian, all loyal Franks wanted to become Christians as well. Altogether, priests baptized some 30,000 Franks that day! Just as the conversion of Constantine helped make Christianity the religion of Rome, so the conversion of Clovis helped make Christianity the religion of Gaul.

After the baptism, Clovis built an even bigger kingdom. His vast kingdom covered nearly all of what is now France— which is why modern-day France is named for Clovis' tribe, the Franks.

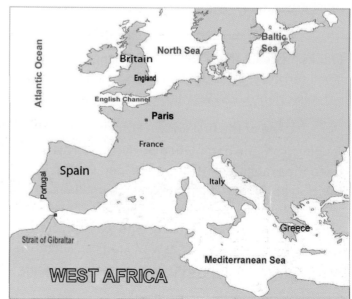

One unusual thing about Clovis and the Franks was that they followed an unusual code of laws: the **Salic Laws**.

Two laws set the Salic Laws apart from most other law codes. One Salic law said that no woman could inherit property— not even a royal woman. When a Frankish king died, his kingdom always went to a male relative, never to a daughter. What the Franks liked about this was that no

The **Salic Laws** were an unusual code of laws named for Clovis' special tribe, the <u>Salian Franks</u>.

Frankish kingdom ever went to a daughter's husband— which meant that no foreign king could take over Frankish lands just by marrying a Frankish princess!

The other unusual Salic law said that when a Frankish king died, his sons divided his territory between them. In most other places, the whole kingdom passed to the eldest son. In France, though, every son received a share— which meant that if a Frankish king had more than one son, then his kingdom would be broken into pieces as soon as he died.

This second law meant bad news for Clovis' huge kingdom. When Clovis died in 511, the kingdom that he had spent a lifetime building was divided between his four surviving sons!

Two French Saints

— stop —

The baptism of Clovis might never have happened without a churchman called **Martin of Tours**. The name "Tours" comes from the city of Tours, Gaul, where Martin became a bishop in 372.

When the future Saint Martin was born, Emperor Constantine sat on the throne of Rome, and Christianity was growing more popular every day. Young Martin longed to study this new faith; but his father insisted that he join the Roman army instead. Martin's army unit was assigned to Gaul.

As Martin's unit was riding up to a city one cold day, he happened to see a nearly-naked beggar freezing beside the road. Even though Martin hadn't been baptized yet, he understood that Christians were supposed to care for the poor. So Martin unsheathed his sword, and used it to slice his warm officer's cloak in two. One half of the precious cloak went to the beggar, and the other half Martin kept for himself.

That night, Martin dreamed that he saw Christ admiring the beggar's half of his cloak, saying, "Look at this cloak Martin gave Me!" Martin already understood what Christ said in Matthew 25:40— that "whatever you did for one of the least of these brothers and sisters of mine, you did for me." The simple act of caring for a penniless beggar was so unusual in Martin's day that

Martin of Tours
(316 – 400)

The future St. Martin of Tours as a Roman soldier, giving half of his cloak to a beggar

he became a Christian hero of Gaul, legendary for his humility and self-sacrifice.

After leaving the army, Martin went on to plant churches all over Gaul. Without Martin of Tours, the Baptism of Clovis might never have happened— for Clovis' wife Clotilda might never have heard the gospel of Jesus Christ!

†††

Genevieve was a Frankish nun who was living in Paris in 451, the year when Attila the Hun sacked city after city in

Saint Genevieve
(422 – 512)

eastern Gaul. Most Parisians were so terrified of Attila that they were ready to flee the city.

Genevieve was braver. Instead of fleeing, Genevieve told the people of Paris to fast, pray and trust in God. When Attila decided to bypass Paris, and sack another city instead, Parisians thanked Genevieve for saving their city. It is partly for this reason that Genevieve became a patron saint of Paris.

Each year on Good Friday, the Friday before Easter, every church bell in France suddenly falls silent. When children ask why, their parents tell them that church bells only seem like regular bells. What they really are, parents say, is *cloche volants*— "flying bells."

In French legend, these flying bells gather the sorrows of all who mourn Jesus' crucifixion. Every year on Good Friday, the flying bells carry these sorrows off to Rome, the center of power in the Catholic Church. When Jesus rises from the dead on Easter morning, He erases all sorrow. Then the flying bells go back to their French bell towers and ring out in celebration.

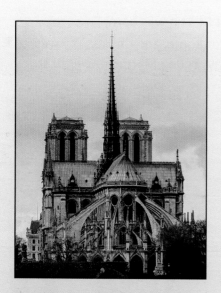

One of the biggest, best-known cathedrals in all the world is the *Notre Dame de Paris*, French for "Our Lady of Paris." **Notre Dame** stands on the *Ile de la Cite*— a large island in the Seine River, the big river that flows through Paris.

Among other things, Notre Dame is famous for its many **gargoyles**. These are gruesome statues which double as long spouts to carry rainwater away from the cathedral's foundation.

The beautiful stone bridge that connects the west end of the *Ile de la Cite* to the mainland is called **Pont Neuf**, French for "New Bridge." Oddly enough, this "New Bridge" was finished in 1607— which makes the *Pont Neuf* the oldest bridge in modern-day Paris!

Gargoyles on a corner of Notre Dame

Gargoyle atop Notre Dame

The *Pont Neuf*, or "New Bridge"

CHAPTER 7:

The Islamic Empire;
The Carolingian Empire

Chapter 5 told of the Islamic Empire built by Muslims. Chapter 6 told of the Christian empire built by the Franks. This chapter tells how these two great empires clashed.

The Islamic Empire

For its first 10 years, Islam knew only one leader: the prophet Muhammad. Beginning with the **Hegira** in 622, Muhammad guided every decision the Islamic Empire made. Unfortunately, Muhammad left one important decision unmade. The question was, who was to lead Islam when Muhammad was gone?

Just 10 years after the Hegira, Muhammad suddenly fell ill and died— leaving behind no clear leader to take his place. Although Muhammad had married more than once, his wives had given him no sons, only daughters. And no good Muslim would follow a woman!

> Remember that Islam began in 622, the year when the prophet Muhammad led his followers on the **Hegira** from Mecca to Medina.

Without Muhammad to hold them together, Muslims started to split.

Some Muslims felt that Allah had already chosen the next leader of Islam. In these Muslims' minds, the right man for the job was **Ali ibn Abi Talib**, also called simply **Ali**. Besides being a great Muslim leader and a close friend of Muhammad's, Ali also had strong family ties to Muhammad. Ali was Muhammad's first cousin; and he was also married to Fatima, Muhammad's favorite daughter.

Other Muslims felt that the best way to choose their next leader was to call an emergency meeting. Soon after Muhammad died, several important Muslim leaders met at Mecca. Since Ali was still in Medina burying

Muhammad receiving a vision from the archangel Gabriel

Muhammad, he wasn't in Mecca when these leaders elected someone else. The man elected to take Muhammad's place was **Abu Bakr**, father-in-law to Muhammad.

If Ali had wanted to fight for Muhammad's place, then many Muslims would have fought beside him. Instead, Ali graciously stepped aside, allowing Abu Bakr to take his place as the first **caliph**.

> The Arabic word *caliph* means "successor." A **successor** is one who takes a leader's place after the leader is gone.
> A **caliph** was a successor of Muhammad, one of the men chosen to lead the Islamic Empire after the prophet died.

Thanks to the graciousness of Ali, most Muslims accepted Abu Bakr. For the moment, everyone agreed that Abu had been Allah's choice, not man's choice.

The same was true of the three caliphs who came after Abu. Most Muslims accepted them as Allah's choices, for two main reasons. First, all four had been close friends of Muhammad. Second, none of the four inherited the job of caliph. Instead, all four were elected by Muslim leaders. For the moment, most Muslims agreed that this was the best way to know the will of Allah.

As a mark of approval, most Muslims call these first four caliphs *rashidun*— Arabic for "rightly guided." The government these four caliphs led is called the **Rashidun Caliphate**.

The Rashidun Caliphate accomplished much for Islam. First, the Rashidun caliphs collected all of Muhammad's visions and wrote them down, assembling the first complete **Quran** (Chapter 5).

Second, the Rashidun caliphs spread Islam like wildfire. By the time the last Rashidun caliph died in 661, the Islamic Empire controlled the whole Middle East, from Arabia and Egypt to Palestine, Syria, Persia and beyond.

One stunning result was that the birthplace of Christianity became Muslim territory. By the mid-600s, the entire Holy Land had fallen to the Islamic Empire!

> A **caliphate** was an Islamic government set up by a caliph or a dynasty of caliphs.
> The first caliphate was the **Rashidun Caliphate**, which ruled the Islamic Empire from 632 – 661. The Arabic word *rashidun* means "rightly guided."

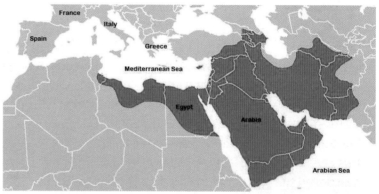

Green shows the Islamic Empire under the last Rashidun caliph

Wherever Muslims conquered, they tried hard to convert their new subjects to Islam. Some converted easily; while others were stubborn. Some stayed faithful to their old religions, even when Muslims threatened to kill them.

Just how many of these stubborn faithful the Islamic Empire killed, no one now knows. It certainly killed very many, and sold many others into slavery.

But Muslims didn't always kill the stubborn faithful. For Muhammad had a certain amount of respect for Jews and Christians, whom he called **People of the Book**.

The "book" Muhammad was talking about was the Bible. Although Muhammad didn't exactly believe in the Jewish Bible, or the Christian Bible, he did accept parts of them as true. So he respected Jews and

A Muslim slave trading caravan

The non-Muslims whom Muhammad called **People of the Book** were mostly Christians and Jews—people who lived by holy books older than the Quran.

The *jizya* was a special tax paid by non-Muslims who lived in the Islamic Empire.

Christians who believed in the Bible. Thanks to Muhammad's respect for People of the Book, Muslims sometimes allowed Jews and Christians to stay Jews and Christians.

On the other hand, Islamic law made it clear that Jews and Christians were inferior to Muslims, and not to be trusted. For example, some Islamic laws forbade non-Muslims to serve in the army or the police. Other laws forbade non-Muslims to own weapons, or even to ride horses.

Besides all this, Muslims forced non-Muslims to pay a special tax called the *jizya*. This tax served two purposes. First, since non-Muslims couldn't send their sons to serve in the army or the police, this tax was their way of paying for army and police protection. Second, the tax helped convince stubborn non-Muslims to convert to Islam. After all, if they became Muslims, then they wouldn't have to pay the tax.

ꌅꌅꌅ

In the process of conquering the whole Middle East, the Rashidun caliphs made a lot of enemies for themselves. Of the four caliphs after Muhammad, only the first died of old age. The second and third were both murdered by their enemies— Persians and Egyptians who were furious with the caliphs for taking over their countries.

The fourth caliph was **Ali**, the beloved cousin of Muhammad whom many Muslims had wanted from the first. Unfortunately, Ali's reign fell during a terrible civil war. Near the end of this civil war, one of Ali's fellow Muslims murdered him with a poison-tipped knife.

The end of Ali set up a contest between two possible caliphs. One was Ali's son **Hasan**. The other was the governor of Syria— a man named **Muawiyah**, leader of an Arab clan called the **Umayya**.

To stop the civil war, Hasan made the same gracious choice Ali had made: he stepped aside, allowing Muawiyah to become caliph. However, Hasan insisted on one condition: that when Muawiyah died, either Hasan himself or some other member of Muhammad's family would be caliph.

The Dome of the Treasury from the Umayyad Mosque in Damascus, Syria

Once Muawiyah became caliph, though, he forgot all about Hasan's condition. When Muawiyah died, his throne didn't go to a member of Muhammad's family. Instead, it went to Muawiyah's son.

Thus Muawiyah's family became the first Muslim **dynasty**— the first family to hand down the throne from father to son. The Umayyad dynasty was named for Muawiyah's clan, the Umayya. The rise of the Umayyads marked the beginning of the second Islamic caliphate: the Umayyad Caliphate.

A **dynasty** is a line of rulers who all come from the same family.

The second caliphate was the **Umayyad Caliphate**, which ruled the Islamic Empire from 661 - 750.

Some Muslims accepted the rise of the Umayyad dynasty as the will of Allah; but others never did. Some insisted that handing down the throne from father to son was wrong— for it meant that men were choosing the next caliph, instead of Allah choosing.

This argument over caliphs was one reason for a long-lasting split between two groups of Muslims.

➢ The larger group, the Sunni, followed the Umayyad caliphs. The name "Sunni" comes from *sunnah*, the religious way of life taught by Muhammad.

➢ The smaller group, the Shia, refused to follow the Umayyad caliphs. Instead, the Shia followed special leaders called **imams**. The name "Shia" means "follower of Ali"— for the Shia believe that Ali was the **First Imam**, the true successor of Muhammad.

Despite the bitter split between Sunni and Shia, Islam grew just as fast under the Umayyad Caliphate as it had before. To the east, Islam spread throughout Persia and beyond, as far as western India. To the west, Islam swallowed up all of North Africa.

Then came a leap that terrified Western Europe. In 711, Islam leapt across the Strait of Gibraltar into the Christian West!

〰〰〰〰〰〰〰〰〰〰〰〰〰〰〰〰〰〰〰〰〰〰〰〰〰〰〰〰〰〰

The Strait of Gibraltar is a narrow waterway that connects the Mediterranean Sea to the Atlantic Ocean, dividing Western Europe from North Africa. North of the strait lies Spain, and south lies Morocco. At its narrowest point, the Strait of Gibraltar is only about 8 miles wide— which means that on clear days, a person standing on the shore of Morocco can easily see the shore of Spain, without using binoculars!

At the eastern entrance to the strait, on the Spanish side, stands one of the best-known landmarks in the world: the Rock of Gibraltar. With its peak rising 1,400 feet above sea level, this enormous chunk of limestone is impossible to miss. Ancient mapmakers marked the Rock of Gibraltar as one of two **Pillars of Hercules**.

The Twelfth Imam

An **imam** is a Muslim spiritual leader. Both Sunni Muslims and Shia Muslims follow imams; however, Sunni imams are different from Shia ones.

The Sunni have many imams. Nearly all Sunni mosques have at least one imam to teach the faithful, and to lead prayers five times each day.

The Shia have only a few imams. Among the Shia, an imam is a perfectly righteous leader sent by Allah as an example to the faithful.

The largest branch of Shia, called **Twelvers**, believe that there have been just twelve imams in all of history. The first was **Ali**, cousin and son-in-law to Muhammad.

The **Twelfth Imam**, Muhammad al-Mahdi, was the son of the Eleventh Imam. Born in 869, al-Mahdi was only five years old when his father was murdered like so many other imams before him.

After leading his father's funeral, the five-year-old al-Mahdi disappeared, and hasn't been seen since! Twelvers believe that Allah has hidden the Twelfth Imam for now— and that when he returns, he will bring perfect Islamic justice on Earth.

Looking across the Strait of Gibraltar from Morocco

The Rock of Gibraltar is named for the Muslim general who leapt across the Strait of Gibraltar in 711. "Gibraltar" is a version of *Jebel Tariq*, which is Arabic for "Mountain of Tariq."

ᓚᓚᓚᓚᓚᓚᓚᓚᓚᓚᓚᓚᓚᓚᓚᓚᓚᓚᓚᓚᓚᓚᓚᓚᓚᓚ

On ancient maps, the **Pillars of Hercules** were two gateposts that marked the entrance to the Mediterranean Sea.

In real life, the pillars were mountains. The northern pillar was the Rock of Gibraltar, and the southern pillar a Moroccan mountain called *Jebel Musa*. An ancient myth says that both mountains were made of rock cast aside by the mighty Hercules as he carved out the Strait of Gibraltar.

Tariq bin Ziyad was probably a **Berber**. The Berbers were an ancient race that lived along the coast of North Africa, west of Egypt.

When the Islamic Empire took over North Africa, most Berbers became Muslims. Some converted sadly, others gladly.

Tariq bin Ziyad was one of the glad Berbers. According to legend, Tariq had once been a slave. The wars that carried Islam to North Africa gave Tariq a chance to show his talent as a military man. It was because of this great talent that his master set him free.

As a military Muslim, Tariq took on the task of building the Islamic Empire.

Tariq's target was Hispania, the future Spain. Like Britannia and Gaul, Hispania had once been a province of the Roman Empire. When Rome fell, Hispania was home to the **Visigoths**— the same Visigoths who had sacked Rome in 410 (Chapter 1). Like the Franks, the Visigoths had since become Christians.

One day in 711, Tariq quietly rowed his army of Berber Muslims across the Strait of Gibraltar. They started in Morocco, and ended in Hispania.

On the way across, Tariq sensed fear in his troops. So he took a bold step to quiet that fear. When they landed near the Rock of Gibraltar, Tariq ordered his men to burn their ships. Without ships to take them home, Tariq's men had two choices: they could either beat the Visigoths, or take up swimming!

As it turned out, Hispania fell to Islam even faster than Arabia had. City after city went from Christian to Muslim. By 718, only 7 years after the invasion began, the Islamic Empire controlled almost all of Hispania!

After taking over Hispania, the Islamic Empire looked forward to an even bigger task: taking over Gaul, land of the Franks.

The Rock of Gibraltar

Remember what the **Salic Laws** were— a unique code of laws which insisted that when a Frankish king died, his territory must be divided between his sons.

The Pippinid Dynasty

Meanwhile, over in Gaul, the **Salic Laws** were making it hard for the Frankish empire to grow as fast as the Islamic Empire did.

The Salic Laws undid a lot of what Clovis had done. The life's work of Clovis, the first great king of the **Merovingian dynasty**, had been to combine all of Gaul into one great Frankish empire (Chapter 6). But when

Coin of Clothar I

Clovis died in 511, the Salic Laws divided his empire between his sons. Since Clovis had four living sons when he died, the Frankish empire split into four pieces!

The same thing happened to Clovis' son. **Chlothar**, the last surviving son of Clovis, reunited his father's empire in 558. But when Chlothar died three years later, the empire once again split into four pieces for four sons.

Remember what the **Merovingian dynasty** was— the first great dynasty of Frankish kings.

The years to come brought a new problem for the Merovingian dynasty. Over time, the Merovingian kings grew too lazy to manage their kingdoms for themselves! Instead, they came to rely on trusted advisers called **majordomos**.

Majordomo is French for "Mayor of the Palace." The first majordomos were just that: palace managers, secretaries to arrange the details of palace life for the Merovingian kings. Later, though, the majordomos grew far more powerful.

Some majordomos rose to power as **regents** for boy kings. When a king was too young to run his government on his own, his majordomo ran it for him.

A **regent** is a government officer who makes decisions for a king who is too young to make decisions on his own.

The problem was that with majordomos to do everything for them, these boy kings grew up lazy and soft. When these soft kings grew old enough to take charge, they didn't want to take charge. Instead of running their governments themselves, they preferred to let their majordomos keep running them.

Over time, the Merovingian kings became what the Franks called *roi fainéant*— "do-nothing kings" who let their majordomos handle everything for them!

As for the majordomos, they now saw

Majordomo Pippin II speaking for his boy king, Clovis III of the Merovingian dynasty

themselves as far more than palace managers. In fact, the majordomos saw themselves as royalty!

The first majordomo with a royal title was **Pippin II**. All by himself, Pippin II managed to unite three Frankish kingdoms. To reward himself, Pippin took the title "Duke and Prince of the Franks."

When Pippin II died, he handed down his royal title to his son, just as if he had been a king. Thus Pippin II founded the **Pippinid dynasty**— a family line of powerful majordomos.

The **Pippinid dynasty** was a family line of powerful majordomos who ruled in place of King Clovis I's descendants— the "do-nothing kings" of the late Merovingian dynasty.

Pippin's son **Charles Martel** took over in 714. Charles was still majordomo in 732, the year when the Islamic Empire invaded Gaul.

The Battle of Tours

— Start —

Actually, the Islamic Empire invaded Gaul before 732. Since 719, Muslims had held a bit of Mediterranean coastline on Gaul's side of the Pyrenees Mountains. Using this coastline as a base, Muslims had launched a few raids into Gaul.

Then came the big push. In 732, the Muslims gathered an enormous army, most of it on horseback. Pushing northwestward, the Muslims surrounded **Bordeaux**, a rich city near the Bay of Biscay. Bordeaux soon surrendered, handing over a fortune in gold and gems.

The treasure of Bordeaux was the key to what happened next.

After seizing the treasure of Bordeaux, the Muslims pressed on toward another rich target: **Tours**. They knew that Gaul's favorite saint, Martin of Tours, had built a big monastery at Tours (Chapter 6). They also knew that this monastery must be stuffed with treasure.

What the Muslims didn't know was that Majordomo Charles Martel was nearby, and was rushing to stop them. Somewhere between Poitiers and Tours, Charles found a wooded hill where he could make his stand. So he arranged his Frankish army atop this hill, and waited for the Muslims to arrive.

In looking at the two armies before the **Battle of Tours**, most people would have said that the Muslims would win. For one thing, the Muslim army was far bigger than the Frankish army— perhaps twice as big. For another, most of the Franks were on foot, while most of the Muslims rode horses. In any physical contest between man and horse, horse usually wins!

Fortunately for the Franks, they too had advantages. Perhaps their biggest advantage was Charles Martel himself— for Charles was the craftiest, steadiest, most experienced general of his day. Another advantage was the battlefield— for with the Franks planted on that wooded hilltop, the Muslims had to charge uphill to attack, dodging trees as they went. With the Franks huddled in tight ranks bristling with long spears, the Muslim horsemen couldn't break through. Against all odds, Charles Martel's Frankish foot soldiers stood up to the Muslim cavalry— for just how long, no one knows.

The end of the Battle of Tours may have turned on a rumor. Some say that on the last day of the battle, someone shouted to the Muslims that a band of Franks had broken into their camp— and was stealing the treasure of Bordeaux! Hearing this, some greedy Muslims forgot all about the battle, and started racing for their tents.

Charles Martel and his troops surrounding the Muslim commander at the Battle of Tours

The name "Martel" wasn't really a name. Instead, it was an honorary nickname given to Charles after his great victory at the Battle of Tours. *Martel* is French for "hammer"— for Charles Martel was the mighty "hammer" who pounded the Muslims out of Gaul.

Stained glass of Charles Martel at a cathedral in Strasbourg, France

Seeing this, other Muslims raced off as well— probably thinking that their general had ordered a retreat. Amid all the confusion of the retreat, the Franks surrounded the Muslim general and killed him.

At sunrise the next day, the Franks were delighted to see the Muslims heading home. The Battle of Tours was over! The Islamic Empire would never conquer Gaul as it had conquered Hispania.

Ever since Charles Martel won the Battle of Tours, historians have wondered what might have happened if he hadn't won. At the time, Charles' army was the strongest army in the Christian world. If Charles hadn't stopped the Muslims, then it is hard to imagine that any other Christian could have stopped them. All of Gaul, and indeed all of Western Europe, might have fallen to Islam.

Instead, Christianity survived in Western Europe— thanks to Charles Martel's victory at the all-important Battle of Tours!

The Carolingian Empire

The Battle of Tours left the majordomos stronger than ever. All could see that Charles Martel had won the Battle of Tours without the least bit of help from his do-nothing Merovingian king. From Charles Martel forward, all of the real power lay with the majordomos.

The next majordomo, Charles' son **Pippin III**, was the one who finally got rid of the Merovingian kings.

After putting up with a do-nothing king for several years, Pippin III finally decided that enough was enough. So in 751, Pippin sent a letter to Rome, asking this question of Pope Zachary:

"In regard to the kings of the Franks who no longer possess the royal power: is this state of things proper?"

Pope Zachary's answer was just what Pippin had hoped it would be. The pope agreed that this state of things was indeed most improper! And so, with the pope's blessing, Pippin III got rid of his do-nothing king. The last of the Merovingian kings, Childeric III, went to live in a monastery for the rest of his life.

As a sign that the Merovingian dynasty was truly at an end, Pippin III removed an important symbol of Merovingian power: the king's hair. Since the time of Merovius, no Merovingian king had ever cut his hair or beard. But when Pippin III forced the last of the Merovingian kings into a monastery, he also forced him to trade his long hair for a **tonsure**— the almost-bald hairstyle of a monk.

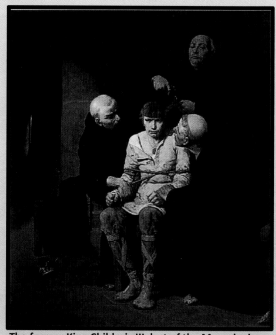

The former King Childeric III, last of the Merovingians, tied to a chair as monks forcibly cut his hair

As for Pippin III, he became the first king of a new Frankish dynasty: the **Carolingian dynasty**, named in honor of his father Charles Martel.

Carolus is the Latin form of "Charles."

This was the beginning of an important new **alliance** between Frankish kings and Roman popes. Each side gained something it needed. — slop —

An **alliance** is an arrangement between two or more parties in which each party hopes to gain something it needs.

The popes gained a fine new country called the **Papal States**. At his pope's request, Pippin III marched an army down into central Italy in 756. There Pippin defeated the **Lombards**, who had been giving popes trouble since the time of Gregory the Great (Chapter 5). After driving the Lombards back into northern Italy, Pippin gave central Italy to the pope!

The **Donation of Pippin** was a rich gift of land given to the Church of Rome by King Pippin III in 756.

Pippin's donation was the beginning of the **Papal States**, a country in central Italy governed entirely by the Church. The Papal States survived from 756 – 1870.

Historians call this incredibly rich gift the **Donation of Pippin**. Pippin's gift was the beginning of a brand-new country in central Italy: the **Papal States**, which were run entirely by the Church. The popes collected taxes, raised armies and even fought wars, just like worldly kings!

As for the Frankish kings, they gained the blessings of the popes. In Christian eyes, the blessings of the popes marked the Kings of the Franks as the rightful rulers of the whole Christian world.

The king after Pippin III was the greatest Carolingian king of all: **Charlemagne**. Like the name Charles Martel, the name Charlemagne is actually part name, part honorary title. "Charlemagne" is short for *Charles le Magne*, which is French for "Charles the Great."

Charlemagne (742? – 814)

Like his grandfather Charles Martel and his father Pippin III, Charlemagne was a great fighting king. With his legendary sword **Joyeuse** in one hand and a cross in the other, Charlemagne built his empire in several directions at once.

➢ To the south, Charlemagne captured northern Italy from the Lombards. He also drove the last of the Muslims out of Gaul, back into Hispania.

"Emperor Charles the Great" by artist Albrecht Durer

- To the north, Charlemagne conquered what are now the Netherlands and northern Germany.

- To the east, Charlemagne conquered what is now southern Germany, and even parts of Eastern Europe.

By 800 AD, Charlemagne had built one of the biggest empires the world has ever seen. The **Carolingian Empire** was enormous, spreading across nearly all of Western and Central Europe!

The vast Carolingian Empire at its largest

Wherever Charlemagne's empire spread, Christianity spread as well. Sometimes, Charlemagne let missionaries convert conquered peoples to Christianity. Other times, he converted them with his sword. It is said that in 782, Charlemagne executed 4,500 rebel Saxons in a single day. The main reason for the Saxon rebellion was that they didn't want to become Christians.

On Christmas Day 800 AD, Charlemagne took Holy Communion at Old St. Peter's Basilica in Rome. As the great king knelt at the altar, Pope Leo III unexpectedly set a new crown on his head.

The pope was doing something no one had done since the fall of the Western Roman Empire back in 476. He was crowning a new *Imperator Romanorum*, or "Emperor of the Romans"! In the pope's mind, Charlemagne was the emperor who finally succeeded in rebuilding the Western Roman Empire.

Poisson D'Avril, French for "Fish of April," is the French version of April Fools' Day.

This tradition began in 1564, the year when King Charles XIV officially moved the first day of the year from April 1 to January 1. Despite the new law, some backward Frenchmen still celebrated the New Year on April 1. To tease these stubborn fellows, some enlightened Frenchmen stuck paper fish to their backs!

Why the French chose paper fish, no one now knows for sure. The French still enjoy eating chocolate fish on *Poisson D'Avril*.

Scandinavia

In northernmost Europe, between the North Sea and the Baltic Sea, lies a region called Scandinavia.

Scandinavia consists of three countries. The first two, **Norway** and **Sweden**, lie on the huge **Scandinavian Peninsula**. Part of the third country, **Denmark**, lies on the much smaller **Jutland Peninsula**. The rest of Denmark lies on islands between the Jutland and Scandinavian Peninsulas. The largest of these **Danish Islands** is called **Zealand**. The capital of Denmark, **Copenhagen**, lies on the east coast of Zealand.

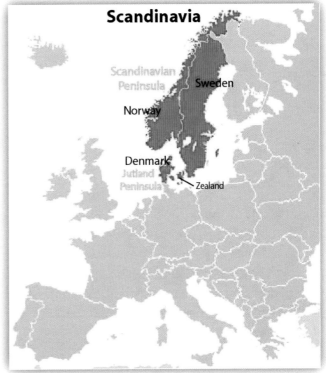

The climate of Scandinavia is very different from place to place. Northern Scandinavia lies within the **Arctic Circle**, where temperatures can be unbearably cold!

The **Arctic Circle** is the part of the globe above 66-1/2 degrees north latitude. Within the Arctic Circle, the sun never rises for part of each winter, and never sets for part of each summer.

Most Scandinavians prefer to live in southern Scandinavia, where the climate is much more bearable than the north. They especially like the coast, where warmth from the sea keeps temperatures from dropping too low. This is one reason why the Vikings, who came from Scandinavia, were such expert seamen.

Norsemen and Vikings

The natives of Scandinavia were called Norsemen— an ancient name which means simply "north-men." Norse tribes lived all along the coasts of what are now Denmark, southern Norway and southern Sweden.

Wherever they lived, all Norsemen had two things in common. First, they all spoke an ancient language called **Old Norse**. Second, they all followed the ancient Norse religion— a warlike religion built around warrior gods. The greatest of all Norse gods was Odin, and the mightiest in battle was Thor.

The warlike Norse religion inspired some of the deadliest warriors of all time: the **Vikings**.

The Vikings were Norse raiders who always struck from the sea, at least at first. Even the very name "Viking" spoke of the sea; for it probably came from an Old Norse word that meant "sea journey."

Just before 800 AD, the Vikings suddenly started raiding monasteries and villages all along the coasts of northern Europe. Viking ships appeared out of nowhere, landing where no one expected them to land. The mostly blonde warriors who strode ashore were uncommonly tall, strong and skilled. After killing everyone who stood in their way, the Vikings stole everything of value, loaded it aboard their ships and then disappeared! This was the beginning of the **Viking Age**— a time when Europeans lived in constant fear of raiders from the north.

The **Viking Age** was a time when Viking warriors launched savage raids all along the coasts of northern Europe. This age began around 793, and lasted until 1066.

Viking Ships

Viking ships came in two kinds: **longships** and **knarrs**.

A longship was a long, narrow vessel built for swift raids. The smallest longships were about 60 feet long, and carried crews of 25 – 30. The largest were twice as long, and carried crews of 100 or more.

Longships could be driven by sails, oars or both. Instead of simple rowing benches, Viking oarsmen sat on clever sea chests that were part seat, part storage locker.

Two special features made longships perfect for Viking raids. First, longships were **symmetrical** from front to back. In other words, their backs were shaped just like their fronts— which meant that if the Vikings needed to turn around quickly, then they could just turn in their seats and row the other way!

Second, longships' bottoms were almost flat. This feature was key to the element of surprise! Flat-bottomed ships could sail along coasts and up rivers that were far too shallow for other ships. Since no one had ever seen ships in these waters before, no one expected the Vikings to land there. Flat-bottomed ships could also land on any beach, with no need for docks.

Vikings landing in England

A third special feature of longships was more decorative, but no less useful for war. Vikings often carved the prows of their longships in the shape of dragon heads! The Vikings loved dragons— partly because Norse legends were full of dragons, and partly because dragons terrified their enemies. Dragon-shaped prows were so common that most people called longships **dragon ships**. The sight of a dragon ship nosing onto a beach was enough to strike terror in any heart!

A knarr was a cargo ship built to carry supplies and trade goods. Knarrs were wider, deeper and shorter than longships. They could carry more weight than longships, but also were slower and harder to turn. With smaller crews and fewer oars than longships, knarrs depended on sails more than oars.

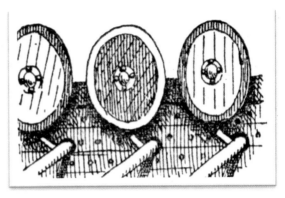

Round Viking shields hung on the side of a longship

Viking warriors used many different weapons, from bows and arrows to spears, swords, battleaxes and pikes. Like their Saxon neighbors to the south, the Vikings favored a special kind of straight sword called a **seax**.

Viking Weapons

For defense, early Vikings carried round shields; while later Vikings carried kite-shaped shields. Their armor was usually chain mail, and their helmets were usually simple ones made of metal or leather.

Contrary to popular belief, no archaeologist has ever found a Viking helmet with horns! Most historians think that horned Viking helmets were only an artists' invention— a way to show the deep terror Europeans felt whenever they saw Vikings.

A **berserker** was a Viking warrior who fought in a mad, violent trance called the *berserkergang*. Berserkers fought like wild animals, with all the strength of bears, the speed of wolves and the viciousness of cornered beasts.

In English, a person who goes violently crazy is said to have "**gone berserk**."

Helmet of a Viking buried in the 900s

Many Viking families lived in special homes called **longhouses**. The usual longhouse was a long, strong building with a stone foundation, walls of stone or wood and a sod roof over a wooden frame.

Living in a longhouse was quite different from living in a modern-day house. One big difference was that longhouses combined home, storehouse and barn under the same roof! The family end held living space; while the barn end held animals, feed, tools and weapons. Wooden benches lined the walls of the family end. Covered with animal skins, these benches served as padded seats by day and warm beds by night. Most longhouses were also windowless which meant that the only light inside came from the doors, the kitchen fire and a chimney hole in the roof.

Viking Longhouses

Another big difference was that a single longhouse might hold several generations of a family at once— from grandparents down to parents, children and grandchildren, all living under the same roof with their animals!

Modern-day reconstruction of a sod-roofed longhouse in Iceland

The harshness of Scandinavia placed harsh demands on Viking children.

The first demand came shortly after birth, when Viking leaders examined every child for birth defects. If a child appeared to have any problems, then its parents were not allowed to feed it. For the Vikings would not waste food on any child whom they feared might weaken their tribe.

Healthy Viking children started working at around age 5. Viking boys learned hunting, fighting, farming, shipbuilding and weapon-making. Viking girls learned mainly homemaking and farming— although some learned fighting as well.

A Viking boy of 15 or 16 was old enough to marry, start a family and take on all the responsibilities of an adult. Viking girls grew up even earlier, marrying at age 12 to 14.

Norse Mythology

MUNINN

Start

Like ancient Greeks and Romans, ancient Norsemen invented flawed gods to explain the flawed world around them. The gods of Norse mythology were gifted with superhuman strength, wisdom and beauty. But they were also plagued with human weaknesses— things like greed, jealousy and wickedness. In the end, the Norse believed, the wickedness of certain gods would lead to a terrible battle that would destroy the whole world.

> Most of what is still known about Norse mythology comes from a pair of books called the **Eddas**. Although the Eddas weren't written down until the 1200s, they record myths far older than that.

The complicated universe of Norse mythology begins with nine worlds, all built around a mighty world tree called **Yggdrasil**. The nine worlds are divided into three levels: three heavens, four earths and two hells.

The highest heaven is **Asgard**, home to the greatest Norse god of all: the mighty, far-seeing Odin.

Odin is the god of war, wisdom and more. Some of Odin's wisdom came from the **Well of Mimir**— one of three hidden wells that watered the world tree. To drink from the Well of Mimir, Odin had to gouge out one of his own eyes and sacrifice it to the well. This explains why Odin is a one-eyed god.

Fortunately, Odin has other ways of seeing. First, Odin has two clever ravens who gather news for him. One is called *Huginn*, or "Thought"; and the other *Muninn*, or "Memory." Second, Odin can see everything that is happening in all nine worlds— but only when he sits on **Hlidskjalf**, his magical silver throne.

Besides Odin himself, the god Norsemen loved most was Thor, Odin's son. The Vikings honored Thor, god of thunder, as the strongest and most battle-ready god in all of Asgard.

Like Odin, Thor owns magical objects which make him even mightier than he already is. The mightiest is **Mjolnir**— a throwing hammer so heavy

Odin seated on his throne *Hlidskjalf*, with his ravens *Muninn* and *Huginn* and his magical spear *Gungnir*

that no one in the universe can lift it, save only Thor. The best parts of Mjolnir's magic are that it never misses its target, and always returns to Thor's hand. Thor also has Járngreipr, a pair of iron gloves for gripping Mjolnir; and Megingjörð, a battle belt that doubles his strength!

Most of the trouble in the Norse universe comes from a mischievous character called Loki. Loki is a half-god, half-giant with the remarkable power to change into any shape he likes, from fly to fish to horse. At first, Loki uses his powers for simple mischief. Later, though, Loki turns to the worst form of mischief: murder.

The human world is called **Midgard**. Between Midgard and Asgard stands a rainbow-colored bridge called the **Bifrost**. A sleepless god called **Heimdal** stands constant guard over the Bifrost, making sure no human comes to Asgard uninvited.

The only way most humans are ever invited to Asgard is if they die glorious deaths in battle. Half of the Vikings who die this way go to **Fólkvangr**, a field ruled by a goddess named **Freyja**. The other half go where every good warrior hopes to go when he dies: **Valhalla**.

Valhalla is a victory hall where great warriors get to live with Odin himself. With a roof made of shields over a frame of spears, Valhalla is a warrior's paradise. Every day, the warriors of Valhalla test their skills in great battles and hunts. Any warrior who dies comes back to life by nightfall, when a great feast begins!

The point of all this fighting and feasting is to keep warriors fit for their last battle: a world-ending melee called the Ragnarok. On one side will fight the gods of Asgard and the warriors of Valhalla. On the other will fight Loki and his kin, the evil giants.

When it comes, the Ragnarok will be a battle with no winners.

➢ The greatest of all warriors, Thor, will manage to kill **Jörmungandr**— a giant serpent long enough to stretch around the world. But then, the serpent's poison will lay Thor low.

For such a heavy hammer, Mjolnir was a bit short-handled. This is because as Mjolnir was being forged, a pesky fly bit the blacksmith's bellows-turner on the eyelid— causing him to stop turning the bellows before Mjolnir was quite finished.

The "pesky fly" turned out to be the trouble-making, shape-shifting Loki in disguise.

A dwarf blacksmith forging *Mjolnir* while the bellows-turner and Loki look on

Thor tackling the world serpent, *Jormungandr*, during the Ragnarok

- An immense wolf called **Fenrir** will swallow Odin whole! But then, one of Odin's sons will tear Fenrir limb from limb.

- As for Loki, Heimdal will manage to slay him— but not without being slain himself.

In the end, a great fire will rage through all of the nine worlds, destroying everyone and everything. The smoldering ruins of Asgard, Midgard and the rest will sink into the sea, leaving only darkness.

The English names for four of the seven days of the week come from Norse gods:

- **Tuesday** is named for a god called Tyr.

- **Wednesday** is named for Odin, which is sometimes pronounced Woden.

- **Thursday** is Thor's day.

- **Friday** is named for a goddess called Frigga.

A **valkyrie** is a heavenly shield-maiden sent by Odin to watch over a battle in Midgard. When a great warrior dies a glorious death in battle, a valkyrie carries him up to Asgard.

Valkyries carrying slain warriors off to Asgard

From Raiders to Conquerors

The Viking Age started in 793— when out of nowhere, a band of Vikings suddenly attacked a defenseless Christian monastery in the British Isles.

This first Viking raid happened on **Lindisfarne**, a small island just off the east coast of Scotland. The Vikings not only stole the monastery's treasures, but also killed many monks, and carried off others to sell into slavery.

One thing the Vikings learned from the famous **Raid on Lindisfarne** was that monasteries made perfect targets for their raids. For one thing, monasteries were filled with donated treasures. For another, most monks were completely helpless in a fight!

Exactly why the Vikings chose this time to attack, no one knows for sure. Some say that the Vikings had outgrown Scandinavia, and needed more room to grow. Others say that Scandinavia suddenly grew colder around this time, making it hard for the Vikings to raise enough food.

Hnefatafl was a popular board game that ran much like a Viking raid. In the center of a checkered board stood a king, defended by a home army of about 8. Around the edges of the board stood a Viking army twice that size. The king tried to reach safety by running for the edges of the board; while the Vikings tried to surround the king.

Hnefatafl remained popular until a new game arrived to replace it: Chess.

Still others say that the Vikings needed no special reason to go to war. They were simply a warlike people— bloodthirsty savages who liked nothing better than a good fight!

Lightning raids like the one on Lindisfarne were only the beginning. As the Vikings grew more confident, they sent bigger raiding parties, striking targets farther inland. In time, they sent armies to conquer new lands for the Norse people.

By the 840s, Viking families were settling into new lands all over northern Europe. Wherever they settled— from Britain and France in the west all the way to Russia in the east— the incredibly tough Vikings changed the course of history.

Viking Explorers in the North Atlantic — STOP —

The Vikings were more than just raiders and conquerors. They were also explorers and adventurers! While some Vikings fought for old lands in Britain and France, others searched for new lands not marked on any map.

The first new lands the Vikings discovered were the **Faroe Islands**, which lie about midway between Norway and Iceland. From the Faroes, they leapt on to **Iceland**; then farther on to **Greenland**; and then farther yet.

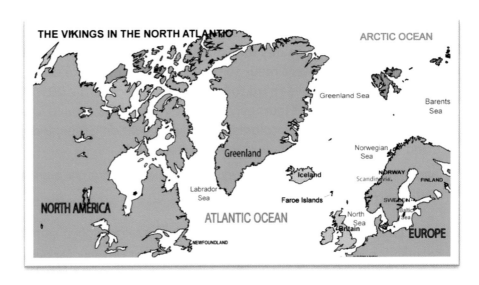

The great mystery is how the Vikings managed to find all these islands! After all, the North Atlantic is a very big place, and there are no signs pointing the way to the next island. Yet somehow, the Vikings managed to find distant islands that no one else had ever found. They also managed to keep finding those islands, going back to them again and again— all without compasses, sextants, star charts or clocks!

The first Viking leader in Iceland was **Ingólfr Arnarson**, who built the first settlement there around 874. Arnarson was the first to realize what a treasure Iceland was— a luscious place filled with fish, seals, walrus and good farmland. When the Vikings back home heard of Arnarson's treasure, they couldn't move there fast enough. Just 50 – 60 years after Arnarson first moved to Iceland, Viking settlers had already claimed all of the best farmland there.

Fifty more years passed before the Vikings moved on to their next big find: Greenland. **Eric Thorvaldsson**, also called

Vikings landing in Iceland

Eric the Red, built the first Viking settlement on Greenland around 986.

There are two possible explanations for Eric's nickname. One is that he had fiery red hair. The other is that he had a fiery temper— for Eric came from a family of convicted killers!

Eric's father, Thorvald Asvaldsson, had been banished from Norway for murder or manslaughter. This is why Thorvald moved his family to Iceland around 960. Twenty-two years later, Eric was convicted of the same crime, and sentenced to three years' banishment.

Eric made good use of this time— for it was during those three years that he found and explored Greenland.

Actually, the name "Greenland" started as an advertising stunt. The moment his three years were over, Eric was back in Iceland looking for settlers to build a colony. To make his island sound more attractive, Eric called it "Greenland"— even though it was really less green, and far more covered with ice, than Iceland was. By this time, though, most of Iceland was already taken— which meant that Eric found plenty of Vikings who were ready to try their luck somewhere else.

Sad to say, luck was hard to find on Greenland. Of the 20 – 30 ships that sailed with Eric in 986, only 14 survived the hard journey. And the ones that did survive found Greenland to be far less green than Eric had promised. The few colonies the Vikings built on Greenland never prospered like the ones on Iceland did. Most of Greenland was simply too cold!

𝕌𝕌𝕌

Leif Ericsson, son of Eric the Red, was to become the most famous Viking of all.

Like his father, Leif Ericsson was a skilled seaman. Leif's first long sea voyage took him from Greenland to Norway— probably to beg the King of Norway for help. If the colonies on Greenland were to survive, then they would need more help than the king had sent so far.

By this time, the King of Norway was a Christian. So Leif became a Christian as well— either because he believed the gospel, or because he wanted to please his king. Either way, the king sent at least one kind of help to Greenland. Thanks to Leif's trip, Greenland received its first Christian church!

Leif's trip to Norway also led to the greatest discovery of his life. One version of Leif's story says that on his way home from Norway, a heavy storm blew him off course. When the big storm finally blew over, Leif found himself sailing along the coast of a place no other European had ever seen: **North America**.

After exploring this unknown coast for some time, Leif named part of it **Vinland**, or "Vine-land"— after the plentiful grape vines he found there. He also built a temporary colony there for the winter. Just where Leif built his colony, no one knows for sure; but the best guess is somewhere in Newfoundland, Canada.

"Leif Ericsson discovers North America" by artist Christian Krohg

The few Vikings who tried to settle in Vinland had even less luck than the ones on Greenland did. Leif's brother, Thorvald Ericsson, died with an arrow in his chest— fired by angry Native Americans whom the Vikings called *Skraelings*.

The death of Thorvald Ericsson brought an end

> The *Skraelings* were probably ancestors of the **Inuit**, a Native American people who still live in northern Canada.

to the Viking colonies in Vinland. Although other Vikings returned there to gather grapes and wood, none settled there permanently.

A long time later, the Viking colonies on Greenland failed as well. As time went on, more and more Vikings gave up on frozen Greenland. By about 1400, the Vikings had all moved back to Iceland or Scandinavia.

Leif Ericsson discovered North America around 1000 AD— nearly 500 years before Christopher Columbus discovered the West Indies! So why do most people know more about Christopher Columbus than they do about Leif Ericsson?

The failures of Vinland and Greenland explain why. When the Vikings left North America, Leif Ericsson's colonies faded from memory. But Columbus' colonies thrived. The Spanish spread out all over the West Indies, Middle America and South America, building one of the richest empires the world has ever seen (Chapter 25).

The East-West Schism

The rise of Islam destroyed most churches in the East. By the end of the **Rashidun Caliphate** in 661 (Chapter 7), only one great Christian city remained in all of the East. This was Constantinople, capital of the Byzantine Empire.

Meanwhile, Rome was still the leading Christian city in the West.

Over time, the churches of East and West grew different from one another. One big difference was that Western priests spoke Latin in church, while Eastern ones spoke Greek. Another was that Eastern priests were allowed to marry, while most Western ones were not. East and West also argued over how to worship— what to read, what to say and what to sing, as well as how to use icons and relics (Chapter 5).

Oddly enough, one of the biggest disagreements between East and West started over a single word: *filioque*.

Filioque is a Latin word that means "and from the Son." Around 400 AD, some Western churches started adding *filioque* to the **Nicene Creed** (Chapter 2). Without the *filioque*, the Nicene Creed read:

"I believe… in the Holy Spirit, the Lord, the Giver of Life, who proceeds from the Father…"

With the *filioque* added, the Nicene Creed read:

> The **Nicene Creed** is an important statement of faith that describes the three persons of the Holy Trinity: God the Father, God the Son and God the Holy Spirit (Chapter 2). This creed was first written by the Council of Nicaea in 325, and expanded by the Council of Constantinople in 381.

"I believe… in the Holy Spirit, the Lord, the Giver of Life, who proceeds from the Father **and from the Son…**"

The difference was small, but important. Western Christians liked the *filioque*. To them, it was another way of saying that Christ the Son was God, just like God the Father. This was important to Western Christians, especially after Arius tried to say that Christ was less than God (Chapter 2).

But Eastern Christians hated the *filioque*. To them, it seemed to say that the Holy Spirit was less than God. Besides, adding the *filioque* was bad manners. The Nicene Creed was one of the most important statements of faith ever written; and yet the West had changed it without even asking the East!

The argument over the *filioque* was only part of a much bigger argument between Rome and Constantinople. The popes of the Church of Rome saw themselves as the leaders of all Christian churches, not just Western ones. The East disagreed. Eastern churches followed a different leader: the **Patriarch of Constantinople**, whose headquarters was the great **Hagia Sophia** (Chapter 4).

> The **Patriarch of Constantinople** was the head of the Church in the East, just as the Pope was the head of the Church in the West.
>
> A **schism** is a church split.

The argument over which was higher, pope or patriarch, was the biggest argument of all. This was the argument that led to one of the biggest church splits of all time: the East-West Schism, also called the **Great Schism**.

The argument came to a head in 1054. That was when **Pope Leo IX** sent his favorite secretary, **Cardinal Humbert**, to Constantinople for a big meeting with **Patriarch Michael I Cerularius**. Basically, the cardinal told the patriarch that he had no choice. If he wanted to be a Christian, then he would have to obey the pope, just like every other Christian in the world!

Naturally, the patriarch didn't see it that way. After a big argument, the cardinal stormed out of their meeting in a rage.

What happened next broke the last tie between the churches of East and West.

In July 1054, Cardinal Humbert marched into the Hagia Sophia and laid a **papal bull** before the patriarch. Upon opening this papal bull, the patriarch learned that the pope had just **excommunicated** him. In other words, the Patriarch of Constantinople was kicked out of his own church! By order of the pope, all Christians everywhere were to cut ties with the patriarch. Most importantly, no Christian church was to serve the patriarch Holy Communion.

> A **papal bull** is a sealed letter containing important statements or instructions from the pope.
>
> To **excommunicate** someone is to cast him out of the Church, cutting him off from Holy Communion.

Naturally, no one in the East obeyed this papal bull. Instead of excommunicating their patriarch, the churches of the East excommunicated Cardinal Humbert!

From then on, the churches of East and West went their separate ways. Churches that followed Constantinople became Eastern Orthodox churches; while churches that followed Rome became Roman Catholic churches. The two have remained separate ever since.

Patriarch Michael I Cerularius seated on his throne at the Hagia Sophia in Constantinople

The Norman Conquest

The English Channel

The **English Channel** is the sea channel that divides Great Britain from mainland Europe. This important body of water measures about 350 miles long, and about 150 miles wide at its widest.

This widest section is home to the **Channel Islands**, two island groups that are well-known to dairy farmers. Two breeds of dairy cattle are named for the two biggest Channel Islands, where farmers developed these breeds: **Jersey** and **Guernsey**. At its narrowest, the English Channel is only about 21 miles wide.

This is the famous **Strait of Dover**, where most travelers go to cross over from England to France and back. The longest undersea rail tunnel in the world, the **Channel Tunnel**, lies beneath the Strait of Dover. Also called the "**Chunnel**," this fantastic engineering project was completed by the Channel Tunnel Group in 1994.

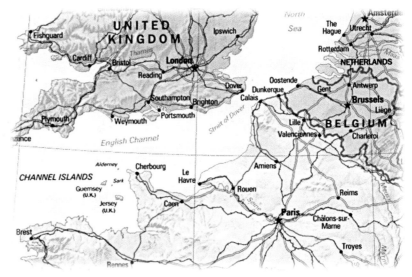

Two well-known landmarks line the Strait of Dover. On the English side stand the **White Cliffs of Dover**. And on the French side stands the port of **Calais**.

The English Channel is one of England's strongest defenses. Over the centuries, many would-be invaders have had their plans shipwrecked by the stormy, rocky English Channel. One was King Philip II of Spain, who sent the Spanish Armada against England in 1588 (Chapter 34). Two others were Napoleon I of France (1805) and Adolf Hitler of Germany (1940).

This chapter tells of an invader who didn't shipwreck: **William the Conqueror**, who led the Norman Conquest in 1066.

A **conquest** is a conquering.

The **Norman Conquest** was the conquest of England by the **Normans**— a Viking people who lived just across the English Channel in Normandy, France.

The **White Cliffs of Dover** are a long set of chalk-white cliffs that line the English side of the Strait of Dover. Against the many invaders who tried to cross the Strait of Dover over the centuries, the White Cliffs stood as a forbidding barrier.

A lighthouse standing atop the White Cliffs of Dover

The Vikings in France

The Viking Age started during the reign of Charlemagne, emperor of the huge Carolingian Empire. The notorious **Raid on Lindisfarne** (Chapter 8) came in 793, just seven years before the pope crowned Charlemagne "Emperor of the Romans" (Chapter 7).

While Charlemagne lived, the Vikings mostly stuck to quick raids like the one on Lindisfarne. The same was true under Charlemagne's heir, the one legitimate son who survived him: **Emperor Louis the Pious**. Throughout Louis' reign, the Vikings were mostly raiders, not conquerors and settlers.

The Salic Laws helped change all that.

The Salic Laws were a special code of laws which insisted that when a Frankish king died, his kingdom must be divided between his sons (Chapter 7). Unlike Charlemagne, Louis the Pious left behind several legitimate sons. So when Louis died, his sons went to war over his throne.

The Vikings took advantage of this war. While the sons of Louis the Pious were distracted, the Vikings seized a big land from the Carolingian Empire. This land lay just across the English Channel from Britain.

An elderly Charlemagne bestowing a crown upon his son Louis the Pious

When it became clear that the Vikings were there to stay, the Franks gave this land a new name. They called it **Normandy**, after the "north-man" Vikings. The capital of Normandy, **Rouen**, stood on the **Seine River** about 40 miles from the coast. The Seine is the same famous river that flows through Paris, the capital of France.

At the end of the Carolingian Civil War, the Carolingian Empire split into three pieces for three sons of Louis the Pious. The western piece, called **West Francia**, went to **King Charles the Bald**.

Since the Vikings' new land lay in West Francia, the task of dealing with these terrible neighbors fell to Charles the Bald!

Two years into Charles the Bald's reign, a Viking army sailed up the Seine River to Paris, where it quickly destroyed half of Charles' army. The rest of Charles' army ran off, leaving Paris defenseless. The Vikings spent that Easter sacking Paris— killing its people, burning its

Viking warriors on the move

buildings and looting its treasure. An infamous Viking called **Ragnar Lodbrok** may have led this first **Sack of Paris**.

The Sack of Paris (845)

In the end, the only way Charles could save Paris was by paying Ragnar off. Ragnar rowed away with a fortune in gold and silver— nearly three tons in all! After that, Viking armies sailed upriver almost every year, hoping for more payoffs as big as Ragnar's.

To better defend his kingdom against the Vikings, Charles the Bald announced a tough new law called the **Edict of Pistres**. First, the edict made it a crime for anyone to sell weapons or horses to the Vikings. Second, the edict created a fast-moving cavalry force to battle the Vikings. Before the Edict of Pistres, nearly all Frankish knights fought on foot, as they had at the Battle of Tours (Chapter 7). After the Edict of Pistres, Frankish knights learned to fight from horseback.

The Edict of Pistres also brought another important change to West Francia. Since Vikings always attacked upriver, the edict ordered new bridges built along big rivers like the Seine. These were no simple bridges! Instead, they were strong ones defended by tall siege towers. If the Franks defended these bridges well, then they might be able to stop the Vikings from sailing upriver every year.

Viking Coins

The first Vikings knew little of coin money— for the ancient Norse traded only in goods, never in coin. Having no other use for the silver and gold coins they captured, early Vikings usually melted them down to make armbands, jewelry or decorations for their weapons.

After the Vikings started trading with other countries, of course, they understood the value of coins very well! Later Viking kings minted their own coins, just like other kings.

The Siege of Paris (885 - 886)

Twenty-one years after the Edict of Pistres, the bridges of Charles the Bald proved their value. In 885, a Viking called Siegfried led a big army up the Seine. Upon reaching Paris, Siegfried found the river blocked by two bridges, each guarded by tall siege towers. No matter how hard they tried, the Vikings could not break past these bridges:

➢ When the Vikings tried catapulting heavy rocks at the towers, the Franks repaired them under cover of darkness.

➢ When the Vikings tried setting fire to the towers, the Franks poured down water to put them out.

➢ The Vikings even tried filling in the river around the towers, piling up tons of earth and rock so that they could come close enough to climb the walls. When the Vikings came too close, though, the Franks poured down hot pitch on their heads.

Scene from the Siege of Paris, 885 – 886

Thus the terrible **Siege of Paris** went on for most of a year, with neither side gaining any ground.

By this time, Charles the Bald had died. The new King of West Francia was his nephew, **Charles the Fat**.

To end the siege, Charles the Fat decided on a new way of handling the Vikings. Instead of fighting the Vikings, Charles bargained with them! In exchange for more silver, Siegfried agreed to go fight for Charles in the east, and leave Paris alone. Once again, the Vikings sailed away happy— for the moment.

A **siege** happens when an attacker surrounds a fort or city, cutting off the food and supplies it needs to survive. Without help from outside, any besieged fort must eventually either surrender or die.

The Franks wanted their king to fight the Vikings, not bargain with them. So when Charles the Fat chose to bargain, he lost his people's trust. Soon after the bargain, the great Carolingian Empire built by Charles Martel and Charlemagne broke apart for the last time.

Rollo the Viking (846? - 931?)

Another Viking who fought at the Siege of Paris was one of the most famous who ever lived: **Rollo the Viking**. According to legend, Rollo was also one of the biggest Vikings who ever lived— a mountain of a man, frightfully large and strong. Rollo's nickname, "Rollo the Walker," may have come from the fact that he was too heavy to ride a horse!

King Charles the Simple, whose nickname may also be translated "Charles the Straightforward"

Twenty-five years after the Siege of Paris, Rollo led another Viking army upriver, where he attacked Paris yet again. After failing to break into Paris, Rollo moved on to another key city: **Chartres**, 50 miles to the southwest.

By this time, Charles the Fat had died. The new King of West Francia was his cousin, **Charles the Simple**. Fortunately for the Franks, Charles the Simple was still strong enough to beat Rollo at the **Battle of Chartres**.

Even so, the Franks were no closer to stopping the Viking raids that came year after year. What Charles the Simple really wanted was to tame the savage Vikings.

With this in mind, Charles the Simple took a page out of Charles the Fat's book: instead of battling Rollo, Charles bargained with him. In a treaty signed after the Battle of Chartres, Rollo agreed to several things. First, Rollo would become a Christian. Second, Rollo and his people would become subjects of Charles the Simple. This meant defending Charles' kingdom against all attacks— including attacks from other Vikings.

In exchange, Charles gave Rollo what the Vikings had already stolen: the land of Normandy. Rollo became the first **Duke of Normandy**. Rollo was now an official member of the Frankish nobility, second in rank only to the king himself.

With a stroke of his treaty pen, Charles the Simple did more to tame the Vikings than his ancestors had done in a century. Instead of savage Vikings, Rollo and his people gradually became the **Normans**— a French-speaking, Christian people of Normandy, a fine duchy in West Francia.

A **duke** is a nobleman who manages a big territory called a **duchy** in the name of his king.

Dukes stand above marquises, who in turn stand above counts (earls), viscounts and barons. Thus a duke is often second in rank only to his king.

~~~ 96 ~~~

The Vikings in England

- Start -

When the Viking Age began, the future England was still divided into the **Heptarchy**— the seven kingdoms that the Angles and Saxons built after the Romans left (Chapter 2). The four largest Anglo-Saxon kingdoms were **Northumbria**, **Mercia**, **Wessex** and **East Anglia**. Three smaller kingdoms lay along the southeast coast: **Essex**, **Kent** and **Sussex**. The lines between these seven kingdoms often blurred, as certain kings ruled more than one of them.

The Vikings attacked the Heptarchy the same way they attacked West Francia: first with raiding parties, then with invasion armies. The first big Viking army in the Heptarchy came from Denmark in 865. This terrifying force, which Anglo-Saxons called the **Great Heathen Army**, easily defeated King Aella of Northumbria in 866. Afterwards, legend says, the Vikings murdered Aella in the most horrifying way imaginable.

When the Great Heathen Army showed no signs of going home, the other kings of the Heptarchy realized that they were in serious trouble. Unless they all stood together, the Vikings would surely pick them off one by one! What the Anglo-Saxons needed was a strong leader to pull together all the kingdoms of the Heptarchy.

The leader who filled that need was **King Alfred of Wessex**, also called **Alfred the Great**.

Born in 849, Alfred was the youngest son of King Aethelwulf of Wessex. With four older brothers ahead of him, Alfred seemed unlikely to inherit the throne. So instead of raising Alfred to be a king, Aethelwulf raised him to be a scholar. In a time when few Anglo-Saxons even learned to read, young Alfred learned law, Bible and much more.

Alfred the Great
(849 - 899)

AELFREDUS
MAGNUS

Alfred was still a young student when his brothers started dying off, one by one. With each brother's death, Alfred drew a little bit closer to the throne. When the Great Heathen Army struck in 866, only one brother remained: **King Aethelred of Wessex**, who had joined forces with the King of Mercia to tackle the Vikings.

In 871, Aethelred died in battle— leaving no one but the 22-year-old Alfred to take his place.

Shortly after his brother died, Alfred signed a peace treaty with the Vikings. Like most Viking treaties, this one didn't last long. Five years later, a Danish Viking called **Guthrum the Dane** launched new attacks deep inside Wessex.

The low point of Alfred's reign came in January 878. In celebration of the Christmas season, Alfred had sent most of his troops home, and was relaxing at a hunting lodge. He may have forgotten that the Vikings were pagans— which meant that they didn't celebrate Christmas. When Guthrum the Dane attacked the hunting lodge, Alfred barely escaped with his life!

Fortunately, Alfred knew a good place to hide. In western Wessex, not far from Bristol, lay a swampy land called **Somerset Levels**. On some forgotten island hidden in the swamps, Alfred spent the early months of 878 planning his next move.

According to legend, Alfred spent part of this time with a peasant family who had no idea that their strange guest was the King of Wessex. One day, the woman set some meal cakes around her fire to bake. Since Alfred was sitting near the fire, she asked him to watch the cakes while she went outside for more firewood. Alfred was so lost in thought that he didn't notice the smell of burning meal cakes. When the woman returned, she gave him a good scolding— not knowing that she was scolding her king!

Alfred in the peasant woman's cottage

Those thoughtful months in Somerset Levels would prove to be time well spent. In the spring of 878, Alfred summoned every fighting man in Wessex to a meeting place called **Egbert's Stone**. After training up his army, Alfred tackled Guthrum the Dane at the **Battle of Edington**, fought about 15 miles northwest of Stonehenge. This time, Alfred crushed Guthrum, leaving him no choice but surrender!

After this great victory, Alfred struck a great bargain with Guthrum the Dane. Like Rollo the Viking, Guthrum agreed to become a Christian. Guthrum also agreed to be satisfied with the land he had already conquered, instead of constantly fighting for new land.

Since Guthrum and his fellow Vikings came mostly from Denmark, Anglo-Saxons called Guthrum's territory the **Danelaw**. What had once been the Heptarchy now became just two kingdoms, more or less: the Danelaw in the northeast, and Wessex in the southwest.

> The **Danelaw** was the part of Britain conquered by Danish Vikings— the part where Danish law ruled, rather than Anglo-Saxon law.

King Alfred's Tower

After the Battle of Edington, Alfred the Great put the education he had received as a boy to good use. Alfred was not only a great military man, but also a great king who brought fairer laws and better education to a people who had never known them before— the once-savage Anglo-Saxons.

Almost 1,000 years after Alfred, the English erected a 160-foot-tall monument to him on the site of Egbert's Stone. A plaque on **King Alfred's Tower** describes the warm feelings the English people hold for Alfred the Great:

"…To him we owe the origin of juries, the establishment of a militia, the creation of a naval force. Alfred, the light of a benighted age, was a philosopher and a Christian, the father of his people, the founder of the English monarchy and liberty."

Alfred died in 899. In all the generations since, no other English king has ever earned the title "Great."

Although some honor Alfred the Great as the first King of England, Alfred never claimed that title— for Alfred never conquered the Danelaw. The first true King of England was Alfred's grandson **Aethelstan**. For in 927, Aethelstan finally conquered the Danelaw, bringing all of what is now England under one crown for the first time. Thus the **Kingdom of England** began in 927!

But the Viking Age wasn't over. For not all of Alfred the Great's descendants did as well against the Vikings as Aethelstan did.

In 1013, a Danish Viking called **Sweyn Forkbeard** seized the throne of England from another descendant of Alfred: **King Aethelred the Unready**. From then on, the throne passed back and forth between two royal houses. One was the **House of Denmark**, founded by the Viking family of Sweyn Forkbeard. The other was the **House of Wessex**, founded by the English family of Alfred the Great.

To make matters even more complicated, there was also a third royal house involved. This is because two kings of England married the same woman: **Emma of Normandy**.

Emma came from the **House of Normandy**— the house that Rollo the Viking had founded over in France back in 911! In fact, Emma was Rollo's great-granddaughter. Emma of Normandy became the knot that tied together the three royal houses of the Norman Conquest: the House of Denmark, the House of Wessex and the House of Normandy.

> The **Kingdom of England** began in 927— the year when King Aethelstan of Wessex finally conquered the Danelaw, bringing all of what is now England under one crown for the first time.

Emma of Normandy with her sons Edward and Alfred, both from her marriage to Aethelred the Unready

The Norman Conquest

To understand how Emma of Normandy tied together three royal houses, we must look back for a moment.

Emma's first husband was King Aethelred the Unready (above). As Queen of England, Emma gave Aethelred two sons: **Alfred Aetheling** and **Edward the Confessor**. When Sweyn Forkbeard seized the throne in 1013, Emma fled across the English Channel with her sons, seeking safety with her family in Normandy.

Fortunately for the House of Wessex, Sweyn Forkbeard died only a few months later. With Sweyn out of the way, Aethelred came back to reclaim his throne. Just two years after that, though, Aethelred himself died!

The death of Aethelred set up a struggle between two sons of two past Kings of England. One was Cnut the Great, son of Sweyn Forkbeard. The other was Edmund Ironside, son of Aethelred the Unready. Edmund was an older son born to an earlier wife, not to Emma of Normandy. Cnut the Great won, claiming the throne of England in 1016.

Since Cnut was a Dane, not an Englishman, he feared that the English people might not trust him. To gain their trust, he decided to marry Aethelred's widow— making Emma of Normandy Queen of England a second time!

Two years later, Emma gave Cnut a son called **Harthacnut**. Since Harthacnut shared a mother with Alfred and Edward, he was their half-brother. However, Harthacnut's father was the sitting King of England; while Alfred and Edward were only sons of a dead king. So Harthacnut became heir to the throne; while Alfred and Edward went to live with Emma's relatives in Normandy.

Poor Alfred died a horrible death in 1036— probably while fighting for his father's lost throne. With Alfred gone, Edward the Confessor was the only surviving heir from the House of Wessex.

Next, young Harthacnut died, just six years after becoming King of England. Harthacnut may have drunk himself to death.

Since Harthacnut died childless, there could be no more heirs from the House of Denmark. So the throne went to the only man alive whose father had been King of England: Edward the Confessor.

Edward the Confessor turned out to be just as childless as Harthacnut. Edward's strange nickname, "the Confessor," came from the fact that he was as religious as a monk. Edward may have even sworn a monk's vow of chastity— guaranteeing that he would stay childless!

The childlessness of Edward the Confessor was one of the main reasons for the Norman Conquest. With a childless king sitting on such a tempting throne, it is no wonder that Edward's neighbors schemed to seize his throne the moment he was gone!

STOP

ꑍꑍꑍꑍꑍꑍꑍꑍꑍꑍꑍꑍꑍꑍꑍꑍꑍꑍꑍꑍꑍꑍꑍꑍꑍꑍꑍꑍ

After a long illness, Edward the Confessor finally died on the night of January 5, 1066. The death of the childless king set up a contest between three rivals, all eager to claim the throne.

The first rival was an English nobleman called **Harold Godwinson, Earl of Wessex**. Harold offered several reasons why the throne should be his. First, he was the richest, most powerful noble in England. Second, he was England's best, most experienced army commander.

Third, the king himself had promised Harold the throne— or so Harold said. Harold swore that in the last moments of his life, Edward the Confessor had come awake just long enough to name Harold Godwinson as his heir.

The second rival was **Duke William of Normandy**, later called **William the Conqueror**. William's claim to the throne came through Edward the Confessor himself. William and Edward were cousins through Edward's mother, Emma of Normandy.

Westminster Abbey is a beautiful church that stands in Westminster, an important section of London. Edward the Confessor started work on the first Westminster Abbey around 1042. The Westminster Abbey that stands today is a replacement church started by King Henry III in the 1200s.

Since the days of William the Conqueror, every monarch of England and Britain has received his or her crown at Westminster Abbey. The church has become a symbol of English royalty, and of the link between God and monarch.

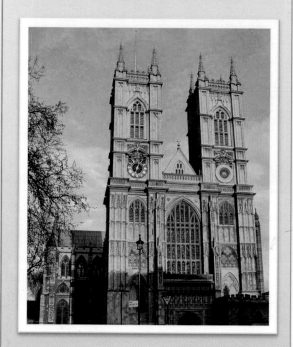

Besides this, William also claimed that both Edward the Confessor and Harold Godwinson had promised him the throne. In fact, William said, Harold Godwinson had sworn this promise on holy relics. By claiming the throne now, Harold was breaking a solemn vow before God!

The third rival was **King Harald III of Norway**. Harald was a Viking king whose claim to the throne of England came through the House of Denmark— the old house that had died out with Harthacnut. King Harald felt that when Harthacnut died, the throne of England should have gone to one of his Viking relatives, not to Edward the Confessor.

〜〜

Without a king to choose between the rivals, the decision lay with the king's council. This was a group of advisers called the **Witan**.

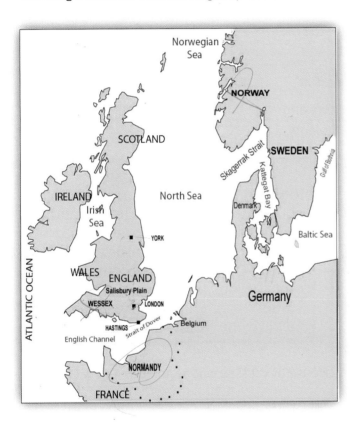

> The **Witenagemot**, also called the **Witan**, was a council that advised the King of England. *Witenagemot* is Old English for "meeting of the wise."

Since Harold Godwinson was the only Englishman on the list, it is not surprising that the Witan chose Godwinson! The day after Edward the Confessor died, Harold Godwinson was crowned King of England.

The moment Godwinson received his crown, both of his rivals started raising armies against him.

The first to strike was King Harald III of Norway. In September 1066, King Harald landed in northern England with about 300 ships, carrying about 15,000 troops. With such a large army, King Harald had no trouble seizing the surprised city of York, England on September 20.

At the time, Godwinson's main army lay at his capital, London. Since York stood 175 miles north of London, and since most armies would need a long time to cross 175 miles, King Harald believed that he had a long time to prepare for Godwinson.

King Harald turned out to be quite wrong. Just a few days later, King Harald was stunned to see Godwinson marching up to **Stamford Bridge**, just east of York. Godwinson had marched his army 175 miles in just four days, making an incredible 44 miles per day! On September 25, Godwinson crushed King Harald at the **Battle of Stamford Bridge**— killing his first rival.

King Harald's loss was William of Normandy's gain.

While Godwinson was busy tackling King Harald, William of Normandy sailed across the English Channel. With 700 or more ships, carrying about 30,000 troops, William's force was twice as large as King Harald's had been! Just 3 days after the Battle of Stamford Bridge, the Normans landed near a place called **Hastings**, about 50 miles southeast of London.

At the time, Godwinson was still in York— which meant that for the second time in two weeks, his army was a long way from where he needed it. Once again, Godwinson had to march his troops a long way in a short time, rushing to put his army between Hastings and London.

The Battle of Hastings (October 14, 1066)

The battle that followed was the key battle of the Norman Conquest.

William of Normandy enjoyed three big advantages at the **Battle of Hastings**. First, William had many archers and crossbowmen; while Harold had few. Second, William had plenty of horse-mounted troops; while Harold had mostly foot soldiers. Third, William's army was well-rested; while Harold's army was exhausted after its long march down from York.

Despite fighting at a disadvantage, Godwinson fought long, bravely and well. In the end, though, a Norman arrow pierced Godwinson, claiming his life. Without its leader, the English army fell apart.

Thus at the Battle of Hastings, William of Normandy not only killed his last rival for the throne of England, but also destroyed the best army in England. The House of Wessex was at an end. A new English royal house had begun: the House of Normandy.

Although the Normans were supposed to be civilized by 1066, they had not quite forgotten their savage Viking roots. After the Battle of Hastings, the Normans mercilessly slaughtered many English troops, and also mutilated the remains of Harold Godwinson.

As punishment for these shameful deeds, Pope Alexander II ordered the Normans to build a new church on the site of the battle. William dedicated the **Battle Abbey** to St. Martin of Tours, patron saint of France.

The **Bayeux Tapestry** is a long, narrow cloth embroidered with about 50 scenes from the Norman Conquest. The tapestry's name comes from Bayeux Cathedral, the church in Normandy where the tapestry has been stored for nearly 1,000 years. The first scene shows Edward the Confessor on his throne.

This scene from the Bayeux Tapestry shows Harold Godwinson and his advisers pointing at Halley's Comet in fear and awe

Halley's Comet is a big, bright comet that appears once every 75 – 76 years, when its long orbit around the sun carries it close enough to be visible from Earth.

It so happened that 1066, the year of the Norman Conquest, was a Halley's Comet year. The comet appeared soon after Harold Godwinson claimed the kingship—leading the superstitious to connect king and comet.

The Normans took the comet to mean that God was angry with Harold Godwinson for breaking his oath to William. They predicted that God would soon end Godwinson's unjust reign. In Norman eyes, that prediction came true when Godwinson died at the Battle of Hastings.

CHAPTER 10:

England after the Norman Conquest

The **Norman Conquest** is a good example of the bad things that can happen when a foreign invader takes over a country. **William the Conqueror** did much more than just invade England and kill its king. He also stole English property, rewrote English law, and killed many innocent Englishmen.

Naturally, the English didn't just put up with all of this! The **Battle of Hastings**, fought in 1066, was only the beginning of the Norman Conquest.

The **Norman Conquest** began in October 1066, when William the Conqueror beat Harold Godwinson at the Battle of Hastings.

Finishing the Norman Conquest

After winning the Battle of Hastings, William the Conqueror marched toward London, where he hoped to be crowned King of England.

But the English people didn't want a foreign king. Instead, they wanted another king from England's old royal house, the House of Wessex. The king they chose was **Edgar Aetheling**, a 15-year-old cousin of Edward the Confessor.

Despite Edgar's young age, William had a hard time breaking into London. Since Hastings lay south of London, William tried to enter London from the south. The easiest way was to take London Bridge, which crossed the Thames River just south of the main city.

Much to William's frustration, Edgar wouldn't let him take the easy way. Try as he might, William couldn't drive Edgar's army off London Bridge. So instead, William took the hard way. He marched far to the west, where he could cross the Thames more easily. Then he circled around, marching toward London from the northwest— where no river stood in his way.

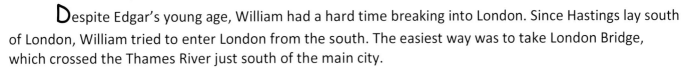

Without a river, Edgar couldn't hope to hold off William's huge army. So Edgar surrendered, leaving William to claim the throne. At Westminster Abbey on Christmas Day 1066, William the Conqueror officially became **King William I of England**.

But Edgar didn't stay surrendered. Instead, he moved up to northern England, where he launched a rebellion against William.

The King of Scotland promised to help Edgar rebel. So did the King of Denmark; and so did several nobles from the north. With that many allies, Edgar stood a good chance of taking back northern England.

William the Conqueror riding a black horse in a scene from the Bayeux Tapestry

To keep that from happening, William launched a **total war** called the **Harrying of the North**.

Total war was a tactic the Romans knew well. Long ago, the Roman army had learned that the best way to beat stubborn rebels was not to destroy their armies. No, the best way was to destroy their homeland! Roman soldiers destroyed everything the rebels might possibly use— not only food, shelter and weapons, but also the innocent civilians who grew food, built shelter and made weapons.

This is what the Harrying of the North was like. Taking a page out of the Romans' book, William laid waste of northern England— killing people, burning towns and farms, destroying crops and livestock. Very few rebels survived William's attack. And even if they did survive, they had nothing to look forward to— for William had ruined their farms, leaving them no way to feed themselves. Northern England took a long time to recover from the cruel Harrying of the North.

〜〜

The Norman Conquest finally wound down in 1072, six years after the Battle of Hastings. After that, William settled down to the business of remaking England's government.

One of William's first jobs as king was to reward the people who had helped him claim the throne.

The Norman Conquest had been a dangerous gamble. It had required thousands of Normans to risk their lives, for no better reason than because their duke wanted to be a king. Even for loyalty's sake, most men wouldn't take that kind of risk— unless William promised them rich rewards.

The rewards William promised were all the treasures he planned to win in the Norman Conquest.

Now that the Norman Conquest was finally over, it was time to hand out rewards. To do that, William simply took lands and treasures away from Englishmen and gave them to his Norman

William the Conqueror leading his Companions into battle in a scene from the Bayeux Tapestry

friends. After the Norman Conquest, almost every property in England belonged to Normans— even though there were far more Englishmen than there were Normans!

No one received more land and treasure than the **Companions of William the Conqueror**. These were the knights who actually fought beside William at the Battle of Hastings. After the Norman Conquest, the Companions became the richest, most powerful nobles in England. Even today, some of the richest families in England still trace their fortunes back to a Companion of William the Conqueror.

Even so, William was careful not to give his Companions too much. For he knew that even a close friend could become a danger to his king, if he gained too much power.

A **Companion of William the Conqueror** was a Norman knight who personally fought beside William at the Battle of Hastings.

So William took steps to keep that from happening.

First, William gave his Companions the lowest noble rank he could. William **created** many new nobles after the Norman Conquest. But he didn't create the higher ranks, such as **dukes**, **marquises**, **earls** and **viscounts**. Instead, he created mostly minor nobles called **barons.** Since **baronies** were small, barons didn't command enough men to rebel against their king.

Second, William scattered his barons' baronies. Some of William's Companions deserved more than one barony. But William didn't give side-by-side baronies to the same baron. Instead, he gave him one in Wessex, one in Kent and maybe another in Northumbria. That way, no baron commanded too many men in any one place.

Third, William insisted that baronies didn't really belong to their barons. Instead, they belonged to the king. If a baron displeased William, then he could take away his barony and give it to someone else.

All of these changes were part of a medieval style of government called the **feudal system**.

> To **create a noble** is to promote a person to a noble rank.
>
> ➤ The lowest noble rank is **baron**, head of a **barony**.
> ➤ The next noble rank is **viscount**, head of a **viscountcy**.
> ➤ Next comes **earl**, head of an **earldom**.
> ➤ Next comes **marquis**, head of a **marquisate**.
> ➤ The highest noble rank is **duke**, head of a **duchy**.

The Feudal System — Stop —

The **feudal system** was a kind of land ownership based on oaths of loyalty between two people. The higher person was the **lord**, or master; while the lower person was the **vassal**, or servant.

> The word "**feudal**" may come from the same root as the word "fealty," meaning "loyalty."

The oath between lord and vassal was like a contract for the use of the lord's land. The vassal received the money earned from selling crops, livestock and so on. In exchange, the lord received taxes from the vassal. The vassal also sent troops for his lord's armies. In exchange, the lord promised to use those armies to protect the vassal.

The same person could be a vassal in one oath, and a lord in another oath. For example, in the oath between king and baron, the king was lord, and the baron was vassal. But then, the baron might decide to place part of his barony in the hands of a knight. In that oath, the baron was lord, and the knight was vassal.

The feudal oath happened in a solemn ritual called a **commendation ceremony**. First came the **Act of Homage**, in which the vassal knelt before his lord and acknowledged him as his master. Then came the **Oath of Fealty**, in which the vassal swore to serve his lord faithfully and never harm him.

The lord made two promises in return. First, he promised to protect his vassal. Second, he promised to give his vassal whatever reward he

A nobleman swearing the Oath of Fealty
to King William I of England

earned. If the vassal kept his oath, then his lord would honor him. But if the vassal broke his oath, then his lord would take vengeance!

At the bottom of the feudal system stood three kinds of peasants: **freemen**, **serfs** and **slaves**. Some freemen were skilled tradesmen, such as blacksmiths and carpenters. Others were farmers who could afford to pay the rents demanded by their lords.

If a farmer couldn't afford to pay, then he became the most miserable of all medievals: a **serf**. Some became serfs because bad harvests or long winters left them too poor to feed themselves. Others did because they needed a lord's protection, or because cruel lords forced them to.

Serfs harvesting wheat for their lord

> To be in **bondage** is to be a slave.
>
> A **serf** was a medieval peasant who was bound to serve his lord. Serfdom started with a harsh oath called the **oath of bondage**.

Serfdom started with the harshest oath imaginable. In the oath of bondage, the serf promised to serve his lord with all his heart— to love what his lord loved, hate what his lord hated, and always strive to please his lord. Once they swore this oath, serfs had only one advantage over slaves: they could not be bought and sold like property. Other than that, serfs were much like slaves.

➤ Like slavery, serfdom was **hereditary**— which meant that if a father and mother were serfs, then their children would be serfs as well.

➤ Like slaves, serfs needed their lord's permission to marry.

➤ Like slaves, serfs could not leave their lord's land without permission. And if the land passed from one lord to another, then the serfs went with the land.

In exchange for the oath of bondage, the lord promised the serf three things: protection, a place to live and help in times of need. Most serfs spent part of the year working the lord's land, and the rest on a small plot their lord set aside for them. Once the oath of bondage was sworn, a serf had little hope of ever becoming a freeman again.

The Beginning of the High Middle Ages

The reign of William the Conqueror marks the beginning of the High Middle Ages. This was the age of castles, knights and chivalry.

William was England's first great castle-builder. Whenever the Conqueror moved into a new part of England, he built at least a small castle there. Each new castle served as an army base— with barracks for troops, stables for horses and storehouses for food and weapons.

Why did the Normans need so many army bases? Because Englishmen were furious about the Norman Conquest! As hostile invaders in a foreign land, the Normans were always in danger of attack. Each Norman castle was like a little island of safety in a big sea of trouble. If the English attacked one castle, then the Normans could usually hold out long enough for help to come from another castle.

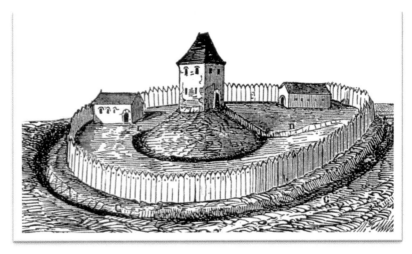

Sketch of a motte and bailey castle

The first type of castle the Normans built was the simplest: a **motte and bailey** castle. The **motte** was a steep mound of earth piled up by the castle's builders. The steepness of the motte made it hard to attack what stood at its top: the **keep**. The keep was the safest part of the castle, a strong building with sturdy defenses.

The **bailey** was a low, level area around the motte, surrounded by strong wooden walls called **palisades**. Baileys were protected places for barracks, stables, blacksmith's shops and so on.

Because the Normans were in a hurry at first, they usually built their keeps out of wood. Later, they wanted to replace these wooden keeps with stone ones— for stone was not only stronger than wood, but also more fireproof.

Unfortunately, mottes built from fill dirt were too soft to support the tremendous weight of stone keeps. Without a solid foundation, any stone building will first crack, and then collapse!

The answer was a type of castle called a **shell keep**. Instead of building stone keeps atop their fill-dirt mottes, the Normans added thin shells of fire-proof stone around their old wooden keeps.

Later, richer lords built a stronger type of castle: the all-stone **courtyard castle**. The simplest courtyard castles had three or four tall, strong **towers** bristling with defenses. **Curtain walls** connected the towers, finishing the defensive ring around the courtyard.

A **gatehouse** was a strong structure built to protect the gate, which was the weakest point of any castle. The best gatehouses actually had two gates, one at each end of a long tunnel. If an attacker managed to break through the first gate, then he still had to break through the second. Meanwhile, defenders fired at him through **arrow slits** that lined the tunnel walls.

A **portcullis** was a heavy latticework gate that slid up to open and down to close. When defenders wanted to seal an enemy inside the gatehouse, all they had to do was drop the portcullis.

A **bastion** was a structure that jutted out from a curtain wall, allowing defenders to fire on their attackers' flanks.

The strongest castle of all, the **concentric castle**, was protected by two sets of walls: a lower outer wall, and a higher inner wall. Any attacker who managed to climb over the outer wall might find

Bodiam Castle in East Sussex, England, a courtyard castle featuring towers, curtain walls and a strong gatehouse

himself trapped in the deadly space between the two walls. — STOP —

⚔⚔⚔⚔⚔⚔⚔⚔⚔⚔⚔⚔⚔⚔⚔⚔⚔⚔⚔⚔⚔⚔⚔⚔⚔

Knights jousting in chain mail

A **knight** was a trained fighting man who swore an oath to defend his lord. In the medieval ranking system, knights stood just below nobles— higher than gentlemen, but lower than barons.

Of course, knights who served their lords well could earn noble titles. Some of William the Conqueror's men started out as knights, but wound up as noblemen.

A long with knighthood went the knight's code of conduct, which

Chivalry was the knight's code of conduct.

went by the strange name of **chivalry**. Both "chivalry" and a similar word, "cavalry," referred to the fact that knights rode horses. Over time, though, "chivalry" stopped referring to horses. Instead, it referred to the way horse-mounted knights were supposed to behave.

The chivalrous knight was both mighty in battle and honorable in character. He was brave, tough, strong and skilled; but he was also courteous, well-spoken, loyal and generous. He never backed down from a fight in fear; never gave up on a task; and never stopped defending the weak.

Above all, the chivalrous knight never broke an oath! He always did his duty to his God, his lord and his lady.

The importance of oaths explains how chivalrous knights could take part in an ugly total war like the Harrying of the North (above). After the Norman Conquest, William demanded the oath of fealty from every noble in England. The nobles of northern England broke those oaths when they rebelled against William. As chivalrous knights, the Normans felt that it was their duty to punish the oath-breaking nobles of the north.

In fact, the whole Norman Conquest was based on an oath that Harold Godwinson supposedly swore to William the Conqueror (Chapter 9). In Norman eyes, Harold broke that oath when he tried to claim the throne.

⚔⚔⚔⚔⚔⚔⚔⚔⚔⚔⚔⚔⚔⚔⚔⚔⚔⚔⚔⚔⚔⚔⚔⚔⚔⚔⚔⚔

The first **knights' tournament** probably happened in the days of William the Conqueror. Tournaments helped train knights for war. They also gave knights a way to test their skills, boost their reputations and win prizes.

Later, tournaments became a kind of entertainment— somewhat like gladiator fights in the old Roman Coliseum.

Early tournaments were divided into two rounds. First came the *melee a cheval*, or "battle on

Tournament knights fighting the *Melee a Cheval*

horseback." Whole teams of knights charged at one another with leveled lances, trying to unhorse as many opponents as possible. After this first charge, any knight who was still on his horse turned to face new opponents. The word "tournament" may have come from this turn.

After the *melee a cheval* came the **melee a pied**, or "battle on foot." As in a real battle, knights fought in teams, not individually.

Some knights preferred a special kind of tournament called the **pas d'armes**, or "passage of arms." The first kind of *pas d'armes* was a standing challenge to any and all passing knights. The challenger set up camp near some narrow spot in the road, such as a bridge or a gate. Any knight who wanted to pass that spot would have to fight the challenger first. If the passing knight refused, then the challenger marked him as a coward— sometimes by taking away his spurs.

The later *pas d'armes* was part of an organized tournament. In this kind of pas d'armes, all knights nailed their coats of arms to a display called the **tree of shields**. To challenge another knight, one simply walked up to the tree of shields and struck his opponent's coat of arms.

Some tournaments included a dangerous fight called a **jousting match**. Two horse-mounted knights raced toward one another as fast as they dared, aiming blunt lances at each other's shields. A good strike would either drive the opponent off his horse or shatter his lance. A bad fall could lead to a concussion, broken bones or worse.

Like other tournament styles, jousting matches changed over the years. Early jousting matches didn't end when one knight unhorsed the other. Instead, the battle continued on foot, ending only when one knight struck the other senseless.

An invention called the **tilt** helped make later jousting matches more civilized. The tilt was a long, low fence that divided the jousting **list** into two lanes, one for each knight. One advantage of the tilt was that it kept knights from colliding at full speed— which sometimes happened in the days before tilts! Another advantage was that it made the lance strike at an angle, reducing the force of its blow.

Scene from the tilt jousting tournament that killed King Henry II of France

Even with the tilt, though, jousting was still highly dangerous. In the 1500s, a long splinter from a broken lance killed a sitting King of France!

England under the House of Normandy

When he wasn't conquering countries, William the Conqueror liked to hunt. The king liked nothing better than to ride through the forest with his noble friends, shooting down wild game.

What William didn't like was sharing the forest with peasants. For hungry peasants often hunted until there was little game left for the king and his friends.

WILLIAM THE CONQUEROR

The solution to this problem was to set aside **royal forests**— private game reserves where no peasants were allowed. The first royal forest was a wood in south central England called the New Forest.

To make his New Forest as private as possible, William wrote a code of laws called Forest Law. Under Forest Law, all royal forests were reserved strictly for the king and his friends. No one could kill any wild animal without permission from the king. Nor could anyone harvest any plant— for plants were food for the wild game William loved.

Scene from the New Forest

The problem with Forest Law was that so many peasants depended on forests. Before Forest Law, England's forests had belonged to everyone. Any peasant who lived near a forest could go there to find meat, berries, firewood and more. With enough hard work, a forest-dwelling peasant could earn a small living selling meat or firewood. At the very least, the forest kept peasants from freezing to death.

After Forest Law, though, royal forests belonged to the king alone. Peasants had to ask the king's permission for everything— even to harvest dead wood from the forest floor!

For peasants who lived near a royal forest, Forest Law was the worst part of the Norman Conquest. The king's selfishness robbed them of their livings! With no way to replace what they had lost, many peasants had little choice but to take the oath of bondage, and become serfs. —STOP—

〰〰〰〰〰〰〰〰〰〰〰〰〰〰〰〰〰〰〰〰〰〰〰〰〰〰〰〰〰〰〰〰〰〰〰〰〰〰〰

Besides being a determined hunter, William was also a determined tax collector.

Near the end of his reign, William ordered a detailed inventory of every person and property in England. The king's men left no stone unturned— carefully counting every barn and mill, every plow and hoe, every ox and horse, every lord, knight, serf and child in the whole kingdom. When they finished, William's men wrote down their counts in a record called the Domesday Book.

Tax collectors also collected money for the church— for the law required every Englishman to pay a **tithe** (one-tenth, or 10%) of his earnings to the church each year. Since most peasants had little money, they paid their tithes the only way they could: in grain or livestock. Many English villages built special buildings called **tithe barns** to store the mountains of grain donated by peasants each year.

William's government used the Domesday Book to decide two things. The first was how much tax the king should demand from each landowner. The second was how many troops each landowner should provide for the king.

The decisions in the Domesday Book were absolutely final. Whatever tax was written in the Domesday Book, that was the tax one paid— or else one went to jail! The purpose of the Domesday Book was simple: to make sure every Englishman paid every penny of tax he owed.

"Domesday" is an Old English word for "Judgment Day." The name "Domesday Book" meant that all judgments in the book were absolutely final— as final as the one God will make on Judgment Day!

Just before William died in 1087, he divided his lands between his three surviving sons. Oldest son **Robert Curthose** received the Duchy of Normandy. Middle son **William Rufus** received the Kingdom of England, becoming **King William II**. As for the youngest son, **Henry**, he received only money— for the moment.

King William II pierced by an arrow in the New Forest

Like his father before him, **King William II** was a cruel Norman who treated Englishmen more like slaves than citizens. But William II may have paid a high price for his cruelty.

One fine day in August 1100, William II was enjoying his favorite hobby— hunting in the New Forest— when an arrow suddenly pierced his lung, killing him. According to his friends, the king's death was a tragic hunting accident. An arrow fired at a fleeing animal had happened to glance off a tree, striking the king instead.

Some people doubt this story. Since William II had so many enemies, historians have always wondered if this so-called "accident" was really an accident at all!

ௐௐௐ

When William II died, his brother Robert Curthose happened to be in the Holy Land, where the First Crusade was just ending (Chapter 12). If Robert had been home in Normandy, then he certainly would have tried to claim his brother's throne. Since Robert wasn't home, his younger brother Henry stepped in!

King Henry I was cut from different cloth than his cruel father and brothers. Like Alfred the Great (Chapter 9), Henry was a younger son who had been raised to be a scholar, not a king— for no one expected younger sons to inherit crowns.

One of the subjects Henry had studied was law. So when Henry became king, he worked to bring fair law to all his lands. Englishmen remember King Henry I as the first fair, wise Norman King of England.

After beating his brother Robert Curthose at the **Battle of Tinchebray**, Henry became Duke of Normandy as well as King of England. Thus Henry ruled all of the lands William the Conqueror had ruled— unlike William II, who never ruled Normandy.

ௐௐௐௐௐௐௐௐௐௐௐௐௐௐௐௐௐௐௐௐௐௐௐௐௐௐௐௐௐௐௐௐ

King Henry I had two legitimate children: a son called **William Aetheling**, and a daughter called **Matilda**.

One evening in November 1120, the 17-year-old William Aetheling set out across the English Channel aboard a brand-new vessel called the **White Ship**. Beside the young prince rode many of his young friends, all headed from Normandy to England. With Christmas coming soon, the prince and his friends were in the mood to drink and celebrate.

The White Ship breaking up on a rock

The captain of the White Ship may have been drinking too. If he was, then that would explain what happened next.

When sailing out of that particular harbor, wise captains always steered south for a while. That way, they could be sure to avoid some dangerous rocks that lay hidden near the coast to the north.

For some reason, the captain of the White Ship didn't follow this wise course. Instead, he steered directly to the north, where he smashed his hull wide open on a hidden rock!

Thus the White Ship sank, taking down with it the only son of the King of England.

The Wreck of the White Ship

Fortunately, the king still had his daughter. When William Aetheling died, Matilda was married to a Holy Roman Emperor in Germany. Instead of Princess Matilda, she was now called **Empress Matilda**.

A few years after her brother died, Matilda's husband died as well, leaving her a widow at age 23.

A few years after that, King Henry arranged a second marriage for his daughter. Matilda's new husband was **Geoffrey of Anjou**— also called **Geoffrey Plantagenet**, heir to a county south of Normandy.

Since Henry had no son to inherit his lands, he wanted Matilda to inherit them. But he knew that his nobles wouldn't want to follow a woman. So before he died, Henry asked his nobles to swear double oaths to him. Out of love for Henry, all promised to accept Matilda as queen when Henry was gone.

> The **White Ship** was much like the **RMS Titanic**, the huge luxury liner that sank in the North Atlantic in April 1912. Both were brand-new ships praised for their luxury. Both carried some of the richest people of their day. And both sailed far too fast into known dangers— things their captains should have been wise enough to avoid!

But when Henry died, his nobles forgot all about their oaths! Instead of following Matilda, the nobles followed her cousin **Stephen of Blois**. Stephen was the count of Blois, a county southeast of Normandy. Stephen was also a grandson of William the Conqueror, just like Matilda. But unlike Matilda, Stephen was a man— which is why the nobles chose him over Matilda.

The Coronation of Stephen of Blois

Matilda and her husband fought hard to take back her lost inheritance. The start of King Stephen's reign was also the start of a long, confusing war called the **Anarchy**.

Midway through the Anarchy, Matilda and her husband managed to take back Normandy. But they never managed to take back England.

After almost 20 years, the Anarchy finally ended with an agreement called the **Treaty of Wallingford**.

The key to this treaty was another royal death. In the last year of the Anarchy, King Stephen's only son died, leaving him without an heir. After that, the agreement was simple. Stephen would remain King of England as long as he lived. But when Stephen died, the throne would go to Matilda's son, whose name was **Henry Plantagenet**.

Thus Stephen of Blois was the last King of England from the House of Normandy. When Stephen died in 1154, Henry Plantagenet became **King Henry II of England**.

Since Henry's family name was Plantagenet, his reign was the beginning of a new English royal house: the **House of Plantagenet**.

-STOP-

The Baltic Sea

The Baltic Sea is a big inland sea in northern Europe. To reach the Baltic Sea from the Atlantic Ocean, ships must first pass into the North Sea. From there, the natural path to the Baltic lies through two straits: first the **Skagerrak**, then the **Kattegat**.

In modern times, there is also a manmade path from the North Sea to the Baltic Sea. This is the **Kiel Canal**, which cuts across northern Germany near the base of the **Jutland Peninsula** (Chapter 8).

Setting aside the Skagerrak and the Kattegat, the rest of the Baltic Sea looks something like a squirrel climbing down a tree. The squirrel's big, bushy tail is the **Gulf of Bothnia**. One of the squirrel's hind legs is the **Gulf of Finland**, and the other is the **Gulf of Riga**. The squirrel's front legs are two much smaller gulfs: the **Curonian Lagoon** and the **Gulf of Gdansk**.

Ten countries line the shores of the Baltic Sea. Going clockwise from the northwest, they are **Norway**, **Sweden**, **Finland**, **Russia**, **Estonia**, **Latvia**, **Lithuania**, **Poland**, **Germany** and **Denmark**.

With so many countries lining its shores, the Baltic Sea is very important for trade. Unfortunately, the Baltic suffers from a problem that can make trade rather difficult: sea ice.

Because the Baltic Sea lies so far north, at least part of it freezes over every winter. Even in an average winter, sea ice may cover almost half of the Baltic Sea— from the northern tip of the Gulf of Bothnia all the way down to the Gulf Riga. Hard winters may freeze over even more.

Before modern times, sea ice meant closed ports. Several important ports used to close for at least part of every winter— including **Stockholm**, Sweden; **Helsinki**, Finland; **St. Petersburg**, Russia; **Tallinn**, Estonia; and **Riga**, Latvia. In modern times, ice-breaking ships keep these ports open all year— for a price.

Lithuania, Latvia and Estonia are called the **Baltic States.**

Kaliningrad is an **exclave** of Russia— in other words, a part of Russia that isn't connected to the rest.

German Beginnings

Magna Germania, or "Greater Germany," was a Roman name for north central Europe. Basically, **Germania** was a big area that lay north of the Roman Empire, south of the Baltic Sea and east of the Rhine River.

Although Rome tried to conquer Germania, it never quite managed it. Instead, one might say that Germania conquered Rome! For the "barbarians" who dragged down the Western Roman Empire came from Germania. The **Vandals** and **Visigoths** who sacked Rome were Germanic peoples (Chapter 1). So were the **Angles**, **Saxons** and **Jutes** who invaded Roman Britannia (Chapter 2). And so were the **Franks**, **Alemanni** and **Burgundians** who invaded Roman Gaul (Chapter 6). Even the **Vikings** were Germanic peoples (Chapter 8).

The Germans started as pagans. Many ancient Germans believed in the same gods the Vikings believed in— Norse gods like Odin and Thor.

That was before the **Carolingian Empire** came.

As we read in Chapter 7, the Carolingian Empire was named for the great Frankish general who won the Battle of Tours: **Charles Martel**. It was Charles Martel's grandson, **Charlemagne**, who finally conquered Germany. And wherever Charlemagne conquered, Christianity followed.

One of the first missionaries to preach the gospel in Germany was **Saint Boniface**. Boniface moved to Germany in 718, when Charles Martel still ruled the Carolingian Empire. Just as Patrick was an Apostle to the Irish, and Martin of Tours was an Apostle to the Gauls, so Boniface became an Apostle to the Germans.

Saint Boniface, Apostle to the Germans (680 – 754)

One way Boniface preached the gospel was by chopping down trees! Many Germans liked to worship at certain special trees— perhaps because these trees reminded them of **Yggdrasil**, the world tree of Norse mythology (Chapter 8).

One favorite tree was **Donar's Oak**. This was a huge old oak tree that stood near a German village called Fritzlar.

Donar was the German version of Thor, the favorite god of many Norsemen. To Germans, Donar's Oak was a symbol of Thor's awesome might. But to Boniface, Donar's Oak was a pagan idol. So Boniface decided to chop down Donar's Oak— which would prove that Thor wasn't mighty at all.

Boniface standing beside Donar's Oak, which he has just felled

When Boniface first set his ax to Donar's Oak, some Germans were probably expecting Thor to strike him down with a bolt of lightning, or perhaps a blow from his hammer *Mjölnir*. Of course, nothing of the sort happened. Donar's Oak went down just like any other tree. To add insult to injury, Boniface even used lumber from Donar's Oak to build a Christian church!

With help from Charles Martel's soldiers, Boniface did the same thing in many other German villages: he tore down pagan shrines, and built Christian churches instead. In 36 years of ministry, Boniface helped spread Christianity over most of Germany.

> Besides being the Apostle to the Germans, Boniface also may have decorated the very first Christmas tree! According to legend, Boniface used a small evergreen that sprouted near the stump of Donar's Oak as a symbol of Christ. The eternal leaves of the evergreen represented eternal life in heaven with Christ.

The Holy Roman Empire

As we've already read, the Carolingian Empire didn't last. Charlemagne's descendants fought among themselves, dividing his empire again and again. As of 870, the Carolingian Empire was divided into three kingdoms:

➤ South of the Alps lay the **Kingdom of Italy**.

➤ West of the Rhine River lay **West Francia**, which would go on to become the **Kingdom of France**.

➤ East of the Rhine lay **East Francia**, which would go on to become the **Kingdom of Germany**.

The last emperor to reign over all three kingdoms was **Charles the Fat**. This was the same Charles the Fat who lost his people's trust by bargaining with the Vikings at the Siege of Paris (Chapter 9). Two years later, in 888, the Carolingian Empire fell apart for the last time.

But the end of Charlemagne's empire didn't mean the end of Charlemagne's family. A descendant of Charlemagne still sat on the throne of East Francia— which meant that the German people were still ruled by a Frankish king.

Louis the Child with his father Arnulf, King of East Francia

That would soon change. After the Carolingian Empire fell apart, the branch of Charlemagne's family that ruled East Francia started dying out. By 899, the only one left alive was a 6-year-old king called **Louis the Child**.

Twelve years later, Louis the Child died as well— leaving behind no heir to take his place. The Carolingian dynasty in East Francia was at an end.

Without a king to hold it together, East Francia was in danger of falling apart. At the time, the kingdom was made up of five **duchies**. Some duchies had Frankish dukes, and some had German ones. Now that the descendants of Charlemagne were all dead, the German dukes longed to be free of the Franks.

> Remember what a **duchy** is— a land governed by a duke.

The dukes of East Francia elected one more Frankish king: Duke Conrad of Franconia, who became **King Conrad I** in 911. But Conrad had a lot of trouble with his German dukes. Just seven years into his reign, Conrad fought a big battle against the Duke of Bavaria, and ended up dying of his wounds.

Before he died, though, King Conrad laid out a plan for holding his kingdom together. Conrad believed that the only way to unite the German people was to choose a German king. The right man to take his place, Conrad said, was a German duke called Henry of Saxony— also called Henry the Fowler.

Conrad's choice of kings led to a strange scene in the forests of Saxony.

Henry the Fowler being surprised by the crown of East Francia while working on his falconry gear

Duke Henry's nickname, "the Fowler," came from the fact that he liked to use falcons for hunting. According to legend, Henry was working on the nets and cages he used for falconry when a crowd of nobles suddenly appeared in the middle of the forest. Just why they were there, Henry had no idea— until they offered him the crown of Germany!

Naturally, Henry accepted. In 919, Duke Henry of Saxony became **King Henry I of Germany**— the first non-Frankish king of all the Germans!

Like most kings of his day, Henry the Fowler was almost always at war. Henry's worst enemies were a people called the Magyars.

The Magyars were a lot like the Huns (Chapter 6). Both were expert horsemen who swept in from the east, conquering everything in their paths. And both demanded tribute payments from the people they conquered.

In Henry's day, the Magyars were newcomers. They had just crossed the **Carpathian Mountains**, settling in what is now Hungary. From there, they launched deadly raids against their new neighbors to the west: Germany and Italy.

At first, the Magyars were more than Henry the Fowler could handle. Then Henry had a stroke of luck. One day in 924, Henry managed to capture the son of an important Magyar prince. With this son as his hostage, Henry was able to strike a hard bargain with the Magyars.

Henry's side of the bargain was to return the prince's son unharmed. In exchange, the Magyars agreed to a 9-year truce with Germany— provided the Germans kept up their tribute payments.

Henry made the most of this 9-year truce. Throughout those 9 years, Henry bought horses for every knight in his kingdom. By training his knights to fight from horseback, Henry took away the Magyars' biggest advantage, their horses.

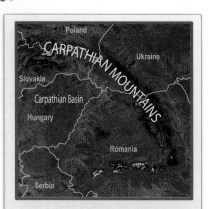

The **Carpathian Mountains** are an Eastern European mountain range that arcs through Romania, western Ukraine and southern Poland. West of this arc lies the **Carpathian Basin,** home of Hungary.

Hungary lies just east of Austria, which was then part of Germany.

By the end of those 9 years, Henry was ready. When the Magyars showed up to demand another year's tribute, Henry refused to pay! In the battle that followed, Henry's new cavalry beat the Magyars so badly that they dared not attack Germany again— at least, not while Henry was alive.

The Magyars crossing the Carpathian Mountains

ⁿⁿⁿⁿⁿⁿⁿⁿⁿⁿⁿⁿⁿⁿⁿⁿⁿⁿⁿⁿ

The next King of Germany was **Otto I**, son of Henry the Fowler. Like Charlemagne before him, Otto had big dreams of rebuilding the Roman Empire.

A strange romance helped Otto claim a key part of that empire: northern Italy.

Otto's romantic tale starts with two teenaged royals who rose to the throne of Italy in 948. One was **King Lothair II of Italy**; and the other was his wife, **Queen Adelaide of Italy**.

Lothair picked a bad time to grow up. In those days, most Italian nobles didn't follow the King of Italy. Instead, many followed **Berengar II**. Berengar was the Marquis of **Ivrea**, a land in northwest Italy.

Most people blamed Berengar for what happened to poor Lothair. Just two years into his reign, the young king suddenly died— probably because he was poisoned by Berengar!

With Lothair out of the way, Berengar seized the throne of Italy— for himself, and for his son **Adalbert**. But Berengar and Adalbert had a problem: their blood was only noble, not royal. No member of their family had ever been a king before. If they were going to keep the throne they had just stolen, then they would have to bring royal blood into their family.

To get that royal blood, Berengar arranged for Adalbert to marry Lothair's widow: Queen Adelaide. With a royal marriage, and hopefully a royal grandson or two, the family of Berengar and Adalbert would soon be royal enough.

Berengar's clever plan would have worked, if not for one important detail. Adelaide didn't want to marry Berengar's son— not when she was sure that Berengar had murdered her husband! So instead of making wedding plans, Adelaide tried to run away.

Side-by-side statues of Adelaide of Italy and her husband Otto I at a German cathedral

At this point, Adelaide's life became just like a storybook. Berengar soon caught the fleeing queen and locked her in a castle prison. Adelaide was now damsel in distress, in need of a knight in shining armor to rescue her.

Instead, she got a priest! Under cover of darkness, a loyal priest called **Warinus** tunneled under the walls of Adelaide's prison, scratching his way toward her night after night until they finally escaped together.

But Adelaide's adventures weren't over— for when Berengar found Adelaide's new hiding place, he quickly surrounded it.

Otto of Germany

This is where Otto of Germany comes into the story. Desperate to save herself, Adelaide hit upon a clever idea: she would write the mightiest king in Europe for help. She promised Otto that if he rescued her from Berengar, then she would marry Otto instead. That way, Otto could claim the throne of Italy through Adelaide!

Otto did just that. With Adelaide on Otto's side, most of Berengar's allies abandoned him before Otto even reached Italy. Otto beat Berengar easily. He then married Adelaide, becoming King of Italy as well as Germany!

Eleven years later, Otto received yet another title. In 962, the pope crowned Otto the first emperor of the Holy Roman Empire. Otto and his heirs, the **Holy Roman Emperors**, would rule Germany and more for the next several hundred years.

The Holy Roman Empire was a strange organization. As the French author Voltaire liked to say, every word of the empire's name was wrong— for it was "neither Holy, nor Roman, nor an Empire."

➤ It wasn't **"holy"** because it was a worldly kingdom, not a spiritual one— even if the emperor did receive his crown from the pope.

➤ It wasn't **"Roman"** because its core was Germany, not Italy. The Holy Roman Empire grew and shrank many times over the centuries. Sometimes it included northern Italy, but sometimes it didn't.

➤ It wasn't an **"empire"** because the so-called "Holy Roman Emperor" wasn't as powerful as a true emperor. German noblemen had a stubborn streak. They often did what they wanted to do, not what their emperor ordered them to do!

Despite its many weaknesses, the Holy Roman Empire would last for 844 years— from 962, when Otto I became the first Holy Roman Emperor, until 1806, when Napoleon I of France dissolved the empire.

One of the best-known Holy Roman Emperors was **Frederick I**, who reigned during the Third Crusade (Chapter 12). Frederick was also called **Barbarossa**— Italian for

The **Imperial Crown of the Holy Roman Empire** is an eight-sided crown made of very pure gold, and studded with dozens of precious gems. The 12 large gems on the front of the crown may represent Christ's twelve apostles.

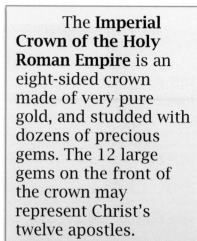

"red-beard"— after the flowing red beard he wore.

When the pope announced the Third Crusade, Frederick led a huge army from Germany toward the Holy Land. One day, Frederick's army started across a narrow bridge over a strong river in Asia Minor.

Frederick was impatient. He wanted to cross the river right away, but didn't want to make his army stop for him. So he decided to swim his horse across, taking some of his knights with him.

But the current turned out to be stronger than Frederick realized. The great old emperor wound up drowning in his own armor, before he ever reached the Third Crusade!

Emperor Frederick I and his knights plunging into the river

The Legend of the Sleeping Hero

According to legend, Emperor Frederick I Barbarossa isn't really dead at all. Instead, he is only sleeping a charmed sleep in some unknown mountain cave. Barbarossa will rest until his kingdom's hour of need, when he will awaken to lead his people to victory.

Barbarossa isn't the only sleeping hero in history. Arthur of Britain, Merlin, Charlemagne and many others also have sleeping hero legends.

The **Rammelsberg** is a mountain in Saxony, Germany that once held one of the richest silver mines in the world. The mountain is named for Ramm, the knight who discovered the silver in 900.

One day while Ramm was out hunting, he tied his horse so that he could chase his prey on foot. As the horse awaited Ramm's return, it impatiently scraped its hooves through the thin turf of the mountain— revealing a glint of silver underneath.

Two Christian Heroes

The Christmas carol "Good King Wenceslaus" is based on a true story. The real Wenceslaus was actually a Duke of Bohemia who lived in the days of Henry the Fowler. At the time, Bohemia was a duchy of Germany.

Unlike most noblemen, Duke Wenceslaus cared about the poor people of his duchy— which is why he wound up in a Christmas carol! The carol is set on a bitterly cold day just after Christmas, when Wenceslaus and his young page are out carrying gifts to the poor. The page grows so cold that he finally complains to Wenceslaus— protesting that if he takes one more step, then he will surely freeze.

In reply, Wenceslaus advises his page to "walk in my footsteps." When the page does, he is stunned to find that they are quite warm! The page is feeling the love of Christ, which fills Wenceslaus' heart so full that it spills over— warming even the frigid snow beneath his feet.

Duke Wenceslaus I of Bohemia
(907? - 935)

ΠΠΠΠΠΠΠΠΠΠΠΠΠΠΠΠΠΠΠΠΠΠΠΠΠΠΠΠΠΠΠΠΠΠΠΠ

Elizabeth of Hungary was another kindly noble like Wenceslaus. By Elizabeth's day, Hungary was no longer an enemy of Germany. Instead, it was a Christian kingdom attached to the Holy Roman Empire. Princess Elizabeth was 14 years old when she married Duke Ludwig of **Thuringia**, a duchy of the Holy Roman Empire.

When Elizabeth was not quite 20, Ludwig left her in charge of his duchy while he took a long trip. Of course, Ludwig also left older advisers to guide his young wife through any tough decisions she might have to make.

Princess Elizabeth of Hungary
(1207 - 1231)

Elizabeth of Hungary handing out bread to the poor at her castle door

While Ludwig was away, a terrible famine struck, starving the poor people of the duchy. If Elizabeth had listened to Ludwig's advisers, then she would have closed the castle gates and left the poor to starve. Instead, Elizabeth listened to the Bible, which told her that she must always help the poor.

So instead of closing her gates, Elizabeth threw them wide open! Elizabeth donated money from the duchy's treasury, handed out grain from the duchy's granaries, and even sold her own jewelry to raise money for a hospital.

When Ludwig returned, his advisers complained that his foolish young wife had emptied his treasury for nothing. Ludwig answered that as long as Elizabeth didn't give away his castle, he would still be far richer than most people!

Russian Beginnings

Russia is a big country that grew up in northeastern Europe. The story of Russia starts with two separate peoples.

➢ The **East Slavs** were natives of Eastern Europe. They lived mainly in what are now western Russia, Belarus and Ukraine.

➢ The **Rus** were a Viking people— Norsemen who lived along the eastern coasts of the Baltic Sea.

The East Slavs far outnumbered the Rus. Yet somehow, a Rus leader called **Rurik the Viking** became a king of the East Slavs. In 862, Rurik founded the **Rurikid dynasty**— the longest-reigning dynasty in Russian history.

What did Rurik the Viking want with Eastern Europe? The answer is trade. As an eastern people, the Rus loved to shop in the best shopping center of the East: Constantinople, capital of the Byzantine Empire (Chapter 4). Constantinople sold everything!

The East Slavs greeting Rurik the Viking, first king of the Rurikid dynasty of Kievan Rus

Besides common goods like grain, tools, sailcloth and rope, Constantinople also sold olive oil, wool and wine from Italy; luxurious silk and porcelain from China; rich spices from India and beyond; and even rare items from Africa.

So why didn't the Rus go to Constantinople by sea, like everyone else did?

The answer is because the sea route was too long and dangerous. The Rus preferred a route that led across Eastern Europe, mostly by river. This route started at the eastern tip of the Gulf of Finland, where St. Petersburg now lies. And it ended at the Black Sea, which of course leads to Constantinople.

The biggest river along this trade route was the **Dnieper**, which flowed into the Black Sea. To control the trade route, the Rus needed to control the Dnieper. And to control the Dnieper, they needed to control a set of high hills overlooking the Dnieper's banks— at a place called **Kiev**. This is why the Rus built their capital at Kiev, and why their kingdom was called Kievan Rus.

〰〰〰〰〰〰〰〰〰〰〰〰〰〰〰〰〰〰〰〰〰〰〰〰〰〰〰〰〰〰〰〰〰〰

Like the rest of the Vikings, the Rus started out as pagans. But they didn't stay pagan. Before long, the people of Kievan Rus learned the religion of Constantinople: Eastern Orthodox Christianity.

The first Christian ruler of Kievan Rus was Olga of Kiev. Olga started as the wife of Igor I, the third king of the Rurikid dynasty. When angry East Slavs murdered Igor, his son Svyatoslav was too young to rule the empire. So Olga ruled in his place.

Sometime during her 17-year reign, Olga went to Constantinople, where she became a Christian. On her return to Kiev, Olga brought along some of the first missionaries to preach the gospel in Kievan Rus.

But missionaries were only part of making Kievan Rus Christian. The other part was a decision made by Olga's grandson, the first Christian King of Kievan Rus: Vladimir the Great.

Olga of Kiev

After a great start, Kievan Rus had stopped growing as fast as Vladimir wanted it to. And Vladimir thought he knew why: because the pagan religion was holding his kingdom back. What Kievan Rus needed, he decided, was a better religion. So Vladimir sent men to countries all around, ordering them to learn more about the four biggest religions: Islam, Judaism, Western Christianity and Eastern Christianity.

Islam he rejected right away. For strict Muslims don't drink; and Vladimir knew that the Russian people loved drinking too much to ever give it up.

After a bit of thought, he rejected Judaism as well. To a fighting king like Vladimir, the fact that the Jews had lost Israel meant that God must have abandoned them. What good was Judaism, he wondered, if the Jews couldn't even defend their own homeland?

In the end, then, it came down to two choices: Western Christianity or Eastern Christianity.

Being a man of the East, Vladimir finally settled on Eastern Christianity. For in Russian eyes, great cathedrals like the Hagia Sophia of Constantinople were the most beautiful places on Earth (Chapter 5). In those days, no Western church could match the Hagia Sophia. So Vladimir decided to be baptized as an Eastern Christian.

Vladimir the Great trying to decide which religion to follow

Naturally, Vladimir expected his people to be baptized as well. One day in 988, Vladimir and his priests led all of their people down to the Dnieper River, where they led a historic ceremony called the **Baptism of Kiev**. Every citizen of Kiev was expected to be baptized, whether he wanted to be or not. As a sign that Kiev's pagan days were over for good, Vladimir tore down the idols he had once worshipped and tossed them into the river!

More mass baptisms followed, all over Kievan Rus. Under Vladimir the Great, Kievan Rus became the second most important Christian empire in the East, behind the Byzantine Empire.

> The Baptism of Kiev was an example of a **mass baptism**, in which hundreds or thousands of people are baptized all at once.

ฅฅฅฅฅฅฅฅฅฅฅฅฅฅฅฅฅฅฅฅฅฅ

Two centuries later, Kievan Rus fell on hard times.

The 1200s brought the rise of one of the biggest, most powerful empires ever: the **Mongol Empire** (Chapter 19). Around 1240, the massive Mongol Empire swallowed Kievan Rus, just as it swallowed almost everything else in the East. The Russian people would pay tribute to the Mongols for well over 200 years.

But like all empires, the Mongol Empire finally faded. In 1480, a descendant of Rurik the Viking called **Ivan III** suddenly stopped paying tribute to the Mongols. Ivan expected a fight; but instead, the Mongols backed down. The Rurikid dynasty was back in power.

> **Khokhloma painting** is a Russian method for making wood look as smooth as gold or glass. Khokhloma artists cover their wood with thick layers of primer made from clay, oils and powdered tin. High-temperature kilns activate the primer, forming a smooth, hard surface for painting.

In 1547, Ivan III's grandson **Ivan IV** claimed a title no Russian had ever claimed before: "**Tsar of All the Russias.**" *Tsar* is the Russian version of "Caesar," another word for "emperor." From then on, Russia was ruled not by princes or kings, but by emperors called the tsars. See Year 3 for more on the tsars.

> The first Tsar of Russia, **Ivan IV**, was also called **Ivan the Terrible**— partly because he was terribly powerful, and partly because so much of what he did was truly terrible!

Stories from the Russian Orthodox Church

Basil, Fool for Christ was a special kind of Christian called a *yurod*— Russian for "God's fool." *Yurodivy* like Basil took the Bible more literally than other Christians did. One of their favorite verses was I Corinthians 3:19, where the Apostle Paul wrote:

> *"… the wisdom of this world is foolishness in God's sight."*

To *yurodivy* like Basil, "wisdom of this world" meant "love of money." Worldly people store up worldly treasures, trying to enjoy life as much as they can before they die. But this is foolishness for Christians, who are supposed to store up treasures in heaven (Matthew 6:20). So the *yurodivy* did the opposite: instead of storing up worldly treasures, they gave away everything to the poor. For they knew that Christ would reward them in heaven. The *yurodivy* acted like fools— but fools for Christ!

Basil, Fool for Christ
(1469? – 1552?)

Basil the Fool was the most foolish *yurod* of all. Even in winter, Basil wandered around Moscow homeless, penniless and nearly naked. He sometimes wandered into taverns, where he begged his fellow Russians to stop drinking so much. Always he reminded people to focus on Christ. Once, he even rebuked Tsar Ivan the Terrible for not paying attention in church!

Naturally, Basil the Fool made of lot of Russians uncomfortable; but he also made a lot of friends. Even a man as suspicious as Ivan the Terrible couldn't help but admire Basil. So when the old saint died, the tsar personally helped carry Basil's coffin into the famous church that bears his name: St. Basil's Cathedral, which still stands on Red Square in Moscow.

St. Basil's Cathedral on Moscow's Red Square

— Skip —

Once upon a Christmas Eve, an old Russian woman carefully cleared all the spider webs from her house, working hard to make everything ready for the coming of the Christ child the next morning. With nowhere else to go, the poor spiders fled to a tiny hiding place in a far corner of the old woman's attic.

The Russian Spider Christmas Legend

When the youngest spiders found that they couldn't see the Christmas tree from their hiding place, they were terribly upset. So they begged and begged until finally, their parents decided to risk a trip to the family room. After the old woman went to bed, the spiders climbed all over her Christmas tree— covering it with their ugly, dirty webs!

When the Christ child came to bless the house, He of course saw the webs. He knew very well how much the old Russian woman hated spider webs! However, He also loved spiders, which are after all part of God's Creation. So He stretched out His arm; and with the touch of His almighty hand, the ugly, dirty cobwebs changed into glistening strands of silver and gold.

The next morning, the old woman was delighted with how beautiful her Christmas tree had become! Every Christmas since, Russians have remembered the love of Christ by hanging two special decorations on their trees: glistening tinsel, and ornaments shaped like spiders!

Babushka was an old Russian grandmother who lived just before the birth of Christ. One night when Babushka was cleaning her house, the Three Wise Men asked her to shelter them for one night before they traveled on in search of the Christ Child. The next morning, the Wise Men invited Babushka to join them on their journey. But Babushka decided that she had better stay home and finish cleaning her house.

The next morning, Babushka changed her mind, grabbed a few gifts for the Christ Child and ran out to follow the Wise Men. Sadly, the Wise Men were long gone. By worrying too much about housecleaning, poor Babushka had missed her only chance to see the Christ child!

Babushka's search continues to this day. Every year on the Eastern Orthodox Christmas, which falls on January 6th, Babushka leaves gifts in children's shoes— hoping that when they find them, they will put on their shoes and help her find the Christ Child!

Babushka and the Christ Child

CHAPTER 12:

The Middle East

The **Middle East** is the part of the world between the **West** and the **East**. "The West" basically means Europe and the Americas. "The East" basically means East Asia— including China, Japan, India and much more. The Middle East is the meeting point between these two very different parts of the world.

Almost all of the Middle East lies in West Asia. The only exceptions are Egypt— which lies in North Africa— and a small piece of Turkey, which lies in Eastern Europe.

At the western tip of Asia, a big peninsula reaches out between the Mediterranean and Black Seas. This peninsula has two names: **Asia Minor** and **Anatolia**. Asia Minor means "lesser Asia"; while *Anatolia* comes from a Greek word that means "east" or "sunrise." Asia Minor now belongs to the Republic of Turkey.

The heart of the Middle East is the land that used to be the **Ancient Near East**. This is where some of the world's oldest known civilizations began, along with some of the world's oldest religions.

₪₪₪₪₪₪₪₪₪₪₪₪₪₪₪₪₪₪₪₪₪₪₪

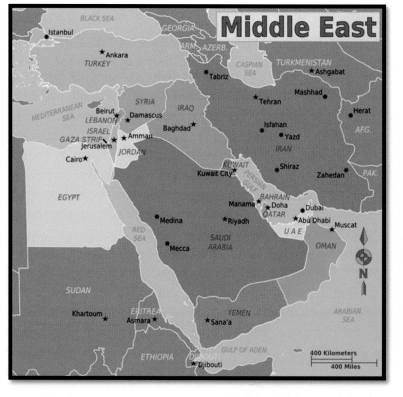

From medieval times down through modern times, the Middle East has been mostly Muslim. Almost every country of the Middle East still has some kind of Islamic government.

The only one that doesn't is Israel; for Israel is Jewish. The Holocaust of World War II almost destroyed the Jewish people. So in 1948, three years after that war ended, the United Nations recreated Israel as a homeland for the Jewish people.

Israel, of course, is where both Judaism and Christianity were born. One city is holy to all three religions: Judaism, Christianity and Islam. That city is 𝒥erusalem, capital of Israel.

➤ Jerusalem is holy to Jews for many reasons. One is because it was the **City of David**, the greatest King of Israel. Another is because the Hebrew **Temple**, where Jews offered sacrifices to God, stood in Jerusalem. All of the land God promised the Jews is now called the **Holy Land**.

> All of what was once ancient Israel is now called the **Holy Land**.

- Jerusalem is holy to Muslims partly because of the **Night Journey**. The **Dome of the Rock**, a monument to the Night Journey, now stands where the Hebrew Temple once stood.

Remember what the **Night Journey** was— the important vision which showed the prophet Muhammad how Muslims should worship (Chapter 5).

Remember who the father of the Arab people was: **Ishmael**, son of **Abraham.**

- Jerusalem is holy to Christians because so many key events of Christ's life happened there. Jesus was dedicated at the Temple in Jerusalem; rode into Jerusalem as a hero on the first Palm Sunday; was crucified on Jerusalem's Calvary Hill; was buried in a Jerusalem tomb; and rose from the dead at Jerusalem on the first Easter Sunday.

The **Holy Land Crusades** were nine holy wars ordered by the popes of the High Middle Ages. The main goal of the Crusades was to take back the Holy Land from Muslims.

As we read in Chapter 7, the Islamic Empire seized Jerusalem in the mid-600s— along with all the rest of the Middle East. 400 years later, the struggle for Jerusalem became one reason for the **Crusades**.

The Battle of Manzikert

Another reason for the Crusades was a problem in the Byzantine Empire (Chapter 4). In the late 1000s, Muslim armies threatened to overrun the whole empire— including Constantinople, the capital of Eastern Christianity!

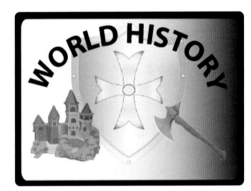

Back in Chapter 7, we read about the **caliphs** who led the Islamic Empire after the prophet Muhammad died. We also read about the first two **caliphates**: the Rashidun Caliphate and the Umayyad Caliphate.

The third caliphate was the **Abbasid Caliphate**, which took over in 750. The Abbasid caliphs reigned from Baghdad, which lies in what is now Iraq.

Over time, the Abbasid caliphs grew weak. The Abbasids were supposed to rule the whole Islamic Empire, just like earlier caliphs. But they really didn't.

For by now, the Islamic Empire was starting to fall apart. Instead of one Islamic Empire, there were now many smaller kingdoms, each ruled by a **sultan** or **emir**. Some sultans and emirs obeyed the caliphs. But others were actually more powerful than the caliphs.

The **caliph** was the one man who ruled the whole Islamic Empire after Muhammad died.

A **sultan** was a governor who ruled part of the Islamic Empire in the caliph's name.

An **emir** was a military leader who ruled part of the Islamic Empire in the caliph's name.

Sultan Alp Arslan of the Great Seljuk Empire

Just before the Crusades, the most powerful men in Islam were the sultans of the **Great Seljuk Empire**.

Before the 900s, the **Seljuk Turks** were much like the Huns and the Magyars. All were ferocious warriors who rode in from the East.

The homeland of the Seljuk Turks lay northeast of Persia (Iran), between the Caspian Sea and China. This part of Asia was once called **Turkestan**— which is why these people were called "**Turks**."

Since ancient times, the Turks had followed a religion called **Shamanism**. In the 900s, though, they switched to the religion of neighboring Persia. That religion, of course, was Islam.

> A **shaman** is a kind of Eastern monk who is supposed to be able to speak with spirits.

A century later, the Seljuk Turks spread far beyond Turkestan. They struck out to the west, seeking to build an empire.

With a string of victories, the Great Seljuk Empire spread steadily westward. By 1040, the Seljuk Turks had conquered most of Persia. In 1055, they won an important prize: Baghdad, capital of the Abbasid Caliphate. With Baghdad under their belts, the Seljuk sultans were now more powerful than the Abbasid caliphs! However, they still hadn't captured the Holy Land.

The farther west the Seljuk Turks conquered, the closer they came to the Byzantine Empire.

The big showdown between the two came in 1071. That was the year when **Emperor Romanos IV Diogenes** of the Byzantine Empire faced **Sultan Alp Arslan** of the Great Seljuk Empire at the famous **Battle of Manzikert**.

> **Manzikert**, also called **Malazgirt**, was a fortress in what is now eastern Turkey.

The strange thing about the Battle of Manzikert was that neither army had set out to fight the other. Diogenes was on his way to Armenia, where he hoped to take back some forts he had lost to Arslan. As for Arslan, he was on his way to conquer the Holy Land— not from Diogenes, but from another Muslim kingdom. Diogenes had no idea that Arslan's army was still nearby.

When Diogenes finally figured out where Arslan was, he turned to attack him. The result was one of the biggest disasters in the whole history of the Byzantine Empire. Diogenes' army collapsed— allowing Arslan to capture Diogenes himself! Legend tells that the sultan set his boot on the neck of the beaten emperor, making it perfectly clear which of them was the master.

After the Battle of Manzikert, the Seljuk Turks seized more and more territory in Asia Minor— edging closer and closer to Constantinople. By about 1090, only a narrow strip of land and water stood between Constantinople and the Turks!

Meanwhile, the Turks seized the Holy Land as well. Just before the First Crusade, the mighty Turks controlled an enormous empire. Their lands stretched all the way from Asia Minor in the West to Turkestan in the East.

Sultan Alp Arslan of the Great Seljuk Empire with his boot on the neck of the Byzantine Emperor

STOP

The Holy Land Crusades (1096 - 1272)

- Start -

With nowhere else to turn for help, the Byzantine Empire turned toward Rome. In March 1095, **Emperor Alexios I Komnenos** sent ambassadors to Italy with an urgent message for **Pope Urban II**. The emperor warned that if the Christians of the West didn't help the Christians of the East— and soon— then Constantinople might fall to the Muslims.

The pope's answer came later that same year. At the **Council of Clermont**, France in November 1095, Pope Urban II announced a holy war against the Muslims. All Christian soldiers of the West, rich or poor, were to go and rescue the Christians of the East at once!

Besides saving the Byzantine Empire, the pope had another big reason for going to war. When the Great Seljuk Empire seized the Holy Land, it stopped Christians from going there! Before then, Christian pilgrims had always been able to visit the places where Jesus walked— places like Jerusalem, Bethlehem and Nazareth. Now all of a sudden, they couldn't. A victory over the Turks would re-open the Holy Land to all Christians who wanted to go— and there were many.

As a reward for Christians who answered his call to war, the pope added a special promise. According to a writer called **Fulcher of Chartres**, the pope promised that any Christian who died fighting— or even on his way to

Pope Urban II announcing the First Crusade at the Council of Clermont

fight— would have all of his sins forgiven! As the keeper of the keys of St. Peter (Matthew 16:19), the pope promised to open wide the gates of heaven for every Christian who died in the **First Crusade**.

With a promise like that, the pope got a big response. Not one, but two armies answered the pope's call to war! Each army fought part of the First Crusade. The first army fought the **People's Crusade**, and the second the **Prince's Crusade**.

The People's Crusade was a disaster led by a French priest called **Peter the Hermit**. After the Council of Clermont, Peter went from town to

The People's Crusade (1096)

town, calling all Christians to come and fight. Tens of thousands answered his call.

Peter the Hermit drumming up support for the First Crusade

The problem was the kind of Christians who answered. Peter's soldiers were the poorest of the poor. They were penniless, weaponless peasants who had no idea how to fight a war, and no business trying. Of course, the Turks destroyed Peter the Hermit's army the moment it set foot in Asia Minor.

The Turks had a lot more trouble with the Prince's Crusade.

In 1097, the year after the People's Crusade, the real soldiers of the West started arriving in the East. These were no unarmed, underfed peasants. Instead, they were skilled knights with the training, experience and money needed to fight a real war. Most of them were either Franks or

The Princes' Crusade (1097)

Normans. One of their leaders was a Frankish lord called **Godfrey of Bouillon**.

Godfrey of Bouillon with other leaders of the First Crusade. Each knight who joined a crusade was said to "take the cross." Part of taking the cross was to mark breastplate and shield with the sign of the cross.

The Princes' Crusade was to be long, hard and horribly violent. The first great victory for the crusaders came at a place that had once been a leading Christian city: **Antioch, Syria**. In winning Antioch, the crusaders won back the home of famous Christians like Ignatius of Antioch (Chapter 1) and John Chrysostom (Chapter 4).

The problem with taking Antioch was that it took almost a year! With both money and spirits running low after the **Siege of Antioch**, the crusaders didn't have time for another long siege when they moved on to their most important target: Jerusalem.

So for the **Siege of Jerusalem**, the crusaders tried something different. According to one version of the story, the crusaders marched around Jerusalem barefoot for 3 days— much like the ancient Israelites marched around Jericho in Joshua 6. The crusaders then pushed siege towers up to the city walls, leapt into the city and killed almost everyone inside.

Crusaders using a siege tower to climb over Jerusalem's city walls

To hold all the land they'd won in Asia Minor and the Holy Land, the crusaders set up four new countries called the **Crusader States**. From north to south, the four Crusader States were: the **County of Edessa** in Asia Minor; the **Principality of Antioch** in Syria; the **County of Tripoli** in Lebanon; and most important, the **Kingdom of Jerusalem**.

The First Crusade would turn out to be the only Holy Land Crusade the Church could honestly say it won.

The **Second Crusade** started after Muslims conquered the northernmost Crusader State, the County of Edessa. This happened in 1144, almost 50 years after the First Crusade. When the knights of the Second Crusade failed to take back Edessa, the first of the four Crusader States was lost forever.

The first crusading knight over the walls at the Siege of Jerusalem was **Godfrey of Bouillon.** For his great heroism in the First Crusade, Godfrey won a place on the list of the **Nine Worthies**— the nine greatest knights of all time.

A **coat of arms** was a colorful symbol designed to tell the achievements of a medieval knight.

The knights of the Dark Ages, such as Arthur of Britain, didn't have coats of arms. So medieval artists designed coats of arms for them. These are called **attributed arms**.

The attributed arms of King Arthur had three crowns, one for each of his three kingdoms: England, Wales and Scotland.

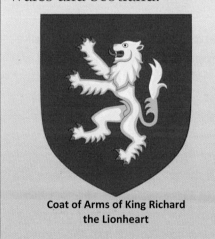

Coat of Arms of King Richard the Lionheart

ᘉᘉᘉᘉᘉᘉᘉᘉᘉᘉᘉᘉᘉᘉᘉᘉᘉᘉᘉᘉᘉᘉᘉᘉᘉᘉᘉᘉᘉᘉᘉᘉᘉᘉ

Between the Second Crusade and the Third Crusade came the rise of a great Muslim leader: mighty **Saladin**, Sultan of Egypt and Syria. Saladin conquered the most important crusader state, the Kingdom of Jerusalem.

Saladin's greatest victory was the **Battle of Hattin**, which

The Battle of Hattin (July 1187)

started with a siege. In the middle of the hot, dry summer of 1187, Saladin suddenly surrounded **Tiberias**. This was a Christian city on the Sea of Galilee, about 75 miles north of Jerusalem. In fear for their lives, the Christians of Tiberias sent word to **King Guy of Jerusalem**, begging him to bring his army.

The key to what happened next was water.

Between King Guy and Tiberias lay a long stretch of near-desert ground. With thousands of thirsty troops and horses, Guy's army needed thousands of gallons of water every day— especially under a hot July sun. Yet in all this stretch of ground, there was not one working well where Guy could refill his water barrels. So Guy would have to make do with whatever water he could carry.

Fortunately, Guy thought, Tiberias stood only about 15 miles away— not too far for a big army to travel in one day.

Guy might have been right— if not for Saladin's army. With Muslim troops blocking their way, Guy's army couldn't make it to Tiberias in just one day. So Guy's water ran out, leaving his troops thirsty and miserable.

That night, Saladin magnified Guy's misery in the most merciless ways imaginable. The Muslims lit fires in the dry grass, sending stinging smoke into Guy's waterless camp. The next morning, they hauled whole wagonloads of water near the camp, just out of the crusaders' reach. As the parched Christians looked on in horror, the Muslims poured out barrel after barrel of precious water on the ground! Thousands of crusaders lost their lives in the terrible battle that followed— or after the battle, when Saladin executed most of the survivors.

The Battle of Hattin was a terrible loss for the Kingdom of Jerusalem. Without King Guy's army to defend the kingdom, city after Christian city fell to Saladin. Later that year, Jerusalem itself fell.

STOP

The Third Crusade was the Church's answer to Saladin. After the Battle of Hattin, Pope Gregory VIII called for a holy war to take back Jerusalem.

In answer to the pope's call, all three of the three mightiest kings in Europe set out for the Holy Land. These were **Holy Roman Emperor Frederick I**, also called Barbarossa; **King Philip II of France**, also called Philip Augustus; and **King Richard I of England**, also called Richard the Lionheart. Barbarossa, of course, never made it to the Holy Land— for Barbarossa was the beloved Holy Roman Emperor who drowned on his way to the Third Crusade (Chapter 11).

The biggest, longest battle of the Third Crusade was the Siege of Acre, which started in 1189. Acre was an important port along the Mediterranean seacoast. This port had once been Christian, but had fallen to the Muslims after the Battle of Hattin. So the Christians laid siege to Acre, trying to take it back.

Muslim leaders surrendering the city of Acre to King Philip II of France, right, and King Richard I of England, left

Kings Philip and Richard reached Acre in the spring of 1191, almost two years into the siege. With fresh troops and fresh ideas, these two quickly turned the tide of battle. The greatest Christian victory of the Third Crusade came in July 1191, when the crusaders finally won the Siege of Acre.

With Acre under their belts, the victorious crusaders might have gone on to capture far more— if they hadn't quarreled among themselves.

The first quarrel was between King Richard I and **Duke Leopold V of Austria**. Leopold was a leader of the German army that had set out with Emperor Barbarossa. After Barbarossa's drowning, Leopold had taken command of some German troops and continued on to the Holy Land.

Having joined the Siege of Acre long before Philip and Richard, Leopold felt that this great victory was partly his. So when the Muslims surrendered Acre, Leopold flew his flag over the city— right beside the flags of Philip and Richard.

But when Richard saw Leopold's flag, he told his men to tear it down and throw it in the moat! For in Richard's proud eyes, no mere duke had the right to fly his flag beside a king's. Enraged at this insult, Leopold gathered his troops and went home to Austria.

Flag of Austria

The second quarrel was between Richard and Philip. Even before the Third Crusade, these two had a long history as sometimes-friends, sometimes-enemies. In the end, Philip went home like Leopold, leaving Richard to command the Third Crusade by himself.

Although Saladin and Richard were bitter enemies, the two kings treated one another with a curious respect. When Richard's old horse died in battle, Saladin sent him a nice new Arabian horse. And when Richard had a fever, Saladin sent him fresh fruit and other hard-to-find luxuries.

About a year later, King Richard gave up on taking back Jerusalem. He had won many battles, and might even have won Jerusalem if he tried. But how could he possibly hold Jerusalem, he wondered— with so many Muslims surrounding it?

So instead, Richard bargained for Jerusalem. In September 1192, Richard and Saladin signed an agreement called the **Treaty of Jaffa**. Richard promised to end the Third Crusade. In exchange, Saladin agreed to let Christians visit Jerusalem— not forever, but only for the next 3 years.

Having settled Jerusalem's affairs as best he could, Richard boarded ship for England. The Third Crusade was over.

〰〰〰〰〰〰〰〰〰〰〰〰〰〰〰〰〰〰〰〰〰〰〰〰〰〰

The Fourth Crusade was the most disgraceful of all nine Holy Land Crusades. On their way to the Holy Land in 1202, the crusaders foolishly took sides in a fight between two Byzantine emperors. Instead of attacking Muslims in the Holy Land, the crusaders wound up attacking Christians in Constantinople!

〰〰〰〰〰〰〰〰〰〰〰〰〰〰〰〰〰〰〰〰〰〰〰〰〰〰

Even after the Fourth Crusade failed, the crusading spirit was still strong enough to inspire many Christians back West— including children.

The Children's Crusades (1212)

In May 1212, legend says, a 12-year-old French boy called **Stephen of Cloyes** announced that God was calling him to lead a children's crusade! A few months later, a 12-year-old German boy called **Nicholas of Cologne** announced the same thing.

Both boys thought they knew why the Crusades were failing. It was because the crusaders weren't faithful enough! The right way to fight the crusades, the boys said, was to send children. For the pure, unquestioning faith of children was far stronger than the doubting faith of grown-ups.

But Stephen and Nicholas disagreed about how to fight the Children's Crusades. Stephen wanted to fight; but Nicholas wanted to preach the gospel to the Muslims.

If the legend is true, then both Stephen and Nicholas led child armies to ports along the

Richard the Lionheart lived to regret the way he insulted Duke Leopold. Although Richard left the Holy Land by ship, bad weather forced him to finish his journey on foot. Most unfortunately, Richard's road home took him through Leopold's territory! Of course, Leopold gleefully locked Richard up. To get Richard out of jail, Richard's mother had to pay an enormous sum— a **king's ransom** worth about twice what England collected in taxes every year!

Richard the Lionheart leaving the Holy Land

The **arabesque** is a Muslim form of art. Since Islamic law forbids idol worship, and since pictures of people and animals look too much like idols, Muslim artists create art with no people and no animals. Arabesques include mostly vines, leaves and flowers, all woven into flowing, never-ending patterns.

southern coast of France. They promised their followers that when they got there, God would part the Mediterranean Sea for them— just as God had parted the Red Sea for Moses in Exodus 14!

Much to their dismay, the waters didn't part. At this, some children gave up and tried to go home. But others boarded ship for the Holy Land. Some were shipwrecked, and others captured by Muslims and sold in slave markets. Very few ever made it home again.

The well-known legend of the **Pied Piper of Hamelin** may be based on the tragedy of the Children's Crusades. The Pied Piper was a magical man in a "pied," or multi-colored, suit. In 1284, legend tells, the town of Hamelin, Germany struck a bargain with the Pied Piper. If the piper could somehow get rid of Hamelin's many rats, then the town would pay him a lot of money.

The Pied Piper held up his end of the bargain. Pulling a flute from his pocket, the Pied Piper piped a tune that drew Hamelin's rats to him like magic. Still piping his tune, the Pied Piper led the rats to the banks of the nearby Weser River, where they all fell in and drowned!

The townspeople should have been pleased; but instead, they were furious. As good Christians, the people of Hamelin distrusted all magicians. So the townspeople refused to pay, even though the Pied Piper had done as they asked.

The Pied Piper took his revenge on the next Saints John and Paul's Day. While all of the townspeople were sitting in church, the Pied Piper used his magical pipe to lure their children out of town, and into a cave. 130 boys and girls simply disappeared, never to be seen again!

In the long run, the nine Holy Land Crusades did none of what the popes had wanted them to do. All four of the Crusader States fell to the Muslims. The road to the Holy Land was still often closed to Christians. And Muslims still threatened the Byzantine Empire!

Analyzing the Crusades

A People Set Apart

The time of the Crusades was a terrible time to be Jewish.

Long before the Crusades began, the Jewish people were already scattered all over the Middle East and Europe. This scattering is called the Jewish Diaspora, and it started in Bible times. The Assyrian Empire conquered the Kingdom of Israel in 722 BC, scattering its people (Year 1). The Babylonian Empire did the same thing to the Kingdom of Judah in 586 BC.

A **diaspora** is a scattering of a group of people.

The **Jewish Diaspora** is the scattering of the Jewish people all around the world— far away from their ancient homeland, Israel.

The scattering grew even worse in Roman times. In 70 AD, Roman soldiers utterly destroyed the last Hebrew Temple. In 135 AD, angry Romans finally kicked all Jews out of Jerusalem— after an uprising called the **Bar Kohkba Revolt**.

Wherever they scattered, Jews held themselves apart from their non-Jewish neighbors. As children of Abraham, Jews saw themselves as God's chosen people. They were heirs to a special promise that God had made to them alone. So they kept to themselves— refusing to worship their neighbors' gods, or to let their children marry their neighbors' children.

In Europe, most of their neighbors were Christians. Even though Jesus Christ Himself was a Jew, many Christians still found reasons to hate Jews.

> A **synagogue** is a house of worship where Jews come together to pray, worship God and learn Torah. The Jews do not sacrifice animals in their synagogues! That form of worship ended when the Romans destroyed the Second Temple at Jerusalem in 70 AD.

- Some Christians called Jews "Christ-killers"— remembering how a crowd of Jews had practically forced Pontius Pilate to crucify Jesus Christ (Matthew 27:22-25).

- Some Christians accused the Jews of sacrificing Christian children in secret worship services. This was ridiculous— for after the Temple was destroyed, the Jews no longer sacrificed any animals, even birds. These false accusations were called **blood libel**.

- Some Christians resented the Jews for loaning out money at interest, the way banks do. Before the Renaissance came, the Church forbade most Christians to loan money at interest (Chapter 26).

- Some Christians resented Jews just for being rich enough to lend money!

As so often happens, hatred turned to violence. Some of the worst attacks on Jews happened during the time of the Crusades.

The First Crusade was especially horrible for Jews. In Germany, the peasant mobs of the People's Crusade robbed and murdered countless Jews— defenseless innocents whose only crime was that they happened to live along the road to the Holy Land. Whole Jewish communities died at the hands of pitiless Christian peasants who were supposed to be doing God's work.

A mob of peasants from the People's Crusade attacking Jews at Metz, Germany

More British Isles

As we read in Chapter 2, the British Isles lie off the northwest coast of mainland Europe. Two of the British Isles are far larger than all the rest. One is **Great Britain**, which is home to three countries: England, Scotland and Wales. The other is **Ireland**, which is home to two countries: Northern Ireland and the Republic of Ireland.

Besides these two main islands, the British Isles also include hundreds of smaller islands. Some of these belong to **archipelagos**, or groups of islands; while others stand more or less on their own.

> An **archipelago** is a group of islands.

The largest archipelago is actually two archipelagos: the **Inner Hebrides** and the **Outer Hebrides**. Both lie off the northwest coast of Scotland. The island of **Iona**, where Saint Columba built his famous monastery (Chapter 3), is one of the Inner Hebrides.

North of Scotland lie two well-known archipelagos: the **Orkney Islands** and the **Shetland Islands**. The Orkneys lie near the northern coast; while Shetland lies more than 100 miles off the coast. Shetland farmers have produced some of the best-known animal breeds in the world— including the small but tough **Shetland pony**.

One well-known island is the **Isle of Man**, which lies midway between Great Britain and Ireland. The name "Man" does not mean the human race! Instead, it may be short for an Irish sea god called

Manannan mac Lir. A few people on the Isle of Man still speak an ancient Celtic language called **Manx**. The Isle of Man is also famous for the **Manx cat**— a breed without a tail.

Another well-known island is the **Isle of Wight**, which lies in the English Channel just off the coast of **Portsmouth**.

The House of Plantagenet

The last son of William the Conqueror to rule England was **King Henry I**. Henry was the wise but unfortunate king who lost his teenaged son and heir, **William Aetheling**, in the awful **Wreck of the White Ship** (Chapter 10).

After Henry I died, a French noble called **Stephen of**

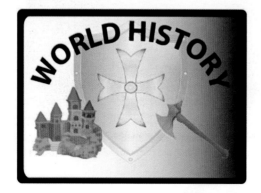

King Henry II

Blois claimed the throne— more or less stealing it from Henry's daughter, **Empress Matilda**. Matilda and her husband, a French noble called **Geoffrey Plantagenet**, fought long and hard to take back her inheritance. In the end, the two sides reached an agreement called the **Treaty of Wallingford**. For as long as he lived, King Stephen kept the throne of England. But when Stephen died, Matilda's son Henry Plantagenet took his place, becoming **King Henry II**.

Since Henry II's family name was Plantagenet, his reign marked the beginning of a new royal house: the **House of Plantagenet**.

Like his great-grandfather William the Conqueror, Henry II held lands in France as well as England. Through William, Henry was Duke of **Normandy**. Through his father Geoffrey of Anjou, Henry was Count of **Anjou**. And through his wife Eleanor of Aquitaine, Henry became Duke of **Aquitaine**.

In fact, Henry II held so many lands that he was almost more emperor than king. Historians call Henry's huge collection of lands the **Angevin Empire.**

> **Normandy** was a big duchy in northwestern France, just across the English Channel from Great Britain.
> **Anjou** was a county south of Normandy. The name **"Angevin Empire"** comes from Anjou— for Henry II's father was the Count of Anjou.
> **Aquitaine** was a big duchy in southwestern France.

Eleanor of Aquitaine
(1122 – 1204)

Eleanor of Aquitaine, queen to King Henry II, lived one of the longest, most fascinating lives of the High Middle Ages. One fascinating fact about Eleanor is that before she was Queen of England, she was Queen of France!

Eleanor was still just a girl in August 1137, when she inherited the rich Duchy of Aquitaine from her dying father. The King of France, who was also dying, wanted the riches of Aquitaine for his son. So he arranged for Eleanor to marry his son, who soon became **King Louis VII of France**.

Eleanor's husband Louis also happened to be her fourth cousin— a fact that would prove most important in years to come.

Like many royal marriages, the marriage between Eleanor and Louis was an unhappy one.

One reason for their unhappiness was the **Second Crusade**, which fell in the middle of their married years (Chapter 12). In a time when women never, ever went to war, Eleanor stubbornly insisted on doing her part. So she followed Louis to the Holy Land— much to her husband's embarrassment.

After she got there, Eleanor embarrassed her husband even worse. Right in front of Louis' nobles, Eleanor shouted that Louis was leading the war all wrong! When the Second Crusade ended in failure, Eleanor blamed Louis, and Louis blamed Eleanor.

Another reason for Louis' unhappiness was the kind of children Eleanor gave him. Both children were daughters— not the sons Louis needed to carry on his dynasty.

Both Eleanor and Louis wanted to end their miserable marriage. But in the High Middle Ages, unhappy couples did not simply call divorce lawyers! For all Christian

King Louis VII of France marrying Eleanor of Aquitaine (left) before sailing off to fight the Second Crusade (right)

marriages were governed by the Church; and the Church almost never allowed an outright divorce.

However, the Church sometimes allowed a tricky kind of divorce called an **annulment**— which is how Eleanor and Louis finally ended their marriage.

After 15 years together, Eleanor and Louis suddenly started complaining that the Church never should have let them marry in the first place. After all, Eleanor and Louis were fourth cousins. And Church law said that fourth cousins couldn't marry— for they were already too closely related by blood.

> To **annul** a marriage is to dissolve it, making it as if the couple had never married.

Of course, the Church had known all along that they were fourth cousins, and had blessed their marriage anyway! Even so, the Church accepted Eleanor and Louis' thin excuse, annulling their marriage in 1152.

What happened next proved what a thin excuse it was. Only two months after the annulment, Eleanor married an even closer relative: her third cousin Henry Plantagenet, who was soon to become King Henry II of England!

Eleanor would go on to give Henry eight children— including several of the boys that Louis had wanted so badly. Three of her boys would grow up to be the next three kings from the House of Plantagenet: **Henry the Young King**, **Richard I** and **John**.

Some storytellers blame Eleanor of Aquitaine for the terrible failure of the Second Crusade. As the story goes, Eleanor was a finicky royal lady who always insisted on traveling in style, even in a war zone. To keep Eleanor happy, Louis had to drag along a lot of ladies, servants and useless baggage— none of which belonged anywhere near a war.

When the French army was on the move, Eleanor's slow-moving baggage train couldn't keep up. So the army started to spread out— most of it forging ahead, and a small part staying behind to defend the queen and her ladies. Sensing weakness, the Turks attacked the thin French rear, and nearly destroyed it. Eleanor's husband barely escaped with his life!

— STOP

𝍖𝍖𝍖𝍖𝍖𝍖𝍖𝍖𝍖𝍖𝍖𝍖𝍖𝍖

Henry II turned out to be a most unpopular king. Even so, the English still honor him for one great accomplishment: establishing **common law** in England.

The long war between King Stephen and Empress Matilda had left England in chaos. Lawless robbers and mercenaries were committing crimes all over the country. Without good law, England couldn't punish these criminals fairly. For example, a court in one English town might lock a thief in the stocks. But another town court might cut off a thief's hand, or even put him to death!

Kings from the Royal House of Plantagenet

1. King Henry II
(Reigned 1154 – 1189)

2. Henry the Young King
(Co-reigned 1170 – 1183)

3. King Richard I
(Reigned 1189 – 1199)

4. King John
(Reigned 1199 – 1216)

King Henry II and his wife Eleanor of Aquitaine

Common law changed all that. Instead of the old town courts, Henry set up new courts called **assizes**. Assize judges traveled from place to place, hearing cases all along their **circuit**.

Once the assizes decided on a fair punishment for a certain crime, all courts punished that crime in the same way. For example, if one court locked thieves in the stocks, then all courts locked them in the stocks. Common law was an important step toward equal justice for all.

Common law is law that is the same for everyone, everywhere. The purpose of common law is to set equal punishments for equal crimes— regardless of where the accused commits his crime, or which judge handles his trial.

The **assizes** were courts that traveled around England. Assize judges held court at each town or county along their **circuit**, or route.

ꙫꙫꙫꙫꙫꙫꙫꙫꙫꙫꙫꙫꙫꙫꙫꙫꙫꙫꙫꙫꙫꙫꙫꙫꙫꙫꙫꙫ

Oddly enough, Henry's love for law was one reason for his downfall. For it led to a deadly argument with his old friend **Thomas Becket**.

Thomas Becket was a brilliant man who stood with one foot in the Church, and the other in the government. For years, Thomas worked closely with the Archbishop of Canterbury, head of all English churches. Then in 1155, the archbishop recommended Thomas for an important government job. As **King's Chancellor**, Becket worked as closely with the King as he had once worked with the archbishop.

In seven years as King's Chancellor, Thomas grew quite friendly with Henry II— so friendly that when the king argued with the Church, Thomas often took the king's side.

The king loved having a smart churchman like Thomas on his side. So when the old archbishop died, Henry appointed Thomas as the new Archbishop of Canterbury— hoping that Thomas would still take his side, even when he was head of the Church.

What Henry didn't count on was how being archbishop would change Thomas. As King's Chancellor, Thomas had lived a kingly lifestyle; but as Archbishop of Canterbury, Thomas took his faith more seriously than before. He even wore a hair shirt and slept on the hard floor, just like a monk. Now when the king argued with the Church, Thomas always took the Church's side!

What king and Church argued about most was common law. Before Henry II, any priest who stood accused of a crime was tried in a Church court. And Church courts were far too easy on priests. Even if a priest murdered someone, the worst a Church court might do to him was remove him from the priesthood. If that same priest had been tried in the assizes, then he probably would have been put to death!

As a believer in common law, Henry wanted priests to be tried in the assizes, just like everyone else. But Thomas didn't. For in Thomas' eyes, priests were too holy to stand trial in common courts.

The King and the Archbishop argued back and forth for years— until finally one day, Henry shouted to no one in particular: "Is there no one who will rid me of this turbulent priest?"

The king may or may not have meant what he said in anger. But whether he meant it or not, someone believed that he meant it.

Shortly afterward, four knights burst into Canterbury Cathedral shouting "Where is the traitor, Thomas Becket?" Becket answered, "Here am I— no traitor, but a priest of God."

Knights cutting down Thomas Becket

Henry's knights commanded Thomas to submit to his king. When Thomas refused, the knights killed him, right there on the altar of Canterbury Cathedral.

Even if Henry wasn't entirely to blame for what his knights had done, people blamed him anyway. The murder of Thomas Becket was the darkest of many dark stains on the reputation of King Henry II.

🔁🔁

If the English people hated Henry II, then his family hated him still more. Each member of Henry's family had a special reason for hating him. Twenty years into Henry's reign, the hatred of his family led to a revolution that almost cost him his throne!

In 1170, Henry II appointed his eldest son Henry as **junior king**. The idea was that if anything should happen to Henry II, then no one would question his son's right to take his place— for young Henry would already be king.

> **Henry the Young King (co-reigned 1170 - 1183)**

For the moment, though, young Henry had no real responsibilities. So instead of learning the duties of a king, he spent most of his time having fun at knights' tournaments.

The problem with tournaments was that they cost a lot of money. Young Henry had to buy weapons and armor, clothes and decorations, prizes, gifts and much more. Most kings raised money by collecting taxes from their lands. But as junior king, young Henry didn't have any lands. And when he asked his father for lands, Henry II wouldn't give him any.

Another problem was jealousy. Young Henry couldn't help but notice that John, his father's favorite son, seemed to get whatever he wanted. In the process of arranging a marriage for John, Henry II gave away a castle that he had once promised to young Henry!

Now furious with his father, Henry the Young King rebelled against Henry II. And he wasn't the only family member to join the **Revolt of 1173 - 1174**. Richard the Lionheart joined— also because Henry II refused to give him lands of his own. Eleanor of Aquitaine also joined— partly because Henry II had been carrying on with other women.

Eleanor of Aquitaine heading off to start her 16 years under house arrest (1174 – 1189)

Somehow, Henry II managed to fight off all of his attackers at once! Once the revolt was over, Henry II forgave Henry the Young King and Richard the Lionheart— but not Eleanor of Aquitaine. The brave queen spent the next 16 years under **house arrest**.

After 1183, Henry II would have no more trouble with Henry the Young King; for that was the year when young Henry died. But Henry II's troubles with Richard were far from over.

As the next brother in line, Richard would have been sure to inherit Henry II's throne— if it weren't for his brother John. Given all the trouble in their family, Richard feared that Henry might make John king instead! For John was Henry's favorite, just as Richard was Eleanor's favorite. Besides, John was Henry's only loyal son— the only one who hadn't joined the ugly Revolt of 1173 – 1174.

> To be under **house arrest** is to be a prisoner in one's own home. House prisoners like Eleanor of Aquitaine were allowed to live at home, but couldn't go anywhere or meet anyone without permission.

To stop Henry from choosing John, Richard attacked his father again. This time, Richard brought a powerful new friend to the fight: **King Philip II of France**, the same Philip who would soon join Richard on the Third Crusade (Chapter 12).

If Henry II had been young and well, then he probably could have beaten both Richard and Philip. By this time, though, Henry was neither young nor well. Sensing that death was near, Henry turned to meet with his son one last time.

In these last meetings of his life, Henry learned one last horrible truth: that his favorite son John, who had always been loyal to Henry, had now sworn loyalty to Richard instead. The news struck Henry like a death blow, sending him into a feverish sleep. Just before he died, though, Henry awakened long enough to speak this bitter curse against Richard:

> *"God grant that I may not die until I have had my just revenge on you."*

Thus Henry II died the loneliest of deaths, leaving Richard I to claim his throne in the ugliest of ways. Anyone who believes that money and power are the keys to happiness must have forgotten the sad story of King Henry II!

STOP

The year of Richard's crowning, 1189, was the same busy year when the Third Crusade began. Right away, Richard made plans to leave for the Holy Land.

The first thing Richard did was to free his mother Eleanor of Aquitaine from her long house arrest. Next, he appointed Eleanor as his regent. Although John had sworn to be loyal, Richard still didn't quite trust his younger brother— with good reason.

Richard the Lionheart as a crusading knight

As we read in Chapter 12, Richard was gone for a long time— not only fighting the Third Crusade, but also sitting in a German jail! During Richard's long absence, two rivals tried to claim his lands:

> One was Richard's old friend **King Philip II of France**. After arguing with Richard in the Holy Land, Philip came home and seized part of Normandy.

King Richard I (reigned 1189 - 1199)

> The other rival was Richard's slippery brother **John**. When Richard didn't come home, John announced that his brother must have died in the Third Crusade. As a dutiful brother, John said, he had no choice but to take Richard's place!

Of course, Richard finally did make it home from the Holy Land— after Eleanor paid Germany a king's ransom. Richard the Lionheart spent the rest of his life in Normandy, trying to win back what Philip had stolen.

To defend Normandy against Philip, Richard built a strong castle called **Chateau Gaillard**. The two fighting kings often teased one another over this great castle. Philip bragged that he could take the castle from Richard "even if its walls were made of steel." Richard replied that he could hold the castle against Philip "even if its walls were made of butter."

The central keep of Chateau Gaillard castle, built by Richard the Lionheart to defend Normandy against King Philip II of France

Sadly, Richard never got a chance to test Chateau Gaillard.

One day in the spring of 1199, Richard was trying to break into the castle of a rebellious noble. While inspecting his army, Richard noticed an amusing sight: an enemy soldier was standing on the castle wall, using a frying pan to knock crossbow bolts out of the air!

Richard was laughing so hard that he didn't notice an enemy archer hiding nearby. The unseen crossbowman took Richard by surprise, burying a bolt deep in the king's shoulder.

As Richard lay dying from his infected arrow wound, he was tormented with guilt over the horrible way he had treated his father. Before he died, Richard asked to be buried at the feet of Henry II— so that the moment his eyes opened on the next life, he could beg his father's forgiveness.

The true story of Richard and John gave rise to the probably-untrue legend of **Robin Hood**. In most versions of the legend, Robin Hood was a noble who defended poor Englishmen against the evil King John while the good King Richard was away fighting the Third Crusade.

What the legend of Robin Hood doesn't tell is that Richard was more French than English! Like his mother, Richard spent most of his life in France, and probably spoke only a little English. When Richard thought of England at all, he mostly thought of it as a place to collect taxes. Once when Richard was raising money for the Third Crusade, he said this about England: "If I could have found a buyer, I would have sold London itself!"

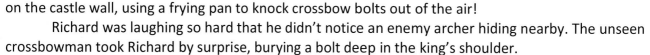

The Magna Carta

King John
(reigned 1199 - 1216)

Upon the death of Richard the Lionheart, the throne passed to one of the worst kings in English history: King John. The cruel John was guilty of many crimes, both as a person and as a king. His worst crime as king was this: that thanks to his foolishness, the great Angevin Empire built by King Henry II came crashing down!

Of all kings in English history, none is more hated than King John. In the centuries since John's reign, there have been other kings of England named Richard, Henry, William and so on. But there have been no more named John— nor will there ever be, as long as England remembers the first King John!

The reign of King John had hardly begun when he had trouble with two special enemies.

John, King of England

A monk/historian who lived in John's day condemned the despised king with this verdict:

"Foul as it is, Hell itself is defiled by the fouler presence of John."

The first enemy was **Arthur of Brittany**, a son to a dead older brother of John. Young Arthur had held high hopes of inheriting Richard's throne. So when John inherited it instead, Arthur was highly disappointed.

The second enemy was a French noble called **Hugh IX of Lusignan**. Hugh was an enemy of John's own making. The year after he became king, John suddenly insisted on marrying a beautiful young woman called **Isabella of Angouleme**. This was despite the fact that Isabella was promised to

King John's beautiful wife Isabella of Angouleme

Hugh! Naturally, Hugh was more than a little upset.

Arthur of Brittany joining forces with King Philip II of France

In 1202, these two special enemies teamed up with a third. This was a man who loved to make trouble for any King of England: Richard's old enemy, King Philip II of France. That summer, Philip planned to attack John from the east, while Arthur and Hugh teamed up to attack him from the south.

The first move Arthur and Hugh made was to surround **Mirabeau Castle**. This was where John's 80-year-old mother, Eleanor of Aquitaine, was living when the war broke out.

Like a good son, John decided to go down to Mirabeau and rescue his mother. This decision led to one of the few successes of John's career: the **Battle of Mirabeau**.

Since Mirabeau stood about 100 miles from where Arthur and Hugh expected John to be, they thought they were safe for a while. So they were most surprised to see John's army riding up, just when they were sitting down to breakfast! Somehow, John had traveled those 100 miles faster than anyone had thought he could. Before Arthur and Hugh could save themselves, John swept in and captured them both!

What happened next was the key to the misery that followed John for the rest of his life.

If John had been a chivalrous knight of the High Middle Ages, then he would have treated his prisoners well— especially his noble prisoners. Instead, John locked Arthur, Hugh and other nobles

The Battle of Mirabeau (August 1, 1202)

in dark dungeons for days at a time— with neither food, nor water, nor bathroom breaks. In a short time, more than 20 French noblemen died in John's filthy, miserable dungeons!

Mistreating his noble prisoners would turn out to be a big mistake.

From the days of William the Conqueror down through John's day, western France was always in a tug-of-war between the King of France and the King of England. To win that tug-of-war, John needed help from French nobles. But after the way John treated his prisoners, no French noble wanted to help him!

Thus the Battle of Mirabeau, which could have been a great beginning for John, was instead the beginning of the end. As more and more French nobles abandoned him, John lost more and more lands in France. By the end of 1204, John lost the most important French land of all: Normandy, home of William the Conqueror. The fall of Normandy meant the end of the great Angevin Empire.

〰〰〰

Normandy was so important to John that he spent the next 10 years fighting to take it back. But instead of taking back Normandy, John almost lost the best land he had left: England.

A King John Penny

Like his brother Richard, John thought of England as a place to raise tax money for wars in France. The noble barons of England thought otherwise. After 10 years of fighting for Normandy, English barons were furious over the high taxes John collected. English traditions set certain limits on taxes, and John had broken these limits.

Besides taxes, English barons listed several other complaints. One was that John showed no respect for the Christian faith. Another was that John liked to flirt with his barons' wives— even though he was already married to one of the most beautiful women in Europe, Isabella of Angouleme!

By 1215, John's English barons had had enough. That May, a group of barons marched on London, which they quickly captured. At a place called Runnymede, just west of London, the barons forced John to sign one of the best-known documents in all of history: the first **Magna Carta**.

Basically, the Magna Carta said that the King of England couldn't simply do whatever he pleased. Instead, a king must always remember that Englishmen had rights!

Most of the rights in the Magna Carta were for barons. For example, the king was not to demand high taxes from his barons, nor seize a baron's land without good reason.

But some of the rights in the Magna Carta were for all free Englishmen. For example, the king was not to seize any freeman's property without paying for it, nor jail any freeman without a proper trial. Thus the Magna Carta declared that all free Englishmen had rights, whether they were nobles or not!

Naturally, King John hated anything that set limits on his power. The slippery John was already looking for ways around the Magna Carta before he even finished reading it.

In no time, the king and his barons were at war again, fighting the **First Barons' War**. This latest war was a low point in English history. For the first time, England almost fell to a King of France! About half of England's barons swore loyalty to King Philip II's son, the future King Louis VIII. To some barons, even the King of France seemed better than their wicked King John!

What saved England from the King of France was an unexpected event that almost no one mourned: the death of King John. While fighting rebel barons in the east, John caught a bad case of dysentery that wrecked his health. One night in October 1216, John died— leaving his 9-year-old son to take his place. The next king from the House of Plantagenet was **King Henry III**.

> ***Magna Carta*** is Latin for "Great Charter." The first Magna Carta was signed at Runnymede on June 15, 1215.
> The purpose of this first Magna Carta was to set limits on King John's power. John's English barons wanted him to stop trampling on their rights.

King John signing the Magna Carta

The First Barons' War (1215 - 1217)

STOP

According to legend, the last journey of King John cost England a priceless set of crown jewels. Since John's men weren't used to eastern England, they didn't know the dangers of crossing a strange piece of coastland called the **Wash**. The Wash was a low area that was dry at low tide, but flooded with rushing currents at high tide. The Wash was dry when John's men set out. But before they could make it across, the tide poured in— drowning John's men, and burying the crown jewels in a thick layer of mud and sand. Even today, treasure hunters still search the Wash for the lost crown jewels of King John!

Christian Heroes of the High Middle Ages

The High Middle Ages were a high point for the Church of Rome. In a time when the pope could call kings from all over Europe to fight in his Crusades, few dared disagree with the pope.

One who dared was **Peter de Bruis**, a priest from southeastern France.

Peter was one of the first Christians to draw a sharp line between Scripture and **Church tradition**. Scripture, of course, means the Word of God. Church tradition, on the other hand, means something that Christians learn from the generations of Christians who came before them.

A **Church tradition** is a belief or practice that Christians learn from the generations that came before them, not directly from the Bible.

Peter de Bruis
(? – 1131?)

Peter decided that when Church tradition disagrees with Scripture, Christians should always follow Scripture. For Scripture comes from holy God; but Church tradition might come from sinful man.

The more Peter thought about it, the more he believed that certain Church traditions disagreed with Scripture.

➢ One Church tradition Peter didn't like was **infant baptism**. The Church baptized children as infants. But Peter only baptized believers who were old enough to understand why they were being baptized.

➢ Another tradition Peter didn't like was **transubstantiation**. The Church taught that when a priest led Holy Communion, the bread and wine actually changed into the body and blood of Jesus Christ. To Peter, transubstantiation seemed to honor priests more than it honored Christ.

➢ Peter also didn't like the tradition of **praying for the dead**. He believed that God would judge people for their own deeds, not for the prayers of others.

Unfortunately, Peter also taught his followers to burn crosses. To Peter, the cross was a symbol of Christ's torture and death, not of His resurrection. So Peter held big bonfires for cross-burning.

Of all the things Peter taught, the Church hated cross-burning most. And so, legend says, a mob of angry Christians killed Peter de Bruis by throwing him into one of his own bonfires.

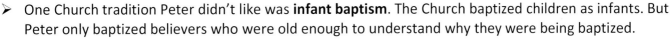

Another medieval Christian who dared disagree with the pope was a once-rich Frenchman called **Peter Waldo**. Peter was quite happy being rich, until he learned this story from Mark 10:17-23:

Peter Waldo
(1140? - 1218?)

"As Jesus started on his way, a man ran up to him and fell on his knees before him. 'Good teacher,' he asked, 'what must I do to inherit eternal life?' ... [Jesus said] 'Go, sell everything you have and give to the poor, and you will have treasure in heaven. Then come, follow me.' At this the man's face fell. He went away sad, because he had great wealth. Jesus looked around and said to his disciples, 'How hard it is for the rich to enter the kingdom of God!'"

Unlike the rich young man in the Gospel of Mark, Peter really did give away his whole fortune to benefit the poor. The faithful Peter Waldo went on to preach the gospel for the rest of his life.

Because Scripture had brought Peter to Christ, Peter liked to preach straight from Scripture. Unfortunately, the Bibles of Peter's day were all written in Latin, which his French listeners couldn't understand (the Vulgate, Chapter 3). So Peter Waldo translated the whole New Testament into French! But while Peter's listeners loved his new translation, the Church of Rome did not.

Translating the Bible wasn't the only thing Peter Waldo did without Church approval. Like Peter de Bruis, Peter Waldo felt that certain Church traditions disagreed with Scripture. Peter didn't believe in praying to the saints. Nor did he believe in **purgatory**, the afterworld where Christians supposedly go to be purged of sin. Peter also didn't believe that only priests should be allowed to preach.

Peter asked the pope to approve his beliefs. Instead, the pope condemned Peter as a heretic. Many of Peter Waldo's followers, the **Waldensians**, were burned to death for believing what Peter taught, instead of what the pope taught.

✝✝

One medieval Christian who didn't disagree with the pope was **Francis of Assisi**. Like Peter Waldo, Francis was a rich young man who gave up his riches because he couldn't stand the suffering of the poor. More than any other Christian saint, Francis is remembered as a tenderhearted servant of the poor. So are Francis' followers, an order of servant monks called the **Franciscans**.

Francis of Assisi
(1181? - 1226)

Clare of Assisi
(1194 - 1253)

Clare of Assisi was a devoted Christian girl who fell in love with Francis of Assisi's beautiful preaching. Clare longed to serve the poor as Francis did; but her parents insisted that she marry instead. So when Clare was 18, she ran away from home and tried to join the Franciscans!

Most monks probably would have sent Clare home, but not Francis. Instead, Francis found a home for Clare in a nearby nunnery. Clare of Assisi went on to found the **Order of Poor Ladies**— an order of nuns that followed the Franciscans, serving wherever the monks served.

Francis of Assisi

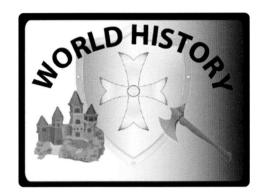

The First English Parliaments

In Chapter 13, we read how angry English barons forced King John to sign the first **Magna Carta**. For the first time, an official document declared that the English people had rights, and that the king must always respect those rights.

The Magna Carta was only the beginning of a long, hard tug-of-war between king and people. The kings pulled for more power; while the people pulled for more rights. Sometimes the kings won, and sometimes the people did.

We also read how King John tried to get around the Magna Carta. In 1215, the same year when he signed the Magna Carta, John went to war against his angry barons. When the **First Barons' War** broke out, many English barons gave up on John, and started looking for a new king.

The Palace of Westminster in London, modern-day meeting place of Parliament

The King of France was happy to help! In 1216, **Crown Prince Louis Capet of France** landed in England. Louis was the son of John's old enemy, Philip II of France. By mid-year, about half of all English barons had sworn loyalty to the Crown Prince of France. For a while there, it looked like all of England might soon belong to the King of France!

But that was only until October, when John suddenly died. The death of John changed everything.

The new King of England was John's son, a 9-year-old boy called **Henry III**. Now that John was out of the way, the barons took a fresh look at their choices. On the one hand stood a full-grown French prince; while on the other stood a half-grown English king. The barons knew that a boy king would be easier to control than a grown prince. And as Englishmen, they wanted an English king.

So in the end, the barons all abandoned Prince Louis, and swore loyalty to King Henry III. England was whole again!

₪₪₪₪₪₪₪₪₪₪₪₪₪₪₪₪₪₪₪₪₪₪₪₪₪₪₪₪₪₪₪₪₪

As a boy king, Henry III didn't mind the Magna Carta. But when Henry grew up, he found that he didn't like the Magna Carta any more than his father had liked it.

To Henry, the worst thing about the Magna Carta was that he couldn't raise taxes without permission from his barons. Like his father, Henry wanted to fight for more lands overseas. So Henry tried to do the same thing his father had done: he tried to use tax money raised in England to fight wars overseas.

> ### More Kings from the Royal House of Plantagenet
>
> **5. King Henry III**
> (Reigned 1216 – 1272)
>
> **6. King Edward I**
> (Reigned 1272 – 1307)
>
> **7. King Edward II**
> (Reigned 1307 – 1327)
>
> **8. King Edward III**
> (Reigned 1327 – 1377)
>
> **9. King Richard II**
> (Reigned 1377 – 1399)

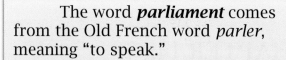

Once again, his nobles stopped him. In 1258, a group of nobles met at Oxford, England to set new limits on the king's power. This meeting, which is called the **Oxford Parliament**, was one of the first English **parliaments**.

The word ***parliament*** comes from the Old French word *parler*, meaning "to speak."

In modern times, **Parliament** is the **legislature** of the United Kingdom. This is the part of the government that writes law, just as Congress writes law for the United States.

The Oxford Parliament insisted that the King of England could not simply do whatever he pleased. Instead, he would have to listen to two groups of nobles. The first was a small group called the **Privy Council**; and the second was a bigger group called **Parliament**. Three times a year, nobles from all over England would gather for Parliament, where they would discuss how the king and his Privy Council were running their country.

The creation of Parliament was another big step toward protecting the rights of all Englishmen. The aim of Parliament was the same as the aim of the Magna Carta: to stop the king from becoming a tyrant. Before making any big decisions, the king would have to listen to people from all over his country.

At first, only nobles were invited to Parliament. Very soon, though, some commoners were invited as well. In time, Parliament gave all free Englishmen a voice in their government.

Like many other kings all over Europe, King Henry III hated Jews. In keeping with a decree from the pope, Henry III commanded all English Jews over the age of seven to wear yellow badges over their hearts. These particular Jewish badges were shaped like the two tablets of the Ten Commandments, brought down by Moses from Mount Sinai (Exodus 32:15).

England under the Edwards

The next king of England was one of the mightiest ever— and also one of the cruelest, in the eyes of the Scots. **King Edward I of England**, son of Henry III, is mostly remembered for two things: conquering Wales, and almost conquering Scotland.

Wales, of course, is one of three countries on the island of Great Britain. It lies on the west side, north of Bristol Channel. Before Edward I, Wales was ruled by a Welsh prince.

In 1282, though, Edward conquered the last Welsh prince— a man called **Llewellyn the Last**. To strengthen his hold on Wales, Edward built an **iron ring** of strong castles there.

From then on, the King of England ruled Wales as well. Since the time of King Edward I, almost every heir to the throne of England has been titled "Prince of Wales."

෴෴෴෴෴෴෴෴෴෴෴෴෴෴෴෴෴෴෴෴

The story of Scotland is quite different from the story of Wales. No matter how hard Edward tried, the Scots stubbornly held onto their independence.

The trouble in Scotland started with a death in the Scottish royal family. In 1290, the last king from the royal **House of**

Caernarvon Castle, part of King Edward I's "iron ring" around Wales

Dunkeld died, leaving no clear heir to the throne. At this, Scottish nobles started arguing over the throne, each insisting that his claim was the best.

To understand what happened next, we must remember the rules of the feudal system. All feudal law was based on **oaths of fealty** sworn by vassals to their lords (Chapter 10). To break the oath of fealty was one of the worst crimes a vassal could commit.

The royal **House of Dunkeld** was a family line that reigned over Scotland from 1034 - 1286. **Macbeth**, the famous Scottish king from the Shakespeare play, came from the House of Dunkeld.

With its nobles all fighting over the throne, Scotland was headed toward a nasty civil war. But there was one way to avoid that war. If the Scots could find a respected foreign king to come and choose their next king, then everyone might accept that king's decision.

The foreign king the Scots chose was Edward I of England. In 1292, Scotland invited Edward to come and help choose its next king.

This would turn out to be a terrible mistake. For when Edward came, the first thing he did was to demand the oath of fealty from every Scottish noble. Why? Because if they swore the oath, then they would have to accept Edward's decision.

After receiving those oaths, Edward chose **John Balliol** as the next King of Scotland. But in Edward's eyes, John was only a junior king. The real King of Scotland was Edward himself— for John had sworn the oath of fealty to Edward.

A few years later, Edward decided to test his new authority over Scotland. At the time, Edward needed more troops to help fight a war in France. So he ordered the Scots to send an army.

King Edward I of England

Edward's order was an insult to Scottish independence! If the King of England could command Scotland's armies, then Scotland was really just a part of England, and not an independent country at all.

THE THISTLE OF SCOTLAND

To protect their independence, the Scots took a bold step: instead of sending an army to fight the French, Scotland formed an **alliance** with France. This was the beginning of the **Auld Alliance**, a long-lasting friendship between Scotland and France.

In Edward's eyes, the Auld Alliance was criminal. For in swearing oaths to France, the Scots broke the oaths of fealty they had sworn to him.

So Edward changed his plans. Instead of attacking France that year, Edward attacked Scotland. This was the beginning of the First War of Scottish Independence.

The **Auld Alliance** was a military alliance between Scotland and France against their common enemy, England. The two countries agreed that if England attacked either of them, then the other would attack England.

Edward's attack was fierce and terrible. The English army seized several Scottish cities in just a few months. One of those cities was **Edinburgh,** the capital of Scotland.

With the fall of Edinburgh, Scotland became an **occupied** country. For the time being, Scotland was no longer ruled by Scots. Instead, the English army ruled Scotland under **martial law**, the law of war.

No one liked living under martial law, least of all the Scots. The English army showed no mercy. English troops robbed Scots, beat Scots and even killed Scots, sometimes for no reason at all.

The cruelty of the English explains why a Scottish noble called **William Wallace** hated them so much. According to legend, an English sheriff murdered the innocent Scottish girl whom Wallace had hoped to marry.

William Wallace made a fierce enemy for the English.

> **William Wallace**
> **(1273? - 1305)**

For one thing, he was unusually tall, strong and smart. For another, he was a born leader with new ideas about how to fight the English.

Early on, it looked like Wallace might win. For in September 1297, Wallace beat a big English army at the **Battle of Stirling Bridge**.

The key to the Battle of Stirling Bridge may have been the bridge itself. According to one version of the story, the wooden bridge collapsed halfway through the battle— leaving half of the English army on one side of the river, and half on the other. With half of the English cut off, Wallace easily beat the other half!

That was before Edward came.

When Edward heard about the Battle of Stirling Bridge, he decided to go to Scotland and tackle Wallace himself. The next year, Edward crushed Wallace's army at the terrible **Battle of Falkirk**.

Scene from the Battle of Stirling Bridge

The Stone of Scone and King Edward's Chair

The **Stone of Scone**, also called the Stone of Destiny, was the coronation seat for Scotland's kings. For centuries, every new King of Scotland sat on the Stone of Scone when he received his crown.[†]

As a sign that the King of England was now the King of Scotland as well, King Edward I stole the Stone of Scone from the Scots! Back in England, Edward built **King Edward's Chair**, a coronation seat for new kings of England. Beneath the seat of this chair was a slot for the Stone of Scone. From then on, any new king who sat on the coronation seat of England was also sitting on the coronation seat of Scotland!

King Edward's Chair in Westminster Abbey, London, with its slot beneath the seat for the Stone of Scone

[†]According to legend, the Stone of Scone is the same stone that Jacob used as a pillow on the night when he saw angels climbing up and down a ladder between heaven and Earth (Genesis 28:10-22).

After the Battle of Falkirk, William Wallace disappeared for a time. He may have gone to France, trying to gain French help in the fight for Scottish independence.

A few years later, the English finally caught up with William Wallace. In 1305, an English court placed Wallace on trial. His crime, the English said, was breaking his oath to his lord King Edward I. In other words, Edward considered Wallace a traitor.

Wallace scoffed. In his eyes, he was a Scottish patriot, and not a traitor all. Wallace insisted:

> "I cannot be a traitor, for I owe [King Edward] no allegiance. He is not my sovereign; he never received my [oath of fealty]; and whilst life is in this persecuted body, he never shall receive it."

The Wallace Monument near Stirling, Scotland

Needless to say, the court didn't agree. At trial's end, the great hero of Scottish independence was put to death in the most horrible way imaginable. *—stop—*

𝍖𝍖𝍖𝍖𝍖𝍖𝍖𝍖𝍖𝍖𝍖𝍖𝍖𝍖𝍖𝍖𝍖𝍖𝍖𝍖𝍖𝍖𝍖𝍖𝍖𝍖𝍖𝍖𝍖𝍖𝍖𝍖𝍖

Fortunately for Scotland, King Edward I didn't live forever; and the next King of England, **Edward II**, wasn't as mighty as his father. In 1328, a King of Scotland called **Robert the Bruce** won back Scotland's independence.

𝍖𝍖𝍖𝍖𝍖𝍖𝍖𝍖𝍖𝍖𝍖𝍖𝍖𝍖𝍖𝍖𝍖𝍖𝍖𝍖𝍖𝍖𝍖𝍖𝍖𝍖𝍖𝍖𝍖𝍖𝍖𝍖𝍖

The third Edward was another mighty one. **King Edward III of England** was the fighting king who started the **Hundred Years' War**— with help from his son, a famous knight called **Edward the Black Prince**.

The Hundred Years' War was a long struggle for the throne of France. From Edward III forward, every King of England claimed that he was also the rightful King of France!

Like the trouble in Scotland, the trouble in France started with a death in the royal family.

For centuries, all kings of France had come from the **House of Capet**. This was the house of Philip II, the same king whose son tried to steal England from King John (above).

Only now, the House of Capet was dying out. The year 1328 brought the death of King Charles IV of France. Since Charles IV had no sons, there could be no more kings from the House of Capet.

On the other hand, Charles IV did have a sister; and that sister had a son. **Isabella Capet**, sister to Charles IV, had been married to King Edward II of England. Isabella's son was **Edward Plantagenet**— in other words, King Edward III of England!

The **Hundred Years' War** actually lasted well over 100 years— all the way from 1337 - 1453.

On the English side, the two greatest heroes of the Hundred Years' War were two fighting kings: **Edward III** and **Henry V**.

On the French side, the greatest hero was no fighting king, but rather a visionary young French girl called **Joan of Arc**.

King Edward III and his son, Edward the Black Prince

What all this means is that the King of England was also the nephew of the King of France. So when the King of France died, leaving no sons to take his place, Edward tried to claim his uncle's throne!

Obviously, the people of France didn't want the King of England to be their king! So instead of choosing Edward, the French chose one of Charles IV's cousins. **King Philip VI of France** was the first king from a new royal house, the **House of Valois**.

A few years later, Edward III and Philip VI were at war. The Hundred Years' War had begun.

The English did well at first. After a great victory in 1346, Edward III took back a small part of Normandy— the important duchy that King John had lost back in the 1200s.

Then, only about ten years into the Hundred Years' War, came one of the worst natural disasters of all time: the Black Death.

The Black Death

Like the Plague of Justinian back in the 500s (Chapter 4), the Black Death was probably an **epidemic** of a very **contagious**, very deadly disease called **bubonic plague**.

Bubonic plague is named for **buboes**, the ugly swellings that appear on its victims' skin. Besides buboes, plague victims also suffered high fevers, trouble breathing and an excruciating cough, among other symptoms even worse.

Churchmen ministering to Italian victims of the Black Death in 1348

Before the days of antibiotic medicines, doctors had no good way to treat plague. Within 2 – 7 days after first showing symptoms, more than half of all plague sufferers were dead.

An **epidemic** is a widespread disease.

Contagious means "easy to catch."

Bubonic Plague is a dreadful disease named for **buboes**. These are ugly black swellings that appear on victims' skin.

The plague spread through grain supplies. The germs that caused plague lived inside fleas, which in turn lived in the coats of rats and mice.

The granaries where cities stored their grain supplies were full of rats and mice. Each time a flea-bitten rat took a bite of grain, it left behind plague germs. After that, catching the plague was easy: all one had to do was carry home a bag of flour!

The Black Death started in the 1330s, somewhere in far-off China. From there, it slowly moved along the Silk Road between East and West. It reached the Crimean Peninsula in 1346.

The Crimean Peninsula is the northern gateway to the Black Sea, which connects to the Mediterranean Sea. From wharves along the Black Sea, rats scurried up the ratlines of trade ships bound for the Mediterranean. Without even knowing it, traders carried these rats to ports all over the Middle East, Europe and North Africa. Along with the rats came their plague-infested fleas.

The Black Death was a catastrophe for Western Europe— a world-changing disaster too terrible to describe or imagine. Within just a few years, the Black Death killed tens of millions of people. It probably wiped out somewhere between one-third and six-tenths of all Western Europeans.

The horrors of the Black Death reached their worst in France in 1347, ten years after the Hundred Years' War began. England's worst year was 1348.

By the end of 1351, the Black Death had run its course. Even so, smaller plague epidemics would continue to trouble Europe for the next 300 – 400 years.

Some victims of the Black Death died because their governments tried to stop the plague without knowing what caused it. For example:

➤ Some governments killed every stray dog and cat they could find, believing that stray animals spread plague. But killing strays only made the plague worse— for strays killed rats, the real villains of the Black Death. Without dogs and cats to kill them, rats multiplied even faster.

➤ Some governments tried to stop the plague by burning houses, or even whole villages, where plague had struck. But these fires killed some of the very people they were trying to protect— uninfected people who had locked themselves inside their homes, trying to avoid the plague.

The Black Death didn't strike Jews as hard as it struck Christians— perhaps because the Jews held themselves separate from the rest of the world. When Christians noticed this, they accused Jews of causing the Black Death! Some Christians insisted that Jews must be secretly poisoning Christian wells.

Sadly, many medieval cities beat, tortured and even killed Jews for the terrible crime of well-poisoning— even though they had absolutely no proof that Jews were poisoning wells.

The **plague doctor's costume** was a special suit that some doctors wore when they examined plague victims. Each feature of this cunning suit was designed to ward off plague:

➤ The beak-like mask was filled with sweet-smelling herbs. By filtering their breath through these masks, plague doctors hoped to block out **miasmas**— the foul airs that they believed to be the cause of plague.

➤ The heavy overcoat, scarf, gloves and boots covered every square inch of the plague doctor's body. All were coated with thick layers of wax or oil to help infection slide off.

➤ The long stick allowed plague doctors to examine plague victims without actually touching them.

This plague doctor's costume was actually made for a later epidemic than the Black Death

About fifty years after the Black Death, and about midway through the Hundred Years' War, came an important change in England's royal family.

The Royal House of Lancaster

When the mighty King Edward III started to grow old, he laid down the law about who would take his place. His oldest son, Edward the Black Prince, was first in line. Next came the Black Prince's son, a boy called Richard.

Sadly, Edward III outlived his oldest son. The Black Prince died in 1376, a year before his father. So when Edward III died in 1377, his 10-year-old grandson Richard took his place— becoming **King Richard II**.

But some Englishmen felt that Richard wasn't the best choice.

For the Black Prince wasn't the only son of Edward III. When Edward III died, his son **John, Duke of Lancaster** was still alive. When a dying king left behind a living son, his throne usually went to that son. If Edward III had followed that rule, then John of Lancaster would have been king. Instead, Edward III left his throne to a grandson.

> ### Kings from the Royal House of Lancaster
>
> **1. King Henry IV**
> (Reigned 1399 - 1413)
>
> **2. King Henry V**
> (Reigned 1413 - 1422)

If John of Lancaster didn't mind not being king, then his son certainly did. In 1399, John's son **Henry, Duke of Lancaster** invaded England, fought off the armies of Richard II and captured the king himself!

After a bit of arm-twisting, Parliament agreed to make Henry the new king. Henry, Duke of Lancaster was now **King Henry IV**— the first King of England from the new royal **House of Lancaster**. As for Richard II, he disappeared into some dark dungeon, where he probably died hungry and alone.

〰〰

At around the same time, France discovered a serious problem of its own— namely, that **King Charles VI of France** was a madman!

There is good reason why King Charles VI is also called **Charles the Mad**. Charles wasn't just a little bit touched in the head. At times, he was completely out of his mind! One day in 1392, Charles was happily riding along when all of a sudden, he drew his sword and started slashing at his own knights! From that day forward, no one ever knew when Charles might fly off into a fit. Some days, Charles couldn't even remember his own name!

> ## The Madness of King Charles VI

Without a sane king to hold it together, France split in two.

➤ Northern France went to the **Burgundians**. The Burgundians were led by the **Duke of Burgundy**, a cousin to Charles the Mad.

➤ Southern France went to the **Armagnacs**. The Armagnacs were led by **Dauphin Charles**, oldest son to Charles the Mad.

> The *Dauphin* was the Crown Prince of France.

King Charles the Mad attacking his own knights

This split meant big trouble for France. Besides the Hundred Years' War against England, now there was also the civil war between Armagnacs and Burgundians.

The next King of England, **Henry V**, took advantage of France's trouble.

The biggest battle of Henry V's career was the

Battle of Agincourt, fought in 1415. In August of that

year, Henry led an English army deep into northern France. He was hoping to take back more of Normandy, the big duchy lost by King John.

But the campaign in Normandy took longer than Henry had hoped. So after a couple of months, Henry retreated northward— back toward the small part of Normandy that Edward III had taken back.

Before Henry could escape, a French army slipped between him and Normandy. Now trapped by an army about six times larger than his, Henry had no choice but to fight for his life!

The first two keys to the Battle of Agincourt were weather and the battlefield. The battle began on the morning after a night of heavy rain, on a field that had just been plowed. When the French knights charged onto this field, it turned to thick, sticky mud. Weighed down by their heavy plate armor, the poor French knights could hardly move— let alone fight!

The other key to the Battle of Agincourt was a powerful weapon called the **English longbow**. With the French stuck in the mud, English archers poured deadly arrows into their midst, killing them by the thousands. Against all odds, Henry V wound up winning the Battle of Agincourt!

After Agincourt, Henry V was well on his way toward winning the Hundred Years' War. Instead of fighting Henry V, the Burgundians now joined forces with him.

With Henry's help, the Burgundians drove the Armagnacs out of Paris and captured Charles the Mad! As for the Dauphin, he retreated southward, making his new capital at a place called **Chinon**.

Now that Henry controlled Charles the Mad, he forced him to sign an important treaty. Under the **Treaty of Troyes**, the Dauphin was no longer the heir of Charles the Mad. Instead, Henry V was his heir!

Once the Treaty of Troyes was signed, all Henry V had to do was wait for Charles the Mad to die. After that, Henry would be King of France as well as King of England— which was the whole point of the Hundred Years' War.

King Henry V fighting the Battle of Agincourt

The **English longbow** was the deadliest weapon of the Hundred Years' War. Edward III wrote a law requiring all able-bodied Englishmen to practice with the longbow in their spare time. By Henry V's day, England had many skilled longbow archers— not only nobles, but also commoners. The English used up so much **yew**, the preferred wood for longbows, that they had to start buying yew from overseas!

Longbow archers had to be very strong. To draw some English longbows was the same as lifting 200 pounds! With that much force behind it, a sharp iron arrowhead called a **bodkin** could pierce any armor of the day— even the heavy plate armor of the 1400s.

Bodkin-point arrowhead

Alas for Henry V, it didn't turn out that way.

A couple of years later, Henry V was leading another campaign in France when he suddenly took sick. To the surprise of all, the great King Henry V died at age 35. He left behind just one legitimate son: an 8-month-old called Henry, who immediately became **King Henry VI of England**.

Just two months later, Charles the Mad died as well!

Now all was chaos. Under the Treaty of Troyes, the English claimed the throne of France for their boy King Henry VI. The Dauphin claimed the throne as well. And so the Hundred Years' War dragged on— with Henry VI king in the north, the Dauphin king in the south, and no one king of all France!

This was the sticky situation when a French peasant girl called **Joan of Arc** came on the scene.

Joan of Arc (1412 - 1431)

With the coming of Joan of Arc, the Hundred Years' War became a holy war for the throne of France. For Joan was more than just a devoted Christian. She was also a **visionary**, a seer of mysterious visions.

In Joan's mind, there was no doubt that her visions came to her straight from God. And what Joan saw in her visions was that the Dauphin was the rightful King of France!

Joan's first visions came to her when she was about 12 years old, a couple of years after Charles the Mad died. Some of her visions told her secrets about the Hundred Years' War— military details which no mere peasant girl should have known.

When Joan was still just 16 years old, she shared some of these details with a knight's squire. In turn, the squire shared them with his knight. When the details turned out to be true, the knight started to believe that Joan might be a prophet.

So the knight took Joan to Chinon, where the Dauphin himself put her to the test. Like most peasants, Joan had never laid eyes on the Dauphin. So the Dauphin decided to take off his royal robes and blend in with everyone else— to see if Joan was prophet enough to recognize him!

When Joan recognized him easily, the Dauphin started to believe in her as well.

After a few more tests, the Dauphin gave Joan a horse, armor and banner, and then sent her off to raise the **Siege of Orleans**.

Orleans was a fortress that guarded an important bridge over the Loire River. At the moment, Orleans was also the key to the Hundred Years' War! For the Loire River was the border between the Dauphin and his enemies, the English and the Burgundians. If his enemies took Orleans, then they took the Loire River. And if they took the Loire, then the Dauphin was in serious trouble.

Joan of Arc raising the Siege of Orleans

When Joan of Arc set out for Orleans, the Burgundians had almost surrounded it. They had also seized the *Tourelles*, a strong gatehouse that guarded the far side of the bridge. With the *Tourelles* in enemy hands, there was no way Orleans could stand for long.

All of that changed when Joan came. For the peasant Joan breathed more life into the French people than the royal Dauphin ever had. When Joan paraded through the streets of Orleans, shouting that God was on France's side, every peasant in France wanted to join her. With help from Joan's peasants, the armies of the Dauphin quickly took back the *Tourelles* and raised the Siege of Orleans!

Joan's next target was **Reims**, a city about 80 miles northeast of Paris.

Actually, what Joan really wanted was **Reims Cathedral**. For centuries, every King of France had received his crown at Reims Cathedral. This is why Joan wanted Reims: so that the Dauphin could receive his crown at Reims Cathedral as well. Driven by her visions, Joan insisted on taking Reims, even though it lay well inside enemy territory.

Reims Cathedral

Reims soon fell to Joan, just as Orleans had fallen! The day after she took Reims, Joan saw her fondest prayer answered. On that day, the Dauphin received his crown at Reims Cathedral. In 1429, seven years after Charles the Mad died, his son the Dauphin finally became **King Charles VII of France**.

Thus it was no splendid fighting king who won the Hundred Years War for France. Instead, it was a peasant girl called Joan of Arc!

In light of everything Joan did for France, the rest of her story is terribly sad.

In May 1430, the Burgundians caught Joan by surprise and took her prisoner. Joan's captors would have been happy to send her home, if her king had been willing to pay a ransom. But for some reason, Joan's beloved king wouldn't pay. So instead, the Burgundians sold Joan to their English allies.

The moment the English got their hands on Joan, they placed her on trial for crimes against God and Church.

Like many trials of medieval times, Joan's trial was a **show trial**. Although the Church pretended to give Joan a fair trial, the court had already made its decision before the trial even began. Vengeful English priests accused Joan of terrible crimes against God. They called her a heretic for saying that her visions came from God. And they accused her of going against God and nature. For Joan had dared to wear battle armor, which was for men alone.

In the end, Joan of Arc suffered the awful death set aside for heretics: she was tied to a stake and burned alive.

A cardinal questioning Joan of Arc in her prison cell

A **show trial** is a false trial designed to make a court look fair, when it really isn't.

The game of **tennis** probably started in French monasteries, where bored monks played handball against monastery walls.

The strange words used in scoring tennis probably also come from French. For example, "love"— the tennis word for zero score— may come from the French word *l'oeuf*, or "goose egg."

Seasons and Tropics

What causes the seasons of the year to change— to go from spring to summer, fall, winter and then back to spring again? The answer is the tilt of Earth's axis!

Once each year, the northern end of Earth's axis leans directly toward the sun, and the southern end directly away from the sun. This is the **summer solstice** of the Northern Hemisphere, which always falls around June 21. This solstice is the start of summer in the Northern Hemisphere, and winter in the Southern Hemisphere.

Six months later, the southern end of Earth's axis leans directly toward the sun, and the northern end directly away from the sun. This is the **winter solstice** of the Northern Hemisphere, which always falls around December 21. This solstice is the start of winter in the Northern Hemisphere, and summer in the Southern.

> Earth's **axis** is the axle on which Earth rotates. It is an imaginary line which runs through the globe from North Pole to South Pole.

The tilt of Earth's axis also marks out five important lines of latitude:

1. The **equator** is the line of 0° latitude. Twice each year, the sun stands directly overhead at the equator. The first time is the **spring equinox**, which comes midway between the winter and summer solstices— always around March 20. The second time is the **fall equinox**, which comes midway between the summer and winter solstices— always around September 23.

2. The **Tropic of Cancer** is the line of 23-1/2 degrees north latitude. The sun stands directly over the Tropic of Cancer once each year, at the summer solstice of the Northern Hemisphere.

3. The **Tropic of Capricorn** is the line of 23-1/2 degrees south latitude. The sun stands directly over the Tropic of Capricorn once each year, at the summer solstice of the Southern Hemisphere.

4. The **Arctic Circle** is the line of 66-1/2 degrees north latitude. For part of each summer, the sun never sets north of the Arctic Circle— for Earth's rotation never carries that part of the globe out of the light. And for part of each winter, the sun never rises north of the Arctic Circle— for Earth's rotation never carries that part of the globe into the light.

5. The **Antarctic Circle** is the line of 66-1/2 degrees south latitude. The Antarctic Circle is the southern equivalent of the Arctic Circle in the north.

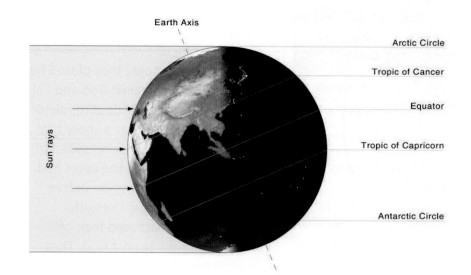

The summer solstice of the Northern Hemisphere, when the sun stands directly over the Tropic of Cancer. Notice how the whole Arctic Circle is always in the light, no matter how Earth rotates.

The End of the Hundred Years' War

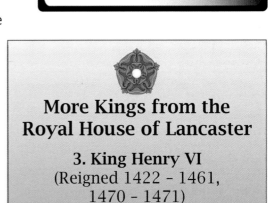

Through faith, Joan of Arc did something that no mere peasant girl should have been able to do: she turned the tide of the Hundred Years' War. With Joan's help, her beloved **Dauphin** received his crown at Reims Cathedral, becoming **King Charles VII of France** (Chapter 14).

But the Hundred Years' War wasn't over yet. For someone else also claimed the crown of France. This was the boy **King Henry VI of England**, son of King Henry V.

> Remember who **Henry V** was— the great English fighting king who won the Battle of Agincourt.
>
> Remember who **Charles the Mad** was— King Charles VI of France, father to King Charles VII.

How could a King of England claim the throne of France? The answer goes back to the **Treaty of Troyes**, which we read about in Chapter 14. The Treaty of Troyes said that when **Charles the Mad** died, Henry V would inherit the throne of France.

> **More Kings from the Royal House of Lancaster**
>
> **3. King Henry VI**
> (Reigned 1422 - 1461, 1470 - 1471)

This same treaty was also important for another reason. To seal the Treaty of Troyes, Charles the Mad had to give away his daughter. In 1420, Charles' daughter **Catherine of Valois** married Henry V. A year later, Catherine of Valois gave Henry V a little boy: the future King Henry VI!

As the son of Catherine of Valois, Henry VI was also the grandson of Charles the Mad— a fact which will become most important later.

As we've already seen, the sons of great fighting kings aren't necessarily great fighters themselves. Just as Edward II lost Scotland (Chapter 14), so Henry VI was to lose France.

Of course, Henry's early losses weren't his fault. Since Henry was still a baby when his father died, older men ran his kingdoms for him. Henry's uncle **John, Duke of Bedford** was in charge of France. It was actually Bedford, not Henry, who lost Orleans and Reims to Joan of Arc.

But when Henry grew up, he found that he didn't like fighting for his French lands. Instead, he often traded them away, getting very little in return.

〜〜〜〜〜〜〜〜〜〜〜〜〜〜〜〜〜〜〜〜〜〜〜〜〜

The boy King Henry VI with his two coats of arms: the arms of England, three lions on a field of red; and the arms of France, three *fleur-de-lis* on a field of blue

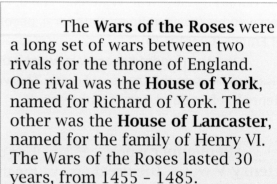

To proud Englishmen like **Richard, Duke of York**, the fact that Henry wouldn't fight for France meant that he wasn't fit to be King of England.

Richard of York was an older cousin of Henry VI. When Henry's uncle John, Duke of Bedford died in 1435, Richard took charge of France in Henry's name.

A few years later, Henry grew old enough to make his own decisions about France. Over the years that followed, Richard watched Henry trade away more and more French lands.

What Richard couldn't forget was that countless Englishmen had given their lives to win those lands. In fact, one of those Englishmen had been Henry VI's own father— the great Henry V! The more lands Henry VI traded away, the angrier Richard grew.

The anger of Richard of York was the spark that touched off some of the ugliest wars in English history.

The Wars of the Roses

Although Richard of York was only a duke, he actually had a strong claim to the throne of England. Richard was descended from the second son of King Edward III: **Lionel, Duke of Clarence**. Henry, on the other hand, was descended from the third son of Edward III: **John, Duke of Lancaster** (Chapter 14). Since Richard was descended from the older son, his claim to the throne was actually stronger than Henry's— in a way.

On the other hand, no one from Richard's branch of the family had ever been king. Whereas Henry's branch had three kings: Henry IV, Henry V and Henry VI himself. In this way, Henry's claim was stronger.

In the end, though, it didn't matter which branch of the family had the stronger claim. It only mattered which branch proved stronger on the battlefield!

The **Wars of the Roses** were a long set of wars between two rivals for the throne of England. One rival was the **House of York**, named for Richard of York. The other was the **House of Lancaster**, named for the family of Henry VI. The Wars of the Roses lasted 30 years, from 1455 - 1485.

The name "Wars of the Roses" came from the badges of the two royal houses. Lancaster's badge was the **Red Rose of Lancaster**; while York's was the **White Rose of York**.

The Red Rose of Lancaster and the White Rose of York

ꙥꙥꙥꙥꙥꙥꙥꙥꙥꙥꙥꙥꙥꙥꙥꙥꙥꙥꙥꙥꙥꙥꙥꙥꙥꙥꙥꙥꙥꙥꙥꙥꙥꙥꙥꙥꙥ

The trouble started in 1451, when Richard of York came to Parliament with an unusual request. It so happened that Henry VI and his wife, **Queen Margaret**, had no sons as yet. So Richard wanted to be named as the official heir to Henry VI.

Naturally, Queen Margaret was furious! For Margaret was still young, and hoped to have sons someday soon. From then on, Margaret saw Richard of York as a traitor to her family.

The year 1453 brought three key events. The first was that after 116 years, the Hundred Years' War finally ended! After losing a big battle that year, Henry VI had almost nothing left in France.

The second key event was that Henry VI lost his mind! Just as Charles the Mad went mad, so his grandson Henry VI went mad. Historians have always suspected that Charles the Mad handed down his madness to Henry VI.

Fortunately, Henry's madness wasn't violent. Instead of slashing at people, the way Charles the Mad did, Henry just lost touch with reality. Even so, Henry was in no shape to run his country!

Coat of Arms of Richard of York

The third key event was that Queen Margaret gave birth to a son: **Edward of Westminster, Prince of Wales**. Now that Henry VI had a son, Richard of York would never be named as Henry's official heir— unless something should happen to Henry's son.

With the king gone mad, and his son too young to take his place, England needed a **Lord Protector of the Realm** to run its government. The question was, who should be Lord Protector?

A **Lord Protector of the Realm** was similar to a **regent**. Both were trusted nobles who managed the government for kings who were too young, or too sick, to manage on their own.

Naturally, Richard of York wanted to be Lord Protector. But Richard was the last person Queen Margaret wanted! For the queen still saw Richard as a traitor to her family. She feared that if Richard took charge, then her son might never inherit the throne.

Just as the madness of Charles the Mad split France in two, so the madness of Henry VI split England in two. Those who stood with Richard of York were called **Yorkists**, after the House of York. Those who stood with Queen Margaret were called **Lancastrians**, after the House of Lancaster. The longer this split went on, the more Yorkists and Lancastrians hated each other.

Besides Richard of York, the most powerful Yorkist was the **Earl of Warwick**. With help from the wealthy Warwick, Richard convinced Parliament to name him Lord Protector in March 1454. This was the first link in a crazy chain of events:

➤ On Christmas Day 1454, King Henry VI suddenly came to his senses! With a sane husband back on her side, Queen Margaret soon drove Richard out of office.

➤ Now came Richard's turn to be afraid. With Henry and Margaret back in power, Richard feared that Parliament might declare him a traitor. If that happened, then any Englishman could kill Richard on sight! Rather than face that danger unprepared, Richard gathered an army to defend himself.

➤ The following May, Henry VI led out an army to tackle Richard. Since Richard hadn't been declared a traitor yet, the king expected Richard to back down without a fight, as a loyal subject should. But Richard feared that if he backed down, then the Lancastrians might take him prisoner— or even put him to death.

Edward of Westminster, son of King Henry VI and Queen Margaret

So Richard didn't back down. Instead, Richard beat Henry at the first battle of the Wars of the Roses: the **First Battle of St. Albans**, fought in May 1455.

The stress of losing the battle caused Henry to lose his mind again. So Richard went back to London, where he took back his old job as Lord Protector.

For the next few years, the government went from Yorkist to Lancastrian and back again. Whenever the king went mad, Richard stood on top. Whenever the king came to his senses, Queen Margaret pushed Richard out. With every change, the hatred between Yorkists and Lancastrians grew a little bit stronger.

Henry VI King of England

Finally, Queen Margaret decided that enough was enough. During one of the king's sane times, Margaret convinced Parliament to declare Richard of York a traitor!

Once again, Henry VI led out an army against the Yorkists; and once again, the Yorkists beat Henry. This time, the Yorkists captured Henry and hauled him back to London.

Back in London, Richard demanded the prize he had been wanting for years: the throne of England! For the first time, Richard formally asked Parliament to get rid of the mad King Henry VI, and name Richard king in his place.

Here Parliament showed how fickle it could be. Just a short time ago, Parliament had declared Richard a traitor. But now, Parliament decided that it had better give Richard at least part of what he wanted.

So instead of naming Richard king, Parliament named Richard as the official heir to Henry VI.

At this, Queen Margaret exploded! This was exactly what Margaret had feared all along— that Richard might come between her son and the throne.

To defend her son, Queen Margaret fled to the north, where she raised the biggest Lancastrian army yet.

This was the start of a deadly chapter in the Wars of the Roses. Until now, both sides had tried to claim the throne legally, through Parliament. Now came an all-out death struggle— with the winner seizing the throne by force, and the loser going to his grave.

෬෬෬෬෬෬෬෬෬෬෬෬෬෬෬෬෬෬෬෬෬෬෬෬෬෬෬෬

In late 1460, Richard went north to tackle Margaret's big army. But Richard had no idea just how big Margaret's army had grown. Margaret may have hired as many as 18,000 troops— about four times Richard's numbers!

Given the size of Margaret's army, Richard should have holed up inside his castle and waited for help to arrive. But he didn't. Instead, Richard bravely rode out to the **Battle of Wakefield**— which he quickly lost.

Queen Margaret, also called Margaret of Anjou

At battle's end, the Lancastrians offered to spare Richard's life if he would just surrender. But Richard knew what happen to him if he surrendered. Since Margaret had declared him a traitor, he would die a traitor's death. Instead, Richard fought on— so that he could die the honorable death of a soldier.

After the Battle of Wakefield, Queen Margaret showed what a merciless enemy she could be. Instead of burying Richard's remains with honor, Margaret ordered his head cut off and set out on a spike. To top off this gruesome sight, Margaret set a paper crown on Richard's head. In her mind, a cheap paper crown was the only kind of crown Richard deserved.

> **The Battle of Wakefield (December 30, 1460)**

> One way to remember the colors of the rainbow is to memorize this short description of the Battle of Wakefield: "**R**ichard of **Y**ork **g**ave **b**attle **in** **v**ain." The colors of the rainbow are <u>r</u>ed, <u>o</u>range, <u>y</u>ellow, <u>g</u>reen, <u>b</u>lue, <u>i</u>ndigo and <u>v</u>iolet.

If Margaret had known what was coming, then she might have shown more mercy.

The army Margaret had just defeated was not the only Yorkist army. To the south stood another army, led by two great commanders. One was Richard's powerful friend the Earl of Warwick. The other was Richard's oldest son **Edward of York**.

With his father out of the picture, Edward was the new head of the House of York. To defend that house, Edward and Warwick marched off to fight one of the bloodiest battles in all of English history: the

Battle of Towton.

The Battle of Towton was the ultimate death struggle for the throne of England. The whole thing started with a dramatic gesture. Just before the battle, Warwick drew his sword and killed his own horse! This was to show Warwick's horseless foot soldiers that he would never run

The Battle of Towton (March 29, 1461)

away, no matter what happened. Warwick meant to either win the Battle of Towton or die trying!

The key to the Battle of Towton was the weather. It so happened that the battle fell on a windy, snowy day. It also happened that the wind blew away from the Yorkists, and toward the Lancastrians— which meant that Yorkist arrows flew farther than Lancastrian ones. Slowed by the wind, Lancastrian arrows never even reached Yorkist lines. Meanwhile, Yorkist arrows pierced countless Lancastrians!

The Earl of Warwick killing his own horse just before the all-important Battle of Towton

When the snow-blind Lancastrians finally realized what was happening to them, they stopped shooting and charged. What followed was one of the ugliest scenes the world has ever witnessed. The hatred between Yorkist and Lancastrian was so bitter that no one asked for mercy, nor gave it. Tens of thousands fell— so many that time and again, the living had to drag off the dead to make room for more fighting. Even when the beaten Lancastrians broke and ran, the Yorkists still didn't stop killing them.

~~~~~~

After losing the Battle of Towton, Queen Margaret and her son fled overseas.

As for the winner, Edward of York, he became King **Edward IV**. Edward was the first king from England's new royal house, the **House of York**.

At the time, the new King Edward was not quite 19 years old. He was a grown man, but still too young to run a kingdom without advice.

Most of Edward's advice came from the noble who had fought so hard at the Battle of Towton: the Earl of Warwick.

<div style="border:1px solid #000; padding:10px; text-align:center">

Kings from the Royal House of York

1. King Edward IV
(Reigned 1461 - 1470,
1471 - 1483)

2. King Edward V
(Reigned 1483, one of the young Princes in the Tower)

2. King Richard III
(Reigned 1483 - 1485)

</div>

Edward owed everything to Warwick. In fact, Edward owed him so much that people called him **Warwick the Kingmaker**.

One of Warwick's first jobs was to arrange a good marriage for Edward. Unfortunately, Warwick and Edward had different ideas about what made a good marriage!

Edward wanted a woman he could love. But Warwick couldn't have cared less about love. What Warwick wanted was a foreign princess— someone who could give Edward new lands and new allies overseas.

What Warwick didn't know was that he was wasting his time. Unknown to just about everyone, Edward had already fallen in love with an English beauty called Elizabeth Woodville. Even worse, he had already married her!

Ordinarily, a royal wedding would have been a grand affair, followed by an even grander coronation for the new queen. But Edward knew how disappointed Warwick would be with his choice of

Elizabeth Woodville as Queen of England

brides. So he kept his wedding secret, even from his top adviser. Imagine how uncomfortable Edward must have felt when he finally broke the bad news to Warwick!

In Warwick's eyes, the worst part of Edward's marriage wasn't the queen, but the queen's family. Before the wedding, the Woodvilles had been minor nobles who had nothing to do with running the government. But after the wedding, Elizabeth's father became the top adviser to Edward— edging out Warwick himself!

In Warwick's eyes, this was a very poor way to treat "the Kingmaker"— the one man who had done more than any other to set Edward on his throne.

The argument between Warwick, Edward and the Woodville family finally led to war. In 1470, Warwick turned against Edward, and instead joined forces with an unlikely ally: his old enemy Margaret, wife of Henry VI! Nine years after the Battle of Towton, Margaret and her son were still waiting overseas, hoping to take back all they'd lost. With Warwick's help, they got their chance. In late 1470, Warwick led Margaret's latest army in an attack on Edward IV.

The attack caught Edward completely by surprise. To save himself, Edward had no choice but to flee the country— for the moment. With Edward out of the picture, Warwick the Kingmaker set the mad King Henry VI back on his throne!

Alas, the second reign of Henry VI didn't last long. Less than six months after fleeing England, Edward IV returned to win two great battles. First came the **Battle of Barnet**. At Barnet, Edward not only crushed Warwick's army, but also killed his old friend Warwick.

After the Battle of Barnet, poor old Henry VI went from the throne of England to a cell in the Tower of London. Not long after, Henry was dead! Just how Henry VI died, no one knows for sure. But historians are fairly sure that the House of York had something to do with it!

> **The Battle of Barnet**
> **(April 14, 1471)**
>
> **The Battle of Tewkesbury**
> **(May 4, 1471)**

The month after the Battle of Barnet came the **Battle of Tewkesbury**. At Tewkesbury, Edward not only crushed Margaret's army, but also killed her son Edward of Westminster. The poor boy was only 17 years old.

After the Battle of Tewkesbury, it looked as if the House of York had finally won the Wars of the Roses! With both Henry VI and Edward of Westminster dead, there could be no more kings from the House of Lancaster. For the next 12 years, no one seriously challenged Edward IV.

Scene from the Battle of Tewkesbury

〰〰〰〰〰〰〰〰〰〰〰〰〰〰〰〰〰〰〰〰〰〰〰〰〰〰〰

One of the saddest stories of the whole Wars of the Roses started when Edward IV died in 1483.

Edward IV left behind two sons: **Edward, Prince of Wales** and **Richard, Duke of York**. Edward was only 12 years old when his father died, and Richard only 9. Both were grandsons to the old Richard of York— the one who died at the Battle of Wakefield.

The new Richard of York lived in London with his mother, Elizabeth Woodville. Prince Edward lived in Wales with his mother's brother, **Anthony Woodville**.

The moment Edward IV died, Prince Edward became **King Edward V**. However, the young king had yet to receive his crown. So when the big news of the old King Edward's death reached Wales, the new King Edward set out for London. At his side rode his guardian and uncle, Anthony Woodville.

Somewhere along the road to London, another uncle showed up: **Richard of Gloucester**. Gloucester was a trusted brother to Edward IV, the one brother who had stood by the old king through thick and thin.

Now that the old king was gone, Gloucester had been named Lord Protector of the Realm. And as Lord Protector, Gloucester insisted that he, not Anthony, would be taking Edward V to London.

Richard of Gloucester as
King Richard III of England

The first sure sign that something was wrong came the following morning, when Gloucester arrested Anthony Woodville. Edward never saw Anthony again.

Even so, Gloucester carried the boy on to London, where he introduced him as King Edward V. So far as most people knew, Gloucester meant Edward no harm.

The widow of King Edward IV knew better. When Elizabeth Woodville heard what was happening, she rushed her second

The Princes in the Tower

son Richard of York to her favorite church: Westminster Abbey.

Elizabeth knew that while Richard lived, it would do Gloucester no good to kill Edward V. For if he did, then the throne would pass to Richard, not to Gloucester. As long as Richard was safe, Edward was safe. And Elizabeth trusted the Church to keep Richard safe.

Sad to say, Elizabeth misplaced her trust.

For Gloucester was very clever— especially when he was talking to priests. Just what Gloucester said to the priests of Westminster Abbey, no one now knows. There may be many ways to explain what happened. But what seems to have happened is that Gloucester talked the priests into handing over Richard of York!

Now that Gloucester had captured both of his brother's sons, both were doomed to die.

For the moment, though, no one knew that the boys were doomed. Gloucester seemed to be doing what any good Lord Protector would do: keeping the precious brothers safe. For safety's sake, Gloucester kept them in the safest fort he had. This just happened to be the **Tower of London**— the same Tower where poor old Henry VI had died!

One reason Edward IV trusted his brother Richard, Duke of Gloucester so much was because of another brother: **George, Duke of Clarence**. All through the Wars of the Roses, Gloucester stayed loyal to Edward. Clarence, on the other hand, switched back and forth— first fighting for Edward, then Warwick, then Edward again. So naturally, Edward trusted Gloucester far more than he did Clarence.

In the William Shakespeare play *Henry VI*, the great playwright calls George, Duke of Clarence a "quicksand of deceit."

It was only later that Gloucester's true plan came to light. And once again, it all started with a priest.

A couple of months later, a priest came forward with a big announcement. Just before Edward IV died, this priest said, the old king had confessed certain sins to him. Deathbed confessions were supposed to be secret. But this one told news that the whole kingdom needed to hear!

What Edward IV confessed was that before he married Elizabeth Woodville, he had promised himself to another woman. In the eyes of the Church, this meant that Edward never should have married Elizabeth! Had the Church but known, it never would have approved Edward's marriage. According to the Church, Edward's marriage was unlawful.

What all this meant was that Edward's children had been born into an unlawful marriage. And no child of an unlawful marriage had any right to the throne of England!

Most Englishmen believed the priest. For in those days, few Christians believed that a priest of God would lie about something as sacred as the deathbed confession of a king. And so, three days after the priest's announcement, a noble council announced that Edward V was no longer King of England.

All of Gloucester's scheming had finally paid off.

Instead of the Duke of Gloucester, he now became King Richard III of England!

After that, people saw less and less of the two young **Princes in the Tower**. In time, they saw nothing at all! What happened to the boys, no one knows for sure— just as no one knows for sure what happened to Henry VI. But historians suspect that all three royals were murdered— either by Richard III himself, or on his orders.

Prince Edward and Duke Richard, the two frightened Princes in the Tower

But for all his scheming, King Richard III didn't hold onto his stolen throne for long. After the Princes in the Tower disappeared, the English people trusted their new king less and less. When the Lancastrians noticed this, they looked around for someone to take Richard's place. The one they found was Henry Tudor.

When one remembers how the Wars of the Roses began, it seems strange that Henry Tudor should try to claim the throne. The wars had started with an argument over whose claim to the throne was strongest. But Henry Tudor's claim was the weakest yet!

On his father's side, Henry Tudor wasn't the son of a king, or even the grandson of a king. Instead, he was the grandson of Catherine of Valois, wife to the old King Henry V. After Henry V died, Catherine married a Welsh soldier called Owen Tudor. Owen was the father of Edmund Tudor, who in turn was the father of Henry Tudor. The only trace of royal blood on this side came from Catherine of Valois.

Henry was only a little more royal on his mother's side. Henry's mother, **Margaret Beaufort**, was a great-granddaughter to John of Lancaster, third son of King Edward III (above). However, John of Lancaster hadn't actually married Margaret's great-grandmother until after their children were born. Because of this, an old law said that no one from Margaret's family could claim the throne.

But the Lancastrians didn't care about that old law. After 30 years of bloody war, Henry Tudor was the closest thing to royalty the House of Lancaster had left. So Henry was the man the Lancastrians chose to invade England get rid of Richard III.

Henry Tudor and his army sailed from Normandy in August 1485. They soon landed in Wales, the home of Henry's father and grandfather. Richard III led his army out to meet them. The clash of the two armies was the last big battle of the Wars of the Roses: the famous **Battle of Bosworth Field**.

The key to the Battle of Bosworth was **Thomas Stanley**. Stanley was a rich noble who commanded a powerful army. And he was married to Henry's mother, Margaret Beaufort— which made him Henry's step-father. So there was a good chance that Stanley might take Henry's side.

Richard couldn't let that happen— not if he could help it. So before the battle began, Richard took one of Stanley's sons hostage, threatening to kill him if Stanley took Henry's side!

The Battle of Bosworth Field (August 22, 1485)

To save his son, Stanley didn't take either side. Instead, he held his army out of the battle, leaving both sides guessing what he might do.

In the middle of the battle, Richard noticed Henry riding toward Stanley, with only a few bodyguards to protect him. At this, Richard charged straight at his rival, hoping to strike him down in man-to-man combat!

Alas for Richard, Stanley chose this moment to join battle. As Richard charged past on his way toward Henry, Stanley's army swept down to attack him from behind. The last Yorkist king went down fighting, crying with his dying breaths: "Treason! Treason!"

Lord Stanley handing the crown of Richard III to King Henry VII after the Battle of Bosworth

Afterward, Stanley picked up Richard's crown and handed it to Henry Tudor. Right there on the battlefield, Henry Tudor became **King Henry VII of England**— the first king from the new royal **House of Tudor**.

Henry VII's first job as king was to let everyone know that the long, horrible Wars of the Roses were finally over.

One of the ways Henry did that was by marrying **Elizabeth of York**. Elizabeth was a daughter to Edward IV, and a sister to Edward V. Since Henry was connected to the House of Lancaster, and Elizabeth came from the House of York, their marriage brought the two royal houses together. Hopefully, this meant the end of the deadly wars between Yorkists and Lancastrians.

Kings from the Royal House of Tudor

1. King Henry VII
(Reigned 1485 - 1509)

King Henry VII was the creator of an elite army unit called the **Yeoman Warders**. The Yeoman Warders guarded the Tower of London, where English kings kept prisoners they couldn't afford to lose.

The Yeoman Warders were also called **Beefeaters**. This funny nickname may have meant that as the king's favorites, Beefeaters ate juicy beef from the king's own table. In a time when few Englishmen could afford beef, this would have been a special treat.

The **Tudor Rose** was the badge of King Henry VII's new royal house, the House of Tudor. As another sign that the long Wars of the Roses were finally over, the Tudor Rose combined two older badges: the Red Rose of Lancaster, and the White Rose of York.

The Divine Comedy by Dante Alighieri

The Divine Comedy is a long poem that describes the **afterworld**, the place where people go when they die. An Italian Christian called **Dante Alighieri** wrote The Divine Comedy over the years from 1308 – 1321. Since then, readers have never ceased to marvel at the images Dante created.

Dante divided The Divine Comedy into three parts: one for hell, one for purgatory and one for heaven. The best-known part is the **Inferno**, which describes hell as Dante imagined it.

Dante's hell is divided into nine circles for nine different kinds of sinners. Dante writes that without Christian baptism, everyone on Earth is doomed to go to one of those nine circles. The worse the sinner, the lower the circle of hell.

Dante's first circle, Limbo, isn't for punishing sinners. Instead, Limbo is for good people who would have gone to heaven, if not for one thing: they were never baptized. Without baptism, Dante writes, even the most innocent people who ever lived can never get to heaven. The saddest sights in Limbo are the countless innocent babies who died before they could be baptized.

The ninth circle of hell is for the worst sinners of all: traitors. The devil Lucifer stands there, frozen waist-deep in ice. Dante's Lucifer is a three-headed monster with three sets of jaws, each set gnawing one of the three worst traitors of all time. The center set gnaws Judas Iscariot, the traitor who betrayed Jesus with a kiss!

Antarctica

Antarctica is the continent where people go to find the South Pole— but only if they don't mind the cold!

The South Pole is far colder than the North Pole. The North Pole lies in the Arctic Ocean, which of course is cold enough. As cold as it is, though, the Arctic Ocean still receives some warmth from the oceans to the south. But the South Pole lies in the middle of vast Antarctica, with no ocean to warm it. Thermometers on Antarctica have recorded temperatures as low as −130° Fahrenheit— more than 160° below freezing!

A **gargoyle** is a statue attached to the outside of a building. Early gargoyles often looked like real animals, especially lions.

Some later gargoyles looked like demons straight out of hell! Even church buildings had demonic-looking gargoyles, to remind sinners how truly terrible hell could be.

A true gargoyle is also a waterspout. The purpose of true gargoyles is to carry rainwater away from their buildings' foundations— usually by pouring it out of their mouths. The words "gargoyle" and "gargle" both come from the Old French word *gargouille*, meaning "throat."

To reach Antarctica, ships must pass through the hazardous Southern Ocean. Glaciers and sea ice can crush any ship that isn't strong enough. The trip is so dangerous that the first explorers didn't set foot on Antarctica until 1821.

Setting foot at the South Pole took another 90 years. The great explorer **Roald Amundsen** planted the flag of his home country, Norway, at the South Pole in December 1911.

If the sea journey to Antarctica was dangerous, then the land journey to the South Pole was even worse. To cross the wasteland of Antarctica safely, Amundsen needed lessons learned from the Inuit people of northern Canada. He wore fur clothes instead of wool, and rode dogsleds instead of horses or tractors!

Roald Amundsen and crew after planting their flag at the South Pole

The Land of the Hindus

India is the biggest country in South Asia, and one of the biggest in the world. In modern times, only six countries on Earth have more land than India: Russia, Canada, China, the United States, Brazil and Australia. And only one country has more people: China. The capital of India is New Delhi.

India used to have even more land than it does today. Until 1948, India was everything east of **Iran**, southeast of **Afghanistan** and south of **China** and **Nepal**. This whole area was called **British India**, and was part of the great **British Empire**.

1948 was the year when India declared independence from Britain. In that same year, India split into two parts for two big religions:

➢ The Hindu part became the **Republic of India**, or simply India.

➢ The Muslim part became **Pakistan**.

At first, Pakistan was also split into two parts: **West Pakistan** and **East Pakistan**. Then in 1971, East Pakistan won independence from West Pakistan. East Pakistan became **Bangladesh**; while West Pakistan became simply **Pakistan**.

Along the northern border of India stands a huge mountain range called the **Himalayas**. Nine of the ten tallest mountain peaks in the world stand in the Himalayas. The tallest of all is **Mount Everest**, which rises 29,029 feet above sea level!

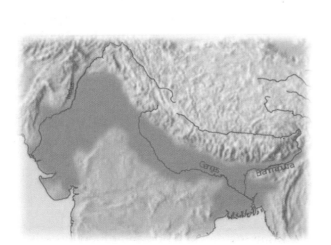

The Indo-Gangetic Plain in purple, just south of the Himalayas

Just south of the Himalayas lies a fertile land called the **Indo-Gangetic Plain**. This complicated name comes from the two most important rivers in India: the **Indus River** in the west, and the **Ganges River** in the east. The Indus River Valley was home to one of the oldest known civilizations: the Harappan civilization.

Southern India is surrounded by huge bodies of water. To the west lies the **Arabian Sea**; to the south lies the **Indian Ocean**; and to the east lies the **Bay of Bengal**. The large island off the southern tip of India is **Sri Lanka**.

> The capital of India is **New Delhi**.

Hindus, Jains and Buddhists

The names "Indus" and "India" both come from the oldest religion in India: Hinduism. "India" means "Land of the Hindus." The Hindu faith is so important to India that it is hard to speak of India without also speaking of Hinduism.

Hinduism

The first rule of Hinduism is that all Hindus are not created equal. Instead, Hindus are born into one of four **castes**, or *varnas*:

> Some societies divide people into different levels called **castes**.

➤ The highest caste is the **Brahmins**. These are priests and teachers of the Hindu faith.

➤ Second come the **Ksatriyas**. These are warriors and government officials.

➤ Third come the **Vaisyas**. These are farmers, businessmen and skilled tradesmen.

➤ The lowest caste is the **Sudras**. These are unskilled laborers who serve the higher castes.

Even in modern times, most Hindus never change castes, or marry someone from a different caste.

Some Hindus are considered too lowly for any caste, even the Sudras caste. These are the **untouchables**, also called **out-castes** or *dalits*. Untouchables handle jobs that the higher castes won't touch— unclean jobs like sweeping streets and scrubbing toilets. Some untouchables work only at night, when no one can see them. That way, upper-caste Hindus don't even have to look at them!

The oldest Hindu holy book is a set of hymns called the **Rig Veda**. The Rig Veda is written in **Sanskrit**, the language of ancient India. *Rig* is Sanskrit for "praise," and *veda* is Sanskrit for "knowledge." So the Rig Veda is a set of praise hymns filled with knowledge about the Hindu world and its gods.

But the Rig Veda is only one of many Hindu holy books. There are different kinds of Hinduism, each with its own favorite scriptures.

Hinduism is a religion of **cycles**— chains of events that repeat themselves over and over again. One well-known cycle is acted out by three Hindu gods. First **Brahma**, the creator god, creates a world. Then **Vishnu**, the preserver god, preserves that world for a time. Then **Shiva**, the destroyer god, destroys that world so that Brahma can create a new one. The three gods Brahma, Vishnu and Shiva make up the **Hindu trinity**. But these are only three of many Hindu gods.

From left to right: Brahma the creator, Shiva the destroyer and Vishnu the preserver

Another example of a Hindu cycle is **reincarnation**, also called *samsara*. Hindus believe that every soul has always been alive, and always will be. When people die, their souls are reborn into new bodies.

Reincarnation is the only way most Hindus can ever rise above the lower castes. If a Hindu does well in this life, then he may move up to a higher caste in the next.

The path to the higher castes lies through good **karma**. Basically, karma is the sum total of the good and bad deeds a Hindu does in life. If the good outweigh the bad, then a Hindu may be reborn into a higher caste.

Besides good deeds, a Hindu may also build good karma through rituals— things like meditation, prayer, worshiping in temples and washing in the Ganges River.

But the highest goal of a Hindu is not to step up to a higher caste. Instead, Hindus work to rise above all castes! The highest goal of Hinduism is to step out of the endless cycle of life, death and reincarnation.

Hindus who reach this goal have reached **nirvana**, also called *moksha*. The Hindu nirvana is a state of perfect peace and rest.

〰〰〰〰〰〰〰〰〰〰〰〰〰〰〰〰〰〰〰〰〰〰〰〰〰〰〰

Nirvana is also the goal of India's second oldest religion: Jainism. But the Jain nirvana is different than the Hindu nirvana. Instead of breaking free from the cycle of life, Jains work to break free from the material world.

Jainism

To Jains, the love of material possessions is the root of all evil. Materialism leads to greed, which leads to theft, violence and many other sins.

To avoid those sins, all Jains live by five strict vows called *mahavrata*. One of these vows is that they will never grow attached to material possessions.

In keeping with this vow, Jains do what Christian monks like Anthony of Thebes did: they become **ascetics**. In other words, Jains own very little, eat very little and sleep very little.

Jains are also strict vegetarians. Why? Because eating meat means killing animals; and Jains vow never to kill.

〰〰〰〰〰〰〰〰〰〰〰〰〰〰〰〰〰〰〰〰〰〰〰〰〰〰〰〰〰〰〰〰〰

One well-known Indian tried the Jain way, but then decided against it. This was **Siddhartha Gautama**, who is also called the Buddha.

Siddhartha's father was a rich king who wanted nothing but the best for his son. He didn't want his precious prince to be troubled by the hard things other people faced— things like suffering, sickness, old age and death. So he built three fine palaces for Siddhartha, and never let him go anywhere else! As long as Siddhartha was a boy, he never saw anyone suffering. He had no idea that most people weren't as fortunate as he was.

The board game "Chutes and Ladders" is based on a very old Indian game called **Snakes and Ladders**.

The Snakes and Ladders game board teaches lessons about Hinduism. The top of the board represents **nirvana**— the state of perfect peace and rest which all Hindus hope to reach someday. The ladders represent good karma, which carries Hindus upward. And the snakes represent bad karma, which carries Hindus downward.

Remember what an **ascetic** is: someone who denies himself material things so that he can focus on spiritual things.

All of that changed when Siddhartha became a man, and took his first trip outside his palaces. The suffering he saw outside horrified him! From that day forward, Siddhartha's goal in life was to find some answer to the terrible problem of suffering.

At first, Siddhartha tried the same answers that other people had already tried. Like the Hindus, Siddhartha tried meditating and doing good deeds— trying to build good

Buddhism

karma. And like the Jains, Siddhartha became an ascetic. He cast off the riches of his princely boyhood, and made himself poor. At times, Siddhartha ate so little that he almost died!

In the end, Siddhartha decided that neither Hinduism nor Jainism could answer his deepest questions. So he sat down under a tree to meditate, vowing never to rise until he finally found the answers he needed.

After meditating for 49 days, Siddhartha had an inspiration. The answer, he thought, was not to be always working toward a higher caste, the way Hindus did. Nor was the answer to deny oneself everything, the way Jains did. Instead, the answer was a middle way between these two extremes.

With this discovery, Siddhartha Gautama became the first **Buddha**. He was the first "enlightened one," the holy man who discovered the answer to the problem of suffering.

Part of the answer Siddhartha found lies in his **Four Noble Truths**:

➢ **Noble Truth #1:** Life is suffering.

➢ **Noble Truth #2:** Suffering starts with the desire for worldly pleasures.

➢ **Noble Truth #3:** To stop suffering, one must free oneself from desire.

➢ **Noble Truth #4:** The Noble Eightfold Path laid out by the Buddha leads to the end of desire, and therefore the end of suffering.

Siddhartha Gautama deep in meditation

> **Buddha** means "enlightened one." Buddhists believe that if they follow the Noble Eightfold Path laid out by Siddhartha Gautama, then they can become enlightened buddhas just like him.
>
> Basically, the Noble Eightfold Path teaches good attitudes, good thoughts and good morals. The eight steps along the path are: right view; right intention; right speech; right action; right livelihood; right effort; right mindfulness; and right concentration.

Empires of Ancient and Medieval India

For most of its history, India was divided into many kingdoms. Only a few empires ever ruled more than a small part of all that is now India.

The first Indian empires all started in the north. The oldest was the **Harappan** civilization, which grew up in the Indus River Valley (Year One). The Harappans kept growing until around 1750 BC, when they mysteriously disappeared!

The next great Indian empire came more than 2,000 years after the Harappans. Around 350 BC, a Hindu called **Mahapadma Nanda** built the **Nanda Empire**. The Nandas stretched across northern India, from the Ganges River Valley in the east almost to the Indus River Valley in the west.

The Nanda Empire lasted until 321 BC, when it was conquered by the **Maurya Empire**. The Mauryas were the first to bring northern and southern India together under the same crown.

But the Maurya emperors had a problem. To build an empire as big as theirs, they had to fight horrible wars that killed countless innocent people. Some emperors couldn't help but feel guilty over all this killing.

The first great Maurya emperor was **Chandragupta**. Like most Indians, Chandragupta started out Hindu. But the Hindu faith didn't soothe the emperor's guilt. So instead, Chandragupta converted to Jainism. After ruling one of the richest empires in the world, he now owned almost nothing!

Chandragupta took the five vows of Jainism so seriously that he wound up starving himself to death.

Emperor **Asoka**, grandson to Chandragupta, felt just as guilty. But Asoka followed a different path. After fighting a bloody war of his own, Asoka converted to peaceful Buddhism. For the rest of his life, Asoka worked hard to spread Buddhism all over India— and even beyond India, into Southeast Asia, China and Japan.

Buddhist missionaries setting up a lion-topped Pillar of Asoka. Asoka set up special pillars like this all over India to help spread the Buddhist faith.

ꡪꡪꡪꡪꡪꡪꡪꡪꡪꡪꡪꡪꡪꡪꡪꡪꡪꡪꡪꡪꡪꡪꡪꡪꡪ

Hundreds of years passed before the next empire arose. The Gupta Empire was the first Indian empire that lasted into medieval times.

The Gupta **maharajas** reigned over a **Golden Age of India**. The Gupta age was a time of peace and prosperity when the Indian people could finally stop thinking of war, and start thinking of better things.

Maharaja is Sanskrit for "great king."

One of those things was art. The **Ajanta Caves** (below) are only one example of the great Indian art crafted in the Golden Age of the Gupta Empire.

The Guptas were also the first great scientists and mathematicians to come from India. Unlike Greek scientists, Gupta scientists understood that the earth revolved around the sun, and not the other way around! The Guptas also created the **Hindu-Arabic numeral system**: 0, 1, 2, 3, 4, 5, 6, 7, 8 and 9. If you don't think these numerals are handy, then just try multiplying Roman numerals!

If the Gupta Empire had survived, then who knows what other discoveries its scientists might have made? Unfortunately, the Guptas faced a terrible enemy: the **Huns**, deadly raiders from the East (Chapter 6).

Just as the Huns threatened the Romans, so too the Huns threatened the Guptas. Although the Huns never conquered the Gupta Empire, they weakened it so badly so that it finally collapsed. With the fall of the last Gupta maharaja, India splintered into pieces again.

COIN FROM THE GUPTA EMPIRE

The Gupta Empire
(320 - 550)

The Ajanta Caves

The Ajanta Caves cut into their mountainside

The Buddha and his bodhisattvas. A bodhisattva is a Buddha in one of his earlier lives, before he achieved enlightenment.

The Ajanta Caves are a set of 29 manmade caves cut into a mountainside in west central India. Buddhist monks spent centuries carving out the Ajanta Caves, probably between about 200 and 600 AD.

The artwork in the Ajanta Caves is stunning. Some of their walls and ceilings are carved into giant statues of the Buddha. Others are painted with murals which tell stories from the Buddha's life. The amount of time and care needed to craft 29 such beautiful caves is almost unimaginable!

Despite all this stunning art, the Ajanta Caves stood empty for hundreds of years. Over the centuries, Buddhism slowly faded out of India, forcing the monks to find new homes elsewhere. Without monks to care for the caves, the jungle grew up around them, and they were forgotten.

It was not until 1819 that a British army officer rediscovered the Ajanta Caves. At the time, the British East India Company ruled India, and the officer happened to be hunting for tigers.

The next Indian empire was neither Hindu, Jain nor Buddhist. Instead, it was Muslim! Even though there were far more Hindu Indians than Muslim ones, Muslims ruled India for more than 650 years— all the way from 1206 through 1857.

Islam spread into India from the west, through Afghanistan and Persia (Iran). The first Muslim rulers of India came from Turkestan, the ancient home of the Turkish people. As we read in Chapter 12, the Turks converted to Islam in the 900s.

Just as Turkish Muslims conquered Asia Minor to the west, so they conquered India to the east! The Turkish sultans of India made their capital at **Delhi**, a city in central India. This is why historians call their empire the Delhi Sultanate.

But India was not like Turkestan, Persia or Afghanistan. In those countries, almost everyone converted to Islam, forgetting all about his old religion. But the Hindu religion was so important to so many Indians that it could never be forgotten. Even after Muslim invaders took over their country, most Indians refused to convert to Islam. They wanted to stay Hindu, no matter what it cost them.

The Delhi Sultanate
(1206 - 1526)

The strange situation of Muslim sultans ruling a Hindu people led to no end of trouble.

As a good Muslim, the Sultan of India was supposed to stamp out all other religions. But he couldn't stamp out Hinduism. For every time he tore down a Hindu temple, Hindus rebelled.

On the other hand, Muslims rebelled if the sultan didn't tear down Hindu temples. So he was in trouble either way.

But the sultan's worst troubles came from outside India. The Delhi Sultanate faced two kinds of invaders, both of them deadly.

The first kind was the **Mongols**. In the early 1200s, **Genghis Khan** of Mongolia set out to conquer the whole world— and almost succeeded! The Mongols threatened India many times, but never quite conquered it. See Chapter 19 for more on Genghis Khan and the Mongol Empire.

The second kind of invader was other Muslims. The worst of these was a fearsome fellow called Tamerlane. This deadly menace came from **Samarkand**, a city in what is now Uzbekistan.

Actually, Tamerlane was both Muslim and Mongol. For Tamerlane was a descendant of Genghis Khan.

Tamerlane's two heritages gave him two great reasons to conquer the world. As the heir to Genghis Khan, Tamerlane wanted to rebuild the Mongol Empire. And as a good Muslim, Tamerlane wanted to stamp out all other religions.

Tamerlane, a.k.a. Timur

This second reason was why Tamerlane marched on Delhi, India in 1398. Since the Delhi Sultanate was already Muslim, India didn't really need another Muslim conqueror. But Tamerlane said that the Delhi Sultanate couldn't really be Muslim— for if it was, then why were most Indians still Hindu?

War elephants at the Battle of Delhi

What happened at Delhi helps explain why Tamerlane is remembered as one of the cruelest villains who ever lived.

On his way to Delhi, Tamerlane crushed several small armies that tried to stop him. By the time he reached the city, he had taken about 100,000 Hindu prisoners.

Ordinarily, Tamerlane would have sold these prisoners into slavery. But with a big battle ahead of him, Tamerlane wanted to make sure that his prisoners couldn't break free and join the other side. So on the night before the **Battle of Delhi**, Tamerlane ordered his troops to kill their prisoners— all 100,000 of them!

After that, the key to the Battle of Delhi was war elephants. As the battle began, the Sultan of Delhi sent 120 armored war elephants charging against Tamerlane. What a fearsome sight that must have made!

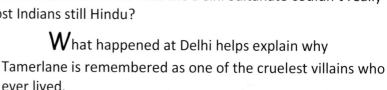

The Battle of Delhi (December 17, 1398)

But Tamerlane also knew how to create fear. Against the sultan's elephants, Tamerlane sent a line of charging camels, their backs piled high with burning wood and straw. The frightened elephants scampered away, leaving Tamerlane to win the Battle of Delhi.

What happened next proved why Tamerlane really invaded India: not because he loved Islam, but because he loved money. After the Battle of Delhi, Tamerlane and his troops carried off a fortune in gems, gold, silver and slaves!

The Battle of Delhi might have meant the end of the Delhi Sultanate, if not for what came next.

Before Tamerlane left, he assigned a Muslim governor to manage India for him. Six years later, Tamerlane died on his way to conquer China. Maybe the governor of India shed a few tears for Tamerlane, but probably not. Either way, the governor took over India— becoming the next sultan of the Delhi Sultanate.

ฌฌฌฌฌฌฌฌฌฌฌฌฌฌฌฌฌฌฌฌฌฌฌฌฌฌฌฌฌฌฌฌฌ

The real end of the Delhi Sultanate came with the next Muslim conqueror: **Babur**. Babur founded the richest Indian empire in history, the **Moghul Empire**.

The word "Moghul" was another version of "Mongol." For Babur was another descendant of Genghis Khan, just like Tamerlane. In fact, Babur was a great-great-great-grandson of Tamerlane.

Just as Tamerlane tried to rebuild the empire of Genghis Khan, so Babur tried to rebuild the empire of Tamerlane. Babur started out fighting for the capital of Tamerlane's empire, Samarkand. When he couldn't take that, Babur tried another of Tamerlane's old haunts: India.

The end of the Delhi Sultanate came at the **First Battle of Panipat**, fought in April 1526. Panipat was a village about 60 miles north of Delhi.

The last Sultan of Delhi brought tens of thousands of troops to tackle Babur at Panipat. He also brought at least 100 war elephants.

As for Babur, he brought far fewer troops, and few if any war elephants. But Babur brought one advantage that the sultan couldn't match: **gunpowder**. Babur was the first general in India to use muskets and cannon in battle.

Imagine how you would feel facing cannon for the first time! The poor sultan and his war elephants never had a chance.

Matchlock Muskets

The **matchlock musket** was an early type of musket that first appeared around 1440.

To use a matchlock, the musketeer first loaded his barrel with gunpowder and ball. He then poured a bit of gunpowder into the **flash pan**. This was a small pan attached to the outside of the barrel. A small hole called a **touchhole** connected the flash pan to the inside of the barrel.

The matchlock's spark came from a slow-burning fuse called **slow match**. A length of slow match was attached to the **lock,** or firing mechanism. To fire, the musketeer simply turned the burning slow match so that it lit the powder in the flash pan. If all went well, then the fire in the flash pan spread through the touchhole to the powder in the barrel— and then boom!

Matchlocks suffered from two big problems. One was that the fire in the slow match was always going out, especially in wind and rain. Later, better firing mechanisms like the snaphance and the flintlock helped solve this problem.

Another problem with matchlocks was that the fire in the flash pan didn't always spread to the barrel. This kind of misfire was called a **flash in the pan**.

A matchlock mechanism with slow match

War elephants and horses terrified by Babur's cannon at the First Battle of Panipat

Babur's grandson was called **Akbar**, which means "the Great." It was the great Emperor Akbar who finally found the answer to the sticky question India still faced: how could a Muslim emperor rule a Hindu people without getting into trouble?

Like Babur before him, Akbar started as a strict Muslim who hated all other religions. But as Akbar grew older, a problem forced him to open his mind.

Akbar's problem was that he had no sons. As of 1570, fifteen years into his reign, Akbar still had no heir to carry on his dynasty. If Akbar couldn't come up with an heir before he died, then the great Moghul Empire would fall.

In need of a miracle, Akbar turned to a man with a reputation as a miracle worker: a Muslim holy man called **Salim Chisti**.

When Akbar shared his problem with Salim Chisti, the holy man blessed Akbar, promising that he would soon have a son. Not long after, Akbar's wives gave him not one son, but three!

To Akbar, this was proof enough that Salim Chisti really was a miracle worker. From then on, Emperor Akbar was a devoted follower of Salim Chisti.

Emperor Akbar

What makes all this so important is that Salim Chisti was no average Muslim. Instead, Salim was a **Sufi**— part of a strange Muslim sect that studied visions and dreams. The Sufis were less strict than other Muslims, and much friendlier to people from other faiths.

In following a Sufi leader, Akbar learned to be friendly to Hindus. Instead of tearing down Hindu temples, as Babur had done, Akbar left Hindus alone.

Naturally, Hindus were happy to have an emperor who didn't tear down their temples. Without all the trouble between Hindus and Muslims, India thrived. The Moghul Empire built by Akbar and his heirs was one of the biggest, richest empires the world has ever seen!

The mark of Akbar's open-minded faith was a special house of worship called the **Ibadat Khana**. This was a place where holy men from all faiths could come together and share their beliefs.

Of course, Akbar invited all kinds of Muslims to the Ibadat Khana. But he also invited Hindus, Jains and Buddhists. He even invited the Catholic priests who were starting to sail in from Portugal (Chapter 24). Akbar listened carefully to what each holy man had to say, honoring them all.

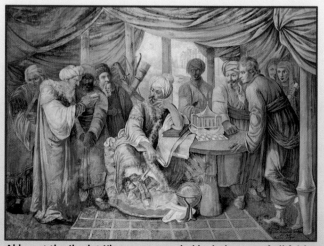

Akbar at the Ibadat Khana, surrounded by holy men of all faiths

CHAPTER 17: China

The Land of Qin and Han

China is one of the biggest countries in the world. In modern times, only two countries on Earth have more land than China: Russia and Canada. And no country has more people than China!

On a map of Asia, the outline of China looks something like a rooster. The big bird's head, beak and crest lie to the northeast, in a part of China called Manchuria. The tail lies to the west, and the belly to the southeast. And the feet are two big islands: one called **Hainan**, and the other **Taiwan**.

Actually, Taiwan has been separate from China since 1949. But the Chinese government would very much like to have Taiwan back!

One way to remember the geography of China is to think of an enormous ramp. The high ground all lies in the west. The low ground all lies in the east, along the coast. And in between, rivers carry torrents of rainwater from high ground to low.

The high ground of western China is the highest in the world. Part of this high ground is the **Himalayas**, which stand along the border with India and Nepal (Chapter 16). Another part is the **Tibetan Plateau**, which stands just north of the Himalayas. The Tibetan Plateau averages almost 15,000 feet above sea level. This is nearly three miles high! This fantastic height explains why people call Tibet the "Roof of the World."

The low ground of eastern China lies along four big seas. The northernmost is the **Bohai Sea**, which lies between China and North Korea. The next sea southward is the **Yellow Sea**, which lies between China and South Korea. Next comes the **East China Sea**, followed by the **South China Sea**. Beyond these four seas lies the Pacific Ocean.

Central China is a land of rushing rivers. Most of China's smaller rivers flow into one of three main river systems: the **Yellow River** in the north, the **Yangtze River** in the middle and the **Pearl River** in the south.

The capital of China is **Beijing**.

A scene from the beautiful Three Gorges region of the Yangtze River Valley

The biggest desert in Asia is the **Gobi Desert**, which lies in northern China and southern Mongolia. The Gobi is a high, cold desert that is mostly covered with rock, not sand.

Dynasties of Ancient China

The history of China reads like a list of dynasties. Over the centuries, China has seen many dynasties rise and fall. Most of these dynasties ruled only part of what is now China— starting with the Yellow River Valley in the north.

WORLD HISTORY

The oldest known Chinese dynasty was the Xia dynasty. **Yu the Great** founded the Xia around 2200 BC.

The Xia Dynasty (about 2200 - 1750 BC)

King Yu is best remembered for his huge water projects. Before Yu, farmers who lived along the Yellow River never knew when a flood might wash away their crops, or when a drought might stunt their crops. With a bit of engineering genius, and a lot of hard work, Yu solved both of these problems. Yu built great dams to control flooding in wet years, and dug great canals to spread water around in dry years.

The third known dynasty was the Zhou dynasty. The Zhou emperors were both strong and weak. On the one hand, the Zhou dynasty reigned for a long time— more than 800 years! On the other hand, the Zhou emperors were weaker than the ones before them.

The weakness of the Zhou emperors led to deadly trouble.

The Zhou Dynasty (about 1100 - 250 BC)

Since the days of King Yu, China had been divided into nine provinces. Without strong emperors to keep them loyal, the leaders of the nine provinces fought among themselves, each hoping to take over the empire. For hundreds of years, peace was nowhere to be found, only war.

The chaos of this terrible time called for new ways of thinking. This explains why two of China's best-known **philosophies**— Confucianism and Taoism— come from Zhou dynasty times.

Confucius was a wise old teacher who lived around 500 BC. To Confucius, the wars of the Zhou dynasty era were a **moral problem**. The leaders of the nine provinces seemed to care only for themselves, and not at all for the poor people who were hurt by their wars. In other words, the leaders lacked good morals.

Confucianism

Confucius

So when Confucius thought about philosophy, he focused on good morals— virtues like honor, decency and caring for others.

➢ One Confucian virtue was *Li*, Chinese for "etiquette" or "good manners." Good Confucians were always humble and respectful toward others, never pushing themselves forward when they shouldn't.

A **philosophy** is a certain way of thinking about life and the world. A **moral problem** is a question about right and wrong.

- Another Confucian virtue was *Xiao*, Chinese for "filial piety." "Piety" means "religion," and "filial" means "of a son." Good Confucians were religious about showing the proper respect for their parents and ancestors. They cared deeply about family honor.

- Above all other virtues, Confucius honored *Ren*— Chinese for "human kindness." The great philosopher wanted everyone to feel true concern for his fellow man. Good Confucians demanded justice for everyone, not just for themselves.

Any man who worked hard at these virtues could become what Confucius called a *junzi*— Chinese for "perfect gentleman."

The great moral teacher Confucius actually taught his own version of the **Golden Rule**— 500 years before Jesus Christ! However, the Confucian Golden Rule is different from the Christian one. Christ said:

"…do to others what you would have them do to you…" (Matthew 7:12).

Confucius, on the other hand, said:

"Don't do to others what you wouldn't want them to do to you."

The difference is that Christ taught Christians to do good deeds; while Confucius taught his followers not to do bad deeds.

Taoism was the teaching of **Lao-Tzu**, another great philosopher from Zhou dynasty times. If you know "Star Wars," then you already know something about Taoism. Jedi philosophy comes straight from Lao-Tzu— with a few changes for dramatic effect!

According to Lao-Tzu, the **Tao** is a force which flows from all things that live, or have ever been alive. This force is not a god. However, it does have a will like a god's. To get along, one must learn to go along with the will of the Tao. Good Taoists take life as it comes, rather than struggling against the will of the Tao.

Taoism

Sculpture of Lao-tzu

The Tao has two sides: a dark side called **yin**, and light side called **yang**. But the dark yin is not bad; nor is the light yang good. Instead, they are two opposite sides of the same whole. There can never be yang without yin. For example, there can never be light without darkness— for without darkness, there would be no need for light.

A *taijitu*, the common symbol for yin and yang

To stay healthy, the Taoist must maintain balance between yang and yin. Among other things, this means living in harmony with others; living in harmony with nature; and eating healthy foods.

〰〰〰〰〰〰〰〰〰〰〰〰〰〰〰〰〰〰〰〰〰〰〰〰〰〰〰〰〰〰〰〰〰〰〰〰〰〰〰

The next two Chinese dynasties are important to remember; for both did important things.

First came the **Qin dynasty**, which took its name from the **Qin province**. Qin was a huge province in western China, far bigger than most other provinces. As the Zhou dynasty grew weaker, the Qin province conquered more and more of the smaller provinces. Finally, all of China belonged to a cruel Qin emperor called **Shi Huangdi**.

The Qin Dynasty
(221 - 206 BC)

One of Shi Huangdi's big accomplishments was to combine the separate provinces of China into a single country.

Since the Zhou emperors had been weak, most Chinese had ignored them. They thought of themselves as citizens of their provinces, not citizens of an empire. But Shi Huangdi would have none of that! He wanted everyone, everywhere to be loyal to him alone. So he forbade the Chinese to speak the names of their old provinces. From now on, all were citizens of the great Qin Empire.

This is probably how China got its name. The word "China" probably comes from the word "Qin."

Emperor Qin Shi Huangdi

Shi Huangdi was also famous for big building projects— including his biggest, the **Great Wall of China**.

The northern border of China was too long for any army to defend all at once. Whenever the army wasn't looking, raiders from the north would sweep down and steal everything in sight. This is why Shi Huangdi built the first sections of the Great Wall: to defend China against raiders from the north.

Over the centuries, other emperors finished what Shi Huangdi had started. By the 1300s, the Great Wall of China was an unbroken barrier more than 5,000 miles long!

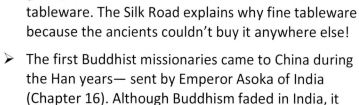

An older section of the Great Wall of China

The years of China's next dynasty, the **Han dynasty**, were years of tremendous change.

➤ The Han years saw the opening of the famous **Silk Road**. Han traders gave the West its first taste of Chinese luxuries like silk and fine tableware. The Silk Road explains why fine tableware is called "china": because the ancients couldn't buy it anywhere else!

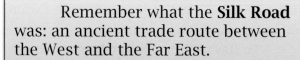

The Han Dynasty (206 BC - 220 AD)

➤ The first Buddhist missionaries came to China during the Han years— sent by Emperor Asoka of India (Chapter 16). Although Buddhism faded in India, it thrived in China.

➤ Han scientists invented two of China's **Four Great Inventions**: the **magnetic compass** and **paper**.

If the Qin dynasty gave China its name, then the Han dynasty gave China's largest race its name. Even today, most Chinese consider themselves members of an ancient race called **Han Chinese**.

Remember what the **Silk Road** was: an ancient trade route between the West and the Far East.

Medieval Dynasties of China

After everything the Qin and Han had done to pull China together, the empire fell apart again. For three hundred years after the last Han emperor fell, different dynasties ruled different parts of China; but no one ruled all of China.

The man who finally pulled China together again was **Yang Jian**, also called **Emperor Wen of Sui**. Yang Jian founded the Sui dynasty, the first great Chinese dynasty of medieval times.

The **Four Great Inventions** are four marvelous technologies that the Chinese developed before any other people on Earth. The first two, the **magnetic compass** and **paper**, come from the time of the Han dynasty. The second two, **gunpowder** and **woodblock printing**, come from the time of the Tang dynasty (below).

The Sui Dynasty (589 - 618)

One reason for Yang Jian's great success was his great marriage. Yang Jian married when he was just 16 years old, long before he came emperor. His wife **Dugu** was the daughter of the northern king whom Yang Jian served at the time. The king gave his daughter as a reward for Yang Jian's excellent service.

Replica of a Han Dynasty compass

Yang Jian was so pleased with the smart, beautiful Dugu that he made her a special promise. He swore that as long as Dugu lived, he would always stay faithful to her.

Yang Jian kept his promise. After he became emperor, Yang Jian could have had all the wives and mistresses he wanted. Instead, he stayed faithful to Dugu. He taught his second son **Yang Guang** the same thing: to honor women and stay faithful to his wife always.

But Yang Guang didn't listen.

After Empress Dugu died, the old Yang Jian took a young mistress. What Yang Jian didn't know was that Yang Guang wanted that mistress for himself. Despite being trained from birth to honor women, Yang Guang actually tried to steal a woman who belonged to his father!

When the mistress told Yang Jian what had happened, the old emperor was furious. So he sent men to arrest his son. But Yang Guang was ready and waiting. When the emperor's men arrived, Yang Guang's men turned the tables on them.

After that, it is said, Yang Guang committed the worst crime a Chinese son could ever commit. He sent one of his servants to smother his old father to death!

And that isn't all. Yang Guang also murdered his older brother, along with all eight of his brother's sons. That way, none of them could ever stand between him and his father's throne.

The strange thing about all this is that the Chinese cared more about family than any other people. Yet somehow, a man who murdered his own father became the second emperor of the Sui dynasty!

Yang Guang, a.k.a. Emperor Yang of Sui

Chinese Vase

Besides caring nothing for his family, Yang Guang also cared nothing for the Chinese people. The cruel new emperor spent countless lives on his biggest building project, the **Grand Canal of China**.

The **Grand Canal of China** is the longest manmade waterway in the world. The modern-day Grand Canal stretches nearly 1,200 miles, starting at Beijing in the north and ending at Hangzhou in the south.

The two biggest rivers in China are the Yellow and the Yangtze; and they both flow mainly from west to east. The valleys around these two rivers were naturally separate, with no good waterways connecting the two.

As long as these separate valleys belonged to separate kingdoms, this wasn't a problem. But when the Sui dynasty brought both valleys together under one empire, it needed a waterway to connect the two. As always, waterways were the best ways to carry heavy loads from place to place.

Since nature hadn't given them a north-south waterway, the Sui emperors decided to build their own! The result was the longest manmade waterway in the world: the Grand Canal.

The amount of work that went into the Grand Canal is almost beyond belief. Both Sui emperors drove their people mercilessly. By law, every able-bodied man had to spend several months working on the huge project. Millions of Chinese came to do their part. Some dug the mountains of earth and rock that had to be moved. Others cut timber or sawed lumber for the many **locks** that had to be built. Still others built bridges over the canal, or roads alongside it.

A **lock** is a set of water gates, pumps and valves that canal operators use to raise and lower ships.

All of this without bulldozers, dump trucks or any other modern-day power tools! The closest thing the medieval world had to a dump truck was an ox-drawn cart.

A scene from the Grand Canal of China in the 1800s

The pressure of finishing all this work claimed many, many lives. Of the 5 or 6 million Chinese who worked to build the Grand Canal, as many as 2 or 3 million died! They died of overwork; or they died of diseases that spread in overcrowded work camps; or they died in cave-ins and drowning accidents. The Grand Canal was a great success for Yang Guang, but a tragedy for the people who built it.

The other tragedy of Yang Guang's reign was the **Goguryeo Wars**.

Goguryeo was a medieval kingdom in what is now North Korea. Both Yang Jian and Yang Guang wanted desperately to conquer Goguryeo. Both sent huge armies against it— sometimes more than 1,000,000 troops at once. But they never conquered Goguryeo, even though countless Chinese died trying.

On the Chinese side, the worst disaster of the Goguryeo Wars was the **Battle of Salsu**. One day in 612, the general in charge of Yang Guang's army sent about 300,000 troops wading across the **Salsu River**. At first, the water was quite shallow. But when the Chinese were about halfway across, the water started rising— first

The **Salsu River** is now called the **Chongchon**. It flows near what is now Pyongyang, North Korea.

The ***Ballad of Mulan*** is an ancient poem that tells one of China's most beloved stories. Fa Mulan is a young Chinese woman who disguises herself as a man so that she can take her father's place in the army— for her father is too old and sick to serve.

If Fa Mulan ever really lived, then she might have lived in Sui dynasty times.

over their waists, then over their heads. At just the right moment, their enemies had opened a dam upriver, sending down a flood to wash away the Chinese. Only about 3,000 troops survived— less than 1 man in 100.

Between the Grand Canal and the Goguryeo Wars, the Chinese finally had enough. The reign of Yang Guang ended in chaos, with rebellions all over China.

One day in 618, Yang Guang's generals decided that the time had come for their emperor to die. But they didn't want to kill him themselves. So instead, they asked him to commit suicide.

Yang Guang would have liked to take a painless poison, but couldn't find any on such short notice. So in the end, he took off his scarf and handed it to a soldier, who used it to strangle him to death.

〰〰〰〰〰〰〰〰〰〰〰〰〰〰〰〰〰〰〰〰〰〰〰〰〰〰〰〰〰〰〰〰〰〰〰〰〰

China thrived under its next great dynasty, the Tang dynasty. The Tang years were a **Golden Age of China**— a time of peace, wealth and discovery. While the Europeans were still muddling through their Dark Ages, the Chinese were making great breakthroughs. Two of these breakthroughs were the last two of the Four Great Inventions: **gunpowder** and **woodblock printing**.

The Tang Dynasty (618 - 907)

Gunpowder is a mixture of three chemicals: charcoal, sulfur and potassium nitrate. The potassium nitrate serves as an **oxidizer,** a source of oxygen. All fires need plenty of oxygen if they are to burn quickly. The chemical formula for potassium nitrate is KNO_3— which means that every molecule of potassium nitrate provides three oxygen atoms to burn.

The Chinese thinkers who discovered gunpowder in the 800s were a special kind of scientists called **alchemists.** One of the breakthroughs alchemists sought was a way to turn cheap metals into precious gold. Alchemists also sought the **Elixir of Life**— a potion which would give eternal life and youth to anyone who drank it.

Woodblock printing is the art of carving a design into a block of wood, and then using that block to print many copies of the same page. Printers who knew this art could copy books far faster than any scribe could copy them by hand!

The other benefit of woodblock printing was that every copy was exactly the same, with none of the mistakes a scribe might make— unless the carver of the woodblock made a mistake.

Besides these great discoveries, the most fascinating fact about the Tang dynasty is that one of its emperors was a woman!

Although Empress Wu Zetian was not the only powerful woman in Chinese history, she was the only **Empress Regnant**. This means that she was the only woman ever to rule China on her own, without a husband or son standing over her.

But all of that came later. At first, Wu Zetian was only a **concubine**. In other words, she was a lower-level wife to an emperor. The Tang emperors had many wives, but only one of them was empress. The rest were all concubines like Wu Zetian. Her first husband was **Li Shimin**, the second emperor of the Tang dynasty.

Unfortunately, Wu Zetian married her emperor too late. He died not long after the wedding, leaving her a widow at age 25.

At this point, it seemed that Wu Zetian didn't have much to look forward to. She was forbidden to remarry. For in Chinese eyes, to marry another man would be to dishonor her emperor husband. Instead, she was locked in a Buddhist monastery, where monks watched over her day and night. The monks even shaved her head, to keep men from noticing her.

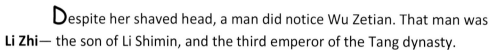

Li Shimin, a.k.a.
Emperor Taizong of Tang

Despite her shaved head, a man did notice Wu Zetian. That man was **Li Zhi**— the son of Li Shimin, and the third emperor of the Tang dynasty.

Actually, Li Zhi had noticed Wu Zetian years before, when she was still his father's concubine. And why wouldn't he notice a woman as beautiful and clever as Wu Zetian? For she was much closer to Li Zhi's age than she was to his father's. Now whenever Li Zhi visited the monastery, he admired Wu Zetian from afar.

Still, Wu Zetian might never have left the monastery— if it weren't for the schemes of Li Zhi's wives. At the time, Li Zhi had two favorite wives: **Empress Wang**, and a concubine called **Xiao**. But Empress Wang lived in constant fear. For Xiao had given Li Zhi children; while Empress Wang had not. Without children of her own, Empress Wang feared that Li Zhi might soon get rid of her, and make Xiao empress instead.

What Empress Wang needed, she thought, was some new woman to make Li Zhi forget about Xiao. And what better woman than the one Li Zhi had admired for years: Wu Zetian?

Thanks to Empress Wang's schemes, Wu Zetian didn't have to spend the rest of her life in a monastery. Instead, she came to the palace as a new concubine for Li Zhi.

Empress Wang didn't know it yet, but she had just made the biggest mistake of her life. Wu Zetian would turn out to be a far worse problem for the empress than Xiao had been.

Right away, Wu Zetian started doing what Empress Wang could not: giving Li Zhi children. Every year brought a new child— first a son, then a second son, then a daughter. With every child, Empress Wang grew a little more jealous of Wu Zetian.

Then tragedy struck. After getting along fine for some time, Wu Zetian's daughter suddenly died. No one had any idea why— until a servant stepped forward, claiming that he had seen Empress Wang coming out of the baby's room!

On the one hand, no one had actually seen Empress Wang hurt the baby. On the other hand, everyone knew that Empress Wang was terribly jealous of Wu Zetian. Putting two and two together, most people decided that Empress Wang must have smothered the poor girl in a fit of jealousy.

Empress Wu Zetian

That was the beginning of the end for Empress Wang. The year after her daughter died, Wu Zetian became **Empress Wu**. The year after that, Empress Wu's oldest son became the official heir to the throne. Later, Empress Wu had both Wang and Xiao put to death!

For most of the next 30 years, Empress Wu took part in every decision her husband made. Whenever Li Zhi sat on his throne, the empress sat right behind him, whispering advice in his ear. But she always sat behind a veil. That way, no one would know that the Emperor of China depended on a woman's advice!

Of course, a few people knew who sat behind that veil. But they didn't criticize; for Empress Wu was a fierce enemy. Anyone who dared to criticize her either disappeared or died.

When Li Zhi died, Empress Wu should have gone into retirement. Instead, she went right on ruling China— but still from behind the veil. Since the next emperor was her son, he usually obeyed his mother. When he stopped obeying, she simply set him aside, and made another son emperor instead.

After a few more years of pretending, Empress Wu finally stepped out from behind the veil. For 15 years, Empress Wu openly ruled China in her own name— the only woman ever to do so!

Medieval Chinese used dragons as symbols of power and authority. The emperor's seat was called the **Dragon Throne**. On flags and other emblems, a five-clawed dragon represented the emperor himself. Dragons with fewer claws represented noblemen.

The next great Chinese dynasty was the **Song dynasty**. Like the Tang, the Song are remembered for important inventions.

The Song Dynasty (960 – 1209)

Paper money from the Song Dynasty

➤ The Song government combined woodblock printing with economics to print the first **paper money**. Of course, the first counterfeiters tried to copy the first paper money the moment it was printed! So the government added complicated designs to its bills, making them almost impossible to copy.

➤ The Chinese printers of the Song era were the first to develop **movable type printing**. Instead of carving a separate woodblock for each new page, they molded ceramic type for each character, and then fastened the characters to an iron plate. Unlike woodblocks, ceramic type could be rearranged to print new pages, and reused again and again.

➤ The Chinese engineers of the Song era built the world's first **iron-cased gunpowder weapons**— including grenades, bombs and hand cannon. Earlier gun tubes had often been made of bamboo.

Like many emperors from the East, the first emperor of the Han dynasty thought of himself as the rightful ruler of the whole world. So when he decided to build a new capital, he wanted it to stand at the center of the world. When he asked his scientists where the center was, they measured out a certain spot in central China. This is where the Han built the city of **Chang'an**, which is now called **Xi'an**.

Centuries later, emperors of the Sui and Tang dynasties rebuilt the ancient Han capital. The new Chang'an was a planned city laid out in a perfect rectangle, 5 miles wide and 6 miles long. In the Golden Age of the Tang years, Chang'an was probably the grandest city on earth.

The Land of the Rising Sun

Japan is an island nation in the farthest part of the Far East. Unless one is going around the world, Japan is about as far east as one can go! This explains why Japan is called the "Land of the Rising Sun."

Like the British Isles, Japan is an **archipelago**. In all, the Japanese archipelago covers more than 4,000 islands. But most of Japan lies on just four main islands. From north to south, these four main islands are **Hokkaido**, **Honshu**, **Shikoku** and **Kyushu**. The largest of the four, **Honshu**, is the seventh largest island in the world. Honshu is just a bit larger than the island of Great Britain.

> An **archipelago** is a group of islands.

Four big seas separate Japan from its closest neighbors. To the north, between Japan and **Russia**, lies the **Sea of Okhotsk**. To the south, between Japan and the **Philippines**, lies the **Philippine Sea**. To the west lie two seas. One is the **Sea of Japan**, which lies between Japan and **Korea**. The other is the **East China Sea**, which lies between Japan and **China**.

Japan is a land of mountains, volcanos, earthquakes and hot springs. **Mount Fuji**, the tallest mountain in Japan, is an active volcano. Fuji stands on Honshu, about 60 miles southwest of **Tokyo**.

The capital of Japan is **Tokyo**.

Most Japanese don't call their home country "Japan." Instead, they call it "Nippon" or "Nihon."

The name "Japan" is a version of "Cipangu," the name Marco Polo learned on his famous trip to the Far East (Chapter 19). "Cipangu" probably meant "Kingdom of the Rising Sun."

The Heavenly Emperors of Japan

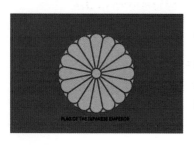

The history of Japan reads very differently than the history of China. Where China has had many dynasties over the centuries, Japan has had only one. This is the **Imperial Dynasty of Japan**, which is sometimes called the **Yamato dynasty**. If the history is true, then all Japanese emperors spring from the same ancestor: **Jimmu Tenno**, the first Emperor of Japan.

Who were Jimmu Tenno's ancestors? According to legend, only some of them were human. The rest were gods. If the legend is true, then the first Emperor of Japan was descended from **Amaterasu**, goddess of the sun!

Where did Amaterasu come from? According to legend, she sprang from a creator god called **Izanagi**. Amaterasu and Izanagi are just two of many gods whose stories are part of the oldest religion in Japan: Shinto.

The Shinto Creation Legend

According to the Shinto creation legend: In the beginning, everything was chaos. The lighter parts of that chaos rose up to form heaven, where the gods lived. But no one lived under heaven; for everything below was still chaos.

Finally, the older gods sent down a couple of younger gods to bring order to the chaos. The male god was **Izanagi**, and the female **Izanami**. To help the young couple, the elder gods gave them a special blade called a **naginata**.

Izanagi dipped this blessed blade into the chaos under heaven. When he pulled it back up, drops of matter clung to it. These drops fell back into the chaos, forming the first solid ground on Earth.

> A **naginata** is a Japanese weapon that is similar to a halberd. Both halberds and naginatas are long poles with sharp blades at one end.
>
> The naginata used by Izanagi was called **Amenonuhoko**.

Izanami and Izanagi bringing order from the chaos under heaven

A long time later, Izanami died in childbirth. The loss of his wife left Izanagi lonely and miserable. He never stopped searching for her— not even when her trail led to **Yomi**, the terrifying Shinto underworld.

The underworld was so pitch-dark that Izanagi couldn't see his wife's face. But he finally recognized her by the sound of her voice. At once, he pleaded with her to come home.

But Izanami said that her husband was too late. She had already eaten the food of the underworld, she said— which meant that she could never go back to the land of the living.

Izanagi wasn't convinced. So instead of leaving his wife behind, he decided to trick her. He waited until she fell asleep, and then struck a light to see how he might help her.

But when the light shone on her, he saw that her once-beautiful face was now riddled with decay. The sight horrified Izanagi! He now realized that his wife was trapped in the underworld forever— and that she meant to trap him there as well.

With a cry of dismay, Izanagi fled the underworld as fast as he could. His cry awakened Izanami, who was instantly furious at her husband's trick. Fortunately, Izanagi made it back to the gate of the underworld before his wife could catch up to him. Breathing a sigh of relief, Izanagi rolled a huge stone over the gate.

What happened next explains how death came into the Shinto world. Still furious with her husband, Izanami screamed out how she meant to destroy his world. Every day, she would drag 1,000 people down into the underworld with her! Izanagi screamed back how he would save his world: by creating 1,500 new people every day!

After his hard time in the underworld, Izanagi felt so filthy that he just had to wash. But even washing wasn't simple for someone as mighty as Izanagi. As he washed his face, three powerful new gods were born! The sun goddess **Amaterasu** sprang from Izanagi's left eye. The moon god **Tsukuyomi** sprang from Izanagi's right eye. And their brother **Susanoo**, god of seas and storms, sprang from Izanagi's nose.

Right away, Amaterasu and Susanoo started arguing. Just as storm clouds frustrate the sun, so the storm god frustrated the sun goddess.

After one bad argument with Susanoo, Amaterasu felt so angry and depressed that she hid herself in a cave. As Amaterasu sulked in her cave, refusing to come out, the sun disappeared from the sky.

The other gods were all anxious to bring back the sun. So they asked Uzume, goddess of laughter, to see what she could do.

The Mirror and the Jewel

Uzume started by hanging two tempting gifts outside Amaterasu's cave. One was a curved piece of **jade**, a lovely green jewel that is treasured in the Far East. The other was a brilliant **mirror** made of polished bronze.

With the jade and the mirror as bait, Uzume gathered the other gods outside the cave and started telling jokes. When they all howled with laughter, Amaterasu peered out of her cave to see what was so funny. Between the laughter of the gods and the beautiful gifts they had given her, Amaterasu cheered up enough to come out of her cave for good.

The brilliant Amaterasu coming out of her cave

Besides this sticky problem with Amaterasu, Susanoo also caused many other problems. In time, Izanagi grew so frustrated with his stormy son that he banished him to the underworld. But Susanoo took his time about getting there. After all, he had never been very obedient.

On his way to the underworld, Susanoo ran into the most terrifying monster imaginable: an 8-headed dragon big enough to swallow whole islands! Fortunately, Susanoo knew this dragon's weakness: it liked rice wine. So before the big fight, Susanoo prepared 8 huge casks of rice wine, one for each head. After the dragon got happily drunk, Susanoo leapt out and cut off all 8 heads!

Nor did Susanoo stop with the heads; for he knew that some serpents can regrow their heads. So he kept slicing at the dragon, trying to cut it into bits too small to regrow.

But one of the dragon's tails wouldn't cut. So Susanoo slit the tail open to see what was wrong— revealing a magnificent **sword** inside! This sword was no ordinary find. It was a treasure, a gift worthy of a god.

Susanoo put the sword to good use. Instead of going on to the underworld, Susanoo turned around and gave the sword to Amaterasu. After the mirror and the jewel, he knew all about her weakness for beautiful objects!

The Sword in the Dragon

Susanoo slaying the dragon

Amaterasu was so pleased with the gift of the sword that she forgave Susanoo. And when Amaterasu forgave him, Izanagi forgave him as well.

ꝰꝰꝰꝰꝰꝰꝰꝰꝰꝰꝰꝰꝰꝰꝰꝰꝰꝰꝰꝰꝰꝰꝰꝰꝰꝰꝰꝰꝰ

The three gifts from these last two legends play an important part in Japanese history. Together, these three precious possessions of Amaterasu— the **sword**, the **mirror** and the **jewel**— are called the **Three Sacred Treasures**.

An artist's vision of the Three Sacred Treasures

According to legend, Amaterasu handed down the Three Sacred Treasures to her grandson **Ninigi**. In turn, Ninigi handed them down to his own descendant: Jimmu Tenno, the first Emperor of Japan.

Since then, every emperor has handed down these family heirlooms to the next emperor. This line has never been broken. Even today, the Japanese still keep the Three Sacred Treasures at three separate Shinto shrines. Although Shinto priests may see one treasure at a time, only the Emperor of Japan may see all Three Sacred Treasures at the same time.

ꝰꝰꝰꝰꝰꝰꝰꝰꝰꝰꝰꝰꝰꝰꝰꝰꝰꝰꝰꝰꝰꝰꝰꝰꝰꝰꝰꝰꝰꝰ

If the emperors of Japan come from gods, then why do they die like ordinary mortals? The legend of Ninigi,

From Immortal to Mortal

grandson to Amaterasu, explains how the emperors lost the gift of immortality.

Soon after Ninigi came down to Earth, he met a lovely young flower goddess called **Sakuya**. Her stunning beauty reminded Ninigi of the chrysanthemum, a flower that is especially treasured in Japan. Ninigi wanted to marry Sakuya at once.

But Sakuya's father had other ideas. It so happened that Sakuya had a sister called **Iwanaga**, who also needed a husband. So when Ninigi asked to marry Sakuya, her father offered him Iwanaga as well.

The trouble was that Iwanaga was no beautiful flower goddess. Instead, she was a plain goddess of stone. Ninigi wanted nothing to do with such a plain goddess. So he refused Iwanaga, but still asked for Sakuya.

Only then did Sakuya's wise old father reveal what was really going on. Flowers, the father said, are beautiful only for a short time. Stone, on the other hand, is permanent. In choosing the short-lived beauty of the flower over the permanent beauty of stone, Ninigi had chosen a short life over a permanent one! Thanks to Ninigi's poor choice, all emperors of Japan lost their immortality— becoming mere mortals like everyone else.

〜〜〜〜〜〜〜〜〜〜〜〜〜〜〜〜〜〜〜〜〜〜〜〜〜〜〜〜〜〜〜〜

Legends like these are only part of Shinto beliefs. Another part is the Shinto belief in *kami*, or spirits.

The chrysanthemum from Ninigi's story is another important symbol of the Imperial Dynasty. The Imperial Seal of Japan is a yellow chrysanthemum. And the seat of Japan's emperors is called the **Chrysanthemum Throne.**

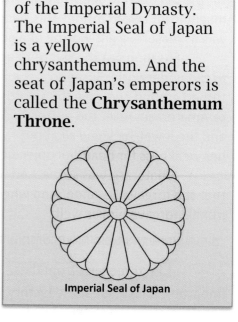
Imperial Seal of Japan

Shinto believers see *kami* in everything— not only living things like gods, people and animals, but also non-living things like mountains, rivers and wind. To approach these kami, Shinto believers worship at special gates called *torii*. Each torii marks a border between heaven and earth, holy and unholy.

One example of a torii, a Shinto symbol of the gateway between heaven and earth

Emperors, Clans and Samurai

The first civilization in Japan came long after the first one in China. In fact, the first people in Japan may have come from China— led by a Chinese magician called Xu Fu.

Xu Fu was a court magician to Shi Huangdi, first emperor of China's Qin dynasty (Chapter 17). Shi Huangdi was terribly worried about what might happen to him after he died. So he assigned his best magician, Xu Fu, to stop him from dying!

Twice, Xu Fu set out from China on long sea voyages, searching far and wide for the magic potion sought by all alchemists. This was the **Elixir of Life**, which bestowed eternal life and health upon all who drank it.

Of course, Xu Fu never found the Elixir of Life. The first time Xu Fu failed, Shi Huangdi sent him back out to search again. The second time Xu Fu failed, he was afraid of what the cruel Shi Huangdi might do to him if he went home empty-handed again. So Xu Fu never went home! Instead, he sailed over to Japan, where he may have built the first Japanese civilization. All of this may have happened around 210 BC. Some people think that Xu Fu and Jimmu Tenno may have been one and the same!

The legend of Xu Fu may not be true. But even if it isn't, the people of ancient Japan certainly learned a lot from the Chinese. For example, the characters used to write the Japanese language came from the ones used to write Chinese.

Xu Fu in search of the Elixir of Life

Japanese characters are called *kanji*, and Chinese characters *hanzi*. Also, early Japanese writing styles were very similar to China's. So were early Japanese law, building styles and much more.

〰〰〰〰〰〰〰〰〰〰〰〰〰〰〰〰〰〰〰〰〰〰〰〰〰〰〰

Despite what all the legends say, it seems that no one emperor ruled all of ancient Japan. Instead, powerful **clans** ruled small kingdoms scattered all over Japan.

> A **clan** is a big, powerful family.

It was only later, in early medieval times, that one clan built an empire. The first Japanese empire lay in southern Honshu, around what is now one of Japan's biggest cities: **Osaka**. The clan that built this empire was the **Yamato clan**— which is why the Imperial Dynasty of Japan is also called the Yamato dynasty (above).

In all the years since, the Yamato dynasty has never fallen. All Japanese emperors are descended from the first Yamato kings. Assuming there have been no mistakes over the centuries, every single Emperor of Japan has had at least a little bit of Yamato blood in his veins!

A *kofun* was a huge burial mound built for an early Japanese emperor. Some *kofun* were shaped like keyholes. The Japanese honor their ancestors so much that even after all these centuries, many *kofun* still lie undisturbed.

Japan's largest *kofun*, which is about the size of 30 football fields, lying undisturbed in the middle of a heavily built-up area. This *kofun* is probably about 1,500 years old, if not even older.

〰〰〰〰〰〰〰〰〰〰〰〰〰〰〰〰〰〰〰〰〰〰〰〰〰〰〰

But the Yamato clan wasn't the only powerful clan. Around 500 AD, another clan grew even more powerful than the Yamato. This was the **Soga clan**, which controlled Japan for nearly 300 years— until the next powerful clan, the **Fujiwara clan**, came along. Later

Emblem of the Fujiwara Clan

came the **Taira clan**, followed by the **Minamoto clan**. If the history of China reads like a list of dynasties, then the history of Japan reads like a list of clans!

The difference is that no one overthrew the Yamato clan. Instead, they simply found other things for the Yamato clan to do.

Basically, the Yamato emperors became the leaders of the Shinto faith. Their jobs were to meet with priests, attend ceremonies, dedicate shrines and so on. Meanwhile, the clan leaders ran the country. Their jobs were to collect taxes, operate courts, raise armies and so on. For hundreds of years, the Yamato emperors were only **figureheads**. The real power in Japan belonged to the clan leaders.

> On a ship, a **figurehead** is a carving that decorates the prow. In government, a **figurehead** is a leader who seems to be in charge, but really isn't.
> Like the figureheads on ships, the figurehead emperors of Japan were there mostly to inspire people, not to lead them.

〰〰〰〰〰〰〰〰〰〰〰〰〰〰〰〰〰〰〰〰〰〰〰〰〰〰〰

Another big difference between China and Japan was the samurai— the Japanese version of knights. The name *samurai* comes from the Japanese word for "servant" or "attendant." This is how the samurai started— as skilled soldiers in the service of Japanese clan leaders.

Like the best knights of the West, samurai were well-trained in all forms of fighting. They could fight with bow, sword or spear, both from horseback and on foot. Unlike the Vikings, some samurai really did wear horned helmets into battle!

But being a samurai meant much more than just being a good warrior. It also meant living by a strict warrior code called *bushido*.

Above all else, *bushido* spoke of honor. In fact, samurai probably cared more about honor than any other people on Earth. When they weren't training for battle, samurai wrote poems about honor, or created art that glorified honor.

What samurai poets wrote about most was how to die with honor. To die an honorable death in battle was the highest calling of the samurai— the only way any good samurai wanted to die. An honorable death meant that a samurai's descendants would honor him forever. On the other hand, a dishonorable death meant being ashamed forever.

Sometimes, the honor of the samurai made it tough to be a Japanese! For example, no Japanese was allowed to insult a samurai's honor. If anyone did, then the samurai could legally draw his sword and cut down his enemy there and then.

Another example of samurai honor was a strange practice called *hara-kiri*. All samurai hated to lose battles; for any loss left a stain on the samurai's honor. Sometimes, the only way a beaten samurai could get his honor back was by committing hara-kiri. This meant killing themselves in the most painful way imaginable. Hara-kiri was the only way could they prove, to themselves and their ancestors, that they weren't cowards.

Samurai Equipment

➢ Most samurai fought with two kinds of swords: a long sword called a **katana**, and a short sword called a **wakishazi**. Both were slightly curved. A third kind of samurai sword, the **tachi**, was for fighting from horseback.

➢ The samurai bow was a **yumi**, and the samurai spear a **yari**.

➢ The samurai suit of armor was called a **yoroi**. Yoroi makers used strips of leather to lace together bands of steel.

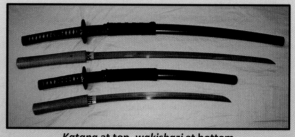

Katana at top, *wakishazi* at bottom

Japanese inventors created the first folding fans around 600 – 800. These first folding fans were simple, with paper blades fastened over thin strips of wood or bamboo.

Naturally, the samurai found ways to turn simple, harmless folding fans into weapons! Some carried fans made of thin sheet metal, honed to a razor-sharp edge. Others carried a special kind of war fan called a *tessen*. Hung on a samurai's belt, a *tessen* looked like an ordinary folded fan. But in a samurai's hand, it turned out to be a heavy iron club or blade! One advantage of *tessen* was that samurai could carry them into places where weapons usually weren't allowed.

A mounted samurai wearing a horned-helmet *yoroi*, and carrying a *yumi*

Example of a *tessen*, an iron club made to look like a folded fan

The Rise of the Shoguns

Bushido was a whole new way of life— not just for the samurai themselves, but for all of Japan. But *bushido* didn't change Japan overnight. For a long time, the samurai remained what they had been in the beginning: soldiers serving in the armies of clan leaders.

It was only later, around the year 1200, that a special kind of samurai took over the government of Japan. These were samurai leaders called **shoguns**.

The Japanese word *shogun* originally meant "commander of armies."

The rise of the shoguns started with the **Insei system**. This was a strange new set of rules for emperors. Basically, the Insei system allowed an emperor to retire early, without really giving up his throne.

When an older emperor grew tired of his duties, he could retire to a peaceful monastery, leaving the next emperor to take over. But handing down the throne didn't mean handing down power. For the new emperor was almost always the son of the old emperor. And Japanese sons always respected their fathers. So the old emperor could usually force the new one to do whatever he asked.

The trouble started in the time of **Toba**, the 74th Emperor of Japan. Toba retired in 1123, leaving his son **Sutoku** to take his place. Despite being retired, Toba kept right on telling Sutoku what to do.

Minamoto no Yoritomo, first Shogun of Japan

Sixteen years later, Toba's favorite young wife gave him a son called **Konoe**. Naturally, the new mother wanted nothing but the best for her son. So she asked Toba to make Konoe emperor— even though Sutoku, Toba's older son, was still on the throne!

To please his wife, Toba agreed. In 1142, Toba forced Sutoku to retire, and set the 3-year-old Konoe on the throne in his place. As an honorable son, Sutoku had little choice but to obey his father— even though he was terribly embarrassed!

Sutoku's next embarrassment came 13 years later, when Konoe died at age 16. With Konoe out of the way, Sutoku expected Toba to set him back on the throne. Or at the very least, he expected Toba to set one of Sutoku's sons on the throne. Instead, Toba chose one of his own sons! The next emperor was a half-brother of Sutoku called **Go-Shirakawa**.

This was too much. When Toba died later that year, Sutoku went to war, trying to take back the throne his father had taken away. The war between Sutoku and Go-Shirakawa is called the **Hogen Rebellion**.

The Hogen Rebellion (1156)

The problem was that neither Sutoku nor Go-Shirakawa had a decent army. Before they could even begin to fight, both needed the samurai armies of the clans. Sutoku hired the samurai army of one powerful clan, the **Minamoto clan**. Go-Shirakawa hired the samurai army of another powerful clan, the **Taira clan**. Without samurai armies, both emperors would have been completely helpless.

The Hogen Rebellion turned out to be short. Emperor Go-Shirakawa soon won, shaming poor Sutoku yet again.

Sutoku

The emperor's victory was great news for the Taira clan! As the clan that won the war and saved the emperor, the Taira clan was now the most powerful clan in Japan.

But the Minamoto clan wasn't finished. The Minamoto's turn came in the next big war, the **Genpei War**.

Like the Hogen Rebellion, the Genpei War started with insults to an emperor. Only this time, the insults didn't come from an older emperor. Instead, they came from **Taira Kiyomori**, the samurai leader of the Taira clan. Kiyomori had a bad habit of bossing around his emperor: **Takakura**, the 80th Emperor of Japan.

The first insult came when Kiyomori forced Takakura to marry one of his daughters. A few years later, that daughter gave birth to a son called **Antoku**.

The second insult came when Antoku was not quite 2 years old. Even though Takakura was nowhere near retirement age, Kiyomori forced him to retire— making little Antoku the 81st Emperor of Japan!

Emblem of the
Minamoto Clan

Now the emperors were in real trouble. Although older emperors had set aside younger emperors before, no mere clan leader had ever dared set aside an emperor!

Desperate to save itself, the Imperial Dynasty called on the only army strong enough to tackle the Taira: the samurai army of the Minamoto clan.

This time, the Minamoto proved stronger. After one big loss to the Minamoto, the Taira samurai gathered up Emperor Antoku and the Three Sacred Treasures and fled.

Emblem of the Taira Clan

The flight of the Taira set up the biggest battle of the Genpei War. This was the **Battle of Dan-no-ura**, a sea battle fought in the waters between Honshu and Kyushu.

The Battle of Dan-no-ura ended with a betrayal. Midway through the battle, a Taira officer suddenly switched sides. Calling out to the Minamoto, this turncoat Taira pointed out the ship that carried Antoku and his family. The Minamoto immediately turned all their bows on this ship, killing its oarsmen and setting it adrift.

When the Taira samurai saw their emperor's ship drifting, they knew that they were beaten. So they did what all beaten samurai were trained

Samurai of the Taira clan drowning themselves after the Battle of Dan-no-ura

to do: they killed themselves. They all leapt over the sides of their ships, where they soon drowned!

One of the dead was Emperor Antoku, who was still not quite 7 years old. The poor child had been manipulated by his powerful family all his life.

After winning the Genpei War, the Minamoto clan took over the government. As always, the Imperial Dynasty emperors stayed in power. But they were only spiritual leaders. The real leaders were the **shoguns**— the generals who commanded the mighty samurai armies of Japan.

The **Heike crab** is a special kind of crab found only near Japan. The odd thing about Heike crabs is that their shells look like human faces—and not just any faces, but the scowling faces of angry samurai!

Any Japanese fisherman who catches a Heike crab automatically throws it back. For legend has it that these crabs carry the souls of the Taira samurai who drowned themselves at the Battle of Dan-no-ura.

Another legend from the Battle of Dan-no-ura tells the fate of the Three Sacred Treasures. Near battle's end, it is said, the Taira samurai tried to throw all three treasures overboard. They knew that without them, the next Emperor of Japan could hardly be a called heavenly emperor. After all, the Three Sacred Treasures were the emperors' only real link to Amaterasu, their heavenly ancestor.

It is also said that the Minamoto samurai leapt aboard just in time to save the jewel. But they were too late to save the mirror or the sword, both of which went to the bottom. Fortunately, the mirror was shiny enough for divers to find. But divers may not have found the sword. Some people think that the sword the Imperial Dynasty now has is only a copy of the one Susanoo found in the dragon's tail!

The Land Down Under

Australia is the smallest of the seven continents, and the second southernmost continent. The name "Australia" comes from the Latin word *australis*, which means "southern."

Long before European explorers discovered Australia, their maps showed a continent called *Terra Australis Incognita*. This is Latin for "Unknown Southern Land." The first Europeans to discover that Unknown Southern Land were the Dutch, who sighted Australia in the early 1600s.

Australia is the lowest, flattest continent— and one of the driest. About two-thirds of Australia is entirely too dry for most people. Nearly all Australians live in wetter regions— mostly near the eastern and southeastern coasts, in and around cities like Sydney, Canberra and Melbourne.

One of Australia's fascinating features is a huge, beautiful coral reef off the northeastern coast. This is the **Great Barrier Reef**, which measures about 1,600 miles long. Other well-known features include the **Great Australian Bight**, a huge bay off the south coast; and **Tasmania**, a big island about 150 miles south of the mainland.

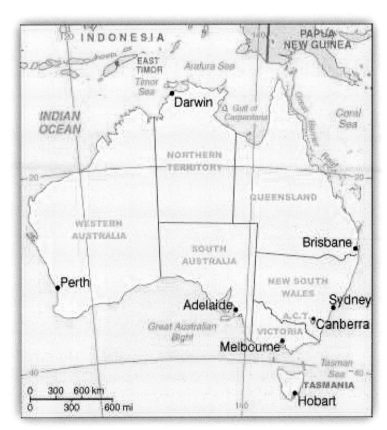

CHAPTER 19

The Mongol Empire

Mongolia

Mongolia is a large, **landlocked** country in East Asia. The Mongols have just two neighbors. Everything north of Mongolia belongs to Russia; while everything west, south and east of Mongolia belongs to China.

Unless you happen to be talking to a Mongol warrior, it is probably safe to say that Mongolia is not the most comfortable place to live! Most of Mongolia is too high, cold and dry for raising crops. In fact, only about 1% of Mongolia is good for crop farming. Most of the rest has only enough grass to feed wandering herds of sheep or goats. In modern times, more Mongols earn their livings as miners than as farmers.

A **landlocked** country is one with no coasts.

The capital of Mongolia is **Ulan Bator**.

In medieval times, most Mongols made their livings as wandering herdsmen, wandering hunters or both. Either way, the Mongols were always wandering— which meant that they didn't need permanent homes. Instead, most Mongols lived in a special kind of tent called a **yurt**.

A modern-day yurt standing on a Mongolian plain near the base of the Gurvansaikhan Mountains, just north of the Gobi Desert

A **yurt** is a round tent made for a single family. The average Mongol yurt was a light frame of wooden poles covered with layers of warm felt. Finding felt was no problem for the Mongols— for felt is made by crushing wool, and the Mongols had plenty of sheep. Finding wood, on the other hand, could be a big problem— for few trees grow on the high plains of Mongolia.

The Mongols always set up their yurts with their doors facing south, the direction that received the most sun throughout the day. Honored guests sat farthest from the door, where the air was warmest. Children and less honored guests sat closer to the door.

The Rise of Genghis Khan

The very first historian, a Greek called Herodotus, wrote that tough lands produce tough peoples. If a land gives plenty of food easily, then the people of that land may grow soft. But if a land gives little food, then the people of that land will grow tough— for they will have to fight hard for every mouthful.

There are few lands on Earth harder than Mongolia. So it is no surprise that Mongol warriors were some of the toughest people who ever lived!

> **Marmots** are big rodents that live in holes burrowed in the ground. The common groundhog is a type of marmot.

Being born to hardship, the Mongols made great warriors. Like the Huns before them, they lived on horseback. Without horses, there would have been no Mongol warriors! From hunting **marmots** on the open plains, Mongol warriors learned to shoot with deadly accuracy. And from spending days with no food, they learned to cross great distances swiftly, carrying almost no supplies.

Since their own land gave little food, the Mongols stole food from other lands. For centuries, the people of rice-rich China lived in constant fear of raiders from the north. These raids were the main reason why Shi Huangdi, first emperor of the Qin dynasty, started building the Great Wall of China (Chapter 17).

Mongol warriors chasing down their enemies

All through ancient times, and well into medieval times, the Mongols were divided into different tribes. The **Khamags**, the **Tatars** and the **Merkits** were just a few of the many tribes that roamed the plains of Mongolia. Without a leader to bring the tribes together, the Mongols raided each other as often as they raided China.

The childhood years of a boy called **Temujin** taught him all about Mongol raids. In fact, Temujin owed his very birth to a raid.

> **Genghis Khan**
> **(1165? - 1227)**

Temujin's father, **Yesugei**, was a leader of the Khamag Mongols. Yesugei was out hunting with falcons one day when he saw a beautiful girl riding by in a horse-drawn cart. The horseman pulling the cart was the Merkit Mongol whom the girl had just married. Wanting the girl for himself, Yesugei chased down the Merkit and stole his wife.

This tearful young woman, whose name was **Oyelun**, would go on to give Yesugei five children. Temujin was the oldest.

According to Mongol legend, Temujin was born "with fire in his eyes and light in his face." In other words, Temujin was the leader who was born to unite all Mongol tribes. In later years, this great leader would be known by his title: Genghis Khan.

When Temujin was nine years old, Yesugei took him to find a bride. He had hoped to find one among Oyelun's family. Along the way, though, a mysterious stranger invited Yesugei to meet his daughter— a 10-year-old called **Borte**.

Yesugei noticed that Borte's eyes glowed with the same "fire and light" as Temujin's. Seeing this, he knew that he had found the right bride for his son. So Yesugei headed home. As for Temujin, he stayed behind to live with Borte's family; for this was the Mongol custom.

Finding a bride for his son would turn out to be the last thing Yesugei ever did.

Along the road home, a group of pleasant-seeming strangers invited Yesugei to share a meal with them. What Yesugei didn't realize was that these were no strangers. Instead, they were angry Tatars who held a terrible grudge against him! Years before, Yesugei had led a raid against these very Tatars. Yesugei didn't recognize the Tatars; but they recognized him very well. So they mixed a bit of poison with the food they gave him— causing him to sicken and die when he got home.

The death of his father was the beginning of the hardest time in Temujin's life. As soon as he heard, Temujin rushed home to take his father's place. But when he got there, the other leaders of his tribe had already abandoned his family— leaving poor Oyelun to feed and raise five children, all on her own. "Apart from our own shadows," Oyelun mourned, "we have no friends."

As Temujin grew older, the other leaders of his tribe grew afraid of him. They had been wrong to abandon his family, and knew that he might take revenge someday. So they ordered the family to hand him over!

But the family didn't hand him over. Instead, they put him on a horse and sent him racing through a forest. He soon found a heavy thicket where he could hide.

A Tatar elder

Alone in his thicket, Temujin waited nine solid days for his enemies to give up the chase. In all that time, Temujin had not one morsel of food to sustain him. When he could stand the hunger no longer, he finally cut his way out of the thicket— allowing his enemies to capture him at last.

As a wandering people, the Mongols didn't have jails to hold

prisoners. Instead, they locked them in miserable contraptions called **cangues**. A rope tied to the cangue helped jailers hold their prisoners.

But Temujin was too strong for his jailer. One summer day, Temujin jerked the rope out of his jailer's hands, hit him on the head and ran!

Even Temujin couldn't run far with a heavy cangue on his neck. So instead of running, he laid himself down in a rushing river, leaving only his face above the surface. When the coast was clear, he waded downriver to the home of some friends, who finally helped him escape.

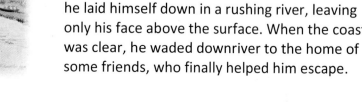

A prisoner locked in a cangue

Afterward, Temujin and Borte were married at last. Alas, the young couple's happiness was short-lived. For just months into their marriage, a band of Merkits kidnapped Borte!

The Merkits had never forgotten how Yesugei had kidnapped Oyelun from them years before. Since Yesugei was now dead, the Merkits took their revenge by kidnapping Borte from his son.

The day when Temujin took Borte back was the day when his fortunes finally turned from bad to good. The key to that turnaround was the oath of loyalty sworn between **anda**— in other words, "blood brothers."

Before setting out to take Borte back, Temujin called on his father's old *anda*— a Khamag prince called **Toghrul Khan**. In honor of the unbreakable vow he had sworn to Yesugei, Toghrul Khan promised 20,000 troops to Yesugei's son. Temujin also called on an *anda* of his own, another Khamag prince called **Jamukha**. With another 20,000 troops from Jamukha, Temujin had more than enough to crush the Merkits and take Borte back.

With this great victory, Temujin finally took his father's place as a great leader of his tribe. Thousands of troops joined Temujin's armies. In time, he grew as powerful as Jamukha and Toghrul Khan.

One secret of Temujin's success was a new way of promoting army officers. Other Mongols always promoted troops who came from the richest, most powerful families. But Temujin promoted the troops with the most skill and courage. That way, Temujin wound up with better officers!

Another secret of Temujin's success was the way he swallowed up other tribes. Each time Temujin conquered a tribe, his mother adopted young princes from that tribe. These princes became half-brothers to Temujin. As the head of the family, Temujin became the head of his half-brothers' tribes.

> *Anda* is Mongolian for "blood brother." *Anda* were special friends who vowed always to be loyal to one another, no matter what. The vows *anda* swore were the most sacred, unbreakable vows in the Mongol world.

> Temujin and Jamukha were *anda* from age 11. To seal their vow as blood brothers, each gave the other a **knucklebone**. This was actually the anklebone of a deer or other animal.
>
> The gift of a knucklebone was more special than it sounds. The odd shape of knucklebones allowed them to be rolled like dice. Mongol **shamans**, or spirit-talkers, rolled knucklebones to try to predict the future.

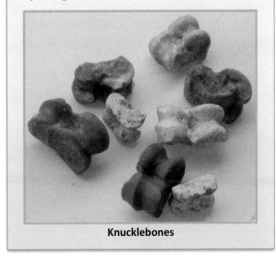

Knucklebones

The more tribes Temujin swallowed, the more he dreamed. Someday, Temujin hoped to bring all Mongol tribes together under a single leader— himself.

Unfortunately, Jamukha dreamed the same dream. The quest to become the **Great Khan**, the one ruler of all Mongols, set up a deadly contest between these two blood brothers.

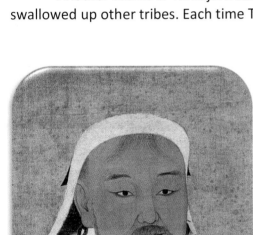

Portrait of Genghis Khan by a Chinese artist

The contest ended in betrayal. In the end, Jamukha's men handed him over to Temujin— probably expecting rich rewards. Instead, Temujin put them to death for betraying their master.

Then, for the sake of old oaths, Temujin offered Jamukha his life. All Jamukha had to do was swear loyalty to Temujin, and he could live out his days in peace and comfort.

But Jamukha couldn't. For one thing, Jamukha was ashamed of the way he had treated his blood brother. For another, Jamukha was too proud to live on as a servant, when he could have been emperor. So Jamukha asked for a quick death, saying:

"As there is room for only one sun in the sky, so too there is room for only one Mongol lord."

With this last rival out of his way, Temujin was no longer called Temujin. Instead, he finally claimed the title he had fought so many battles to win: **Genghis Khan**, ruler of all Mongol tribes.

Temujin enthroned as Genghis Khan, great ruler of all Mongol tribes

ⁿⁿⁿ

After uniting the Mongol tribes, Genghis turned his attention to conquering the Chinese.

The timing was important. When Temujin became Genghis Khan in 1206, the Song dynasty still ruled China (Chapter 17). But the Song didn't rule all of China. Northern China, the part around the Yellow River, had broken away from the Song dynasty. Even worse, the western half of northern China had broken away from the eastern half.

This breakup helped the Mongols pick China apart piece by piece. By 1215, Genghis Khan had conquered all of northern China! But he didn't conquer southern China. The Song dynasty still ruled there.

After conquering all of the east he could, Genghis Khan turned westward. The lands between China and the Caspian Sea were the next to fall. The Mongol Empire now stretched all the way from the Caspian Sea to the Pacific Ocean!

Genghis Khan died in 1227. But before he died, he said to his four sons:

"With heaven's aid I have conquered for you a huge empire. But my life was too short to achieve the conquest of the world. That task is left for you."

The sons of Genghis Khan took their father's last words seriously. Before the end of the 1200s, the Mongol Empire was the biggest empire in all of history— at least on land. Almost all of Asia, and even a big chunk of Eastern Europe, belonged to the Mongols!

Genghis Khan capturing Beijing, the capital of northern China

If the Huns were the most terrifying warriors of ancient times, then the Mongols were the most terrifying of medieval times. Hordes of Mongols appeared out of nowhere, catching cities completely by surprise. If anyone dared to put up a fight, then the Mongols slaughtered everyone.

Several times, Mongol hordes left nothing but grim mounds of skulls where there had once been thriving cities. Hundreds of thousands of people, if not millions, died in the Mongol invasions of the 1200s.

Even so, Mongol historians like to point out that Genghis Khan wasn't all bad. For example:

➤ Mongol historians give Genghis Khan credit for bringing law and order to Mongolia. His code of laws, the *Yassa*, was the first written law in Mongolian history.

➤ Genghis Khan also built the *Yam*, a clever communications network that could move messages incredibly fast. Like the Pony Express of the old American West, the *Yam* was a set of postal stations spread out along main roads all over the empire. Each station kept plenty of fresh horses, food and water. By riding hard from station to station, horsemen could carry messages across thousands of miles in just a few days.

➤ The Mongol Empire took great care to protect the **Silk Road**— the ancient trade route that connected the West to the Far East (Chapter 17). At the height of their power, the Mongols controlled almost the whole length of the Silk Road.

Since the Mongols were always on the move, their government needed to move with them. But the government of the Great Khan could hardly meet inside a common yurt! So instead, the Mongols built huge, movable yurts called **ordos**. Some ordos were so big and heavy that they needed teams of 22 oxen to pull them.

Genghis Khan Coin

The Mongols had two good reasons for protecting the Silk Road. One was because the Silk Road helped make them rich. Mongol tax collectors demanded high tolls from traders who used their road!

The other reason was because the Silk Road was the only place where the Mongols could buy certain goods. As a nation of wandering raiders, the Mongols knew more about stealing fine goods than they did about making them for themselves. So if they wanted fine goods— for example, silk cloth from southern China— then they bought those goods along the Silk Road.

A darughachi inspecting a tribute payment from a Russian village

To control their vast empire, the Mongols divided it into smaller sections called **darugha**. Each darugha was governed by a Mongol officer called a **darughachi**.

The most important job of any darughachi was collecting tribute payments. As conquerors, the Mongols demanded regular payments of gold, silver, grain, fur or whatever else a darugha produced. Any village that paid less than its share could expect a visit from a Mongol horde!

The Yuan Dynasty

The Song dynasty fought hard to keep the Mongols out of southern China. For a long time, the Song succeeded— partly because Chinese technology was much better than Mongol technology.

Back in Chapter 17, we read that Song dynasty engineers were the first to pack gunpowder into iron bombs. The Song also knew how to build a much older, simpler weapon: the catapult. Putting two and two together, the Song catapulted iron bombs at the Mongols. Even warriors as tough as the Mongols couldn't ignore iron bombs!

In the end, though, not even the clever Song dynasty could stand up to the Mongols forever. Although none of Genghis Khan's sons conquered southern China, one of his grandsons did. This was the mighty **Kublai Khan**, who would turn out to be the last emperor of the whole Mongol Empire.

Kublai Khan (1215 - 1294)

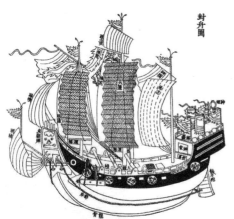

A Chinese junk from Yuan dynasty times

Like his father and grandfather before him, Kublai Khan intended to conquer the whole world. After finally conquering all of China, he set out to conquer Japan as well.

The trouble was, Mongol warriors knew a lot more about horses than they did about ships! Twice, Kublai Khan sent huge fleets of ships to invade Japan; and twice, Mongol troops drowned by the thousands.

Nor was Japan the only country Kublai Khan failed to conquer. He also invaded both Vietnam and Burma, yet conquered neither.

> Some Japanese thank their Shinto gods for keeping the Mongols out of Japan. Both times the Mongols tried to invade Japan, heavy storms called **typhoons** drove them back. The typhoons that saved Japan from the Mongols are called *kamikazes*— Japanese for "heavenly winds."

When he wasn't at war, Kublai Khan enjoyed all of the good things China had to offer. The Chinese had great science, beautiful art and interesting literature to share. Kublai Khan wrote poetry in Chinese, and even converted to Chinese Buddhism.

He also gave himself a Chinese title. Outside China, Kublai Khan was still the Great Khan of the Mongols. But inside China, he was the Emperor of China. His family was the **Yuan dynasty**, the next great dynasty to rule China after the Song dynasty.

For most of every year, Kublai Khan ruled from his capital in northern China. This was Beijing, which is still the capital today. As the capital of the greatest empire on Earth, Beijing drew visitors from all over— including a few from Western Europe.

Kublai Khan's battle command center, built across the backs of four war elephants

Brothers **Niccolo** and **Maffeo Polo** were traders from Venice, Italy. Around 1260, the Polos set out along the Silk Road, hoping to find better fortunes than they had found closer to home.

In 1264, a Mongol ambassador invited the brothers to Beijing. Kublai Khan had never met anyone from Venice before, and wanted to know more about Italy.

Crossing the Silk Road took a long time. Two more years passed before Niccolo and Maffeo finally made it to Beijing.

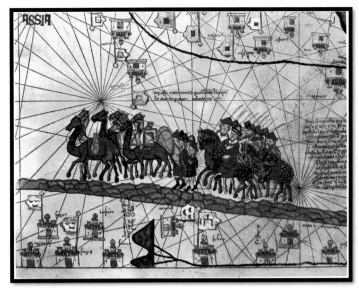

The Polos' trade caravan traveling the Silk Road

After meeting the Polo brothers, Kublai Khan wanted to know more about the Christian faith. So he sent the brothers home with a letter for the pope, asking him for two items. One was a bit of holy oil from the Church of the Holy Sepulcher in Jerusalem. The other was 100 Christian men to teach his people Western religion and science.

Back home in Venice, Niccolo Polo ran into someone he barely even knew: his own son, **Marco Polo**! When Niccolo had last seen Marco, he was a little boy being raised by his mother.

By the time the Polos set out for Beijing again, Marco was 17 years old. And when they finally reached Beijing, Marco was 21. Marco Polo grew from boy to man along the Silk Road, seeing more of the world in a few years than most people saw in a lifetime.

The sights didn't stop when Marco reached Beijing. Kublai Khan was so pleased with the Polos that he took them with him wherever he went. Marco Polo spent 17 years traveling all over China, seeing the Far East as no European had ever seen it before.

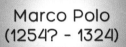

Marco Polo
(1254? - 1324)

To aid the Polo brothers in their travels, Kublai Khan gave them a special emblem called a *paiza*. The holder of a *paiza* could demand free food and fresh horses from any *Yam* station in the Mongol Empire, courtesy of the Great Khan himself. Even with their valuable *paiza*, the Polo brothers still needed 3 years to travel from Beijing to Italy!

The Polo brothers receiving their paiza in the court of Kublai Khan

Back home in Venice, Marco Polo wrote one of the first bestsellers ever written. This was *The Travels of Marco Polo*, which he first published around 1300. Some publishers called the book *Marvels of the World*. For Marco Polo described marvels that no one in the West had ever seen!

For example, he described the great Kublai Khan commanding half a million Mongol horsemen at once— from a tower built across the backs of four war elephants! He also described wonders of science which the West had yet to discover. The Chinese had fireproof cloth made of asbestos fibers; "burning rocks," also known as coal; and paper money that worked just as well as gold and silver coins.

Not everyone believed Marco Polo's book. Some Westerners refused to believe that the East had discovered all these wonders, when the West had not. Italians were so doubtful that they gave Polo's book a third title: *Il Milione*, "The Million Lies."

But Marco Polo wasn't lying— at least, not about everything. In medieval times, Chinese technology really was better than Western technology.

卍卍卍卍卍卍卍卍卍卍卍卍卍卍卍卍卍卍卍卍卍卍卍卍卍卍卍

How did the great Mongol Empire end?

A Yuan Dynasty Jade belt featuring an Azure dragon

One way to mark the end of the Mongol Empire is by the end of Kublai Khan. When Kublai Khan died in 1294, the Mongol Empire split into four parts. The **Yuan dynasty** continued to rule China. The **Chagatai Khanate** ruled the lands west of China. The **Ilkhanate** ruled the Middle East; while the **Golden Horde** ruled Western Asia and Eastern Europe. The more time passed, the less these four parts had to do with one another.

Another way to mark the end of the Mongol Empire is by the end of the Yuan dynasty. In 1368, a Han Chinese called **Zhu Yuanzhang** overthrew the last Yuan emperor. Zhu was the first emperor of the next great Chinese dynasty: the **Ming dynasty**.

One by one, the other pieces of the Mongol Empire all collapsed. As we read in Chapter 11, the Russians stopped paying tribute to their Mongol khans in 1480. By this time, the empire was all but gone.

When he wasn't in Beijing, Kublai Khan liked to spend time at a special place called **Xanadu**.

Xanadu was a fantastic retreat that served as summertime capital, when Beijing was too hot. Marco Polo wrote of two palaces at Xanadu: one made of marble, and one made of lacquered bamboo tiles. As was fitting for a Mongol lord, the bamboo palace could be taken down, hauled away and then set up again wherever the Great Khan wished!

The Ming emperors reigned from a special section of Beijing called the **Forbidden City**. The name "forbidden" came from the fact that no one could enter or leave without the emperor's permission.

The number 9 is very important to the Chinese. Because of this, the original plans for the Forbidden City called for 999 buildings containing a total of 9,999 rooms.

Two strong barriers surround the Forbidden City: a wall about 25 feet high, and a moat more than 50 yards wide.

One of many palaces inside the Forbidden City

Some medieval Chinese kept an unusual kind of pet: crickets. Some liked crickets because they believed that these musical insects brought good luck. Others favored crickets just for their music. Still others enjoyed crickets for a less noble reason: because they liked to watch crickets battle to the death.

A gourd and stopper used as a cricket cage

The Church of the East

Unlike most medieval empires, the Mongol Empire didn't care what its people believed. As long as the Mongols' subjects didn't miss their tribute payments, they could believe whatever they liked— whether they were Shamanist like most Mongols, Buddhist like most Chinese, or Muslim like most Turks and Persians.

The Mongols' subjects could even follow a religion that was barely known in the Far East: Christianity. Without meaning to, Genghis Khan brought new life to an old church that had been struggling along for centuries. This was the Church of the East, which was also called the **Nestorian Church**.

The name "Nestorian" came from Nestorius, a Syrian priest who lived from about 386 – 450. Nestorius became Archbishop of Constantinople in 428, just before the Coptic Orthodox Church of Egypt split off from all other churches (Chapter 4). Poor Nestorius got trapped in the same sticky web that caught the Egyptians, but in an opposite way.

Nestorius' problems started with a single Greek word: *Theotokos*, meaning "Mother of God." This was a word that priests had been using to describe Mary, the mother of Jesus, since long before Nestorius came on the scene. Nestorius didn't like calling Mary "Mother of God." For he believed that God had created all things, including Mary. If God created Mary, Nestorius asked, then how could Mary possibly be the "Mother of God"?

An icon of Mary as Theotokos

The strange way Nestorius answered this question was to cost him his job as Archbishop.

Most Christians believed that Christ blended two natures: the divine nature of God, and the human nature of man. Nestorius believed that those two natures were completely separate. According to Nestorius, a Christian could say that Mary was the mother of Christ's human nature— *Christotokos*. But one could never say that Mary was the mother of Christ's divine nature— *Theotokos*. For the divine nature was part of God; and God was never born.

In other words, Nestorius taught the opposite of what Egyptian Christians taught. The Egyptians believed that Christ's divine nature absorbed his human one (Chapter 4). But Nestorius believed that Christ's divine nature remained completely separate from his human one.

Most Christians believed that both were wrong! As Athanasius said, Christ must be both divine and human— fully God and fully man, both at the same time (Chapter 2). If Nestorius was right, and Christ's divine nature was never born, then it also never died on the cross— which meant that Christ never could have conquered sin and death.

Despite what most Christians believed, Nestorius stuck to his own beliefs. And even though Nestorius lost his job as Archbishop, he still had plenty of followers. So when the rest of the Church condemned Nestorius, his followers moved east, into Persia. There they joined the **Church of the East**— a struggling church in Persia.

Although the Church of the East never really thrived, it never died either. Nestorian missionaries won believers not only in Persia, but also in India, China and even Mongolia. Since Genghis Khan didn't mind, whole Mongol tribes became Nestorian Christians. Even the wife of **Mongke Khan**, the fourth Great Khan, was a Nestorian Christian.

CHAPTER 20:

The Rise of the Ottoman Empire

Osman's Vision

The **Ottoman Empire** was the biggest, longest-lasting Islamic empire of all time. From its birth in 1299 through its fall in 1923, the Ottoman Empire lasted more than 600 years!

> The name "Ottoman" comes from the founder of the empire, **Sultan Osman I.**

The heartland of the Ottoman Empire was **Anatolia**, also called **Asia Minor**. As we read in Chapter 12, Anatolia is an Asian peninsula that juts out between the Mediterranean Sea and the Black Sea. In modern times, Anatolia belongs to the **Republic of Turkey**.

Over in Europe, just across the **Bosporus** from Anatolia, stood one of the richest cities in the whole medieval world. This was **Constantinople**, capital of the Byzantine Empire.

Many a Muslim ruler dreamed of conquering Constantinople. For one thing, they coveted its riches. For another, Constantinople was the capital of Eastern Christianity. The fight for Constantinople was another **crusade**— another holy war between Christians and Muslims.

The Christians lost that crusade in 1453, when Constantinople finally fell to the Ottoman Empire.

> Remember what the **Bosporus** is: the narrow strait that connects the Black Sea to the oceans of the world. Constantinople sat on the west side of the southern entrance to the Bosporus.

But that comes later. The story of the Ottoman Empire actually starts with an older empire: the Great Seljuk Empire, which we first met in Chapter 12.

The Seljuk Turks started out as wandering warriors from the East. They came from Turkestan, an ancient land between China and the Caspian Sea.

The Seljuk Turks converted to Islam around 950. After that, they set out to build an Islamic empire. The Great Seljuk Empire spread swiftly westward— from Turkestan into Persia, and then on to the Middle East.

By the 1070s, the Seljuk Turks had reached Anatolia. Their greatest victory came in 1071, when **Sultan Alp Arslan** crushed a Byzantine army at the **Battle of Manzikert** (Chapter 12).

But the Great Seljuk Empire didn't last.

After the Battle of Manzikert, Alp Arslan assigned one of his generals to conquer the rest of Anatolia. As for the sultan himself, he rode on to fight more battles in the east.

A scene from the Battle of Manzikert

A **caravanserai** was a roadside inn built along a trade route of the East, such as the Silk Road. After a long, hot day of desert travel, traders could stop at a caravanserai to water their camels, buy supplies, bathe and sleep with a roof over their heads.

A still-standing caravanserai in Iran

After one of those battles, the sultan's men brought him a beaten enemy leader to judge. Alp Arslan sentenced the man to death, as he had sentenced many others. But this man was different. When the sultan announced his sentence, the man pulled out a hidden dagger and rushed at him!

As dangers went, this was a fairly small one. The sultan was surrounded by guards, all armed and ready to defend him. But Alp Arslan was terribly proud of his bravery, and also of his skill with a bow. So he waved his guards aside, planning to shoot the man down himself.

Ordinarily, Alp Arslan never missed. But this time, his foot slipped, sending his arrow wide! Before the guards could react, the rushing man plunged his dagger into Alp Arslan's chest. The mighty sultan died the year after his great victory at the Battle of Manzikert.

The loss of Alp Arslan was a heavy blow to the Great Seljuk Empire. Back in Anatolia, Alp Arslan's general was still winning battles, seizing more and more land from the Byzantine Empire. But he was doing it all without any help from the Great Seljuk Empire.

The longer this went on, the more the general realized that he didn't need any help. In 1077, the general set up a new country of his own: the **Sultanate of Rum**.

Other generals also broke away, tearing the Great Seljuk Empire to pieces.

The **Sultanate of Rum** was a country led by Turkish Muslims in Anatolia.

The name "Rum" was a Turkish version of "Rome." Before the Turks came, Anatolia had always belonged to the Eastern Roman Empire, a.k.a. the Byzantine Empire.

ꠁꠁꠁꠁꠁꠁꠁꠁꠁꠁꠁꠁꠁꠁꠁꠁꠁꠁꠁꠁꠁꠁꠁꠁꠁꠁꠁꠁꠁꠁꠁꠁꠁꠁꠁ

The sultans of Rum faced two great enemies: one near the beginning of their reign, and one near the end.

The first enemy was the Christian knights of the First Crusade. The sultans had no trouble at all with the first army to arrive— the poor peasants of the People's Crusade (Chapter 12). But when the trained knights of the Prince's Crusade came along, they drove the sultans back, well away from Constantinople.

The second enemy was the Mongol Empire. As we read in Chapter 19, the Mongols set out to conquer the whole world— and almost succeeded! The sons of Genghis Khan came to the Middle East in the mid-1200s. The sultans of Rum were soon making tribute payments to the Mongol Empire, just like everyone else.

But the Mongols only conquered the eastern side of Rum. The western side stayed strong. When the eastern side started to collapse, the generals of the west declared independence from Rum— just as the sultans of Rum had declared independence from the Great Seljuk Empire.

A **ghazi** was a Muslim holy warrior who fought to spread Islam all over the world. The Turkish Muslims who fought for the Great Seljuk Empire and the Sultanate of Rum thought of themselves as ghazis.

One of those western generals was **Ertugrul Ghazi**, who had a son called **Osman**. In the years ahead, Osman would become **Sultan Osman I of the Ottoman Empire**.

Osman was a man with a dream.

As a young man, Osman paid a lot of visits to a wise old holy man called **Sheikh Edebali**. Although Osman loved Islam, that was only one reason why he spent so much time with Edebali. The other reason was Edebali's beautiful daughter: **Mal Hatun**, whom Osman longed to marry.

Osman was lying down to rest one night, thinking about his future, when a vision appeared to him. The first scene he saw was himself and Edebali, lying asleep side-by-side. As Osman looked on, a full moon rose from Edebali's chest, and then set in Osman's chest. Next, a huge tree pushed up from Osman's chest, its branches covered with strangely curved leaves. The tree spread out over all three of the known continents: Asia, Europe and Africa.

Everywhere the tree spread, prosperity spread as well. Fountains gushed from the tree's roots, watering great harvests. Mosques sprang up, filled with Muslims praying thanks to Allah. And in the middle of it all, glittering like a diamond ring, stood the city of Constantinople.

Osman was about to set this precious ring on his finger when the vision ended, and he awoke.

Sheikh Edebali was a special kind of Muslim holy man called a **dervish**.

Dervishes are mystics who try to meet Allah in visions and trances. A **whirling dervish** is one who dances a whirling dance, trying to bring on a trance that will carry him closer to Allah.

Dervishes dancing their whirling dance

When Osman shared his vision with Sheikh Edebali, the wise old man revealed the hidden meanings of everything Osman had seen.

➢ The moon represented Islam, which Edebali loved with all his heart. That love had now spread to Osman's heart— which meant that Osman was the perfect leader to build a new Islamic empire. Now that Edebali knew Osman's heart, he was happy to let Osman marry Mal Hatun.

➢ The great tree represented the great empire that Osman was about to build. The Ottoman Empire would one day spread out over three continents.

➢ The curved leaves represented the curved **scimitars** that Osman and his **ghazi** warriors would use to build the Ottoman Empire.

₪₪₪₪₪₪₪₪₪₪₪₪₪₪₪₪₪₪₪₪₪₪₪₪₪

Despite all the good omens in Osman's vision, the Ottoman Empire took a long time to build.

A **scimitar** was a kind of curved sword used mostly by Muslim warriors.

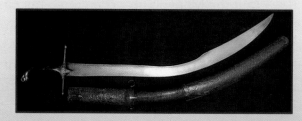

Since the mighty Mongols still ruled eastern Anatolia, Osman built his empire in western Anatolia. In a way, the Mongol Empire actually helped Osman. The longer the Mongols ruled the east, the more Turkish Muslims moved west to join Osman's armies.

Even so, Osman never conquered any lands in Europe or Africa. Constantinople, the glittering ring of Osman's vision, was never his to hold.

Sultan **Orhan**, son to Osman, was the first to conquer lands in Europe. Orhan seized the peninsula of **Gallipoli**, southwest of Constantinople, in 1355.

Sultan **Murad I**, son to Orhan, conquered much more. In Murad's day, the Ottoman Empire added as much land in Europe as it already held in Asia. After Murad, Constantinople was surrounded by Muslims! The great city was now like a small Christian island in a huge Muslim sea.

> **Gallipoli** is a narrow European peninsula that lies just across the Dardanelles Strait from Asia Minor.

Sultan Osman I inspiring his ghazis with words from the Quran

ௌௌௌௌௌௌௌௌௌௌௌௌௌௌௌௌௌௌௌௌௌௌௌௌௌௌௌௌௌௌௌௌௌௌௌௌ

One of the secrets of Murad's success was the kind of soldiers he used. Before the 1300s, most countries didn't have **standing armies** filled with professional soldiers. Instead, they had part-time armies filled with farmers and tradesmen— ordinary men whose everyday jobs had nothing to do with fighting.

Murad had a better idea. Around 1365, Murad created a new kind of soldier called the **janissaries**. These "**new soldiers**" were raised from boyhood to do nothing but fight. The janissaries had the best of everything: the best weapons, the best training, the best horses and uniforms. When a janissary fought an enemy farmer, the janissary usually won.

> A **standing army** is one that is always ready to fight, whether there is a war on or not.
> **Janissary** is Turkish for "new soldier."

Most janissaries weren't born Muslims. Instead, they were Christian boys who were taken from their parents and raised as Muslims!

When an Ottoman sultan conquered a Christian land, he ordered Christian parents to hand over their boys. He especially wanted the younger boys, about 6 – 10 years old; for these were easier to train.

The sultans called this system *devshirme*, Turkish for "child tax." Christian parents called it by a less flattering name: the **blood tax**. *Devshirme* boys went straight from Christian homes to military schools, where teachers raised them as janissaries.

Collecting the blood tax from Christian parents

Because *devshirme* boys were young, most of them forgot all about their pasts. Hearing nothing but Turkish, they forgot their old languages. Hearing nothing but Islam, they forgot their old Christian faith. And hearing nothing but praise for the sultan, they grew up loyal to the sultan. The janissaries were the sultan's special new soldiers, raised from boyhood to fight for the sultan alone.

〰〰〰〰〰〰〰〰〰〰〰〰〰〰〰〰〰〰〰〰〰〰〰〰〰〰〰〰〰〰〰〰〰〰

Beside *devshirme* boys, Sultan Murad I had at least two strong sons of his own. The older son, **Bayezid**, commanded the left wing of the sultan's armies. And the younger, **Yakub**, commanded the right wing. When Murad was killed in battle in 1389, no one knew which son would be the next sultan.

No one, that is, except Bayezid. As soon as Bayezid learned of his father's death, he sent a carefully-worded message to Yakub. He ordered Yakub to come to the sultan's tent, without telling him why. Like the dutiful soldier he was, Yakub came at once— probably expecting to receive orders from his father. Instead, Bayezid's men strangled Yakub the moment he stepped into the tent!

Sultan Bayezid I was only one of many sultans to murder his brothers. Ottoman sultans weren't like the kings of the West. Those kings usually handed down their thrones to their oldest sons. But the sultans let their sons fight it out among themselves. The last brother alive, they believed, would be the strongest— which made him the right brother for the job.

〰〰〰〰〰〰〰〰〰〰〰〰〰〰〰〰〰〰〰〰〰〰〰〰〰〰〰〰〰〰〰〰〰

For a while, it seemed that Bayezid I might be the Ottoman sultan who finally captured Constantinople. Bayezid laid siege to Constantinople in 1394, and kept it up for nearly 8 years.

Unfortunately, Bayezid was so busy fighting in the west that he forgot to look east.

Sultan Bayezid I

Back in Chapter 16, we read about **Tamerlane**— the deadly menace who sacked Delhi, India in 1398. A few years after the Battle of Delhi, Tamerlane attacked the Ottoman Empire! In 1402, Tamerlane crushed Bayezid's army at the **Battle of Ankara**. Afterward, Tamerlane hauled Bayezid off in chains. The Sultan of the Ottoman Empire died a prisoner in Tamerlane's capital, **Samarkand**.

Tamerlane soon died as well. By then, though, the Ottoman Empire was in chaos, and needed a long time to get back on its feet.

The Fall of Constantinople (1453)

So it wasn't Bayezid I who captured Constantinople. Nor was it Bayezid's son, **Sultan Mehmed I**; nor even his grandson, **Sultan Murad II**. The Ottoman sultan who finally captured Constantinople was Bayezid's great-grandson, Sultan Mehmed II— who is also called Mehmed the Conqueror.

How did Constantinople stand for so long against such a strong enemy? The answer is that Constantinople was probably the strongest city on Earth. The whole city was surrounded by high, strong walls that had been hundreds of years in the making. Some sections had two walls,

or even three. If an enemy broke through the outer wall, then he still had more walls to go. And to reach even the first wall, attackers on the land side had to cross a broad, deep moat.

On all other sides, attackers had to cross three huge bodies of water. To the south lay the **Sea of Marmara**. To the east, of course, lay the **Bosporus Strait**. And to the north lay Constantinople's natural harbor: the long, calm, beautiful **Golden Horn**.

Mehmed would have loved to sail his warships into the Golden Horn; but the Byzantines wouldn't let him. Whenever enemies attacked, the Byzantines stretched a long, strong chain across the harbor's entrance. Floating logs kept the chain near the surface of the water, making it impossible to cross. And with the Byzantine navy defending the chain, Mehmed couldn't cut it.

Mehmed also tried **sapping**— in other words, tunneling underneath the city walls. With a finished tunnel, Mehmed's troops might have sneaked into the city and attacked the Byzantines from behind. Or they might have piled enough gunpowder under the walls to blow them sky-high!

But the Byzantines had faced sappers before, and knew how to beat them. Wherever the Byzantines heard digging sounds, they dug holes of their own— collapsing the tunnels on the sappers' heads.

When both sailors and sappers failed, Mehmed turned to a weapon that was still fairly new in Europe: the cannon.

The **Golden Horn** is a fine harbor just north of Constantinople. Two advantages make the Golden Horn the perfect place to load and unload trade ships. First, it is deep enough for big, heavy ships to sail in. Second, it doesn't have all the high waves that trouble ships outside the harbor.

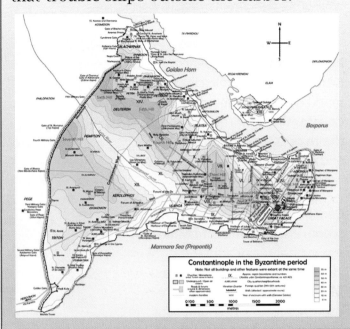

Constantinople in the Byzantine period

A **sapper** was a special kind of soldier trained to tunnel underneath city walls.

Before the Siege of Constantinople, a Hungarian cannon-maker called **Orban** had offered to forge a huge cannon for the city. But the Byzantines couldn't afford Orban's price. So Orban offered his cannon to Mehmed II, who was rich enough to afford any price! Orban's cannon should have been used to defend Constantinople. Instead, it was used to attack it.

The size of Orban's cannon was breathtaking. Even broken down into two pieces, the cannon needed 60 oxen and 400 men to haul it into place. Once it got there, it could hurl a 2-foot stone cannonball a mile through the air! Weighing in at 600 – 1,200 pounds each, these cannonballs could smash any wall to rubble— even Constantinople's.

But Mehmed needed more than just cannon to break into Constantinople. Before his troops could even get close to the walls, they had to build **causeways** over the city moat. To build causeways, they had to dump tons of earth and rock into the moat— with the Byzantines firing down on them all the while.

A **causeway** is a low road across a body of water, made by piling earth and rock into the water.

The end of the siege came on May 29, 1453. When his causeways were finally ready, Mehmed sent thousands of troops streaming over them at once. One set of troops broke through a small gate that someone had foolishly left open.

Meanwhile, janissaries surged over a wall that had been crushed by cannonballs. Each time the Byzantines threw down one janissary, two more leapt up to take his place. With Muslims pouring over the walls in two places at once, the city was lost.

The last Byzantine emperor made a brave end. Casting off the purple cloak that marked him as emperor, **Constantine XI** threw himself into the thickest part of the fighting, and died fighting for his city.

Scene from the battle inside Constantinople

The Fall of Constantinople was a very ugly scene, even for the Late Middle Ages. After waiting hundreds of years for Constantinople, the Muslims were thrilled to have captured it at last! Triumphant Muslims raced from street to street, killing every Christian in sight— even women and children. It was only after the Muslims calmed down that they remembered how much slaves were worth. So they started capturing Christians instead of killing them.

Mehmed the Conqueror riding into Constantinople

A lot of things ended at the Fall of Constantinople.

One thing that ended was the Middle Ages. The Fall of Constantinople marked the end of medieval times, and the start of the Renaissance (Chapter 26).

Another thing that ended was the Byzantine Empire— a Christian empire that had stood for almost 1,000 years. In a way, the Roman Empire also ended; for the Byzantine Empire had started out as the Eastern Roman Empire (Chapter 4).

Another ending happened at the **Hagia Sophia**, the finest church in Constantinople.

The grand old Hagia Sophia had been the capital of Eastern Christianity since the 500s, when Emperor Justinian first built it (Chapter 4). But Mehmed the Conqueror turned it into a mosque! On the very day when Mehmed rode into Constantinople, an imam started chanting the *Shahada* from the altar of the Hagia Sophia—

saying over and over, "There is no god but Allah, and Muhammad is his prophet." After 900 years of glorifying Christ, the Hagia Sophia now stood for Allah.

The years to come brought more changes to the Hagia Sophia. Muslims were offended by all the Christian mosaics inside the old church. So they covered the mosaics with plaster and paint—after first prying out all the golden tiles. They also added four **minarets**, the towers used to call Muslims to prayer five times each day.

౼౼

With Constantinople as its capital, the Ottoman Empire grew faster than ever. **Sultan Selim I** tripled the size of his empire, conquering Arabia, Egypt and more. After starting in Asia and spreading to Europe, the empire now spread to the third continent from Osman's vision: Africa!

Sultan Suleiman I, son to Selim I, was probably the richest Ottoman sultan ever. As a great figure from history, Suleiman has two historic nicknames. The West calls him **Suleiman the Magnificent**; while the East calls him **Suleiman the Lawgiver**.

The Ottoman Empire was truly magnificent in Suleiman's day— not only huge, but also incredibly rich and prosperous. Muslim writers, artists and builders all did some of their best work in Suleiman's day.

One of Suleiman's many projects was the **Dome of the Rock**, which still stands in Jerusalem as a monument to Muhammad's Night Journey (Chapter 5). By Suleiman's day, the original Dome of the Rock was crumbling. So Suleiman restored it, making it much better than the original.

Suleiman the Magnificent

The East remembers Suleiman as a writer of law. Like the Byzantine Emperor Justinian, and like King Henry II of England, Suleiman established one common law over his whole empire. Even today, some Middle Eastern law is still based on Suleiman's laws.

౼౼

Like all Ottoman sultans, Suleiman kept many women in his **harem**. A harem was a special section of the palace set aside for a sultan's many wives.

When a harem woman gave birth to a sultan's child, the sultan usually sent both woman and child away. That way, the harem women couldn't fight over this all-important question: which of their sons would be the next sultan?

But one of Suleiman's women was different from all the others. His wife **Roxelana** was so smart, pretty and fun that Suleiman couldn't bear to send her away. Instead, he kept Roxelana at his side for the rest of his life, raising six children with her.

As the sultan's favorite wife, Roxelana felt that one of her sons should be the next sultan. The trouble was, her sons were only boys; whereas some of Suleiman's sons were grown men. Roxelana was especially worried about one of Suleiman's older sons— a powerful man called **Mustafa**. Wasn't it true that many Ottoman sultans had murdered their own brothers? Knowing this, Roxelana had good reason to fear that Mustafa might murder her sons!

Suleiman and Roxelana
by Anton Hickel

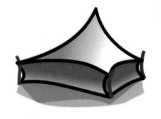

But not if Roxelana murdered him first.

The story of how Mustafa died is really more legend than history. But if the legend is true, then Roxelana planted a false rumor about Mustafa. All of a sudden, Suleiman's spies started hearing that Mustafa was planning a rebellion.

To stop the rebellion, Suleiman summoned his son to his tent. Having no idea that anything was wrong, Mustafa came— probably expecting new orders from his father. Instead, Suleiman calmly looked on while his guards strangled his own son to death.

See Year Three for more on Suleiman the Magnificent.

Muslim Food Laws

Islamic law forbids Muslims to eat certain foods. Any food that Muslims are allowed to eat is **halal**— Arabic for "permissible." Any food that Muslims aren't allowed to eat is **haraam**— Arabic for "sinful."

Two kinds of foods are especially *haraam*: pork and alcohol. Good Muslims never eat any food that comes from a pig. They also avoid alcohol, although not all Muslims live by this rule.

Good Muslims also observe good table manners like these:

➢ They carefully wash their hands before and after each meal.

➢ They don't start eating until their host starts, nor stop until their host stops.

➢ They eat only with their right hands, never their left. And they use at least 3 fingers.

➢ They do not blow on their food to cool it.

➢ During the day, they stand to drink water; but at night, they sit or lie down to drink.

Saint George

Saint George is the patron saint of England. But St. George came from nowhere near England. Instead, he came from somewhere in the Eastern Roman Empire. As we've read, the Eastern Roman Empire became the Byzantine Empire, which later fell to the Ottoman Empire.

The story of St. George is part real and part legend. The best-known legend tells how St. George came to slay a dragon!

As the story goes, George was wandering through North Africa when he met a hermit with a sad tale. A dragon had taken over the little kingdom where George now stood. This evil menace had already eaten all of the kingdom's livestock, and was now eating its way through the children. The dragon wanted a new child to eat every day, or else it would attack the city.

Every day, the king faced a terrible choice. If he obeyed the dragon, then one precious child would surely die. But if he disobeyed the dragon, then his whole kingdom might die.

So far, the king had made his choice in the fairest way he could: by drawing names from a pot. But today, the hermit said, was the worst day yet— for the name that had come from the pot that day belonged to the king's own daughter. At that very moment, the princess was on her way to the dragon's lair, never to return.

Like the hero he was, George immediately galloped off to slay the dragon and save the princess. But this was no easy dragon to slay! When George thrust his spear at the dragon, the spear broke against its scales. His sword was also powerless to pierce the dragon's scales. Meanwhile, poisonous smoke spewed from the dragon's mouth, almost suffocating the brave knight.

Fortunately, the smoke wasn't thick enough to hide the dragon's one weakness. There was a soft spot with no scales, right between breast and wing. When George stabbed this vulnerable spot, the dragon fell dead!

Later, the king asked George how he could thank him for saving his daughter. The only thanks George wanted was this: that everyone in the whole kingdom should become a Christian!

The real story of St. George isn't as romantic. The future St. George was a Christian soldier who served under one of the most Christian-hating Roman emperors ever: Diocletian. When Diocletian found out about George's faith, he ordered George to give it up. And when George refused, Diocletian killed him.

Greek icon of St. George the Dragon-slayer

The Caspian Sea

The Caspian Sea is a huge inland sea east of the Black Sea. But the Caspian Sea is no ordinary sea. Unlike most seas, the Caspian Sea isn't connected to the oceans of the world. Fresh water flows into the Caspian Sea from the Volga River, the Ural River and many others. But no water flows out of the Caspian Sea. The only way water leaves is by evaporation.

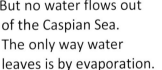

When fresh water evaporates from the Caspian Sea, it leaves behind minerals— including salts. Just as the oceans have built up salt over time, so the Caspian Sea has built up salt. On average, the water of the Caspian Sea holds about one-third as much salt as ocean water.

The Caspian Sea is a great place to catch a kind of fish called **sturgeon**. Russian fishermen make sturgeon eggs into a fancy food that most people can't afford: **caviar**. As of 2016, some kinds of caviar cost well over $100 per ounce!

The Dark Continent

Africa is the second-largest continent. Of the seven continents on Earth, only Asia is larger than Africa.

The easiest way to study such a big continent is to divide it into regions.

The first region, **North Africa**, is home to one of the biggest, driest deserts in the world: the **Sahara**. Next to Antarctica, the Sahara is probably the last place on Earth where most people would want to live. Water is extremely scarce there. On the other hand, sand is extremely plentiful! High winds whip the Sahara sands into deadly sandstorms, piling them into sand dunes up to 500 feet high.

Only two parts of North Africa aren't part of the Sahara.

Africa is the hottest continent. Many of the hottest temperatures ever recorded on Earth come from Africa! This is because most of Africa lies in the **tropics**.

Remember what the tropics are— the warm part of the globe between the **Tropic of Cancer** and the **Tropic of Capricorn**.

➢ One is the **Nile River Valley** in Egypt and Sudan. Egypt is where one of the oldest known civilizations began.

➢ The other is the **Maghreb**, a mountainous region along the Mediterranean Sea. The coasts of Morocco, Algeria, Tunisia and Libya are all part of the Maghreb.

With a total length of more than 4,100 miles, the Nile is the longest river in the world.

Just below the Sahara, between the dry desert and the wetter lands to the south, lies a half-dry region called the **Sahel**. In wet years, the Sahel receives enough rain for crops. But in dry years, stunted crops can leave the people of the Sahel starving.

Along the southern coast of West Africa lies a region called **Guinea**. Since medieval times, Guinea has been known for its gold mines. Near the end of medieval times, Guinean gold helped launch the Age of Discovery (Chapter 24).

Southeast of Guinea lies a region called the **Congo**. The Congo is home to Africa's deepest jungles and wildest animals. Gorillas, leopards and pythons all live in the Congo, as do many other wild species.

East of the Congo lies the **African Great Lakes region**. The biggest lake in Africa, **Lake Victoria**, is also the second biggest lake in the world. Only Lake Superior in North America is bigger.

East of the African Great Lakes region lies a grassy plain called the **Serengeti**. The Serengeti is where the wild herds go to graze— including gazelles, wildebeests, zebras and more. The Serengeti is also where lions and hyenas go to prey on the herds.

A lioness taking some sun on a rock in the Serengeti

In medieval times, most people knew very little about any part of Africa south of the Sahara. Everyone knew all about North Africa, especially Egypt. But the Sahara was so hot, so dry and so wide that only a few people ever dared to cross it. **Sub-Saharan Africa** was the **Dark Continent**— a mysterious world filled with unknown dangers.

Sub-Saharan Africa is the part of Africa south of the Sahara Desert.

Medieval Empires of West Africa

Traders were especially curious about the Dark Continent. Sub-Saharan Africa offered valuable goods that many traders wanted to buy— rare items like gold, ivory and black pepper.

The problem was, most traders were afraid to go and get those goods. For they all knew how deadly the Sahara could be.

WORLD HISTORY

An **oasis** is a place to find water in the middle of a desert. Oases are like tiny green islands amid a huge sea of sand.

A Sahara oasis in Libya

Fortunately, one kind of trader knew how to cross the Sahara without dying. The **Tuaregs** were a tough people who lived all around the Sahara, and sometimes in it. As natives of the desert, the Tuaregs had learned how to survive there— what to wear; how to travel; and above all, where to find water.

As dry as the Sahara is, it does offer a few **oases** where travelers can find water. However, crossing the Sahara is not as simple as hopping on a camel and setting out for the next oasis! For one thing, the sand dunes are always shifting— which makes it easy to get lost. For another, the oases lie many days apart— which makes it easy to run out of water. And in the Sahara, even a few hours without water can be enough to kill.

To solve this water problem, the Tuaregs built a small village at each oasis along their trade routes. When a **trade caravan** started to run out of water, it sent a messenger to the next oasis ahead. Then the villagers sent a caravan loaded with water to meet the trade caravan.

A modern-day salt caravan crossing the Sahara

So far, so good. But if anything went wrong— for example, if the water caravan couldn't find the trade caravan, or found it too late— then the traders might still run out of water. Then everyone would die a hot, dry, sandy Saharan death.

A **trade caravan** is a group of traders who travel together for safety. Sahara trade caravans almost always used camels.

௶௶௶௶௶௶௶௶௶௶௶௶௶௶௶௶௶௶௶௶௶௶௶௶௶௶௶௶௶௶௶

What did traders buy with all of that gold and ivory from sub-Saharan Africa? The answer is mostly salt. In the middle of the western Sahara, halfway between Morocco and Guinea, lay a salt mining town called **Taghaza**. The slaves of Taghaza worked at one of the most miserable jobs ever— mining slabs of rock salt.

What made salt mining so miserable was that the salt got into everything. All of Taghaza was salty— from the drinking water and the food to the miners' clothes, skin and eyes. Even the walls of the miners' huts were made from stacked slabs of rock salt. The miners' jobs were so hard that even today, when people think of jobs they'd rather not do, they speak of going "back to the salt mines."

Why did miners keep doing those hard jobs? Because salt was so valuable— especially to the Africans of hot, humid Guinea. People who sweat a lot lose a lot of salt, and need a way to replace it. Livestock need salt to thrive. Salt is also used to preserve meat and fish, or simply to flavor meals.

௶௶௶௶௶௶௶௶௶௶௶௶௶௶௶௶௶௶௶௶௶௶௶௶௶௶௶௶௶௶௶

Wherever trade grew, empires grew. Taxing trade was a great way for emperors to grow rich. Just as the Mongol Empire taxed trade along the Silk Road, so the empires of West Africa taxed trade across the Sahara.

Stacked slabs of rock salt

The medieval era saw the rises and falls of three great West African empires. The first was **Ghana**; the next was **Mali**; and the last was **Songhai**.

All three empires arose in the Sahel, just south of the Sahara. They stood between Guinea and the Sahara, collecting taxes on gold from Guinea and salt from the Sahara.

Just how the **Ghana Empire** began, no one knows for sure. Some say that the first kings of Ghana were traders who came down from the north to take advantage of the locals. Others say that it was the locals who founded Ghana. Since it all happened so long ago, before anyone in West Africa learned to write, no one can say for sure.

The Ghana Empire
(300? - 1235?)

What is sure is that the Emperor of Ghana owned a lot of gold! One writer who visited Ghana in the 800s saw gold everywhere. Gold jewelry was only the beginning. He also saw golden swords, shields, clothes, hats— even dog collars and horse harnesses!

〰〰〰〰〰〰〰〰〰〰〰〰〰〰〰〰〰〰〰〰〰〰〰〰〰〰〰〰〰

Between Ghana and the next empire, the Mali Empire, came a big change. The people of Ghana believed in ancient African religions, which differed from tribe to tribe. But Mali was a Muslim empire.

A **griot** is a special kind of singing historian found only in West Africa. Griots memorize long, detailed songs about West African history. Before writing came to West Africa, the only way to learn this history was to listen to griot songs. Many important stories would be forgotten today, were it not for the excellent memories of griots.

Learning history from a griot is nothing like opening a history book. To share what they know, griots must sing their songs from beginning to end— which can take more than a day!

The founder of Mali was a mighty Muslim prince called **Sundiata Keita**. Sundiata belonged to the **Mandinka**, one of the first West African tribes to go Muslim.

According to **griot** legend, Sundiata wasn't born mighty. Instead, he was born with a spine so crooked that he couldn't walk!

But there came a day when Sundiata needed his strength. That was the day when a half-brother insulted Sundiata's poor mother, who also had a crooked spine. Sundiata longed to punish his half-brother; but he needed strength to do it.

So Sundiata went to a blacksmith, who gave him a heavy iron rod. Sundiata pulled and pulled on that iron, straining with all his might— until finally, his spine went straight, while the iron went crooked! After that, Sundiata wasn't a bent weakling anymore. Instead, he was a mighty warrior with a backbone stronger than iron!

With a mighty king like that at their head, the Mandinka soon conquered all other tribes

Griots from Mali

around them. As Emperor of Mali, Sundiata Keita took on a new title: *mansa*, Mandinka for "king of kings."

The most famous mansa of Mali, **Mansa Musa**, also rose to power in an interesting way.

The mansa before Mansa Musa wanted to explore the world. So he sent 200 ships out into the Atlantic, ordering their captains to report back whatever they found. Only one of those captains ever came back— and with a frightening story to tell! At the far edge of the Atlantic, the captain said, churned a huge whirlpool that had sucked down all the other ships. It would have sucked him down as well, had he not been last in line.

But the mansa didn't believe his captain. To prove him wrong, the mansa led an exploration of his own— this time with 2,000 ships. Sadly, not one of those 2,000 ever returned, not even the mansa's ship.

With the old mansa out of the picture, his second-in-command took over Mali. That was Mansa Musa.

Mali terracotta horseman

If the Ghana Empire had a lot of gold, then the Mali Empire had even more. For Mali grew larger than Ghana— large enough to swallow some of the gold mines down in Guinea. Instead of just taxing gold, Mansa Musa mined gold of his own.

Under the law of Mali, any gold nuggets found in the mines automatically belonged to the *mansa*. Others could own gold dust; but the big chunks all went to the emperor. On a famous map published all over Europe in the 1300s, Mansa Musa eyes a gold nugget bigger than his fist!

Mansa Musa on a Spanish map published in 1375

The *Hajj* is a yearly pilgrimage to the place where Islam was born: Mecca, Arabia. All Muslims who are able must take the *Hajj* at least once in their lives.

Like all good Muslims, Mansa Musa took the *Hajj* to Mecca (Chapter 5). But with that much gold, Mansa Musa's *Hajj* was like no one else's. As pocket money for his journey, Mansa Musa's caravan carried tons of gold dust— enough to pay for a brand-new mosque at every city where Mansa Musa happened to stop on a Friday night!

Mansa Musa also spent gold to make Mali more Muslim. On his return from Mecca, he brought home a trained architect to build new mosques in Mali. He also brought home imams and books, hoping to teach his people a purer form of Islam.

〰〰〰〰〰〰〰〰〰〰〰〰〰〰〰〰〰〰〰〰〰〰〰〰〰〰〰〰〰〰〰〰〰〰〰〰〰

The Songhai Empire (1200? - 1600?)

The next empire, the **Songhai Empire**, started as a kingdom that broke away from the Mali Empire.

Over time, the Songhai conquered more and more cities that had once belonged to Mali. The greatest of these cities were **Timbuktu** and **Djenne**. Both lay on or near the most important river in West Africa, the **Niger River**.

The rest of the world learned of Timbuktu from a Muslim traveler called **Leo Africanus**. Just as Marco Polo stunned the West with news from China, so Leo Africanus stunned the West with news from Timbuktu.

A sketch of medieval Timbuktu

According to Leo, the emperor of Songhai owned a bar of gold that weighed almost 1,000 pounds! Leo also wrote that Timbuktu was filled with wise men; and that its people strolled casually through its streets each night, serenading one another with fine music. Ever since Leo Africanus' book, travelers have seen Timbuktu as a far-off place of mystery and wonder— hard to reach, but definitely worth the trouble.

The Great Mosque of Djenne in modern times

Djenne is known for the largest mud brick building in the world: the **Great Mosque of Djenne**. The craftsmen of Mali and Songhai built mostly with sun-dried mud bricks, all covered with plaster. The result was a curious style of building found nowhere else in the world.

Of the three great empires of medieval West Africa, Songhai was the greatest. Its territory was even bigger than Mali's, and its riches were beyond count.

Unfortunately, the Songhai emperors failed to keep up with the times.

In the late 1500s, the Sultan of Morocco needed gold to defend himself against the Portuguese. So he decided to steal it from Songhai. The sultan's armies brought weapons the Songhai had never seen before: muskets and cannon. Without muskets and cannon of their own, the poor Songhai warriors never had a chance.

Thus the Songhai Empire collapsed, as all empires collapse. From the 1590s forward, there were no great empires in West Africa, only scattered kingdoms.

The logs that jut from the sides of mud-brick buildings like the Great Mosque of Djenne are called **toron**. Toron serve two purposes:

➢ One is to tie the building together.

➢ The other is provide a permanent scaffold for workers who keep the outside walls sealed with plaster. Without a tight coat of plaster, rainwater would seep in and dissolve the mud bricks.

Besides the Great Mosque, Djenne is also known for the **Djenne terracotta figures**. These strange statuettes were first sculpted by artists of the Mali Empire.

The Mamluk Sultanate of Egypt

On the far side of the Sahara from West Africa, Egypt suffered a different set of troubles.

Unlike West Africa, Egypt had been Muslim for a long time. As we read in Chapter 7, the **Rashidun Caliphate** took over Egypt in the mid-600s. The next caliphate, the **Umayyad Caliphate**, kept a firm grip on Egypt.

After that, the story of Egypt gets a bit more complicated.

The next caliphate was the **Abbasid Caliphate**, which took over in 750. Like the caliphs before them, the Abbasid caliphs claimed to rule the whole Islamic Empire.

But they were wrong. In truth, there was no longer any such thing as the Islamic Empire. Instead, there were many separate Islamic kingdoms, each ruled by a sultan or emir (Chapter 12).

During the Crusades, Egypt fell to a family of sultans called the **Ayyubid dynasty**. The Ayyubids were the heirs of **Saladin**, the Muslim hero who battled Richard the Lionheart in the Third Crusade. Saladin's dynasty ruled not only Egypt, but also the Holy Land, Syria and part of Arabia.

> **Mamluk** is an Arabic word that can be translated "the owned" or "slave-soldier."

Over time, the Ayyubid sultans came to depend on a special kind of soldier called a **Mamluk**.

Mamluks were a lot like the janissaries of the Ottoman Empire (Chapter 20). The first Mamluks came from non-Muslim lands that were conquered by Muslims. They were taken from their parents as boys, and then raised as slave-soldiers to serve a sultan or caliph.

Just as the Ottoman sultans depended on janissaries, so the Ayyubid sultans depended on Mamluks. The Mamluks did everything for their sultans, from defending their country to running their government.

The more the Mamluks did for their sultans, the more they wondered why they couldn't be sultans themselves. After all, they were already doing everything sultans were supposed to do!

The Mamluks' big chance came during the **Seventh Crusade**. In 1249, **King Louis IX of France** sailed across the Mediterranean to a landing in Egypt. Louis planned to take Egypt first, and then use it as a base to take back the Holy Land.

Mamluk lancers

Like all of the Holy Land Crusades, the Seventh Crusade was filled with trouble for the crusaders. The trouble this time was that the Nile River happened to be flooding when Louis landed. Instead of taking Egypt by surprise, Louis had to sit around for months, waiting for the water to go down so that he could attack.

All of that waiting gave the Ayyubids plenty of time to prepare. When Louis finally attacked, the Ayyubids were ready for him. Instead of Louis capturing Egypt, the Ayyubids captured Louis! The Egyptians collected a huge ransom for Louis before finally letting him go.

Thus the Seventh Crusade ended in victory for Egypt. But it was also the beginning of the end for the Ayyubid dynasty.

King Louis VII of France embarking on the Seventh Crusade

Mamluk warrior

Early in the crusade, the old Ayyubid sultan suffered a deep leg wound. When the wound grew infected, the sultan was in danger of blood poisoning. So his doctors cut off the leg, trying to save the sultan's life. Alas, it was too late— for the sultan died anyway.

Fortunately, the dead sultan had a son to take his place.

Unfortunately, the sultan's son made a foolish mistake. Given everything his father's Mamluks had done for him, the new sultan should have treated them with respect. But he didn't. Instead, he ordered them to step aside so that he replace them with new favorites of his own.

As the most powerful men in Egypt, the Mamluks didn't have to step aside for this disrespectful new sultan. Instead, they simply killed him! With their enemy out of the way, the Mamluks named one of their own to take his place.

Thus the Mamluks managed an incredible rise— all the way from slave-soldiers to sultans! As of 1250, the Ayyubid dynasty no longer ruled Egypt. A new government had arisen in Egypt: the **Mamluk Sultanate**.

Ten years later, the Mamluk Sultanate faced one of the worst tests any government could face: an invasion from the Mongol Empire (Chapter 19).

By 1260, Genghis Khan had been dead for more than 30 years. But the Mongol Empire was still growing. **Mongke Khan**, grandson to Genghis Khan, now ruled the Mongol Empire. **Hulagu Khan**, brother to Mongke, was in charge of conquering the Middle East.

As always, the Mongols conquered swiftly. The **Sack of Baghdad**, Iraq in 1258 was a huge victory for Hulagu Khan. Two years later, Hulagu conquered all of Syria as well.

Hulagu Khan leading a Mongol horde

The next big target was Egypt. As he prepared to invade Egypt, Hulagu Khan sent this terrifying message to the Mamluk Sultanate:

"… You should think of what happened to other countries and submit… We have conquered vast areas, [killing] all the people. You cannot escape from the terror of our armies. Where can you flee? …Our horses are swift, our arrows sharp, our swords like thunderbolts, our hearts as hard as the mountains, our soldiers as numerous as the sand. Fortresses will not detain us, nor arms stop us. Your prayers to God will not avail against us… We will shatter your mosques and reveal the weakness of your God and then will kill your children and your old men together."

When they least expected it, the Mamluks had a great stroke of luck. Around the time Hulagu sent this message, he learned that Mongke Khan had died. Now he would have to go back to Mongolia, where there would be a big meeting to choose the next Great Khan. To the delight of the Mamluks, Hulagu took most of his army with him— leaving only a small army to invade Egypt.

Instead of waiting for that army, the Mamluks rode out to meet it. The Mongols and the Mamluks locked swords in the Holy Land, at a place called **Ain Jalut**.

The key to the **Battle of Ain Jalut** was the Mongols' favorite battle plan: the **feigned retreat**.

When facing a Mongol horde, most armies formed a Roman-style **shield wall**. This was a tight wall of shields bristling with long, strong spears. A well-handled spear could skewer any horse that tried to leap the shield wall.

But the Mongols were too clever to leap the shield wall. Instead, they made a feigned retreat. First, they made a half-hearted try at breaking through the shield wall. When that failed, they pretended to run away in fear. Seeing this, most enemies gave chase— which was exactly what the Mongols wanted them to do. Once their enemies left the safety of their shield wall, the Mongols turned and attacked!

But at the Battle of Ain Jalut, the Mamluks turned the feigned retreat back on the Mongols.

Just before the battle, the Mamluks split their army in half. The first half they hid. The second half attacked the Mongols, and then ran away— straight toward the place where the first half was hiding. When the Mongols gave chase, the first half leapt out of hiding and attacked!

In winning the Battle of Ain Jalut, the Mamluks did something that no one had done since before the days of Genghis Khan: they actually defeated a Mongol horde. Thanks to this victory, the Mongol Empire never conquered Egypt. Instead, the Mamluks ruled Egypt for the next 250 years— until 1517, when Sultan Selim I of the Ottoman Empire finally conquered them.

The Avignon Papacy

The end of the Holy Land Crusades raised an important question about authority in the Christian world. The question was, which was greater: the kings' authority, or the popes' authority?

While the Crusades lasted, the popes' authority was probably greater. For example, when the pope announced the Third Crusade, the three mightiest kings in Europe all answered the call. Frederick Barbarossa, Philip II and Richard I all set out for the Holy Land. So in a way, the pope was mightier than all three.

Things were different after the Crusades. For no one could deny that the Crusades had failed. All four Crusader States had fallen; and the Holy Land had stayed Muslim.

After that many failures, it was hard to believe that the popes were really as close to God as they said they were. So some Christians paid less attention to their popes, and more attention to their kings.

Thirty years after the last Holy Land Crusade, an Italian pope called **Boniface VIII** lost a big argument with **King Philip IV of France** over whose authority was greater.

King Philip IV of France   Pope Boniface VIII

As usual, the argument started over money. King Philip needed money to refill his empty treasury. To raise that money, Philip raised taxes on the richest organization in France: the Church.

But the Church also needed more money. So Pope Boniface wrote an angry **papal bull** against Philip (*Clericis laicos*, 1296). Boniface warned that if any king tried to tax the Church without permission from the pope, then the pope would have that king arrested and thrown out of the Church!

Philip answered with another blow to the pope's pocketbook. Under a new law Philip wrote, no French church could send any money at all to the Church of Rome!

Boniface answered back with his harshest words yet. In a papal bull called ***Unam Sanctam***, Boniface wrote that the pope was the highest authority on Earth. If a king

A **papal bull** is an open letter containing a special announcement from a pope. The name "bull" comes from *bulla*, the Latin name for the pope's official seal.

A papal bull from the 1600s with a stamped lead *bulla*

did wrong, then the pope had the power to judge that king. But only God had the power to judge a pope! *Unam Sanctam* ended with this strong warning about heaven and hell:

"… it is absolutely necessary for salvation that every human creature be subject to the Roman [Pope]."

In other words, no one could be saved without the pope. So Philip had two choices: he could either obey the pope, or he could literally go to hell!

At this, Philip decided that enough was enough. In 1303, Philip sent a small army to arrest Boniface. Philip's men caught up with the pope at his home in Anagni, Italy, just outside Rome. Seizing Boniface, Philip's men threw the old man in jail for three days, giving him neither food nor water.

At the end of those three days, an Italian army chased off Philip's men. But before they left, one of Philip's men slapped the old pope hard across the face. This famous episode has two names: the **Anagni Slap** and the **Outrage at Anagni**.

Between the slap, the jail time and the wound to his pride, the Outrage at Anagni was too much for Boniface. The old pope died less than a month later.

A **papal conclave** is a special meeting to decide who will be the next pope. When an old pope dies, the College of Cardinals locks itself inside the Sistine Chapel at Vatican City, Rome. While the cardinals vote, discuss and then vote some more, black smoke rises from the chapel's chimney. But when the cardinals finish voting, white smoke rises.

The whole affair ends with the head cardinal joyfully announcing *Habemus papam*— Latin for "We have a pope!"

The next pope was an Italian who served for less than a year. The pope after that, **Clement V**, was a loyal Frenchman who did whatever King Philip asked.

One of the things Philip asked was to move the Church from Italy to France! In 1309, Pope Clement V moved the offices of the Church from Rome to **Avignon**, a city in southeastern France. This was the beginning of the **Avignon Papacy**, which was to last almost 70 years— all the way from 1309 – 1377. The next seven popes were all Frenchmen, and all lived and worked at Avignon.

The **Avignon Papacy** was a time when the popes lived and worked not in Rome, but in Avignon, France.

The Americas

North America is the third-largest continent on earth, and **South America** the fourth-largest. Together, the two Americas are much larger than the second-largest continent: Africa. Even together, though, the two Americas are not quite as large as the largest continent: Asia.

Two oceans separate the Americas from Asia, Africa and Europe. The enormous **Atlantic Ocean** lies east of the Americas; and the even more enormous **Pacific Ocean** lies west.

Between North and South America lie two more big bodies of water. The northern body is the **Gulf of Mexico**; and the southern is the **Caribbean Sea**.

Just north of Central America, a big peninsula juts out between the Gulf of Mexico and the Caribbean Sea. This is the **Yucatan Peninsula**. In modern times, most of the Yucatan belongs to Mexico. But Belize also owns part, and Guatemala another part.

For a long time, the only way ships could cross from the Atlantic to the Pacific was to sail all the way around South America. Of course, they might have sailed around North America too— but only if the water wasn't clogged with sea ice, which it always was.

The trip from Atlantic to Pacific got a lot easier after engineers finished their work on a certain **isthmus**.

The narrow part of North America that connects to

> An **isthmus** is a narrow bridge of land that connects two larger bodies of land.

South America is called **Central America**. And the narrowest part of Central America is the **Isthmus of Panama**. At its narrowest, Panama is less than 50 miles wide.

The narrowness of the Isthmus of Panama is why engineers chose it for one of the biggest projects ever built. The **Panama Canal** is a man-made waterway connecting the Atlantic to the Pacific. United States engineers finished the canal in 1914. By sailing through the Panama Canal, ships can cross from Atlantic to Pacific in about 8 hours— instead of spending weeks sailing around South America!

Empires of Middle America and South America

Long before Leif Ericsson, and even longer before Christopher Columbus, native kings built great empires in the Americas. Several empires arose in **Middle America**, which is another name for Central America and Mexico. And one empire arose in western South America, home of the **Andes Mountains**.

This is not to say that there were no great empires north of Mexico, in what are now the United States and Canada. Archaeologists have found signs of large civilizations north of Mexico. What they have not found, though, are the long-lasting stone buildings that other empires left behind. Without stone buildings, and without any writing, it is hard to learn much about any empires that might have grown up north of Mexico.

> The **Andes Mountains** of western South America stretch about 4,350 miles from north to south— which makes them by far the longest mountain chain in the world.

Down in Middle America, one mysterious empire left plenty of stone buildings, but very little writing. The capital of this empire was Teotihuacan, an ancient city about 30 miles northeast of what is now Mexico City.

The people of Teotihuacan, whoever they were, probably started their city around 100 BC. They went on to build some of the biggest buildings ever built in Middle America.

One such building was the **Pyramid of the Sun**, a massive pyramid that

A view down Teotihuacan's Avenue of the Dead with the Pyramid of the Sun on the left

still stands almost 250 feet tall! Actually, the Pyramid of the Sun used to be even taller; for a temple once stood at its peak. But that temple collapsed long ago.

The Pyramid of the Sun and its partner, the Pyramid of the Moon, stand on a long street called the **Avenue of the Dead**. So do many other big buildings, all lined with curious paintings of Teotihuacan's gods. These paintings give good clues about what the people of Teotihuacan believed; but without more writing, it is hard to know for sure.

> The people of Teotihuacan may have been the first to build temples in a Middle American style called **talud-tablero**. *Talud* is Spanish for "slope," while *tablero* is Spanish for "board" or "table." The walls of talud-tablero temples go back and forth between steep slopes and level tables.

YYY YYY YYY YYY YYY YYY YYY YYY YYY YYY YYY YYY YYY

We know much more about the Maya civilization, a great civilization that arose on the Yucatan Peninsula. For the Maya not only built temples, but also wrote books.

Maya writing carved into stone

The Maya writing system was the best in Middle America. But Maya writing was nothing like English writing! Instead, it was more like Egyptian hieroglyphics. Like the Egyptians, the Maya didn't use the letters of an alphabet to represent sounds. Instead, they used symbols to represent words, ideas and sometimes syllables.

From Maya writing and art, historians have learned all sorts of strange facts about the Maya. For example, the Maya believed in strange-looking gods with peaked skulls, crossed eyes and fangs like snakes'. Maya kings were supposed to be descended from these gods.

Maya queens wanted their sons to look like their god ancestors. So they tied sandwich boards to their babies' foreheads, clamping them down hard for hours at a time. That way, their babies' soft young skulls would grow in the peaked shape of a god's. Mothers also tied small toys close to their babies' eyes— so that in looking at the toys, their babies would grow cross-eyed. Mothers even filed their babies' teeth into fangs.

Like their neighbors in Teotihuacan, the Maya built tall temples to worship their gods. At the tops of some Maya temples stood round-backed pulpits for the king. The reason for the roundness was to focus the king's voice so that all could hear. When the **acoustics** worked right, a Maya king could talk down to his people with a voice that echoed from on high, as if he were a god!

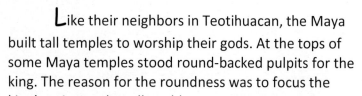

Acoustics is the science of sound.

The Maya built most of their temples from a special kind of rock called **limestone**. One of the many good qualities of limestone is that it is soft when it comes out of the quarry, but hardens in the air. Fresh limestone is soft enough to cut, but then hard enough to make long-lasting buildings. Maya stoneworkers could cut fresh limestone into blocks so smooth that they didn't need mortar to hold them together. All they needed was their own weight.

One reason the Maya built with limestone was because they were missing an important piece of

A **codex** is a kind of book from before the days of the printing press. The plural of codex is **codices**.

The **Maya Codices** were hand-written, hand-illustrated books made of folded paper. The Maya wrote many codices, recording all sorts of facts about their history and religion.

Sadly, only a few Maya Codices still survive. The Spaniards who conquered Middle America in the 1500s wanted to stamp out the Maya religion. In doing so, they burned almost all of the Maya Codices.

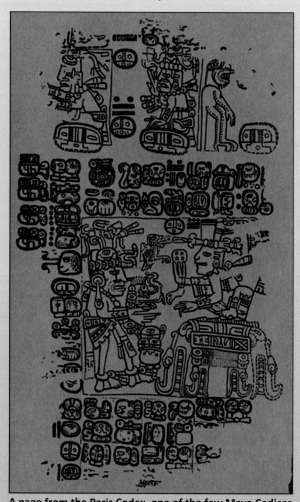

A page from the Paris Codex, one of the few Maya Codices that still survives

technology: **iron tools**. Unlike ancient peoples of Africa, Asia and Europe, the ancient Americans never learned to make iron tools. Instead, the Maya made their cutting tools from hard stones like **obsidian**. Since stone tools can be brittle, Maya stoneworkers needed the softest building stone they could find.

Obsidian is a hard stone that comes from volcanoes.

Temple I at the Maya city of Tikal, with its pulpit at the top

Medieval Americans were also missing two other important pieces of technology: **wheels** and **pulleys**. The Maya knew enough about wheels to use them in small ways. But they never seemed to use them as tools— to roll heavy loads on a cart, or to lift heavy loads with pulley and rope.

One science the Maya knew well was **astronomy**— the study of the heavens. Maya astronomers followed the motions of the sun, moon and planets very carefully. For example, they knew that the **solar year** lasted 365 days. So they made a solar calendar with 18 months of 20 days, plus 1 month of 5, for a total of 365.

One **solar year** is the length of time it takes the Earth to revolve around the sun.

Another Maya calendar focused on Venus. Maya astronomers watched Venus appear as the morning star for 263 days; then disappear for 50 days; then reappear as the evening star for 263 days; and then finally disappear for 8 days. So the total number of days on their Venusian calendar was 263 + 50 + 263 + 8 = 584.

One might say that the Maya were obsessed with calendars! For any given day, Maya astronomers could name a date from the solar calendar, the Venusian calendar and other calendars. Dates were so important to the Maya that they even built birthdates into their children's names.

ᵞᵞᵞ ᵞᵞᵞ ᵞᵞᵞ ᵞᵞᵞ ᵞᵞᵞ ᵞᵞᵞ ᵞᵞᵞ ᵞᵞᵞ ᵞᵞᵞ

The next great empire in Middle America was the **Aztec Empire**. The Aztecs arose in what is now Mexico. But the Aztec people weren't originally from Mexico.

Both the Maya and the Aztecs worshiped a strange creator god who combined the body of a serpent with the feathers of a bird. The Maya called their feathered serpent **Kukulcan**; while the Aztecs called theirs **Quetzalcoatl**.

Quetzalcoatl bridged the gap between heaven and earth. His feathers tied him to the sky, and his snakelike body to the ground. The swishing of his tail caused the wind, and the writhing of his body caused earthquakes.

Quetzalcoatl gleefully swallowing a victim

Instead, the Aztecs sprang from an older people called the **Nahua**. According to legend, the Nahua started as seven tribes living in seven caves, all hidden in a mysterious place called **Chicomoztoc**.

Sometime later, the seven tribes moved to a second mysterious place: **Aztlan**. Just where either place was, no one now knows for sure. But the name "Aztec" comes from Aztlan, the lost second home of the Nahua people.

Later still, the seven tribes struck out from Aztlan in search of another new home. One by one, they all settled in the **Valley of Mexico**. The last tribe to arrive was the **Mexica**. This was the tribe that would wind up giving Mexico its name.

The **Valley of Mexico** is a high valley in south central Mexico. The average elevation in the Valley of Mexico is over 7,300 feet— almost one and a half miles above sea level.

In medieval times, five marshy lakes covered much of the valley floor. The biggest was **Lake Texcoco**, where the Aztecs built their capital: **Tenochtitlan**.

In modern times, all five lakes have been filled in to make room for one of the biggest cities in the world: Mexico City.

By the time the Mexica reached the Valley of Mexico, the other tribes had already taken all of the best land. The only land the Mexica could find was a rocky hill that no one else wanted, at a place called **Chapultepec**. The Mexica pitched their tents at Chapultepec, but kept looking for a good land to call their own.

The Mexicas' priests told them to watch for a sign. They promised that the god of war would show his warrior people the land he wanted them to have.

The coat of arms of Mexico, which comes from the famous vision of the Mexica priests

The Mexica hardly expected to find their new land in a lake. Yet that is just where they found it!

Just east of Chapultepec lay a marshy lake called **Lake Texcoco**. Looking out over the lake one day, Mexica priests noticed a peculiar sight. On an island not far from shore, a golden eagle stood perched on a prickly pear cactus, eating a snake it had just caught.

This was the sign that the priests had been waiting for. Since the Mexica could find no good land of their own, they would take the land the eagle marked for them. They would fill in Lake Texcoco!

A **causeway** is a low land bridge made by piling earth and rock into a shallow body of water.

The Aztecs deliberately left gaps in the causeways that led to Tenochtitlan. Most of the time, wooden bridges spanned these gaps. But when the city was threatened, the Aztecs could raise the bridges and cut off their enemies!

Fortunately, most of the lake wasn't too deep. By carrying in tons of earth and rock, the Mexica built a **causeway** over to their island. With more earth and rock, they added more dry land to their island. They also added two more causeways. Over time, they built their little island into a big city called **Tenochtitlan**.

But where did the Mexica raise crops, if all they owned was an island? The lake filled that need as well.

In certain sections of the lake, Mexica farmers walled off watery gardens called *chinampas*. These were raised planting beds made by piling earth on the floor of the lake.

Chinampas were just a few feet wide, with narrow canals in between. With the water that close, crops always stayed moist, whether it rained or not. And with weather as warm as Mexico's, the Mexica could raise three or four crops per year!

To raise that many crops required careful planning. Mexica farmers didn't plant seeds on their *chinampas*; because raising crops from seed takes too long. Instead, they planted seeds in separate, smaller seedbeds. Only after seeds grew into seedlings did they transplant them to *chinampas*, where they grew to full size. Mexica farmers were always raising two crops at once: seeds in seedbeds, and seedlings in *chinampas*.

Of course, seedbeds also needed space. So Mexica farmers wove reed mats, and then floated them in the lake. With thin layers of soil spread over them, these well-watered mats made perfect seedbeds.

The Mexica tribe grew quickly, now that it had plenty of food and a good place to live. Soon the tribe was strong enough to conquer other tribes, including its brother tribes from Aztlan.

As Tenochtitlan grew, it became a capital for more than just the Mexica. In time, it became a capital for a new people: the **Aztecs**. These were all of the Nahua tribes who had once lived at Aztlan, plus more besides.

ɣ/ɣ ɣ/ɣ ɣ/ɣ ɣ/ɣ ɣ/ɣ ɣ/ɣ ɣ/ɣ

In the middle of Tenochtitlan, on the very spot where the priests had seen their golden eagle, stood the **Sacred Precinct** where the Aztecs worshiped. The biggest of the many temples in the Sacred Precinct was the **Templo Mayor**. This was a double temple in honor of two favorite Aztec gods: **Huitzilopochtli**, god of war; and **Tlaloc**, god of water and storms.

A model of the Sacred Precinct inside Tenochtitlan

If even a few of the stories told about the Aztecs are true, then their worship was horribly cruel. The Aztecs would do anything to please their gods. Sadly, what pleased their gods was blood— lots and lots of human blood.

Most of that blood came from enemy soldiers. When Aztec warriors fought, they tried hard to capture their enemies, rather than kill them. But this wasn't because the Aztecs were kind. It was only because they wanted to haul their enemies back to Tenochtitlan, where they could drag them to the top of a temple and shed their blood as a sacrifice to their gods.

The Aztecs believed they had good reason for shedding so much blood. For the gods of Aztec mythology were cruel and demanding.

One Aztec creation myth divided the whole history of the world into five eras called the Five Suns. Why Five Suns? Because cruel Aztec gods had destroyed the first four.

> The first sun, the **Sun of Water**, ended in a great flood sent by the gods. The people of that sun hid in the water, becoming the first fish.

Huitzilopochtli, the cruel war god of the Mexica tribe

- The second sun, the **Sun of Jaguars**, ended with jaguars eating everyone and everything.

- The third sun, the **Sun of Fire**, ended with a fiery rain that wiped out everything. The people of that sun hid in the air, becoming the first birds.

- The fourth sun, the **Sun of Wind**, ended with a ferocious windstorm. The people of that sun hid in the trees, becoming the first monkeys.

As for the Aztecs themselves, they lived under the fifth sun: the **Sun of Earthquakes**. Aztec priests warned that this would be the last sun. One day, angry gods would send earthquakes and volcanoes to grind this world into a smoldering ruin. After that, there would be no more new worlds.

This was why the Aztecs shed so much blood: to keep the gods from destroying their world. According to one Aztec myth, two good gods had sacrificed their lives so that the Sun of Earthquakes could begin. But it was the Aztecs' job to keep that sun going. To do that, the Aztecs believed, they had to make the same sacrifices those two gods had made.

Tlatchli **goal mounted on the wall of a ball court**

Tlatchtli, or the Middle American Ball Game

In once-forgotten cities all over Middle America, archaeologists have uncovered playing courts for an interesting ball game.

The **Middle American Ball Game** was a bit like basketball— in that the object of the game was to shoot a rubber ball through a high hoop. But Ball Game players didn't dribble like basketball players. In fact, they didn't use their hands at all. They struck the ball only with their hips, thighs and chests— which made scoring goals extremely difficult! In fact, scoring was so difficult that the first team to score usually won.

The losers sometimes faced terrible consequences. Like everything else in Middle American life, the Middle American Ball Game could be tied to the gods. Each team might represent a certain god or gods. When the game was over, the winners might receive all the honor due to a god; while the losers might be sacrificed to the gods.

The Aztec Empire was still growing in 1438, when a king called **Pachacuti** started a new empire down in South America. Pachacuti started out as the **Inca** of **Cusco**, a kingdom in what is now Peru. The people of Cusco were part of a larger people called the **Quechua**.

Before Pachacuti, Cusco was only one of many kingdoms in the Andes. But Pachacuti conquered all other kingdoms, bringing them together to form the **Inca Empire**.

Peru lies in west central South America, the very heart of the Andes Mountains.

The Inca Empire
(1438 - 1533)

Actually, the name "Inca Empire" isn't quite right. The Quechua name for the empire was **Tawantinsuyu**, or "the four corners together." The capital, Cusco, stood near the middle of the Andes mountain chain. So Pachacuti divided his empire into four corners, with Cusco at the center. The governors of the four corners all answered to the Inca of the Four Corners.

So why do most people say "Inca Empire"? Because that was the name the Spaniards used when they came to Middle America in the 1500s.

The biggest problem with building an empire in the Andes was transportation. As the Romans learned long ago, big empires needed good roads. Only with good roads could an emperor send troops and supplies to all corners of his empire when he needed to.

Unfortunately, roads were hard to build in the Andes! For the Andes were not only high and rocky, but also thousands of miles long. And they were cut with countless **chasms**— gaps so deep and dangerous that only mountain climbers could cross them.

A **chasm** is a deep, narrow cut between two pieces of higher ground.

Unless, of course, someone built bridges.

So the Incas became great bridge builders. Up and down the Andes, they built long rope bridges to fill in the gaps in their roads. The emperor kept close watch over his bridges. Whenever a rope bridge started to sag, as they always did, the emperor ordered the locals to replace the ropes. That way, he could always count on his bridges when he needed them.

A rope bridge over a chasm in the Andes. Like other American peoples, the Incas didn't use wheeled carts. However, they did use llamas to carry heavy loads. So Inca rope bridges had to be strong enough to carry loaded llamas.

Just as Lake Texcoco affected farming for the Aztecs, so the rugged terrain of the Andes affected farming for the Incas. When Inca farmers tried planting on steep slopes, heavy rains washed their crops downhill. So instead, they built **terraced farms**.

First they dug into the slope, carving out a level space for planting. This was the first **terrace**. A few feet downhill, they carved out a second terrace. Another few feet downhill, they carved out a third terrace— and so on all the way down. Terracing didn't stop the rain, but it did slow it down enough to save crops from washing away.

Besides rope bridges, terraced farms and a lot of great stonework, the Incas are known best for their gold— tons and tons of gold.

An Inca terraced farm

The fact that the Incas never learned to work with iron didn't stop them from working with gold. Inca goldsmiths made all sorts of beautiful objects, enough to fill whole rooms with gold. But they didn't make gold coins; for the Incas never traded in coin. Instead, they traded in useful items like food and cloth.

Ⅴ⅄Ⅴ Ⅴ⅄Ⅴ Ⅴ⅄Ⅴ Ⅴ⅄Ⅴ Ⅴ⅄Ⅴ Ⅴ⅄Ⅴ Ⅴ⅄Ⅴ Ⅴ⅄Ⅴ Ⅴ⅄Ⅴ Ⅴ⅄Ⅴ Ⅴ⅄Ⅴ Ⅴ⅄Ⅴ Ⅴ⅄Ⅴ Ⅴ⅄Ⅴ Ⅴ⅄Ⅴ Ⅴ⅄Ⅴ Ⅴ⅄Ⅴ Ⅴ⅄Ⅴ Ⅴ⅄Ⅴ Ⅴ⅄Ⅴ

If the Incas could have known how much trouble their gold would bring them, then they might have left it in the ground.

For when the gold-hungry Spaniards reached the New World, rumors of Inca gold drew these dangerous people down to South America. In 1532, a Spanish **conquistador** called **Francisco Pizarro** conquered the Incas. This was 11 years after another Spanish conquistador, **Hernan Cortes**, conquered the Aztecs. See Chapter 25 for more on the sad fates of the Aztecs and Incas.

> *Conquistador* is Spanish for "conqueror."

The conquistadors left no stone unturned in their fanatic search for Inca gold. But they did miss one stony place: a mountain sanctuary called **Macchu Picchu**.

Macchu Picchu is a beautiful set of about 200 Inca buildings, all made from dry-stacked stone. It stands about 50 miles from Cusco, but far higher than Cusco—which may be why the conquistadors missed it. Exactly what Macchu Picchu was, no one now knows for sure; but it may have been a country home for Pachacuti.

Actually, the conquistadors weren't the only ones who missed Macchu Picchu. After the Inca Empire fell, everyone but the locals forgot all about the place. It lay mostly abandoned until 1911, when a Yale University professor called Hiram Bingham rediscovered it.

John Wycliffe and the Lollards

CHURCH HISTORY

After all the failures of Holy Land Crusades, more and more people challenged the pope's authority. In Chapter 21, we read how a King of France challenged the pope's authority over kings. This chapter tells of an Englishman who challenged the pope's authority over all Christians.

John Wycliffe was a Bible professor at **Oxford**, one of the two best universities in England. The more Wycliffe studied the Bible, the more he loved it, and wanted to share it with others.

John Wycliffe (1330? - 1384)

The problem was, how to share it? Before Wycliffe's day, all Bibles were written in Latin. The only time most Christians ever even heard the Bible was when their priests read from the **Vulgate** in church. And since most Christians couldn't understand Latin, it did them little good to hear the Vulgate.

To solve this problem, John Wycliffe did something astonishing: he translated the whole Vulgate into English! That way, Englishmen could read for themselves what the Bible said, instead of waiting on priests to tell them. The **Wycliffe Bible** was the first complete Bible in the English language.

> Remember what the **Vulgate** was— the Latin version of the Bible translated by St. Jerome around 400 AD (Chapter 3).

Even after he finished translating, Wycliffe still faced two big problems. The first problem was that the Catholic Church didn't want anyone but priests reading the Bible. The pope feared that without trained priests to guide them, some Christians might interpret the Bible differently than the Church interpreted it. If enough Christians did that, then the Church might split!

The other problem was that Wycliffe lived before the invention of the printing press. This meant that every single copy of the Wycliffe Bible had to be written out by hand. And hand-copied books cost a fortune! Few Englishmen could afford such an expensive book, no matter how badly they wanted one.

Wycliffe's answer was to train a new kind of preacher. Since the **ordained** priests of the Catholic Church refused to preach from the Wycliffe Bible, Wycliffe gave it to un-ordained preachers who didn't refuse. These were the Lollards.

> To **ordain** someone was to officially install him as a priest of the Church of Rome.

John Wycliffe sharing the Wycliffe Bible with the Lollards

The Lollards were unofficial ministers who traveled all over England, reading the Wycliffe Bible in English to all who would listen. The Lollards didn't know Latin, nor how to lead priestly rituals. But they did know the Bible! In a time when Christians were starting to doubt the Catholic Church, the Lollards took them back to the original Word of God— spoken in a language they could understand.

The Iberian Peninsula

Three large peninsulas jut out from the southern edge of Europe. The eastern one is the **Balkan Peninsula**, home to Greece and several other countries (Chapter 4). The middle one is the **Italian Peninsula**, home to Italy (Chapter 26). And the western one is the Iberian Peninsula, home to Spain and Portugal.

The name **"Iberia"** probably comes from the **Ebro River**, which runs across the northeast corner of the peninsula. *Sierra Nevada* is Spanish for "snowy mountain range."

A strong barrier divides Iberia from the rest of Europe. That barrier is the **Pyrenees**, a high mountain range that stands between Spain and France. Only a few mountain passes cut through the Pyrenees, and even those are very high.

The Pyrenees are only one of many mountain ranges in Iberia. Another well-known range is the **Sierra Nevada of Spain**, which lies in the southeast. Yet another is the **Cantabrian Mountains**, which hug the northern coast.

To sail around Iberia, ships must pass through several big bodies of water. North of Iberia lies the **Bay of Biscay**, which opens on the **Atlantic Ocean** to the west. Southwest of Iberia lies the **Gulf of Cadiz**. And to the south lies the narrow **Strait of Gibraltar**, which opens on the **Mediterranean Sea** to the east.

The best-known mountain in Iberia is probably the **Rock of Gibraltar**, which stands just north of the Strait of Gibraltar (Chapter 7).

As of 2016, Gibraltar doesn't belong to Spain. Instead, it belongs to Britain! The British seized Gibraltar from Spain in 1705, and have never given it back.

Well out in the Mediterranean, but still close to Spain, lie a group of islands that are known around the world for their fine weather. These are the **Balearic Islands**, where temperatures are almost never too hot or too cold. Many Europeans own vacation homes on the three biggest Balearic Islands: **Majorca**, **Minorca** and **Ibiza**.

Balearic Islands

The Re-conquest of Iberia

The last time we read about Iberia was in Chapter 7. At the time, almost all of Christian Iberia had fallen to Islam!

Way back in 711, a Muslim general called **Tariq bin Ziyad** leapt across the Strait of Gibraltar to attack Christians in Iberia. Within 10 years, the Islamic Empire conquered almost all of Iberia. And it didn't stop there. If Charles Martel hadn't won the Battle of Tours, Gaul in 732, then Islam might have conquered all of Europe!

Fortunately for Christians, Charles Martel did win the Battle of Tours. And even though most of Iberia was lost, Christians could still hope. For in the northwestern corner of Iberia, a small Christian kingdom called **Asturias** still stood strong against its Muslim enemies, the **Moors**.

What saved Asturias was the Cantabrian Mountains. **King Pelayo**, the first King of Asturias, used these mountains against the Moors. One day in 722, Pelayo lured a Moorish army into a valley that he knew well. The Moors had no idea that Pelayo's army was hidden in the slopes above. At just the right moment, the Christians leapt out of hiding and rained down arrows on the Moors— thus winning the **Battle of Covadonga**.

The Battle of Covadonga was the beginning of a long war to take Iberia back from the Moors. Historians call this war the **Spanish Reconquista**.

But the Battle of Covadonga was only one Christian victory. Everywhere else, the Moors had already won. So the Moors forgot about their one loss, and settled down for a long stay in the rest of Iberia— which they called **Al-Andalus**.

> Christians called the Muslims who lived in Iberia **Moors**, and their kingdoms **Moorish**.
>
>
>
> **A drawing of Moorish troops from the Alhambra Castle in Granada, Spain**

> *Reconquista* is Spanish for "re-conquering." The **Spanish Reconquista** was a long crusade fought by Christians who wanted to take back Iberia from the Moors. This was the longest of all crusades. The Reconquista lasted 770 years, all the way from 722 - 1492.

At first, Al-Andalus belonged to the Muslims who had conquered it: the Berbers of western North Africa (Chapter 7).

But it wasn't long before Arabs took charge of Al-Andalus. In Muslim minds, Arabs outranked Berbers. After all, the Arabs had been Muslim since Islam began; while the Berbers had turned Muslim more recently. Al-Andalus crowned its first genuine Arab prince, **Abd al-Rahman I**, in 756.

> **Al-Andalus** was another name for **Muslim Iberia**. At least part of Iberia was always Muslim for nearly 800 years, from 711 - 1492.

Who was Abd al-Rahman I? To answer, we must remember the first two **caliphates** to rule the Islamic Empire after Muhammad. First came the **Rashidun Caliphate**, then the **Umayyad Caliphate**. Abd al-Rahman was a son of the Umayyads, a mighty dynasty that ruled from Damascus, Syria.

Abdul al Rahman I

So why did Abd al-Rahman move all the way from Syria to Al-Andalus? Because the Umayyad dynasty was overthrown! In 750, a powerful Arab called **Abul Abbas As-Saffah** killed the last Umayyad caliph. The Umayyad Caliphate was now at an end. As-Saffah was the founder of the third caliphate to rule Islam: the **Abbasid Caliphate**.

The **Abbasid Caliphate** made its capital at Baghdad, Mesopotamia (Iraq). The Abbasids reigned from 750 until 1258, when the Mongol Empire sacked Baghdad (Chapter 22).

Afterward, As-Saffah sent hunting parties to track down and kill the rest of the Umayyads. He especially wanted to kill the 19-year-old prince, Abd-al Rahman.

When he heard about the hunters, Abd al-Rahman gathered up what little family he had left and ran for his life. He and his brother were standing beside the Euphrates River, probably looking for a boat, when the hunters caught up with them. Desperate to save themselves, both brothers dove into the river.

The hunters weren't desperate enough to swim the raging Euphrates. So instead, they tried a trick: they called out to the brothers from the shore, promising to spare their lives if they would turn back.

Abd al-Rahman knew better than to believe the hunters' lie. His brother, alas, did not. Whether because he was drowning, or because he hoped for mercy, the brother turned back. Of course, the hunters murdered him the moment he stepped ashore. Abd al-Rahman wept for his dead brother all the way across the Euphrates.

Six years later, al-Rahman turned up in Al-Andalus, where his royal name carried him to the top of the government. In 756, Abd Al-Rahman I declared himself the emir of a huge new country in Al-Andalus: the **Emirate of Cordoba**. This name came from the emirate's capital: **Cordoba**, a city in south central Iberia.

Thus the Umayyads didn't die out, as the Abbasids had hoped. Instead, the Umayyads built a new empire in the west.

More than 150 years later, a different Abd al-Rahman gave himself a big promotion.

In 929, Emir **Abd al-Rahman III** decided that the Emirate of Cordoba should be more than just an emirate. So he declared himself caliph of a new caliphate: the **Caliphate of Cordoba**.

In his own mind, Caliph Abd al-Rahman III was now the rightful ruler of the whole Islamic Empire. In reality, though, the Cordoba caliphs ruled only in the west. The Abbasid caliphs still ruled in the east. For the first time, there were two Sunni caliphates at once.

As caliph, Abd al-Rahman III needed a capital fit for the ruler of all Islam. So he built **Medina al-Zahara**, a fine new city near Cordoba. In its day, Medina al-Zahara was probably one of the most beautiful cities on Earth; for Abd Al-Rahman used only the best materials and craftsmen money could buy.

Medina al-Zahara, capital of the Caliphate of Cordoba, was a 3-tiered city.

➤ The **alcazar**, a grand palace for the caliph, stood on the top tier. So did the mansions of the caliph's highest nobles, along with the headquarters of his army.

➤ The middle tier held a mosque; a **souk**, or open-air market; and lovely gardens filled with fountains, flowers and exotic animals.

➤ The bottom tier held army barracks, along with stables for the caliph's beloved horses.

Part of the ruins of Medina al-Zahara

Meanwhile, up in northwestern Iberia, the little Christian Kingdom of Asturias was growing. One thing that helped Asturias grow was a special place called **Santiago de Compostela**.

The Basilica de Santiago, a grand cathedral built over the tomb of St. James at Santiago de Compostela

Santiago is Spanish for "Saint James." The Apostle **James, son of Zebedee** is a hero to Spanish Christians. Tradition says that after Jesus rose from the dead, James preached the gospel in faraway Iberia. Without James, the Spanish might never have heard the good news of Jesus Christ.

James later went back to Jerusalem, where King Herod Agrippa killed him for his faith— as we learn in Acts 12:1-2.

CROSS OF SAINT JAMES

The next tradition picks up where the Bible leaves off. After James died, it is said, two loyal followers loaded his body on a boat and sailed it back to his beloved Iberia. When they got there, the followers buried James in a hidden tomb made of marble. Later, when the two followers died, they were buried in that same hidden tomb.

The tomb stayed hidden for about 800 years, until 840. Then, tradition says, a Christian hermit from Asturias received a vision from God telling him just where to find the tomb.

The hermit showed the tomb to his bishop, who in turn showed it to his king. The bishop noticed the tomb's great age, and the fact that it held three bodies. After studying the story of James and his two followers, the bishop announced that this must be the real tomb of Saint James!

What an incredible find this was— a real relic of a real apostle of Jesus Christ, right here in Western Europe! Before now, Christians had had to go all the way to the Holy Land to see such sights. Now they had only to go to Asturias. Countless Christians came from all over Europe to see the tomb of St. James.

And the more Christians came, the more they wanted to help their Christian brothers in Asturias fight off the Moors.

Camino de Santiago is Spanish for "Path of St. James." The **Camino de Santiago** is the much-traveled path that leads to the tomb of St. James at Santiago de Compostela. Even today, Christian pilgrims from around the world still take this path every year.

The most familiar symbol of the Camino de Santiago is the scallop shell. The many lines on the scallop shell represent all the different paths Christians follow to reach the tomb. Just as the lines on the shell all come together, so Christians from around the world all come together in the same place.

By this time, Asturias wasn't the only Christian kingdom in Iberia. There were also the Christian kingdoms of the **Spanish March**.

As we read in Chapter 7, the Franks built a great empire after the Battle of Tours. Under Charlemagne, grandson to Charles Martel, the Carolingian Empire grew into one of the greatest empires the world has ever seen.

With strong enemies like the Moors on his southern border, Charlemagne needed strong armies there. So he set up several counties in the Spanish March.

EMBLEM OF ASTURIAS

Over time, those counties came together to form kingdoms. The three strongest kingdoms of the Spanish March were **Navarre** in the west, **Aragon** in the center and **Catalonia** in the east.

Meanwhile, over in northwestern Iberia, the Kingdom of Asturias was growing.

Around 910, Asturias changed its name to **Leon**, after its new capital. The kings of Leon founded more Christian kingdoms. East of Leon lay **Castile**, named for the castles built there to protect Leon from the Moors. South of Leon lay **Portugal**, named for a big city called Porto.

The word "march" can mean "borderland." **Spanish March** was another name for the borderland between France and Iberia during the Spanish Reconquista.

The noble title **marquis** comes from the word march. Marquises stand below dukes, but above earls, viscounts and barons.

The Spanish Reconquista was not 770 years of non-stop war. At many times, and in many places around Iberia, Christians and Muslims lived together in peace.

Even in times of war, things weren't as simple as they seemed. Christians didn't fight only Muslims; nor did Muslims fight only Christians. Instead, both sides also fought among themselves. And soldiers often switched sides— fighting first for Christianity, then Islam, then Christianity again. Some didn't care which faith they were fighting for, as long as they were getting paid.

One Christian who switched sides was the greatest warrior of the Reconquista: **Rodrigo Diaz de Vivar**, better known as **El Cid**.

Rodrigo was a minor noble born in Castile around 1040. He spent his youth training and serving in the Castilian army. By the time Rodrigo reached his mid-20s, he was already an experienced general in the service of Castile.

When Rodrigo was young, a king called Ferdinand I reigned over both Castile and Leon. But when Ferdinand died, he divided his kingdoms among his children. Castile, where Rodrigo lived, went to Ferdinand's oldest son: **Sancho**. Leon went to Ferdinand's second son, **Alfonso**.

From the moment Ferdinand died, the battle was on to see which of his sons would come out on top.

At first, it seemed that Sancho would come out on top. With help from his friend Rodrigo, Sancho won victory after victory.

Sancho's greatest victory came in early 1072, when he finally defeated Alfonso! In fear for his life, Alfonso fled southward, seeking safety with a Muslim ally. Meanwhile, Sancho became what his father Ferdinand had been: King of both Castile and Leon.

Rodrigo Diaz de Vivar,
better known as El Cid (1040? – 1099)

Sadly, Sancho didn't hold onto his crowns for long. Just a few months after his big win over Alfonso, an assassin stabbed Sancho to death!

Rodrigo was furious. According to legend, Rodrigo leapt on his horse and chased the assassin, desperate to catch the murderer of his friend and king. Above all, Rodrigo wanted to know who had hired the assassin. But the villain slipped out of the city through a little-known gate, leaving Rodrigo's burning question unanswered.

Even so, Rodrigo thought he had a pretty good idea who had hired the assassin. For Rodrigo couldn't help noticing that one person had more to gain from Sancho's death than anyone else.

That person, of course, was Sancho's brother Alfonso. With Sancho dead, and with no sons to take his place, Alfonso became **King Alfonso VI of Castile and Leon**!

Rodrigo wasn't the only one who distrusted Alfonso. To win his people's trust, Alfonso finally had to stand in church with his hand on a Bible, swearing before God and man that he had had nothing to do with his brother's murder!

Alfonso's oath was enough to satisfy most Christians— but not Rodrigo. Since Rodrigo didn't trust Alfonso, and Alfonso didn't trust Rodrigo, the two didn't get along. In 1080, Alfonso sent Rodrigo away— leaving the best general in Iberia without a king to serve.

King Alfonso VI of Castile and Leon taking the Oath of Santa Gadea, swearing that he had nothing to do with the murder of his brother Sancho

By this time, the old Caliphate of Cordoba had fallen apart. But there were still plenty of smaller Muslim kingdoms in Iberia. After two Christian kings turned him away, Rodrigo finally offered his services to a Muslim emir— who gladly accepted! This is how the best Christian general in Iberia came to join forces with the Muslims.

When Rodrigo's Muslim troops learned what a clever general he was, they gave him a new nickname: *El Sayyid*, Arabic for "the Master." Over time, *El Sayyid* shortened to **El Cid**.

Meanwhile, Alfonso was earning the nickname he would carry into history: "**Alfonso the Valiant**." As King of Leon, Castile and more, Alfonso led the fight against Islam, swallowing up more and more Muslim kingdoms.

To save themselves from Alfonso the Valiant, the Muslims called for outside help. In 1085, a general from Muslim Morocco led a huge army into

> **El Cid** was a shortened version of *El Sayyid*, Arabic for "The Master."

Iberia. Some say that El Cid commanded one wing of this army, and some say he didn't. Either way, the Muslims crushed Alfonso the Valiant at the **Battle of Sagrajas**, fought in 1086.

Now came Alfonso's turn to be desperate. The year after his big loss, Alfonso swallowed his pride and begged El Cid to come back to the Christian side!

El Cid still didn't trust Alfonso; so he didn't exactly fight for Castile. But he did turn against his Muslim allies. El Cid spent the rest of his life trying to carve out a Christian kingdom around **Valencia**, a city in eastern Iberia.

A soldier to the end, El Cid went down fighting the Muslims in 1099.

The next great leader of the Reconquista was **King Alfonso VIII of Castile**. This new Alfonso was born more than 100 years after Alfonso the Valiant. Around 1180, Alfonso VIII started pressing hard against the Muslims, seizing more and more of their kingdoms.

Then came a major setback. Once again, the Muslims called for outside help. In 1195, another general from Muslim Morocco crushed another Christian army. Alfonso VIII lost so many troops in the **Disaster at Alarcos** that he needed years to grow strong again.

But the Muslims weren't the only ones who could call for help. By now, the Holy Land Crusades had been going on for 100 years (Chapter 12). Pope Innocent III, the same pope who announced the Fourth Crusade, also announced a crusade against the Muslims of Iberia.

Pope Innocent's call led to one of the biggest battles of the whole Reconquista: the **Battle of Las Navas de Tolosa**, fought in 1212.

The Battle of Las Navas de Tolosa brought together Christian knights from all over Iberia— not only Castile, but also Leon, Portugal, Navarre and Aragon. Even French knights came down to join the crusade, complaining all the while about the terrible heat south of the Pyrenees.

At first, the crusaders had a hard time finding their enemy. The Muslim army had set up camp in the mountains of southern Iberia, where there were very few roads. The crusaders were at a loss— until they met a local shepherd, who of course knew all about the mountains. This shepherd showed them **Despenaperros Pass**, a little-known mountain pass that led straight to the Muslim camp.

Scene from the Battle of Las Navas de Tolosa

Terrible dangers awaited the crusaders at the far side of the pass. For one thing, the Muslim army turned out to be far larger than the Christian one— perhaps five times larger!

For another, the Muslim general had built a strong defense. A ring of 3,000 camels and 10,000 slaves surrounded the general, all chained together to keep them from running away. The general clutched a scimitar in one hand, and a Quran (Muslim holy book) in the other.

As the crusaders closed in around him, the general screamed out promises from the Quran. If his soldiers died fighting for Islam, he said, then they would surely go to heaven. But if they ran away, then they would surely go to hell!

Despite the general's threats, the crusaders somehow managed to break through the circle. When the general finally fled in defeat, Alfonso VIII won one of the greatest victories of the whole Reconquista.

The next hero of the Reconquista was **King Ferdinand III of Castile**. Ferdinand conquered almost everything the Muslims had left. By 1238, the Muslims were down to just one kingdom in Iberia: the **Emirate of Granada.**

Granada was a fine country along the southern coast of Iberia, east of the Rock of Gibraltar. Two advantages helped keep Granada strong. One was the Sierra Nevada mountains, which formed a strong barrier between Granada and Castile. The other was the Strait of Gibraltar, which was the only seaway between the Mediterranean and the Atlantic. The traders who passed through the Strait of Gibraltar paid Granada a fortune in taxes.

Every year, the Emir of Granada sent part of that fortune to the King of Castile. By paying tribute to Castile, Granada survived for another 250 years— long after every other Muslim kingdom in Iberia was gone.

King Ferdinand III of Castile

ꙥꙥꙥ

The job of conquering Granada fell to two famous royals: Ferdinand and Isabella. **Princess Isabella of Castile** was born in 1451, and **Prince Ferdinand of Aragon** in 1452.

By this time, the three kingdoms of Castile, Aragon and Portugal were the strongest in Iberia. Portugal held western Iberia, and Castile the center. Aragon held eastern Iberia, plus lands over in Italy.

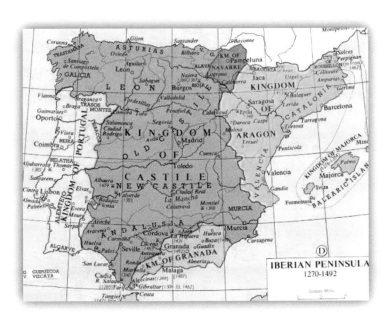

Iberia before 1492, with Portugal in tan, Castile in red, Aragon in bright green and Granada in dark green

Isabella was the second child of King John II of Castile. The princess barely knew her father; for he died when she was only 3. After that, **Enrique IV** took over as King of Castile. Enrique was a much older half-brother to Isabella, born to a different mother.

As the new head of the family, Enrique was supposed to arrange a good marriage for his sister. But Enrique didn't really see Isabella as a sister. Instead, he saw her as a chess piece— a pawn to be sacrificed by her king. Every noble in Europe dreamed of marrying a princess as rich as Isabella. So Enrique arranged several marriages for her! He promised her to first one, then another, trading her for whatever he needed most at the time.

Isabella's first fiancé was the one she would wind up marrying: Ferdinand of Aragon. Enrique promised Isabella to Ferdinand when they were both very young, hoping to bring Castile and Aragon together.

But when Isabella was 10 years old, Enrique changed his mind. Instead of marrying Ferdinand, Isabella was now to marry Charles of Navarre— a man 30 years older than she! Four years later, Enrique changed his mind again. The 14-year-old Isabella was now to marry 42-year-old Pedro Giron, a wealthy warrior who could help Enrique fight his battles. The only thing that saved Isabella from Pedro was the fact that he died on his way to claim her.

ROYAL CROWN OF SPAIN

Three years after that, Enrique promised Isabella to King Alfonso V of Portugal. This was probably the worst match yet, for a couple of reasons. First, Alfonso was almost 20 years older than Isabella. Second, Alfonso's first wife had died young— maybe because Alfonso had poisoned her!

And Enrique still wasn't finished. When Isabella refused to marry Alfonso, Enrique promised her to a brother of the King of France.

At this, Isabella took matters into her own hands. One day when she was 18, Isabella lied her way out of Enrique's castle. She told Enrique that she was going to visit the grave of her younger brother. But she was really going to a secret meeting with Ferdinand of Aragon!

Although Isabella had never met Ferdinand face-to-face, she had secretly traded letters with him. After reading those letters, Isabella felt sure that Ferdinand would make a better husband than anyone Enrique might choose for her. So the young couple arranged a secret meeting in Castile. To enter Castile in secret, the rich Prince Ferdinand had to dress up as a poor trader's servant!

In October 1469, just days after they first met, Isabella of Castile married Ferdinand of Aragon. After that, all the young royals had to do was wait. Enrique died in 1474, leaving Isabella as Queen of Castile. Ferdinand's father died in 1479, leaving Ferdinand as King of Aragon. Later, the two great kingdoms of Castile and Aragon would combine to form an even greater kingdom: **Spain**.

Queen Regnant Isabella I of Castile

The marriage of Ferdinand and Isabella was the beginning of the end for Granada. Both royals were crusaders— strong Christians who were driven to defeat the Muslims. The war to conquer Granada started in 1482, just three years after Ferdinand became king.

Ten years later, the war was over. The last Emir of Granada surrendered in 1492, handing over the last Muslim kingdom in Iberia. After 770 years, the Spanish Reconquista was finally finished!

The following year, the last Emir of Granada left Iberia forever, headed for Muslim Morocco. As he looked back over his shoulder, the emir couldn't help crying over all he had lost. At the sight of his tears, his old mother exploded at him:

"You are weeping like a woman for something that you could not defend like a man!"

Breathing one last sigh, the last emir turned his back on Granada for the last time. The mountain pass where he looked back is still called "The Last Sigh of the Moor."

The last Emir of Granada looking back on his lost kingdom with longing

STOP

One reason why the last Emir of Granada wept as he left was because he couldn't stand losing his favorite castle: the **Alhambra**. The emirs of Granada spent a fortune on this stunning castle, using only the finest materials and craftsmen money could buy. Nothing about the Alhambra was plain! Everywhere one turned, surprising beauties met the eye.

Many of those beauties were **arabesques**, the Muslim pattern art that we saw in Chapter 12. Since Islamic law forbade idol worship— and since carvings of people and animals tended to look like idols— Muslim artists didn't carve people and animals. Instead, they carved mostly vines, leaves and flowers, all woven into never-ending patterns. Some artists deliberately carved small mistakes into otherwise-perfect arabesques, to remind their fellow Muslims that only Allah was perfect.

Great castles like the Alhambra and Medina al-Zahara marked Granada as one of the most advanced kingdoms in the world. In some ways, Granada was more advanced than the Christian kingdoms that took over in 1492.

A view from a lovely court inside the Alhambra

The Spanish Inquisition

Both Ferdinand and Isabella were devoted to the Catholic Church. In fact, they were so devoted that they even had a special nickname: *los Reyes Catolicos*, Spanish for **"the Catholic Monarchs."**

As devoted Christians, the Catholic Monarchs wanted their people to be devoted as well. But in trying to make their people more Christian, the Catholic Monarchs did things that hardly seem Christ-like— especially to modern eyes.

When Isabella was young, she made all of her confessions to a priest called **Tomas de Torquemada**. The two became close friends. Even after Isabella became queen, Tomas was often at her side, sharing his thoughts with her.

Tomas thought a lot about two kinds of people: Moriscos and Marranos. **Moriscos** were Muslims who had switched to Christianity; while **Marranos** were Jews who had switched to Christianity. Some switched because they truly believed in Christ. Others switched because Christian kings had now conquered their homelands, and they wanted to please their kings.

What Tomas didn't like about Moriscos and Marranos was that some of them only pretended to be Christians. In public, they did everything Christians did— attending church, taking communion

Tomas de Torquemada, Grand Inquisitor of Castile

Emblem of the Inquisition

and so on. But in private, some of them still followed their old religions. Some even tried to convince Christians that Islam or Judaism was better than Christianity. Tomas warned Isabella that if she didn't get rid of these pretend Christians, then Castile would never be as Christian as she wanted it to be.

The answer to this problem, Tomas said, was a new court. With permission from the pope, Tomas and Isabella created a Church court to hunt down false Christians. In 1483, Tomas became the first **Grand Inquisitor** of a special new court called the Spanish Inquisition.

When the Inquisition came to a new town, the first thing that happened was a **Catholic Mass**. This was a special church service that always included communion. During this service, the inquisitors asked all good Catholics to examine themselves and confess their sins. They also asked them to examine their neighbors, to see if any of them might be false Christians.

> The **Spanish Inquisition** was a special Church court that started in Castile, and later spread to other parts of the Spanish Empire. The main mission of the Inquisition was to hunt down people who pretended to be Christians, but secretly weren't.

Next came the accusations. Any Christian could accuse anyone of anything, without ever having to face the accused. If a Christian believed that his neighbor might secretly be a Muslim or Jew, then he had only to tell the inquisitors.

Then came the trials. The inquisitors asked tough questions, trying to trick the accused into saying something wrong. One might ask a Morisco, "Why don't you buy wine? Is it because you still follow Islamic law, like the Muslim you really are?" Or one might ask a Marrano: "Why do you buy extra food on Friday afternoons? Is it because you still keep the Sabbath on Saturdays, like the Jew you really are?" If an inquisitor didn't get the answer he wanted, then he might torture the accused until he did.

Last of all came a dreaded Mass called the *Auto-da-Fe*, or **Act of Faith**. If the inquisitors decided that the accused was lying, then they ordered him punished. Some victims of the Spanish Inquisition were only strangled to death; but many others were burned alive.

Because the Inquisition was a Christian court, it had no authority over anyone who still called himself a Jew or Muslim. Even so, the Inquisition caused no end of trouble for Jews and Muslims.

> The **Alhambra Decree** was a 1492 law that expelled all Jews from Aragon and Castile.

For Jews, the worst trouble was the **Alhambra Decree**. In 1492, just after they captured Granada, Ferdinand and Isabella suddenly banished all Jews from their kingdoms! The Alhambra Decree gave every Jew in Castile and Aragon just four months to sell everything he owned and get out.

The catch was that Jews couldn't take money with them. They could take with them only what they could carry. Countless Jews had to start all over in new countries, with little more than the clothes on their backs. This was only one of many times when the Jews of the **Diaspora** had to pack up and leave their homes for good.

For Muslims, the worst trouble was a new Grand Inquisitor called **Jimenez de Cisneros**. In 1502, Cisneros gave the last Muslims in Castile a hard choice: they could either become Christians or get out. Cisneros also burned countless Muslim books, doing his best to stamp out the Muslim faith.

> Remember what the **Diaspora** was— the scattering of the Jews.
> The descendants of the Jews expelled by Ferdinand and Isabella are called **Sephardi Jews**. Some Sephardi Jews still speak a form of Spanish.

CHAPTER 24

Explorers from Portugal and Spain

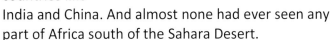

The Age of Discovery

In medieval times, Europeans knew just three of the seven continents: Europe, Asia and Africa. Europe, of course, they knew well. They also knew West Asia and North Africa; for both touched the Mediterranean Sea. But only a few Europeans had

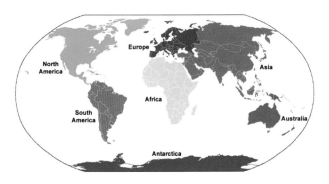

ever ventured beyond West Asia, to far-off countries like India and China. And almost none had ever seen any part of Africa south of the Sahara Desert.

As time went by, Europeans grew more and more curious about the far-off places of the world. Around 1300, *The Travels of Marco Polo* introduced them to the many wonders of China (Chapter 19). A few years later, they heard about the tons of gold that Mansa Musa spent on his *hajj* from Mali to Mecca (Chapter 21).

The more Europeans heard about such wonders, the more they wanted to go and see them with their own eyes.

Many wanted to go for trade. The Chinese made luxuries that no European knew how to make— fine materials like silk and porcelain. The Indians sold tasty spices that Europeans loved. As for West Africans, they sold bountiful gold and beautiful ivory. If European traders could only get their hands on these goods, then they could sell them for fortunes back home.

Others wanted to go for their faith. The Christians of Europe wanted to preach the gospel of Jesus Christ to the rest of the world. To many medieval Christians, preaching the gospel also meant bringing the whole world under the authority of the pope.

The problem was, how could Europeans get to these far-off places? The roads over land were terrible. Marco Polo's father had needed four years to cross from Constantinople to China. And only a handful of Tuaregs knew how to cross the Sahara Desert without dying of thirst!

Besides, heavy loads were hard to carry by land. As always, water was the best way to carry heavy loads. So if European traders wanted to bring back heavy loads from far-off places, then they would have to go by ship.

Replicas of Christopher Columbus' three ships, *Santa Maria*, *Nina* and *Pinta*, in a photo from 1912

Thus began the **Age of Discovery**, a time when Europeans sailed off in search of better routes to the far places of the world. No one dreamed how much they would find.

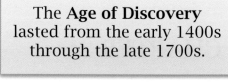

🔁🔁🔁🔁🔁🔁🔁🔁🔁🔁🔁🔁🔁🔁🔁🔁🔁🔁🔁🔁🔁🔁🔁🔁🔁🔁🔁🔁🔁🔁

The Age of Discovery started in Portugal, near the end of the Spanish Reconquista (Chapter 23).

By 1400, the Portuguese had chased most of the Moors out of Portugal. The Moors had fled across the Strait of Gibraltar, seeking safety in Muslim North Africa.

But not all Muslims stayed in North Africa. Every so often, pirates sailed over to raid the Portuguese coast. Besides stealing treasure, these deadly pirates killed many Christian villagers, and sold many others into slavery. These were the first **Barbary Pirates**— Muslim pirates from the **Barbary Coast** of North Africa.

The **Barbary Pirates** were Muslim pirates who launched raids from the **Barbary Coast**— in other words, the coast of North Africa. The name "Barbary" comes from the Berbers, the same North African race that had once conquered Iberia.

A BARBARY PIRATE

The Portuguese soon learned where the Barbary Pirates came from. Most of the attacks on Portugal started from a place called **Ceuta**. This was a thriving Muslim port at the east end of the Strait of Gibraltar, just across from the Rock of Gibraltar.

In the early 1400s, the Portuguese started to think of attacking Ceuta. If they could seize Ceuta from the Muslims, then two things would happen:

➢ First, the Barbary Pirates would lose their favorite base. Hopefully, this would put a stop to their raids.

➢ Second, Portugal would gain a rich port city teeming with gold. For not all African gold went to emperors like Mansa Musa. A lot of it found its way into the hands of Muslim traders in Ceuta.

Acting on this plan, **King John I of Portugal** sailed over and attacked Ceuta in 1415. Part of John's plan went well; for the city's defenses quickly collapsed. In no time, Ceuta went from Muslim to Christian, forcing the Barbary Pirates to move out.

The other part of John's plan didn't go as well. When Ceuta went Christian, Muslim traders simply found other places to take their gold. Despite winning Ceuta, the Portuguese were no closer to their African gold.

Until the king's son thought of a better way to get that gold.

Infante Henry was the fourth son of King John I. In Portugal and Spain, only the oldest son carried the title "prince." The others were all *infantes*— younger sons who never expected to be king.

Since Henry would never be king, he turned his attention to other matters. *Infante* Henry is also called **Henry the Navigator**. The life's work of Henry the Navigator was to find a way for Portuguese ships to sail around the west coast of Africa. That way, the Portuguese wouldn't have to buy gold from traders in North Africa. Instead, they could get it from the source— straight from the gold mines south of the Sahara.

One possible picture of Henry the Navigator

A caravel rigged with triangular lateen sails

Despite his grand nickname, "the Navigator," Henry didn't personally sail around the west coast of Africa. Instead, Henry made it easier for others to sail around Africa.

One of the ways Henry made sailing easier was by building a kind of sailors' college. He hired teachers to train Portuguese sailors in the new science of navigation. And he hired mapmakers to draw the best, most accurate maps the world had yet seen. The better the maps, the more sailors knew about hidden dangers that might wreck their ships.

Besides making better sailors and better maps, Henry also made better ships. Henry didn't build the heavy, slow ships that traders used on the Mediterranean Sea. Instead, he built lighter, faster ships called **caravels**. Caravels had two or three masts, all rigged with triangular sails called **lateens**. By moving their lateens from side to side, caravels could make the most of whatever wind they had. Caravels were more maneuverable than older ships— which made them much better for exploring the shallow shores and rivers along the west coast of Africa.

〰〰〰〰〰〰〰〰〰〰〰〰〰〰〰〰〰〰〰〰〰〰〰〰〰〰〰〰〰

The first great find of the Age of Discovery came in 1419, just four years after Portugal captured Ceuta. That was when **John Goncalves Zarco**, one of Henry's sailing captains, discovered an island group where not a single person lived.

This was **Madeira**, which lies about 500 miles off the west coast of Morocco. After Portugal planted a colony there, Madeira grew famous for its fine wine.

The next big island group to the south didn't need discovering. Since the **Canary Islands** lie near the coast of Morocco, plenty of people already lived there. Castile, not Portugal, built the first European colonies on the Canaries.

Just east of the Canaries lay the next big problem for Henry the Navigator. His sailing captains needed about 10 years and 15 expeditions to get around **Cape Bojador**, a point of land on the coast of Morocco.

One problem with Cape Bojador was that it was a terrifying place. The water was shallow there, and the rocky ocean floor seemed to glow an evil red. Strong currents kicked up a thick ocean spray, warning of grave dangers ahead.

Henry the Navigator (1394 - 1460)

No sailing ship can sail directly into the wind; for the wind will simply blow the ship backward, out of control. Even so, a maneuverable ship like a caravel can still travel upwind. Instead of sailing straight into the wind, sailors **"tack"** back and forth across the wind. The long, slow process of tacking into the wind is called **beating to windward.**

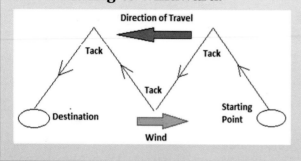

This first problem fed into a second problem: superstition. All of Henry's sailors had heard legends like the one Mansa Musa told— how a great whirlpool at the edge of the Atlantic had sucked down 2,200 Malian ships (Chapter 21). There were also legends of boiling seas in the hot south, and of falling off the edge of the sea. To sailors raised on such legends, passing Cape Bojador seemed like suicide.

On the other hand, some of Cape Bojador's dangers were quite real. In shallow water, any wrong turn could send a ship crashing into hidden rocks. And if a storm blew up at the wrong moment, then a ship might crash anyway, wrong turn or no. Few people led more dangerous lives than medieval sailors.

In spite of all these problems and dangers, a Portuguese captain called **Gil Eanes** finally sailed past Cape Bojador in 1434.

Even then, the discoveries still came slowly. Twenty-six years passed before a captain called **Antonio de Noli** found the next big island group to the south: the **Cape Verde Islands**. Like Madeira, the Cape Verdes were empty of people— until 1460, when Portugal built its first colony there.

The year 1460 was also when Henry the Navigator died. It was only after Henry's passing that the Portuguese finally found what they had been searching for since 1415: African gold.

Soon after 1460, the Portuguese rounded the corner that led to **Guinea**. At last, they had reached the legendary mines where Mansa Musa had found so much gold!

As soon as they could, the Portuguese built a trading post in Guinea. They called their post *El Mina*, Portuguese for "The Mine," after the gold mines nearby.

Elmina Castle, capital of the Portuguese Gold Coast

Later, King John II of Portugal built a strong castle to defend El Mina. **Elmina Castle** became the capital of an important colony: the **Portuguese Gold Coast**, where traders grew rich off African gold.

With growing colonies spread out on islands and coasts thousands of miles apart, Portugal was now more than just a kingdom. Portugal was becoming the Portuguese Empire, the first great overseas empire in the history of the world.

Remember what **Guinea** was— a region along the southern coast of West Africa.

The **Portuguese Gold Coast** was a rich colony along the coast of what is now Ghana, Africa. Besides gold, Portuguese traders bought and sold liquor, ivory, guns— and, sadly, African slaves (Chapter 25).

The modern-day Republic of Ghana lies on different land than the old Ghana Empire (Chapter 21).

The Portuguese Empire didn't stop at the Gold Coast. A big colony down in Guinea meant more ships and more supplies farther south. These were just what Portuguese explorers needed to sail on around Africa, toward their next goal: India.

At first, no one knew if sailing to India was even possible. For all anyone knew, the Indian Ocean might be an inland sea surrounded by land.

The man who proved otherwise was a clever Portuguese called **Bartolomeu Dias**. In 1488, Dias finally sailed around the southern tip of Africa— proving that ships really could sail from the Atlantic Ocean to the Indian Ocean.

The **Cape of Good Hope** is a rocky outcropping near the southern tip of Africa.

Although Bartolomeu Dias was the first European to spot the Cape of Good Hope, it was not Dias who chose its cheery name. The first time Dias approached the southern tip of Africa, strong storms blew him past the cape. So Dias marked "Cape of Storms" on his map.

Later, King John II feared that this gloomy name might frighten off other explorers. So John chose a cheerier name: "Cape of Good Hope."

ꑰꑰꑰꑰꑰꑰꑰꑰꑰꑰꑰꑰꑰꑰꑰꑰꑰꑰꑰꑰꑰꑰꑰꑰꑰꑰꑰꑰꑰꑰꑰꑰꑰꑰ

When Ferdinand and Isabella heard what Dias had done, they started to worry. The Portuguese Gold Coast was already making King John II of Portugal rich. Now he was well on his way to India, where he might grow richer still. With that much money, John might do almost anything. He might even drive Ferdinand and Isabella off their thrones!

Remember that Ferdinand was King of Aragon, and Isabella Queen of Castile. These were the two big kingdoms that would soon unite to form the even bigger Kingdom of Spain.

It wouldn't be the first time a King of Portugal had tried.

Back in 1475, Isabella had inherited the throne of Castile from her half-brother, King Enrique IV (Chapter 23). But not every Castilian wanted Isabella to be queen. Some preferred Enrique's daughter, a 13-year-old called Juana.

One of Isabella's old fiancés tried to take advantage of this. In that same year of 1475, **King Alfonso V of Portugal** barged into Castile and married Juana. This was despite the fact that Alfonso was Juana's uncle, and was 30 years older than she! Obviously, Alfonso and Juana didn't marry for love. They only married so that Alfonso could claim the throne of Castile through Juana.

Alfonso's bold move touched off a five-year struggle called the **War of the Castilian Succession**. The outcome of this war would prove most important to the Age of Discovery.

In the end, as we already know, Isabella won the throne of Castile. But Isabella only won the war on land. Alfonso won the war at sea. This meant that Portugal kept all of its overseas colonies. The only colonies Castile kept were the ones on the Canary Islands.

Without colonies farther south, the Castilians could never reach India the way the Portuguese could— by sailing around Africa. So if Isabella and Ferdinand wanted to trade in India, then they would have to find some other way to get there.

King Alfonso V of Portugal

Which is where **Christopher Columbus** comes into the story.

Columbus was probably born in **Genoa**, a republic along the northwest coast of Italy. The richest families of Genoa all earned their livings at sea. Columbus went to sea as a boy, and stayed there for the rest of his life. By his mid-20s, Columbus was already a skilled, experienced ship's captain.

Christopher Columbus (1451 – 1506)

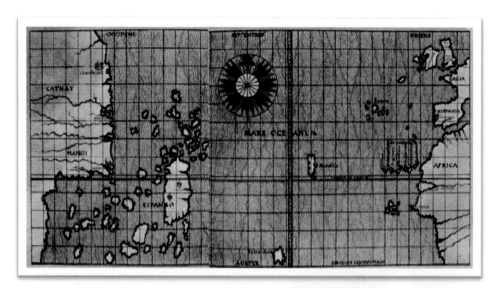

Christopher Columbus

What made Columbus different from other captains was his deep interest in books. When most captains were relaxing, Columbus was reading every book he could find— especially books about geography.

The Age of Discovery was an exciting time for geography, with new maps showing new places every year. Some of those maps showed the farthest places on Earth: China and Japan.

But these maps were only guesses. At the time, no one knew for sure how big the world was, or how far away China and Japan might really be. And of course, no map showed the Americas— for Columbus hadn't discovered the Americas yet!

Columbus tried to fill in the guesses on those maps with real numbers. Based on his reading, and on letters from other mapmakers, Columbus calculated the following: that if a ship sailed due west from the Canary Islands, then it might strike Japan in about 3,000 miles.

What an idea! If Columbus was right, then Japan was only about half as far from Europe as the southern tip of Africa was. Which

A map drawn by Italian geographer Paolo Toscanelli in 1463. The map shows Europe and Africa on the right, China and Japan on the left, and the "Ocean Sea" in between.

meant that ships shouldn't bother sailing around Africa to reach the Far East. Instead, they should sail around the world to the west!

Of course, Columbus wasn't right. The real distance from the Canary Islands to Japan is more like 12,000 miles than 3,000. If the Americas hadn't stood directly across Columbus' path, then he would have starved to death long before he reached Japan!

At the time, though, Columbus had no idea how wrong he was. The only way to know for sure was to sail out and see. To do that, Columbus needed some rich ruler to give him two things: permission and money.

The first ruler Columbus asked was King John II of Portugal. Since the Portuguese were so determined to reach India, John seemed like a good choice. But John turned Columbus away, for a couple of reasons. First, explorers like Bartolomeu Dias were already well on their way toward sailing around Africa. Second, John's scientists warned him that Columbus' calculations were wrong— which turned out to be quite true!

After trying a couple of other rulers, Columbus turned to King John's biggest rivals: Ferdinand and Isabella. With Portugal blocking the way around Africa, Ferdinand and Isabella really needed another way to reach India. This was exactly what Columbus offered.

Unfortunately, Columbus' timing was wrong. When Columbus first spoke to Ferdinand and Isabella, they were still fighting the Spanish Reconquista (Chapter 23). With an expensive war on, they couldn't afford to waste money on an expedition that might not work.

"Columbus before the Queen" by artist Emanuel Leutze

Even so, Ferdinand and Isabella didn't want Columbus taking his ideas anywhere else. So they offered him a small salary, and told him to wait.

After the caravel, the next great new ship design was the **carrack**. Carracks were bigger, taller and heavier than caravels, which meant that they could carry more supplies. Any crew that planned to sail thousands of miles without stopping needed plenty of supplies!

It all came together in one critical year: 1492. In January 1492, Ferdinand and Isabella finally finished the Spanish Reconquista. Now that the war wasn't draining their treasury, they could afford to give Columbus the answer he wanted— the "yes" he'd been seeking for seven years, ever since 1485.

Columbus used the money Ferdinand and Isabella gave him to hire three ships: *Nina*, *Pinta* and *Santa Maria*. *Nina* and *Pinta* were probably caravels; while *Santa Maria* was probably a newer, bigger kind of ship called a **carrack**.

Columbus led his three ships out of Palos, Castile on August 3, 1492. After a short stop at the Canary Islands, they sailed west on September 6.

Five weeks later, in the dark of the morning of October 12, one of Columbus' lookouts spotted a flickering light that could only be one thing: a fire burning on dry land.

The West Indies

The first land Columbus sighted wasn't North America, Central America or South America. Instead, Columbus sighted a big island group called the **West Indies**. The curve of the West Indies divides the Atlantic Ocean from the Caribbean Sea.

The West Indies are divided into three main island groups: the Greater Antilles, the Lesser Antilles and the Lucayan Archipelago.

➤ The **Greater Antilles** are mainly four big islands: **Cuba**, **Jamaica**, **Hispaniola** and **Puerto Rico**. The far smaller **Cayman Islands**, which lie west of Jamaica, also belong to the Greater Antilles.

➤ The **Lesser Antilles** are a string of smaller islands that begin east of Puerto Rico, arc to the south for about 500 miles, and then turn west along the northern coast of South America. This string starts with the **Virgin Islands**, and ends with the "ABC islands"— **Aruba**, **Bonaire** and **Curacao**, just off the northern coast of Venezuela.

➤ The **Lucayan Archipelago** lies just north of the Greater Antilles. The **Bahamas**, where Columbus first struck land, are part of the Lucayan Archipelago.

> Columbus called these islands the **"West Indies"** because he hoped that they were somewhere near the place he was really looking for: India. He called the islands' natives **"Indians"** for the same reason.
>
> As long as he lived, Columbus never admitted that the West Indies were really nowhere near India— although he did admit some doubts.

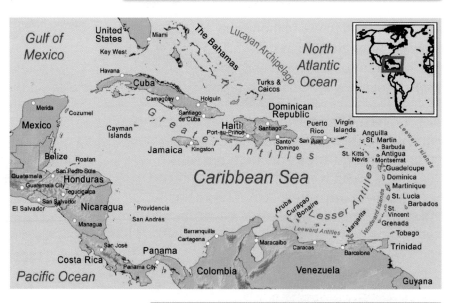

Just which of the Bahamas Columbus struck first, no one is quite sure. It may have been a Bahamian island called **San Salvador**.

Whichever it was, the natives he met there were peaceful and primitive. Many of them walked around completely naked. Like the Maya, Aztecs and Incas, they used no iron, wheels or pulleys (Chapter 22).

After exploring the Bahamas for a while, Columbus moved on to the big island of Cuba. The last stops of this first voyage were on the island of Hispaniola.

> In modern times, Hispaniola is divided between two countries: **Haiti** and the **Dominican Republic**.

The New World

On Christmas Day 1492, *Santa Maria* ran aground off the northern coast of Hispaniola. Try as he might, Columbus couldn't float his biggest ship off the bottom. In a few hours, *Santa Maria* broke up— leaving Columbus and crew thousands of miles from home, with too few ships to carry them all back!

Fortunately, plenty of crewmen volunteered to stay behind. Using lumber from the wreck of *Santa Maria*, 39 members of Columbus' crew built the very first European colony in the New World. They called their colony **La Navidad**, Spanish for "Christmas," after the Christmas day wreck of *Santa Maria*.

Back home in Castile, Columbus dazzled Ferdinand and Isabella with all the wonders he'd collected on his first voyage. Columbus had brought along strange new plants, a few natives— and even a bit of gold.

To say that the Spaniards were excited would be a huge understatement. At the mere mention of the word "gold," every soldier in Spain was ready to board ship for the New World! Now that the Spanish Reconquista was over, soldiers had been wondering what they would do next. Now they knew: they would go to the New World and find fortunes in gold.

Thanks to all the excitement, Columbus' second expedition was far bigger than his first. Seventeen ships, carrying about 1,200 colonists in all, sailed with Columbus on his second voyage to the West Indies.

Columbus returned to *La Navidad* in November 1493, just eleven months after he'd left. With so many new mouths to feed, Columbus needed a lot of money; so he was hoping to find happy colonists telling glad tales of all the gold they'd found.

Instead, Columbus found the little fort destroyed, and the colonists all dead! The long, ugly war between Spaniards and Native Americans had begun.

൚൚൚൚൚൚൚൚൚൚൚൚൚൚൚൚൚൚൚൚൚൚൚൚൚൚൚൚൚൚

Just when Europe was starting to recover from the shocking news of Spain's discoveries, Portugal started making headlines again.

➢ In 1498, a Portuguese explorer called **Vasco da Gama** finally sailed around Africa, all the way to India! After building their first trading post at Calicut, India, the Portuguese started sending trade *armadas* to India every year.

➢ In 1500, the leader of the second **Portuguese India Armada** made a huge discovery. Oddly enough, this discovery lay nowhere near India. Instead, **Pedro Alvares Cabral** discovered Brazil, South America! This explains why it was Portugal, not Spain, that built colonies in Brazil.

The next big discovery was another Spanish one. In 1513, a Spaniard called **Ponce de Leon** became the first European ever to set foot in Florida.

In all, Christopher Columbus made four voyages to the West Indies. He touched land in South America on his third voyage, and spent part of his fourth exploring Central America.

Columbus also spent part of his fourth voyage stranded on Jamaica, depending on the natives to bring him food. In time, the natives started grumbling about how much Columbus and crew were eating.

To keep from starving, Columbus played a trick on the natives. His almanac told him that a lunar eclipse would soon block the sun. So Columbus announced that if the natives stopped bringing him food, then he would take the moon away from them! When the moon went dark, just as Columbus had said, the natives were so scared that they gladly brought him whatever he needed.

Armada means "fleet of armed ships" in both Spanish and Portuguese.

The **Fountain of Youth** is a mythical spring whose waters give eternal life and health to all who drink.

The usual myth about Ponce de Leon is that he went looking for the **Fountain of Youth**. But what he was really looking for was a way to escape the shadow of the great Christopher Columbus.

Juan Ponce de Leon was a young army officer who moved to the West Indies in 1493, with Columbus' second voyage. Like everyone else on that voyage, Juan dreamed of becoming a big success. He thought he had made it in 1509, when the governor of Hispaniola named Juan Governor of Puerto Rico.

Two years later, all of Juan's hopes came crashing down. Although Christopher Columbus had died back in 1506, his son Diego still had the right to name governors for all islands his father had discovered. When Diego Columbus came to Puerto Rico, he took away Juan's job as governor, and set someone else in his place.

The name **"Florida"** comes from *Pascua Florida*, the name of a Spanish Easter celebration.

Juan realized that if he was ever going to be a governor again, then it would have to on some island Columbus hadn't discovered. In early 1513, Juan set out to find such an island. As he hopped from island to island in the Bahamas, the natives told him about a far larger land to the west. That Easter, Juan Ponce de Leon discovered Florida!

The Western Schism

Back in Chapter 21, we read how the pope moved from Rome to Avignon, France. The **Avignon Papacy** lasted nearly 70 years, all the way from 1309 – 1377. This chapter tells how the pope finally moved back to Rome.

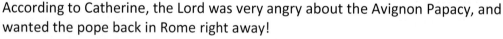

The story starts with **Catherine of Siena**, an honored nun from Siena, Italy. Around 1370, Catherine started writing letters to the pope over in Avignon. According to Catherine, the Lord was very angry about the Avignon Papacy, and wanted the pope back in Rome right away!

After 7 years of pleading, Catherine finally won. To the delight of every Italian, Pope Gregory XI moved from Avignon to Rome in 1377. The Avignon Papacy was over— or so it seemed.

Unfortunately, the beloved Pope Gregory XI died the following year; and the next pope, Urban VI, wasn't beloved at all. The fiery Urban made his cardinals terribly angry— so angry that they soon elected a new pope to take his place.

But Urban refused to leave! After trying in vain to take his seat in Rome, the new pope gave up and moved to Avignon. Now there were two popes at the same time: one in Rome, and another in Avignon!

This time of two popes is called the **Western Schism**. For the next 40 years, the Church did little else but argue over which was the true pope. Since Avignon was in France, most Frenchmen followed the Avignon popes. Most other countries followed the Roman popes. With each pope calling the other a heretic, and claiming that the other pope's followers were all going to hell, the Church was in chaos!

It all ended in 1417, when three things happened. First, two Roman popes stepped down— for by this time, there were actually three popes! Second, the **Council of Constance** excommunicated the Avignon pope. Third, the council elected a new Roman pope that everyone could accept. The Avignon pope didn't step down; but he did lose most of his followers. When he died in 1423, few Christians even noticed.

The **Western Schism** lasted about 40 years, from 1378 - 1417.

CHAPTER 25: Slavery in the New World; the Conquistadors

A Bright Beginning Gone Bad

On Christmas Day 1492, Admiral Christopher Columbus' flagship *Santa Maria* accidentally ran aground off the northern coast of the island of Hispaniola (Chapter 24).

> An admiral's **flagship** is the lead ship of his fleet.
>
> To **run aground** is to strike bottom.

The accident never should have happened. According to Columbus' journal, the wind was still that Christmas Eve, and the sea as smooth as glass. No one expected trouble on a night so calm. Thinking all was well, Columbus left an officer in charge of the rudder and went off to bed at 11 p.m. He certainly deserved a good night's sleep; for he hadn't slept at all the night before.

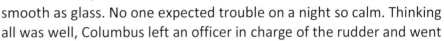
Santa Maria

Unfortunately, Columbus wasn't the only one sleeping. After Columbus went off to bed, the officer in charge decided that he deserved sleep as well. So he handed off the rudder to a younger sailor— probably thinking to himself, "What could possibly go wrong?"

Something soon went very wrong indeed. If the older, more experienced sailor had stayed at the rudder, then he might have noticed the telltale signs of shallow water ahead. The younger sailor noticed nothing— until around midnight, when he felt the sickening crunch of *Santa Maria* running aground.

Columbus tried desperately to save his flagship. His best chance was to make *Santa Maria* as light as possible, in hopes that she might float off the bottom. So he threw her cannon overboard, and even chopped down her masts. Alas, she was still too heavy to float. For the accident had split her seams, filling her hold with water. Despite anything Columbus could do, *Santa Maria* finally broke up.

Fortunately, Columbus had friends nearby.

The natives of Hispaniola were a people called the **Taino**. When Columbus came, the big island was divided into five sections, each ruled by a Taino chief called a *cacique*. The chief for northwestern Hispaniola was a kindly man called **Guacanagari.**

Columbus and Guacanagari were already friends. So when *Santa Maria* shipwrecked, the chief sent his people to help. Taino canoes swarmed around the dying ship, saving everything they could. Without all the tools, lumber and supplies the Taino carried ashore, Columbus might never have made it home from his first voyage.

"Landing of Columbus" by John Vanderlyn

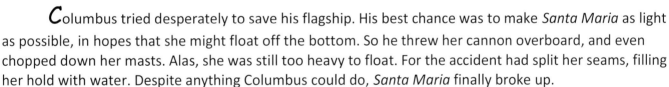

What Columbus liked most about Guacanagari and his people was that they weren't greedy. The Taino could have stolen anything they wanted from *Santa Maria* that night. They must have been tempted by the fascinating trinkets the Spaniards had brought to trade— all the beads, bells and so on. Yet they stole nothing. And when the shipwrecked Spaniards needed a place to stay, the chief offered them the two best houses in his village. Columbus wrote to Ferdinand and Isabella:

"I assure your Highnesses that there is no better land nor people. They love their neighbors as themselves, and their speech is the sweetest and gentlest in the world…"

What happened next is sad. After this bright beginning, the Spaniards and the Taino could have become great friends. Instead, they became deadly enemies.

As we read in Chapter 24, Columbus soon sailed home, leaving behind a little colony called *La Navidad*. When he came back eleven months later, he hoped to find *La Navidad* thriving. Instead, he found the little fort in ruins, and the colonists all dead! What on Earth had gone wrong, Columbus wondered?

Guacanagari knew. According to Columbus' friend, the colonists of *La Navidad* had kidnapped some Taino women from one of the other chiefs. The furious chief had answered by destroying the little fort, killing every Spaniard inside! These were the first blows in a long, ugly war that would leave countless innocent people dead— most of them Taino.

The first big battle of that war came in 1495, while Columbus was still on his second voyage.

With an expensive expedition to pay for, Columbus needed a lot of gold on this second voyage. So he pressed inland, trying to seize the mines where the Taino found their gold. Only one chief fought for Columbus: Guacanagari. The other four chiefs raised a big army against Columbus, hoping to drive him off Hispaniola once and for all.

The two armies met at the **Battle of Santo Cerro**, named for a high hill overlooking the gold mines.

The battle started badly for the Spaniards. Back in 1492, Columbus had believed that he could conquer all of Hispaniola with just a few well-armed Spaniards. Now he worried that his whole army might not be enough! Even sharp steel and heavy cannon were no match for thousands of Taino, all attacking at once. Instead of gaining ground, Columbus lost ground, retreating farther uphill every day.

After several days of losses, Columbus feared that the next day might be his last on Earth. So instead of going to sleep that night, Columbus planted a big wooden cross on Santo Cerro, and spent the night praying.

The Battle of Santo Cerro (1495)

While Columbus was praying, a nearby priest was having a vision. The priest saw the Taino try to burn Columbus' cross; but the fire wouldn't catch. He also saw them try to chop down the cross, and pull it down; but the cross wouldn't fall. Finally, the priest saw the Virgin Mary and the Baby Jesus standing beside Columbus' cross, bathed in white light.

At sunrise the next day, Columbus received the shock of his life: the Taino army was gone! Instead of pressing their attack, the

"The Virgin of Navigators" by Alejo Fernandez

Taino had melted away. Just why the Taino left, no one knows for sure. But Columbus thought he knew why. To him, the priest's vision meant that Christ and His Church would never be driven off Hispaniola.

Whether Columbus was right or not, the Taino never again raised such a large army against him. The Spaniards seized more and more land, conquering more and more Taino.

As a conquered people, the Taino had to do as they were told. Columbus made slaves of the Taino. All conquered Taino over 14 years old had to bring the Spaniards a certain amount of gold dust every month. If they didn't, then the Spaniards punished them in horrible ways. Columbus also sent Taino back to Castile to be sold at slave auctions. Within 25 years after Columbus first landed on Hispaniola, only a few Taino remained on the whole island.

〰〰

Meanwhile, the Portuguese were making slaves of a different kind of people: Africans.

Of course, slavery was nothing new. Since ancient times, the winners of battles had been selling the losers into slavery. Even in peacetime, some people made money by kidnapping their neighbors and selling them into slavery. And when poor people couldn't pay their debts, they sometimes had no choice but to sell themselves into slavery.

But the Age of Discovery made slavery much worse.

The Portuguese started trading slaves in the 1460s, when they first built the Portuguese Gold Coast (Chapter 24). Some Portuguese slavers carried slaves from Africa to old auctions around the Mediterranean Sea. Others carried them to new auctions around the Portuguese Empire. With growing

"The Slave Trade" by artist Francois-Auguste Biard

colonies on Madeira, the Cape Verdes and more, Portugal was hungry for more slaves.

When the Americas opened up, the Spaniards also grew hungry for slaves. A few years after Columbus, slave ships started following the **Middle Passage** from Africa to the West Indies.

〰〰〰〰〰〰〰〰〰〰〰〰〰〰〰〰〰〰〰〰〰〰〰〰〰〰〰〰〰

> The **Middle Passage** was a sea route that slave ships used to carry slaves from West Africa to the West Indies.

Why did the Spaniards buy so many African slaves?

As we already know, the Spaniards eventually found a lot of gold in South America (Chapter 22). But they didn't find much in the West Indies. The gold mines that Columbus won at the Battle of Santo Cerro all ran empty in a few years. After that, the Spaniards of the West Indies needed a new way to earn their livings.

For many, that new way was farming **sugarcane**. The West Indies were the perfect place to raise sugarcane. The climate was hot, and the soil just right.

> **Sugarcane** is a tropical plant with a thick stalk. When the stalk is pressed between heavy rollers, sweet juice comes out. Cane juice can be processed to make molasses and sugar.

African slaves cutting sugarcane while an overseer looks on

The problem was that raising sugarcane took a lot of hard work. Besides planting, tending and cutting plants, there were also endless jobs like pressing stalks, refining juice, barreling molasses and loading ships.

The less a farmer paid for these jobs, the more money was left over for the farmer— which is why the Spaniards bought so many African slaves.

What did the world do with so much molasses? Mostly, the world turned it into rum. Any kind of sugar can be fermented and distilled to make alcohol. Distilleries in Europe could turn molasses from the West Indies into a sweet rum that customers loved.

Sugarcane, rum and slaves— these were the three corners of an ugly new business called the **Triangle Trade**. A song from the musical play "1776" tells the whole story of the Triangle Trade in just five words: "Molasses to Rum to Slaves."

➢ Farmers in the West Indies raised sugarcane, turned it into molasses, and then shipped molasses off to Europe.

➢ Factories in Europe turned molasses into rum, and then shipped rum off to Africa.

➢ Traders in Africa traded rum for slaves, and then shipped slaves off to the West Indies to grow more sugarcane.

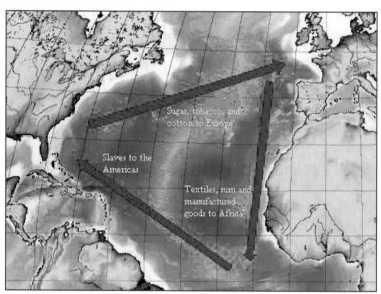
The Triangle Trade

The Door of No Return

After buying or capturing African slaves, traders herded them into strong buildings to wait for the next slave auction. One such building was **Elmina Castle**, which guarded the Portuguese Gold Coast (Chapter 24).

After the auction, the poor slaves were locked inside again until it was time to board ship for the West Indies. When the big day finally came, they passed through one final door on their way out of the building.

Over time, doors like these became symbols of the mournful fact that these slaves were leaving home forever, and would never see their families again. Some call these symbols "Doors of No Return"; while others call them "Portals of Sorrow."

A Door of No Return

Slave Ships

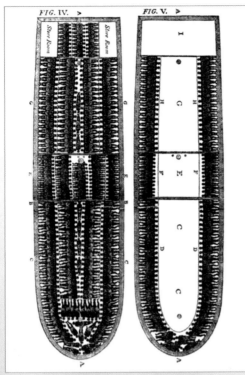

Layout of a large slave ship

The ugly job of carrying so many slaves to the West Indies required a special kind of ship. Instead of the usual cargo hold, slave ships had special decks built just for slaves. The ceilings of these decks were often less than five feet high. Some carried slaves lying down, crowded in head-to-foot. Other carried slaves in a seated position, crowded in back-to-chest. Slavers almost never let slaves up on the main deck, for fear they might take over the ship.

The journey from West Africa to the West Indies usually took about two months. Imagine spending two long months chained in the same place— unable to move, even to go to the bathroom. Imagine being seasick, hot, filthy and crowded for two solid months. Imagine the person next to you dying of fever, as many slaves did. These were just a few of the many horrors aboard slave ships.

The Conquistadors

Conquistador is Spanish for "conqueror."

Between searching for gold and raising sugarcane, brave young Spaniards had two ways to strike it rich in the West Indies. So naturally, they came by the thousands. After taking over Hispaniola, they moved on to Cuba, Puerto Rico and other islands.

These were the first Spanish **conquistadors**— the soldiers who conquered the New World for the Spanish Empire.

From the West Indies, the conquistadors moved on to **Middle America**. The first conquistador to build a colony in Middle America was **Vasco Nunez de Balboa**.

Remember that **Middle America** is another name for Central America and Mexico.

Balboa was born into a family of minor nobles over in Spain. Unfortunately, he was his father's third son— which meant that he would never inherit as much as his older brothers. So Balboa moved to the West Indies, hoping to get rich a different way.

Quinto Real is Spanish for "King's Fifth." Under a Spanish law called the **Quinto Real**, the King of Spain automatically received one-fifth of any gold, silver or other precious metals found anywhere in his empire.

The first way Balboa made money was through the **Quinto Real**, or "King's Fifth." The king gave certain nobles permits to search certain parts of the New World for gold. In exchange, these nobles gave the king one-fifth of any gold they found.

Since Balboa wasn't rich enough to have a permit of his own, he worked for a noble who did have one. After five years' work along the coasts of South and Central America, Balboa had enough gold to buy a big farm on Hispaniola.

Unfortunately, Balboa wasn't much of a farmer. He borrowed a lot of money trying to save his farm, and wound up losing both money and farm!

With no way to repay his debts, Balboa was likely to wind up in jail, if not worse. So he saved himself in the only way he could think of: by sneaking aboard a conquistador's ship and hiding in an empty barrel.

When the captain found out, he almost cast Balboa away on the nearest island! In the end, though, he let Balboa join his crew.

Balboa made a much better conquistador than he did a farmer. Just a few years after he hid in that barrel, Balboa was already the governor of a little colony. His capital, **Dariena**, lay near the northern end of what is now the border between Panama and Colombia.

One day, a Native American prince told Balboa about an "other sea" on the far side of Panama. Since the distance to this other sea was only about 70 miles, Balboa decided to march over and see it for himself.

In 1513, Balboa and his men became the first Spaniards ever to cast eyes on this other sea— which turned out to be the Pacific Ocean! Striding out into the water, Balboa dramatically raised his sword and claimed the entire coast for the Spanish Empire. If Balboa was right, then the west coasts of Central America, South America and North America all belonged to Spain.

Of course, Balboa wasn't right. The people who really owned those coasts were the ones who lived there. Even so, Balboa's expedition made Spain the first country in Europe to claim part of the Pacific coast.

〰〰〰〰〰〰〰〰〰〰〰〰〰〰〰〰〰〰〰〰〰〰〰〰〰〰〰〰〰〰〰〰

The next great Spanish conquistador was **Hernan Cortes**, the man who conquered the Aztec Empire. —STOP—

Balboa claiming every shore of the Pacific for the Spanish Empire

Like Balboa, Cortes was a minor noble who moved to the West Indies as a young man, hoping to strike it rich. He spent five years helping his governor conquer Cuba, the biggest island of the West Indies.

In 1519, Cortes' governor trusted him to lead a big expedition to Mexico. His orders were to claim Mexico in the name of the governor. But Cortes had other ideas. When he reached Mexico, Cortes wrote a letter to the King of Spain— asking him to make Mexico a separate colony, with Cortes himself as governor!

Without waiting for the king's answer, Cortes set out to conquer the capital of the Aztec Empire. This was Tenochtitlan, the beautiful city in the lake (Chapter 22).

Cortes made a lot of friends on his way to Tenochtitlan. The Aztecs' neighbors all hated them, and were happy to help Cortes destroy them. The Aztecs were about to pay a high price for the horrible way they had always treated their neighbors.

Remember why the Aztecs' neighbors hated them so much. The Aztecs had a cruel habit of kidnapping their neighbors and sacrificing them to their gods.

Portrait of Hernan Cortes

When Cortes came, **Emperor Montezuma II** ruled the Aztec Empire.
Montezuma acted strangely around Cortes. After all he had heard about the Spaniards, the emperor must have known that Cortes was up to no good. But instead of standing up to Cortes, Montezuma welcomed him as a friend. He invited Cortes to stay at one of the best palaces in Tenochtitlan. He also gave him many gifts, including a fortune in gold.

One of the gifts Montezuma gave was especially interesting. For some reason, Montezuma gave Cortes the headdress of **Quetzalcoatl**, the feathered serpent god of the Aztecs (Chapter 22).

In Spanish eyes, this gift could mean only one thing: that Montezuma saw Cortes as a god. But this may not be true. Some historians believe that Montezuma was only pretending to honor Cortes. What he was really doing, they say, was watching and waiting— trying to learn more about Cortes so that he could destroy him later.

If watching and waiting were really Montezuma's plan, then things didn't go as planned. In no time, Cortes seized Montezuma and held him hostage. With their emperor in enemy hands, the Aztecs couldn't attack, for fear Cortes might kill him.

All of that changed a few months later, when someone killed Montezuma anyway.

Cortes meeting Montezuma and the Aztecs

What happened to Montezuma? According to the Spaniards, the Aztecs were rioting outside Montezuma's palace, furious with the Spaniards for many reasons. So Cortes sent Montezuma out on a balcony, with orders to calm his people down.

But the Aztecs didn't want to calm down. They wanted Montezuma to stand up to Cortes, not act like Cortes' puppet. So when Montezuma showed up on that balcony, saying just what Cortes wanted him to say, the Aztecs stoned their own emperor to death!

Others tell a different story. Some believe that the Spaniards murdered Montezuma themselves, and then lied about it to cover up their cruelty.

Either way, the death of the emperor left the Spaniards in serious trouble! Without Montezuma to hold them off, the Aztecs would surely kill every Spaniard in Tenochtitlan.

Knowing this, the Spaniards planned to sneak out of the city under cover of darkness. This was the beginning of *La Noche Triste*, "The Sad Night" when most of Cortes' soldiers died.

For of course, the Aztecs were ready and waiting for the Spaniards. Even though they left as quietly as possible, the Aztecs spotted them. As the Spaniards sped over one of the **causeways**, Aztec warriors bore down on them in canoes.

Only a few Spaniards managed to escape. These were mostly the ones on horseback, like Cortes himself. As for the poor soldiers without horses, almost all of them died.

> Remember what the **causeways** of Tenochtitlan were— land bridges connecting the island city to the mainland.

The saddest thing about *La Noche Triste* was the way Cortes' foot soldiers died. Before they left, Cortes let them stuff their packs with as much gold as they could carry. But when the Aztecs stormed the causeway, they drove many foot soldiers into the lake— where the weight of all that gold carried them straight to the bottom. They had carried that gold because they believed that it would buy them richer lives. Instead, gold wound up ending their lives.

Cortes spent the next several months gathering a big army to surround Tenochtitlan. Only a fraction of Cortes' soldiers were Spaniards; the rest were all angry neighbors of the Aztecs. Less than a year after *La Noche Triste*, Cortes laid siege to Tenochtitlan, cutting off all supplies from outside the city.

Besides Cortes' army, the Aztecs also faced another bad enemy: disease. Ever since the Spaniards came, the Aztecs had been sicker than usual. Without meaning to, the Spaniards had brought deadly diseases to the New World— especially **smallpox**.

Soon after *La Noche Triste*, a smallpox epidemic swept through Tenochtitlan. Thousands of Aztecs died; and many others were too sick to work.

Faced with two such deadly enemies, Cortes and smallpox, the Aztec Empire finally collapsed. The last Aztec emperor surrendered to Hernan Cortes in August 1521.

𒊹𒊹𒊹𒊹𒊹𒊹𒊹𒊹𒊹𒊹𒊹𒊹𒊹𒊹𒊹𒊹𒊹𒊹𒊹𒊹𒊹𒊹𒊹𒊹𒊹𒊹𒊹

In conquering the Aztecs, Cortes became the richest conquistador so far. But one conquistador became even richer. This was **Francisco Pizarro**, the man who conquered the Inca Empire.

Pizarro started as an officer in the army of Vasco Nunez de Balboa (above). When a Native American prince told Balboa about the "other sea," Pizarro was right there listening.

That same prince told of something even more interesting to Pizarro. Far to the south, this prince said, lay a huge kingdom that had far more gold than any kingdom in Middle America.

That kingdom, of course, was the Inca Empire. Right then and there, Pizarro decided to either conquer the Incas or die trying.

Pizarro's first problem was finding the Incas. He needed three expeditions to South America before he finally found a good road into the Andes mountains of Peru.

Pizarro's next problem was how to beat the Incas. The size of his expedition was pitiful— less than 200 Spaniards, against tens of thousands of Incas! However, Pizarro did have two advantages.

Francisco Pizarro

Smallpox was a deadly virus that brought on a terrible skin rash and severe breathing problems. The worst form of smallpox killed about 4 out of every 10 people who caught it.

The reason why smallpox killed so many Aztecs, but so few Spaniards, was because Spaniards were used to it. The Spaniards had grown up in Europe, where smallpox was common. So their immune systems knew how to fight smallpox. But the Aztecs had grown up in America, where no one had ever faced smallpox before.

The Aztecs weren't the only ones who died of smallpox. Epidemics struck cities and villages all over the Americas, killing countless thousands. Just how many Native Americans died of smallpox, no one knows; but it may be that smallpox killed more than the conquistadors did.

Native Americans dying of smallpox

Francisco Pizarro
(1475? - 1541)

- The first advantage was that Pizarro's men carried weapons the Incas had never seen before— powerful muskets and cannon that would terrify Inca warriors.

- The second advantage was that when Pizarro showed up, the Incas were just finishing a civil war between two rival emperors. This war had killed many Incas, leaving the empire weaker than before.

Inca Atahualpa

The winner of this civil war was **Inca Atahualpa**, whom Pizarro first met in November 1532. Pizarro made sure to get to the meeting place before Atahualpa. That way, he could hide most of his men behind buildings, ready to leap out and attack.

The moment Atahualpa arrived, Pizarro sent a priest to read him the **Spanish Requirement of 1513**.

Like all Spaniards, the conquistadors were supposed to be good Christians. So how could they treat Native Americans as cruelly as they did? The answer lies in an important paper called the **Spanish Requirement of 1513**, also known as *El Requerimiento*.

The Requirement explained that in the beginning, God created Adam and Eve. All people on Earth were children of Adam and Eve, no matter where they lived. And as God's creatures, all people owed obedience to God.

The only way to obey God was to obey the Catholic Church. The man God had chosen to rule His people was the Apostle Peter— the first pope, the head of the Church. When Peter died, he handed down his authority to the next pope in line, and then the next, all the way down to the present-day pope.

Now the pope had given the Americas to the King of Spain. Which meant that if Native Americans didn't obey the King of Spain, then they were going against God! At least, that is what the conquistadors believed, and told Native Americans each time they read the Requirement.

Of course, Pizarro didn't forget about the gold. Besides reading the Requirement, Pizarro's priest also told Atahualpa that he must pay the King of Spain a lot of gold— starting right now.

At this, Atahualpa laughed in the priest's face! With thousands of troops at his back, Atahualpa saw no reason to fear a few Spaniards. So he tossed away a small book of Scripture the priest had given him, swearing that he would never pay tribute.

Tossing away Scripture was just the sign Pizarro had been waiting for. Now that Atahualpa had disobeyed God, Pizarro's men leapt out of hiding and blasted the Incas. Most of the Incas ran off, allowing Pizarro to capture Atahualpa!

Next, Pizarro did to Atahualpa just what Cortes had done to Montezuma. He held Atahualpa hostage, threatening to kill him if the Incas attacked.

The building where Pizarro held Atahualpa hostage was about the size of a one-car garage. Its name, the **Ransom Room**, comes from a bargain that Atahualpa struck with the gold-hungry Pizarro.

Atahualpa promised that if Pizarro would spare his life, then the Incas would fill the Ransom Room with gold. They would also fill two rooms just like it with silver, and give the whole lot to Pizarro. With that much treasure, Pizarro would be the richest conquistador ever!

The Ransom Room where Pizarro held Atahualpa

Sad to say, Pizarro didn't hold up his end of the bargain. The Incas held up their end, giving Pizarro the huge fortune that Atahualpa promised. But instead of letting Atahualpa live, Pizarro placed him on trial, and wound up strangling him to death.

Without an emperor to hold it together, the Inca Empire collapsed in 1532— eleven years after the Aztec Empire collapsed.

〰〰〰〰〰〰〰〰〰〰〰〰〰〰〰〰〰〰〰〰〰〰〰〰〰〰〰〰〰〰〰〰〰〰〰〰

Around the World in Three Years

In between the mighty deeds of Cortes and Pizarro came another mighty deed. In 1522, an expedition led by **Ferdinand Magellan** became the first to sail around the world!

Ferdinand Magellan

After Vasco da Gama built the first Portuguese trading post in India (Chapter 24), traders sailed on beyond India. There was so much more to discover! East of India lay the **Spice Islands**, where traders could buy valuable spices like cinnamon, nutmeg and cloves.

This was how Ferdinand Magellan got his start: as a Portuguese naval officer defending trading posts in India and the Spice Islands.

Later, Magellan got in trouble with the Portuguese; so he went to work for the Spanish. Magellan promised Spain the same thing Columbus had promised: that he could reach the Far East by sailing around the world to the west. Although no one had ever done it before, Magellan believed that he could sail around the southern tip of South America, just as Bartolomeu Dias had sailed around Africa.

It took a long time, but Magellan and crew finally found a way around South America. Once they reached the Pacific, the Far East couldn't be far off— or so Magellan believed.

> The **Spice Islands** were part of what is now Indonesia.
> **Cape Horn** is a point of land that lies near the southern tip of South America, just as the **Cape of Good Hope** lies near the southern tip of Africa. Magellan didn't actually sail around Cape Horn. Instead, he passed through South America by a narrow waterway called the **Strait of Magellan**.

Magellan was as wrong about that as Columbus had been. The distance to **Guam**, the first island Magellan found on his way west, was almost 10,000 miles! By the time he reached Guam, four months had passed. Since his ships carried only about two months' worth of food, his starving men were reduced to eating anything they could find— including rat meat and boiled leather.

Continuing west from Guam, Magellan struck the **Philippines**, where he made his last mistake. On one of the Philippines, a friendly chief asked Magellan to help him fight a war. Magellan agreed— perhaps because he trusted Spanish steel to save him from the primitive weapons of the natives. But it didn't. Instead of winning the war for his friend, the great navigator Ferdinand Magellan went down fighting.

After that, one of Magellan's ship's captains took over. It was actually **Juan Sebastian Elcano**, not Ferdinand Magellan, who finished the first full voyage around the world. Magellan had sailed out of Spain with five ships and 270 men. Three years later, Elcano sailed back to Spain with just one ship— and only 18 men!

Victoria, **the only ship from Magellan's expedition that made it back to Spain**

John Hus (1369? – 1415)

Back in Chapter 22, we read about a Christian professor from Oxford, England called John Wycliffe. This chapter tells of a priest who loved John Wycliffe's teaching, and what happened to him because of it.

John Hus was a priest and professor at the University of **Prague**, Bohemia. As a Catholic priest, Hus was supposed to obey the Catholic Church. But Hus didn't always agree with the Catholic Church— especially after he read John Wycliffe. Like Wycliffe, Hus believed that the Bible was more important than Church tradition. He also believed in holding church services in a language his people could understand. In Hus' case, that language was Czech.

> **Prague** is the capital of what is now the Czech Republic.

The archbishop in charge of Bohemia did everything he could think of to change Hus' mind. He tried ordering all of Wycliffe's books burned. When that failed, the archbishop excommunicated Hus. By order of the archbishop, no Christian was to have anything to do with John Hus.

But the people of Bohemia didn't obey; for they loved John Hus, and hated their stuffy archbishop. Instead of leaving the Church as ordered, Hus kept right on teaching what John Wycliffe had taught— and in Czech, not Latin.

John Hus

The Church finally did to John Hus what it had almost done to John Wycliffe. In 1414, a Church court charged Hus with heresy and placed him on trial.

The trial of John Hus was no real trial; for no one defended Hus. The priests simply read out their accusations, announced that Hus was wrong, and then ordered him to change his beliefs.

> The trial of John Hus took place at the **Council of Constance**, Germany in 1414 - 1415. This was the same church council that would soon end the Western Schism (Chapter 24).

Hus answered that he would be happy to change his beliefs, if anyone could prove him wrong. However, they would have to prove it from the Bible— for Hus believed in the Bible, not Church tradition.

When the Church couldn't change Hus' mind, it sentenced him to death. Executioners stripped Hus of his priestly robes, and then buried him up to his neck in a pile of wood and straw. On his head they set a mocking paper crown labelled "Leader of Heretics." Then they burned poor, faithful John Hus to death.

John Hus using a Bible to defend himself at the Council of Constance

CHAPTER 26:

The Printing Revolution; the Renaissance in Florence

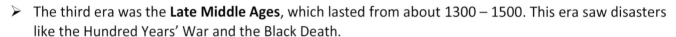
WORLD HISTORY

The End of Medieval Times

Way back at the beginning of this book, we learned that the medieval era can be divided into three shorter eras.

➢ The first era was the **Dark Ages**, which lasted from about 400 – 1000 AD. This era saw the birth of Islam, the rise of Charlemagne and the Viking invasions.

➢ The second era was the **High Middle Ages**, which lasted from about 1000 – 1300. This was the era of knights, castles, the Norman Conquest and the Holy Land Crusades.

➢ The third era was the **Late Middle Ages**, which lasted from about 1300 – 1500. This era saw disasters like the Hundred Years' War and the Black Death.

We also learned why the Dark Ages are called "dark": because the light of Greek and Roman learning went out in Western Europe. Doctors forgot how to heal; engineers forgot how to build great buildings; and sculptors forgot how to carve fine art.

Learning was the biggest difference between

> *Renaissance* is a French word that means "rebirth." The **Renaissance** was the era that fell after the medieval era. Renaissance times started in the 1400s, and lasted into the early 1600s.

the medieval era and the next era: the **Renaissance**. The name "renaissance" means a rebirth of learning. In the Late Middle Ages, Europeans started re-learning all the Greek and Roman knowledge their ancestors had forgotten.

Where does the line between the medieval era and the Renaissance fall? The answer is that there is no one line. Instead, different historians point to different lines.

Some point to the **Age of Discovery**, which started with Henry the Navigator around 1415 (Chapter 24). When explorers from Europe sailed out into the unknown, they left behind the old superstitions of the Dark Ages— crazy stories about boiling seas to the south and giant whirlpools at the edge of the Atlantic.

Others point to the **Fall of Constantinople**, which came in 1453 (Chapter 20). As the capital of a Greek empire, Constantinople was also the capital of Greek learning. When the Ottoman Empire seized Constantinople, some great old scholars moved to Western Europe— bringing along some great old learning that the West had forgotten.

Still others point to one very important invention: the movable-type printing press.

Leonardo da Vinci, a leading thinker of the Renaissance

The Printing Revolution

In medieval times, books were so expensive that only the richest people owned them. The average household owned no books, not even a family Bible. Nor did the average household have any use for books— for most people couldn't read.

Part of the problem was that books were so expensive. In those days, the usual way of making books was to copy them by hand— which took forever! The average scribe needed a whole year to copy out a Bible. And scribes had to be paid— which meant that every Bible cost at least a year's wages. Add in paper, bookbinding and profit, and a Bible might cost two years' wages, or even three. Imagine spending your whole salary for three whole years, just to buy one Bible!

A scribe at work with quill and ink in a monastery scriptorium

Of course, there was also woodblock printing. A printer could carve a page into a flat block of wood. He could then coat the block with ink and press it onto paper to print a page.

But woodblocks came with problems of their own. One problem was that each block took several days to carve! Another was that each block printed only one page, not the hundreds of pages that went into Bibles. Worst of all, woodblocks wore out, forcing the tired printer to carve new blocks. Woodblock printing was fine for a few pages, but not for long books.

All of this was before 1450, when a German printer called **Johannes Gutenberg** figured out a better way.

Just how Gutenberg figured it out, no one knows for sure. His father seems to have worked with the **mint** at Mainz, Germany. This might mean that Gutenberg also spent time at the mint. As a boy with talented hands, Gutenberg might have learned many useful skills at the mint. He might have learned how to engrave words and pictures; how to make molds, and pour metal into molds; and how to make many copies of the same coin.

Years later, Gutenberg turned those skills to the problem of printing. He soon discovered that printing pages could be a lot like minting coins. One by one, Gutenberg's great ideas answered all of the problems that had made woodblock printing so slow and expensive.

> Johannes Gutenberg
> (1398? - 1468)

> A **mint** is where a government makes its coins.

Johannes Gutenberg

Gutenberg's best idea was **movable metal type**. Instead of carving pages into wood, he molded individual letters out of metal. He then clamped his letters to a plate, coated them with ink, and pressed them on paper to print a page.

What a difference movable type made! It took only a few hours to set a page in movable type— far less than the several days it took to carve a page in wood. Since Gutenberg's type was movable, he could re-arrange it to print as many pages as he liked. And since his type was made of metal, it lasted far longer than wood.

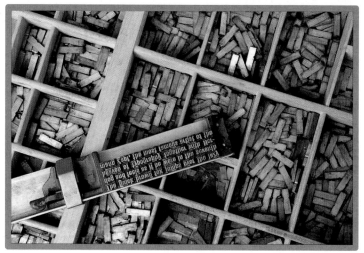

Movable metal type

The movable-type printing press spread like wildfire. Less than fifty years after Gutenberg invented it, print shops all over Europe were churning out books in different languages. And the more books they printed, the more people learned to read.

This was how the Renaissance began: with reading. Reading changed everything. In fact, reading changed so many things that it was like a revolution. This is why historians call this time the **Printing Revolution**.

Two things that reading changed were news and politics. Before the printing press, most people heard only the news their kings wanted them to hear. But after the printing press, people could read books and newspapers— which sometimes contained news their kings didn't want them to hear. More news meant a bit more power for average citizens.

Reading also changed science. Before the printing press, most scientists had no idea what other scientists were working on. One might spend years working on a problem, only to find that someone else had already solved it. But after the printing press, scientists could publish their work in books and journals. Without new books on geography, Columbus might never have discovered the New World!

Reading even changed Christianity. Before the printing press, all Bibles were in Latin— a language only priests and scholars could read. And the Catholic Church wanted to keep it that way. When John Wycliffe translated the Bible into English, the Church did all it could to stop him (Chapter 22).

The reason for this was simple. The Church didn't want people reading the Bible on their own— for fear that if they did, then they might interpret the Bible differently than the Church interpreted it.

The first full books ever printed on a movable-type printing press, at least in Europe, were the **Gutenberg Bibles**. Sometime before 1455, Gutenberg and crew printed and bound about 175 beautiful Bibles. The 48 Gutenberg Bibles that have survived into modern times are some of the rarest, most valuable books in the world.

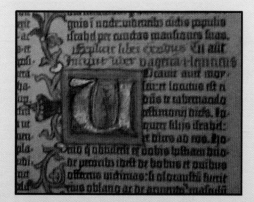

To win buyers for his machine-printed Bibles, Gutenberg had to make them as beautiful as hand-written **illuminated manuscripts** (Chapter 3). So he coated the edges of his pages with gold, and hired artists to hand-decorate certain letters.

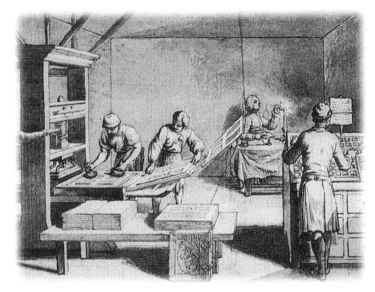
A Gutenberg-style printer's shop at work

Which is exactly what ended up happening. In 1517, a Bible-loving German called **Martin Luther** started complaining that the Church was wrong about certain things.

Before the printing press, most people never would have read Martin Luther. But after the printing press, many people read him— and liked what they read.

Luther went on to lead one of the biggest splits in the history of the Church. This was the **Protestant Reformation**, which we'll study in Chapter 27.

The Renaissance in Florence

But we are getting ahead of ourselves. The Renaissance didn't start with Protestants in Germany, but with Catholics in Italy. The **Cradle of the Renaissance** was Florence, a city in northern Italy.

Renaissance Italy was a broken place. After Roman times, no one king ruled all of Italy— although some claimed to. Instead, different kings ruled different parts of Italy at different times.

Northern Italy, where Florence stood, was especially broken. When the Renaissance began, northern Italy was divided into a dozen or more different countries. Some belonged to the Holy Roman Empire; while others were more or less independent **republics**.

> Remember what a **republic** is: a country governed by representatives who are elected by the people.

At the beginning of the Renaissance, the three biggest republics of northern Italy were Venice, Genoa and Florence.

Italy is a land of mountains.

➤ The **Alps** divides Italy from the rest of Europe. This is the biggest mountain range in Europe. **Mount Blanc**, the tallest mountain in Europe, stands near the corner where Italy, France and Switzerland meet.

➤ A long mountain chain called the **Apennines** runs almost all the way down the Italian Peninsula.

➤ Even the islands around Italy are mountainous. The big island of **Sicily**, which rests at the toe of the Italian boot, is home to the tallest active volcano in Europe: **Mount Etna**.

"A View of Mount Blanc" by artist Karl Friedrich Schinkel

As a republic, Florence didn't follow the old feudal system of lords, vassals and the oath of fealty (Chapter 10). Instead, Florence elected its leaders.

At election time, the names of the leading men of Florence were all written on little slips of paper. The slips were all rolled up, tied off and placed in a leather bag. Then an election officer reached into the bag and pulled out several names. This is how Florence elected the representatives who sat on its governing council: the **Signoria of Florence**.

But who were these "leading men of Florence"— the ones whose names went into the bag? The answer is that they were all **masters** in one of Florence's trade guilds.

Trade guilds were especially important in Florence. No one could work a respectable job without first joining a trade guild.

All guild men stood at one of three levels: apprentice, journeyman or master. An **apprentice** was an unskilled tradesman who was just starting out. A **journeyman** was a skilled tradesman who journeyed from shop to shop, practicing and learning more about his trade. A **master** was a highly skilled tradesman with enough experience, and enough money, to open his own shop.

This last item was key: money. Without extra money, a journeyman might stay a journeyman all his life. Usually, the only journeymen who could afford to open their own shops were the ones with rich families or friends. Only the rich could become guild masters.

What all this means, in the end, is that Florence was ruled by the rich. Since only the rich could become guild masters— and since only masters' names went into that leather bag at election time— only the rich could sit on the Signoria of Florence.

Remember what the **Iron Crown of Lombardy** was: the crown of the King of Italy (Chapter 4). The iron ring that lines the crown is supposed to have come from one of the iron spikes that held Jesus on the cross.

A **trade guild** was an organization that controlled a specific business in a specific town. For example, everyone who made or sold wool in Florence belonged to a wool makers' guild.

Coat of arms of the *Arte della Lana*, the wool makers' guild of Florence

Thus Florence was indeed a republic; but it was not a **democratic republic**. In a democratic republic, every citizen has a voice in government, whether he is rich or poor. Since the poor of Florence had no voice, Florence was a **plutocracy**— a government in which only the rich had voices.

ꄱꄱꄱꄱꄱꄱꄱꄱꄱꄱꄱꄱꄱꄱꄱꄱꄱꄱꄱꄱꄱꄱꄱꄱꄱꄱꄱꄱꄱ

When the Renaissance began, the richest man in Florence was **Cosimo de Medici**. Cosimo was the head of the **Medici family**, and a master of the bankers' guild.

The Medicis had a great talent for managing money. Cosimo's father had built his family bank, the **Medici Bank**, into the richest business in all of Europe. Cosimo carried on that tradition when he inherited the Medici Bank.

Cosimo de Medici
(1389 - 1464)

Portrait of Cosimo de Medici

With that much money, Cosimo could do almost anything he liked. And Cosimo de Medici was an energetic man who liked a great many things.

One of the things Cosimo liked was Greek and Roman learning. And it was a good thing he did; for Cosimo lived at an important time. The Fall of Constantinople came in 1453, when Cosimo was at his richest. After the fall, the Greek scholars of Constantinople needed new places to live.

Cosimo was there to help. Around 1462, Cosimo set up a new college for some of those Greek scholars from Constantinople. The **Platonic Academy of Florence** was named for **Plato**, the great philosopher from ancient Greece. The Platonic Academy was the first school in Italy where students could study under great old Greek professors from Constantinople.

Cosimo also liked beautiful buildings and art. In fact, some of the best Renaissance art might never have been created without him. For Cosimo de Medici was the first great **art patron** of the Renaissance.

Why did artists need patrons? Because great art costs a fortune to create! Even the most talented artists on Earth are not born knowing how to create great art. So the patron must first find talented young artists, and then pay older artists to train them. This means paying for food, clothes, travel and lodging— not only for the artist himself,

> An **art patron** is a rich person who spends part of his fortune to help talented artists create fine art.

but also for his fussy teacher. Then there are the artist's studio; his assistants; his choice materials; his expensive tools— the list is endless. No one could afford those expenses better than Cosimo de Medici.

Still, why would Cosimo want to spend so much money on art?

Some of Cosimo's reasons were unselfish ones. First, Cosimo truly loved art. He also admired the amazing skills of the artists who created it. And he adored the city of Florence, which became a showcase for all the art his money paid for. Between the fortune he spent on art, and the other fortune he spent on buildings, Cosimo left Florence far more beautiful than he found it.

But Cosimo also had selfish reasons. One was because he wanted people to remember him forever, as he said in this famous quote:

> "All those things have given me the greatest satisfaction and contentment because they are not only for the honor of God but are likewise for my own remembrance. For fifty years, I have done nothing else but earn money and spend money; and it became clear that spending money gives me greater pleasure than earning it."

Another selfish reason was Cosimo's banking job.

Before Cosimo's day, most people didn't like bankers. The Medicis earned some of their money by **usury**— in other words, by charging interest on money loaned to the poor. The Bible frowns on usury, as it says in Exodus 22:25:

> "If you lend money to one of my people among you who is needy, do not treat it like a business deal; charge no interest."

This stunning statue of John the Baptist was carved by Donatello, a great Renaissance artist and friend of Cosimo de Medici

In medieval times, the Church outlawed usury. But when the Renaissance came, the Church changed its mind— partly because of huge donations from rich bankers like the Medicis.

Even so, plenty of Christians still didn't trust bankers. Cosimo knew that if he didn't spent part of his fortune to benefit Florence, then the people of Florence might turn against him.

ᘊᘊᘊ

After Cosimo de Medici, the next great art patron was his grandson

Lorenzo de Medici. The two greatest artists of the Renaissance,
Leonardo da Vinci and **Michelangelo**, were both friends of Lorenzo's. Michelangelo may have even lived with Lorenzo for a time.

But the wealth of Lorenzo de Medici bought him more than just great art. It also bought him deadly enemies called the **Pazzis**.

The Medici Bank wasn't the only bank in Florence. There were also the Pazzi Bank, owned by the Pazzi family; and the Salviati Bank, owned by the Salviati family. Both families were terribly jealous of the Medicis.

Besides jealousy, the Pazzis also had a second reason for hating the Medicis: they considered Lorenzo a tyrant. Florence was supposed to be a republic, the Pazzis said. But Lorenzo treated Florence like his personal kingdom! Elections couldn't stop Lorenzo; for no guild master would dare criticize someone as rich and powerful as Lorenzo. Even if Lorenzo couldn't control the elections, the Pazzis said, he could still control the guild masters who won those elections.

At least part of what the Pazzis said was true. The Medicis really did hold tremendous power in Florence. But was Lorenzo really a tyrant? That was a question for the people of Florence to decide.

Either way, the Pazzis decided to murder Lorenzo, along with his younger brother Giuliano. With both Medici men out of the way, the Pazzis would be the new leaders of Florence— or so they hoped.

Lorenzo de Medici
(1449 - 1492)

Portrait of Lorenzo de Medici with Florence in the background

Portrait of Giuliano de Medici by Sandro Botticelli

Their first plan was a quiet one. The Pazzis had heard that the Medicis were going to Rome for the pope's special Easter service in 1478. So they thought, why not kill the brothers in Rome? If an assassin murdered them far from home, then the people of Florence might forget about them sooner.

Unfortunately for the Pazzis, this first plan didn't work out. For some reason, the Medicis decided not to go to Rome that year; so the Pazzis needed a new plan.

The Pazzi
Conspiracy (1478)

Their second plan was much more daring. The Pazzis wanted to kill both brothers at once, but weren't sure when both brothers might be together. Until they asked themselves: why not kill them in church? Both brothers attended Sunday Mass at the **Duomo**, a huge church in the middle of Florence. So the Pazzis decided to kill them at Sunday Mass— in front of 10,000 people!

When the big Sunday arrived, the brothers were separated: Lorenzo stood near the front of the Duomo, and Giuliano near the back. So the attackers split up, agreeing to strike when the priest reached a certain moment in the Mass.

When that moment came, Francesco de Pazzi turned, raised his dagger and stabbed Giuliano de Medici. He kept on stabbing until the young man was dead.

But the Pazzis missed Lorenzo. At the last second, Lorenzo somehow sensed that an attack was coming. So he raised his arm to block his enemies' daggers. Although his arm was badly cut, Lorenzo managed to keep away from his attackers long enough to lock himself inside a room of the Duomo.

Francesco de Pazzi striking down Giuliano de Medici

After that, nothing went right for the Pazzis.

Since the killers couldn't get to Lorenzo, they paraded through the streets of Florence, shouting that the Medici tyrants were dead. They expected the people of Florence to rejoice with them; but instead, the people were furious with them.

A little later, the wounded Lorenzo walked out of the Duomo, very much alive. At this, the people of Florence turned on the Pazzis. First they hanged the attackers to death, along with everyone who might have known about the attack. Then they banished every last Pazzi from Florence forever.

For the Pazzis had been quite wrong. The people of Florence didn't hate the Medicis. Instead, they honored the Medicis for making Florence such a beautiful place to live.

CHURCH HISTORY

The Bonfire of the Vanities

Times change. While Lorenzo de Medici lived, Florence thrived. But when Lorenzo lay down to die in 1492, all of Italy was about to come on very hard times.

At the bedside of the dying Lorenzo sat a strange priest called **Girolamo Savonarola**.

The two men could hardly have been more different.

Girolamo Savonarola (1452 - 1498)

Savonarola was a strict monk who believed in self-denial and simple living. He ate very little, slept in a plain monk's cell, and wore a hair shirt to remind him of Christ's suffering (Chapter 3). Lorenzo, on the other hand, was probably the richest man in Italy. He enjoyed every luxury money could buy, including the best art collection in the world.

How could two such different men become friends? The answer was that the people of Florence were having doubts about the pope. For one thing, the **Papal States** had been an enemy to Florence for years.

For another, the Church went a bit crazy when the Renaissance began. Every pope, cardinal, bishop and abbot wanted the best of everything— the grandest churches and monasteries, all filled with the greatest art. The popes of the Renaissance seemed to love luxury more than they loved God.

Remember what the **Papal States** were: a country in central Italy governed by the pope (Chapter 7).

Michelangelo's Moses

Of course, the people of Florence loved luxury too. But when Savonarola came, they started to wonder if they loved luxury too much.

Savonarola was a fiery preacher with a powerful message. The riches of Florence did not belong to Florence, Savonarola shouted. No, they belonged to God; and God wanted His people to give them up. Christians should never waste God's money on fine art and fancy clothes. Instead, they should give to the poor:

> "O my brothers, to you I say: Renounce your extravagance, your paintings, and your vain ornaments. Make your robes less full and of thinner material. Do you not realize that your extravagances are taking alms away from the poor?"

Savonarola also shouted a warning to all Italians. If Italy didn't give up its luxuries, he said, then God might soon send some foreign king to invade Italy.

Girolamo Savonarola preaching before a huge crowd in Florence

Which is exactly what happened. In 1494, two years after Lorenzo de Medici died, the King of France invaded Italy. This was the beginning of the **Italian Wars**, awful wars that would plague Italy for years to come.

Lorenzo's son **Piero de Medici** had no idea what to do about the French invasion. But Savonarola knew just what to do. After meeting with the King of France, Savonarola came home with a treaty that kept Florence out of the Italian Wars— at least for a while.

> The **Italian Wars** lasted 65 years, from 1494 - 1559.

Savonarola now had two great successes under his belt: he had predicted the Italian Wars, and he had saved Florence from the French. With a record like that, Savonarola seemed far wiser than Piero de Medici. So the people of Florence cast out Piero, and set Savonarola in his place!

Savonarola had big ideas for Florence. The new Florence would be a **theocracy**— in other words, a country led by God. If the people would obey God, Savonarola said, then Florence could take Rome's place at the head of the Church. Florence could be the **New Rome**— the way the old Rome would have been, if the greedy popes of the Renaissance had stayed true to Christ.

At first, the people of Florence went along with Savonarola's big ideas. But they thought he went too far with his big bonfires.

To Savonarola, all luxuries were **vanities**— useless garbage that kept people's eyes on Earth, when they should be looking toward heaven. If his people really wanted to look toward heaven, he said, then they should live like monks did: they should get rid of all vanities.

> The word **vain** can mean "useless."

So Savonarola held big public bonfires, inviting his people to come and burn up all their vanities. The biggest was the famous **Bonfire of the Vanities**, which was held just outside the Signoria building in 1497.

The problem was that some of the things Savonarola burned didn't seem like luxuries. Savonarola didn't just burn expensive clothes, jewelry and makeup. He also burned non-Christian books, non-Christian music and non-Christian art. For the art-loving people of Florence, burning art was especially hard.

Besides all these, Savonarola also burned dice, game boards and playing cards— as if playing any game was automatically a sin!

Shortly after the fire, the pope excommunicated Savonarola. But Savonarola went right on criticizing the pope, insisting that the Church had turned away from God.

If the people of Florence had still admired Savonarola, then they might have ignored the pope. Instead, they started to turn away from Savonarola, going back to the pope.

GIROLAMO SAVONAROLA

Even then, Savonarola might have lived out the rest of his days in peace— if it weren't for one of the pope's friends. The year after the pope excommunicated Savonarola, a friend of the pope challenged Savonarola to the Ordeal by Fire.

The Ordeal by Fire was a test based on a Bible story. In the Book of Daniel, Chapter 3, King Nebuchadnezzar tried to punish Daniel's friends Shadrach, Meshach and Abednego by sending them into a fiery furnace. Since the three men were innocent, the Lord protected them from the flames.

Some Christians believed that the Lord would still protect the innocent from the flames. Back in the Dark Ages, the Ordeal by Fire had been a legal way of deciding questions in court. Two enemies willingly stepped into a fire, or else thrust a hand into a fire— believing that God would protect the innocent one from the flames.

The trouble was, the Ordeal by Fire never worked anymore. Instead of the innocent one being protected, both enemies got burned. To decide between them, the judge usually waited to see whose burns healed faster.

By Savonarola's day, no court had taken the Ordeal by Fire seriously for hundreds of years. Even so, Savonarola's enemy challenged him to test his faith in the flames— to prove once and for all who was right, Savonarola or the pope.

Savonarola never actually agreed to the Ordeal by Fire. One of his friends did, vowing to brave the flames in Savonarola's place. And the Ordeal never actually happened; for a rainy day cancelled the whole affair.

Despite all of this, the people of Florence seemed to think that Savonarola had failed an important test of faith. In any event, they turned their backs on Savonarola. When the pope sent churchmen from Rome to arrest Savonarola, no one tried to stop them.

The Church convicted Girolamo Savonarola of heresy in 1498. The same man who had once ruled Florence was now hanged and burned to death, on the same public square where he'd held the Bonfire of the Vanities a year before.

Savonarola being hanged and burned to death for heresy outside the *Palazzo della Signoria*, where the Signoria of Florence met

CHAPTER 27: *Star* The Protestant Reformation

All Christians agree on certain things. For example, all Christians agree that Jesus Christ is the Son of God, sent down from Heaven to save sinners.

But what happens when Christians disagree on certain things? The answer is that the church often splits. We have already seen several **schisms** over the centuries.

> Remember what a **schism** is: a church split.

➤ The Coptic Orthodox Church of Egypt split off from the rest of the Church around 451 (Chapter 4).

➤ The Church of the East, also called the Nestorian Church, split off around the same time (Chapter 19).

➤ The Eastern Orthodox Church split off from the Catholic Church around 1054. This was the East-West Schism, also called the Great Schism (Chapter 8).

➤ The Catholic Church even split off from itself for a time. During the Western Schism of 1378 – 1417, there were two popes at once: one in Rome, and another in Avignon, France (Chapter 24).

This chapter is about one of the biggest splits of all: the **Protestant Reformation**, which started with a German monk called **Martin Luther** in 1517.

The Renaissance Popes

Martin Luther (1483 – 1546)

Martin Luther didn't set out to split the Catholic Church. At first, he only wanted to **reform** the Church— in other words, fix what was wrong with it. In Luther's eyes, the first thing that needed fixing was the **Renaissance popes**.

The biggest problem with the Renaissance popes was greed. To Luther, this was why the Church needed fixing: because instead of following God, the Renaissance popes were spending all their time raising money for fancy church buildings.

> The **Renaissance popes** were the popes who led the Catholic Church in the 1400s and 1500s.

ഇഇഇഇഇഇഇഇഇഇഇഇഇഇഇഇഇഇഇഇഇഇഇഇഇഇഇഇഇഇഇ

By the time the Renaissance began, the glory of ancient Rome was 1,000 years in the past. Most of what remained was crumbling ruins. The Catholic Church was more than ready to spruce up its tired old capital.

But the Renaissance popes weren't satisfied with just sprucing up Rome. They wanted nothing but the best new buildings, all decorated with the greatest works of the most talented Renaissance artists.

The best example was **Saint Peter's Basilica**. St. Peter's is a beautiful church that still stands on St. Peter's Square in Vatican City, Rome. Both church and square are named for the Apostle Peter.

Peter, of course, was very important to the Catholic Church. According to tradition, Peter was the first pope, the first to hold the keys to the kingdom of heaven (Matthew 16:18-19). All of the popes who came later were heirs to the awesome power handed down to Peter by Christ.

This is why the Renaissance popes built St. Peter's Basilica: as a symbol of the awesome power they inherited from Peter.

They designed that symbol to be as big and impressive as possible. The floors of St. Peter's covered more than 5 acres, and its dome soared over 400 feet!

Even better than the building itself was the art inside. Every single space was filled with the most beautiful art imaginable. Some of the best artists of all time— famous names like Michelangelo, Raphael and Bernini— did their best work at St. Peter's Basilica.

St. Peter's Basilica

St. Peter's Basilica took 120 years to build, all the way from 1506 - 1626.
Some of the marble used to build St. Peter's came from the ruins of the old Roman Coliseum.

What Martin Luther didn't like about all this was that it cost too much. In Luther's eyes, St. Peter's Basilica wasn't a symbol of the popes' authority— no, it was a symbol of greed! Why on Earth, Luther wondered, was the Church spending so much money on itself, when it could be helping the poor?

A view inside St. Peter's Basilica

Greed also showed in the way the Renaissance popes handed out Church jobs. The best jobs should have gone to the people who could do those jobs best. But these popes didn't care how well Church jobs were done. They cared only about money and power. So the best jobs always went to the popes' nephews— even if those nephews had never worked in the Church.

If no nephew wanted a job, then the Renaissance popes sold that job to the highest bidder— again, even if the bidder had never worked in the Church.

Pope Julius II, the "Warrior Pope" who reigned from 1503 – 1513

But the worst thing about the Renaissance popes was their wars. As unbelievable as it may seem, some popes actually strapped on swords and led armies into bloody battle. The worst was Pope Julius II, who fought so many wars that he was nicknamed the "Warrior Pope."

In 1514, the year after Julius died, an unknown author wrote a funny story about him. "**Julius Excluded from Heaven**" imagines what might have happened to the Warrior Pope when he tried to get into heaven.

The story starts with Julius standing before the gates of heaven. Behind him stand thousands of soldiers who have died fighting his wars. Like the popes of the Crusades, Julius has promised that all who die fighting for the Church will go to heaven, no matter what sins they might have committed before.

The problem is, the gates of heaven won't open. Julius still has the key to his private treasure chest, and thinks that this same key ought to unlock the gates of heaven. But for some reason he can't understand, the key won't work. Julius is about to try breaking down the gates when St. Peter peers out of a grated window, asking:

Peter: But oh…. what a sewer-stench is this! …Who are you, and what do you want?

Julius: Open the door, will you? …And if you were really doing your job, it should have been open long ago, and decorated with all the heraldry of heaven.

Peter: …What sort of unnatural arrangement is it, that while you wear the robes of a priest of God, under them you are dressed in the bloody armor of a warrior?

Julius: Enough words, I say. If you don't hurry up and open the gates, then I'll unleash my thunderbolt of excommunication with which I used to terrify great kings on earth and their kingdoms too…

Peter: Perhaps you used to terrify people with that bluster, but it counts for nothing here. Here we deal only in the truth. This is a fortress to be captured with good deeds, not ugly words.

Besides being funny, "Julius Excluded from Heaven" also made a serious point. Why wouldn't the key to Julius' treasure chest unlock the gates of heaven? Because heavenly treasures are completely different from earthly treasures (Matthew 6:19-21). The Renaissance popes forgot this. All popes were supposed to represent Christ; but Pope Julius acted nothing like Christ.

Although no one knows for sure, "Julius Excluded from Heaven" may have been written by **Desiderius Erasmus**. Erasmus was a Dutch author who was well-known for his sharp mind and clever wit.

Why do people think Erasmus wrote "Julius Excluded from Heaven"? Partly because it is a lot like "In Praise of Folly," which Erasmus definitely wrote.

Desiderius Erasmus (1466 – 1536)

"In Praise of Folly" was another funny-but-serious work that pointed out problems in the Church. In Erasmus' opinion, the Renaissance popes could never have gone so far wrong if the rest of the Church hadn't followed them. So Erasmus criticized the whole Church. Monks, friars, priests, bishops, cardinals, even scholars like Erasmus himself— all had forgotten what it really means to follow Jesus Christ.

But for all his mocking words against the Catholic Church, there was one thing Erasmus would never do. No matter what happened, Erasmus would never leave the Church. Erasmus wanted to reform the Church, not tear it down. See Chapter 34 for more on how Erasmus and others tried to reform the Church.

Martin Luther (1483 – 1546)

At first, Martin Luther wanted reform as well.

Martin Luther grew up in Eisleben, a town in Saxony, Germany. His father, Hans Luther, wanted young Martin to become a rich lawyer. So he sent him to the best schools he could find, trying to prepare him for the tough challenges of law school.

But Martin didn't want to learn law. Instead, Martin wanted to learn how God forgave sin.

Young Martin suffered from something he called **Afflictions**. These were terrible times when the fear of dying was more than he could stand. Martin knew that he was a sinner. He also knew how God punished sinners: by sending them to hell when they died. Knowing all this, he was terrified that he might die and go to hell before God forgave his sins.

Like all Catholics, Martin also knew that he could confess his sins in church. And when Martin did confess, his priests assured him that his sins were forgiven. This was supposed to make him feel better; but for some reason, it didn't. Despite all the comforting words of his priests, Martin never felt sure that he was truly forgiven.

It was fear of death and hell that made Martin Luther a monk. One day when Martin was 21 years old, a bolt of lightning struck terrifyingly close to him. In fear for his life, Martin shouted a vow to the mother of the Virgin Mary: "Save me, St. Anna, and I shall become a monk!" When the storm didn't kill him, Martin kept his vow— much to his father's disappointment.

A few years later, Luther took his first classes at the University of Wittenberg, Germany. A few years after that, Wittenberg hired Luther to teach Bible. For the rest of his life, Luther would remain a professor of Bible at the University of Wittenberg.

While preparing lessons for his Bible students, Luther found himself drawn to a certain scripture over and over again. This was Romans 1:17, which reads:

> "For in the gospel the righteousness of God is revealed — a righteousness that is by faith from first to last, just as it is written: 'The righteous will live by faith.'"

Luther wearing the tonsure, a monk's hairstyle

Right there in the Bible, Luther finally found the answer to the Afflictions that had troubled him for so long.

What does "righteousness" mean? Before now, Luther had always believed that being righteous meant doing good deeds. The way to heaven was to work hard at doing good deeds; for that was the only way to buy God's forgiveness. Or so Luther had always thought.

But this wasn't what Romans 1:17 said. What Romans said was that "righteousness is by faith from first to last." In other words, righteousness doesn't come from doing good deeds— no, righteousness comes from faith. The people God forgives are the ones who have faith in his Son, the Savior Jesus Christ.

What a relief! For the first time in his life, Martin understood that he didn't need to work his way into heaven. As long as he had faith in Jesus Christ, he was already on his way to heaven!

〰〰

Luther's new understanding came at an important time. It so happened that when Luther was just becoming a monk, the Renaissance popes were just laying the foundations of St. Peter's Basilica (above).

Pope Leo X, the next pope after the Warrior Pope Julius II, needed a fortune to pay for this huge new church. So Leo struck a deal with the new **Archbishop of Mainz**, head of all German churches.

The pope's deal involved something called indulgences.

An **indulgence** was a special paper that was supposed to have special powers over sin. The Catholic Church taught that all popes inherited great powers from the Apostle Peter. One of these was the power to "bind" or "loose" sinners from the penalties of their sin (Matthew 16:19). If a sinner received an indulgence from the pope, then he wouldn't have to pay the penalties of his sin— or so the Church said.

This, then, was the deal between Pope Leo X and the Archbishop of Mainz. First, the pope sent the archbishop a big supply of indulgences. Then the archbishop sent priests all over Germany, granting indulgences to any Christian who made a big donation to the Church. Half of these donations went to the pope, and the other half to the archbishop.

This is where **Johann Tetzel** comes into the story. Tetzel was one of the German priests who handled the pope's indulgences for the Archbishop.

Tetzel's job was to raise money for the Church; and raise money he did. In fact, Tetzel acted more like a salesman than he did a priest. To hear Tetzel talk, indulgences were like tickets to heaven. If a sinner would only buy an indulgence, then he would never again have to worry about going to hell!

The boldest words Tetzel spoke were about sinners in **purgatory**.

In Catholic teaching, most Christians didn't go straight to heaven when they died. Instead, they went to purgatory to get rid of their sin. Only after purging their sins in purgatory could most Christians move on to heaven.

Any Christian who had ever lost a loved one dreaded the thought of purgatory. Believers mourned to think of their dear mothers, fathers and grandparents suffering in purgatory, when they could be in heaven.

A mocking picture of Johann Tetzel (1465 – 1519) with one hand on a money-chest. Behind Tetzel are indulgences for sale at different prices.

But Tetzel said that now, believers need mourn no more! Besides buying an indulgence for oneself, one could also buy an indulgence for a lost loved one in purgatory. The moment the Church received the money, that lost loved one would leap out of purgatory and go straight to heaven! To make his point as clear as possible, Tetzel even wrote this little rhyme about indulgences:

"As soon as the coin in the coffer rings / The soul from purgatory springs."

Tetzel's little rhyme horrified Martin Luther. In Luther's eyes, it seemed that the Catholic Church was selling God's forgiveness. But the Church had no right to sell forgiveness, Luther raged! For the Bible said that forgiveness was a gift from God, freely given to all who had faith in Jesus Christ.

The Diet of Worms

It was because of indulgences that Martin Luther published his first great writing of the Protestant Reformation: the Ninety-five Theses.

According to tradition, Luther nailed his Ninety-five Theses to the door of All Saints' Church, Wittenberg. This happened on the eve of All Saints' Day: **October 31, 1517**, the first day of the Protestant Reformation. With help from the printing press, the Ninety-five Theses soon spread all over Germany and beyond.

> A **thesis** is a statement to be defended in a debate or argument.
> The **Ninety-five Theses on the Power and Efficacy of Indulgences** were 95 thesis statements first published by Martin Luther on October 31, 1517.

Basically, the Ninety-five Theses said that the Catholic Church had no right to sell God's forgiveness. Forgiveness, Luther wrote, was for all true Christians— not just the ones who could afford special indulgences from the pope.

Besides, the poor were suffering. Instead of donating to the poor, Christians were now spending all of their extra money on indulgences. Even the poorest Christians, the ones who couldn't afford food some days, were spending what little they had on indulgences— believing that they could never get to heaven without indulgences.

Meanwhile, the pope was one of the richest men on Earth. Why didn't the pope spend his own money, Luther wondered, instead of stealing food from the very mouths of the poor?

The Ninety-five Theses were Martin Luther's first step down a deadly path. He knew very well what had happened to John Hus (Chapter 25) and Girolamo Savonarola (Chapter 26). Anyone who criticized the Church could be burned at the stake, just like Hus and Savonarola.

The same thing surely would have happened to Luther, if he hadn't found powerful friends.

Martin Luther nailing his Ninety-five Theses to the door of All Saints' Church in Wittenberg, Germany on October 31, 1517

Pope Leo X was certainly no friend to Luther. If the pope had had his way, then the world would never have heard another word out of Luther. In 1518, the year after the Ninety-five Theses, the pope ordered Luther's fellow monks in Germany to cast him out.

At any other time, the monks might have obeyed. But these were different times. For Martin Luther was a beloved German scholar; while Leo X was an Italian Renaissance pope with a reputation for greed. So instead of casting Luther out, his fellow monks asked him to tell them more of what he had learned from the Bible.

When Luther did, it turned out that indulgences weren't the only Catholic teaching he didn't like. In fact, Luther disliked a great many Catholic teachings!

What Luther disliked most was the Catholic teaching about **salvation**. To Luther, the Church seemed to be teaching **salvation by works**. In other words, the Church seemed to be saying that the only way Christians could be saved was by obeying the Ten Commandments perfectly. If a person behaved perfectly, then even a perfect God couldn't find fault. Then God would have to let that person into heaven; for that person would have earned it.

The problem was, the Bible taught **salvation by faith**. What Luther read in the Book of Romans was that no one was saved by works. The Ten Commandments were so strict that no one could follow them perfectly— no one, that is, except Christ the Son of God. The way to be saved was not by doing good deeds, but by faith in Christ.

> **Salvation** means being saved from sin and death, so that one can go to heaven instead of hell.
>
> **Salvation by works** means doing good deeds in order to buy one's way into heaven.
>
> **Salvation by faith** means trusting Christ as Savior and Lord.

Martin Luther appearing before an angry cardinal

The more time passed, the longer Luther's list of dislikes grew. He didn't like praying to the saints— not even the Church's favorite saint, the Virgin Mary. He also didn't like adoring relics of the saints. Luther even disliked the **Catholic Mass**— in other words, the way Catholics celebrated Holy Communion. He felt that in some ways, the Mass seemed to honor priests more than it honored Christ.

With all of these dislikes, Luther couldn't possibly like something the Church had been saying for centuries: that the pope and his Church councils were never wrong.

How had the Church gone so far wrong, in Luther's eyes? By following something called **Sacred Tradition**.

The Church didn't just follow the Bible. It also followed **traditions**— beliefs and rituals that had been handed down from Christian to Christian for centuries. In Luther's opinion, some of these traditions went directly against the Bible.

This pointed out something else Luther disliked. Why, he wondered, did the Church insist on reading the Bible in Latin— a language only priests could understand? Luther wanted Christians to read the Bible for themselves, in their own languages. He believed that when they did, they would see what he had already seen: that in many ways, Sacred Tradition went against the Bible.

This line of thinking led to one of Luther's most important ideas: **Sola Scriptura**, Latin for

> **Sacred Tradition** is a set of beliefs, rituals and practices that have been handed down through the Catholic Church for centuries. The Church considers these traditions just as holy as the Bible, even though they may not appear in the Bible.

"Scripture alone." Luther believed that the Bible alone was inspired by God, and that Sacred Tradition wasn't inspired at all. In Luther's eyes, the Bible came straight from God, and everything Christians needed to know was written there.

This meant that when Sacred Tradition went against the Bible, Christians should always obey the Bible. The Bible had never led Christians wrong. Sacred Tradition, on the other hand, had led to the greedy Renaissance popes— who were wrong about almost everything, in Luther's eyes!

> *Sola Scriptura* is Latin for "Scripture Alone." It means that the Bible alone is inspired by God.

〰〰

The more Luther said and wrote, the angrier the Catholic Church grew. *STOP*

At first, Luther wrote only to change the Church's mind about certain things. Before long, though, Luther realized that no words of his could ever change the Church's mind. Not long after that, Luther realized that the Church meant to kill him.

In 1519, a smart priest called **Johann von Eck** challenged Luther to debate him in public. In the middle of the **Leipzig Debate**, von Eck asked Luther a tricky question. What did Luther think of **John Hus**, von Eck wanted to know?

Luther was trapped. As von Eck knew very well, Luther agreed with Hus in many ways. So if Luther said that Hus was wrong, then he would be admitting that he himself was also wrong. On the other hand, Hus was a condemned heretic whom the Church had burned alive. So if Luther said that Hus was right, then the Church might burn him alive as well.

> Remember who **John Hus** was— the Czech-speaking priest who the Church convicted of heresy and burned to death in 1415 (Chapter 25).

Johann von Eck, Luther's opponent at the Leipzig Debate

Luther was too brave to deny what he truly believed. So instead, Luther admitted that he agreed with John Hus. From that moment forward, Johann von Eck was determined to bring Martin Luther down.

In 1520, the year after the Leipzig Debate, Pope Leo X issued his first **papal bull** against Martin Luther. By order of the pope, no Christian was to read anything Martin Luther had written. Instead, Christians were to burn all of Luther's writings. As for Luther, the pope gave him 60 days to take back all the ugly things he had written about the Catholic Church.

> Remember what a **papal bull** was— an official letter containing a special statement from the pope.

With papal bull in hand, Johann von Eck rode triumphantly back to Germany, planning to burn all of Luther's books in big public bonfires. But von Eck soon learned that Germans didn't want to burn Luther's books. In fact, some Germans muttered about burning von Eck instead! For the German people loved their feisty Martin Luther far more than they loved the pope.

With that many friends, Luther didn't need to burn his books. Instead, he burned a copy of the papal bull!

Pope Leo X's Papal Bull
against Martin Luther

A few months later, Pope Leo issued a second papal bull against Luther. This time, the pope declared Luther an enemy of the Church— an "infected animal" whose sickness might spread to the whole flock. No faithful Christian was to have anything to do with Martin Luther, nor with any of Luther's friends. In the eyes of the Church, all **Lutherans** were heretics.

> A **Lutheran** was a follower of Martin Luther.

Pope Leo didn't actually say that Luther should be burned to death. But he did say that Luther should be punished the same way other heretics had been punished. Since the Church had burned John Hus, everyone knew that the pope meant to burn Luther too.

This second papal bull set up one of the most dramatic scenes of the whole Reformation.

After the way his first papal bull had failed, the pope knew that no one would obey his second papal bull either. Luther had many friends in Germany; whereas the pope had few friends. So if the pope wanted Luther arrested, then he needed a powerful friend of his own.

The friend the pope chose was one of the most powerful men who ever lived. This was **Holy Roman Emperor Charles V**, who was also **King Charles I of Spain**. Charles was a loyal Catholic who believed in a strong Catholic Church. Since Martin Luther was a danger to that Church, Charles summoned him to appear before the **Diet of Worms**.

> The **Diet of Worms** was a special meeting of the German government held at Worms, Germany in 1521.

Despite its funny-sounding name, the Diet of Worms had nothing to do with eating worms! A **diet** was a meeting of the German government; while **Worms** was a city in Germany. So the Diet of Worms was a special meeting of the government held in Worms, Germany. The main purpose of this meeting was to try Martin Luther for crimes against the Catholic Church.

Luther's trial started like John Hus' trial, or like a trial before the Spanish Inquisition. Such trials were nothing like modern-day trials. The court didn't need to decide whether Luther was guilty or innocent; for the pope had already declared him guilty. The only thing left to decide was how Luther should be punished.

However, Luther did have one thing in his favor: a crowd of German friends outside the court, angrily shouting "Death to Rome!"

Martin Luther defending himself before Holy Roman Emperor Charles V at the Diet of Worms

The priests who tried Martin Luther didn't want him making any long speeches. So they asked him just two quick questions. Pointing to a pile of Luther's books, they asked: Did you write these books? And, will you **recant**— in other words, take back— all of the lies in these books?

Of course, there was no use denying that the books were Luther's. But when it came to the second question, Luther asked for one more day to think about his answer. His accusers would have liked to say "no," but couldn't— for fear that Luther's friends outside might riot.

Luther Rose

The next day turned out to be just what the priests had feared. Instead of taking back his words, Luther told the whole world what he thought of the Catholic Church. He spoke furiously against the pope, accusing him of greedily lining his own pockets while the poor suffered. Luther's dramatic speech ended:

"I cannot and I will not recant. **Here I stand**; I can do no other. God help me."

After the Diet of Worms, many loyal Catholics would have liked to kill Martin Luther. But the Holy Roman Emperor had promised not to arrest Luther just then; and he kept his promise. Instead, Luther's friends whisked him away for his own good. He spent most of the next year hiding at **Wartburg Castle** in Eisenach, Germany, where he worked on his German translation of the New Testament.

By the time Luther returned home to Wittenberg, the Protestant Reformation was in full swing. Churches all over Germany were leaving the Catholic Church and setting out on their own. Luther spent the rest of his life teaching, writing and building a new church in Germany: the Lutheran Church.

ꙮꙮꙮꙮꙮꙮꙮꙮꙮꙮꙮꙮꙮꙮꙮꙮꙮꙮꙮꙮꙮꙮꙮꙮꙮꙮꙮꙮꙮ

Katharina von Bora (1499 – 1552)

One big difference between Catholics and Lutherans was that there were no Lutheran monks or nuns. Since the Bible said nothing about monks, Luther and his friends released all monks and nuns from their vows.

Which freed Luther to do something he never could have done as a monk: get married.

Luther's future wife, **Katharina von Bora**, had been living at a nunnery school since she was about five years old. Not all girls who attended these schools went on to become nuns. But Katharina did, taking her nun's vows when she was about sixteen.

Katharina was about eighteen when the Reformation started. Although older nuns tried to keep younger nuns from reading Luther's books, Katharina and her friends still heard all about Luther. The bold new ideas of Martin Luther soon took hold in the young nuns' hearts, just as they were taking hold in hearts all over Germany.

When Luther and his friends announced that there would be no Lutheran monks or nuns, Katharina and her friends wanted to go home. But the older nuns held them at the nunnery, insisting that they must keep their vows before God.

In desperation, Katharina wrote to the man who had inspired her: Martin Luther. It was Luther who came up with a simple plan to rescue the trapped girls.

Luther happened to know a fish-seller who often visited Katharina's nunnery. This man would enter the nunnery with wagonloads of barreled fish, and leave with empty barrels. So on Easter eve, 1523, Luther's friend simply hid Katharina and her friends in some empty fish barrels. Under cover of darkness, the young nuns rode a smelly fish wagon out of their nunnery prison.

Martin and Katharina soon fell in love. But at first, Martin wasn't sure he should marry; for he feared that the Reformation was changing things too fast. After all, both he and Katharina had sworn before God that they would never marry. Was it really safe to break such a vow?

In the end, though, Luther decided that monks' vows were just another Catholic tradition he couldn't agree with. The couple married in 1525, and went on to have six children.

CHAPTER 28

The Renaissance in Art

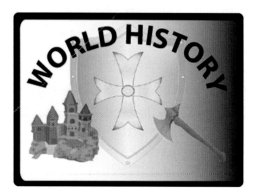

Amazing Artists of the Renaissance

Back in Chapter 26, we read that Florence, Italy was a great place to be a Renaissance artist. The fabulously rich Cosimo de Medici, owner of the Medici Bank of Florence, spent two huge fortunes: one on great art, and another on beautiful buildings.

But the Renaissance in art didn't start with Cosimo de Medici. It actually started long before. The art world needed a long time to learn the skills that made Renaissance art so much more exciting than medieval art.

One difference between medieval art and Renaissance art started with a difference in the Church. The medieval Church didn't like art that looked too much like the real thing. Medieval artists feared to break the Second Commandment, in which God warned:

> Remember what **Renaissance** means: a rebirth of learning.

"You shall not make for yourself an image in the form of anything in heaven above or on the earth beneath or in the waters below. You shall not bow down to them or worship them; for I, the Lord your God, am a jealous God…"

Out of respect for God, medieval artists didn't make their images too lifelike. Instead, they kept them flat and unrealistic. That way, viewers would be sure to worship the God behind the images, and not the images themselves.

Things were different when the Renaissance came. The Renaissance popes seemed to forget all about the Second Commandment! They spent fortunes on art, filling their churches with the most realistic sculptures and paintings money could buy.

A quote from a Renaissance pope explains the change. According to Pope

Two paintings of Mary and the baby Jesus in two very different styles. On the left is a flat Eastern Orthodox icon from the 900s. On the right is a realistic painting done by the great Renaissance artist Raphael in 1505.

Nicholas V, the purpose of all this fine art was "to strengthen the weak faith of the populace by the greatness of that which it sees." In other words, the church buildings of the Renaissance were designed to impress. One look at a beautiful church like St. Peter's Basilica, and no one could doubt that the pope was truly the heir of St. Peter! Or at least, this was what the Renaissance popes believed.

The first great Renaissance artist, **Giotto di Bondone**, was born more than 100 years before Cosimo de Medici. As the son of a shepherd who lived near Florence, Giotto was well on his way to becoming a shepherd as well.

Until one day, when an older artist called **Cimabue** noticed the fine pictures this shepherd boy drew of his sheep. Giotto's pictures looked so much like real sheep that the artist decided to take him into his studio and train him.

Giotto di Bondone
(1267? – 1337)

The student was soon a better painter than his teacher. One day when Cimabue was out of the studio, Giotto decided to play a trick on him. So he painted a lifelike fly on the canvas Cimabue had been working on. When Cimabue came back to work, he swatted at the fly several times before he realized that it was only a painting!

This was Giotto's gift: creating lifelike paintings. His style was like a stepping stone between two other styles: the flat, unrealistic style of medieval times, and the realistic style of the Renaissance. For example, the faces in Giotto's paintings showed strong feelings—unlike medieval icons, which showed little feeling at all.

Giotto was more than just a painter. He was also an architect! The same artistic eye that made Giotto a great painter also made him a great designer of buildings.

In 1296, Florence started building a huge new church. Although its full name was **Cathedral of Saint Mary of the Flowers**, most people just called it **Florence Cathedral**. Later, people called it by an even shorter name: the

"The Kiss of Judas" by Giotto, from the Arena Chapel in Padua, Italy. A yellow-robed Judas stands at center, betraying Jesus with a kiss on the night before the crucifixion. A red-robed Peter stands at left, slicing off a servant's ear (Matthew 26:48-51).

Duomo, after its dome-shaped roof. This was the same Duomo where the Pazzi family murdered Giuliano de Medici, and tried to murder Lorenzo de Medici as well (Chapter 26).

Like most Renaissance cathedrals, the Duomo took a long time to build. The beautiful bell tower that Giotto designed for the Duomo was hardly begun when Giotto died in 1337.

The next great Renaissance artist was

Filippo Brunelleschi. Brunelleschi built the best-known part of the Duomo: its domed roof.

Domed roofs are hard to build— especially huge, heavy ones like the Duomo's. If the builder doesn't know what he's doing, then the weight of the dome can cause it to spread in the middle, bringing the top crashing down.

Of course, the ancient Greeks and Romans had known how to build domes. The biggest dome in the world covered an ancient Roman building called the **Pantheon**. But in Brunelleschi's day, no one had built anything like the Pantheon for a very long time.

In 1418, the city of Florence announced a contest to decide who would build the dome over Florence Cathedral. Brunelleschi won this contest in an interesting way.

Filippo Brunelleschi
(1377? – 1446)

Brunelleschi had been studying Florence's dome problem for years. He had even gone to Rome to study Roman architecture. He knew just how to build the dome; and he had even built a small model to test his ideas. This model, Brunelleschi said, proved that he alone was the right man to build the dome.

Naturally, the other architects all wanted to see Brunelleschi's model. But Brunelleschi refused; for he didn't want the others learning his secrets.

Florence Cathedral, better known as the Duomo. The domed roof built by Brunelleschi stands at right, the bell tower designed by Giotto at left.

Instead of showing his model, Brunelleschi announced a challenge. The man to build the dome, he said, should be the one who could figure out how to make a chicken egg stand on one end!

This seemed to be a problem that no one could solve. Until Brunelleschi solved it— by striking the egg lightly on a table, making a flat end for it to stand on.

Of course, the other architects complained that they could all do that! To which Brunelleschi replied, "Of course you could— now that I have shown you how. Just as you could all build the dome, after I showed you my model." The city fathers gave Brunelleschi the job.

The next great Renaissance artist,

Donatello, was a close friend to Brunelleschi. When Brunelleschi went to Rome to study Roman architecture, he took Donatello with him.

While Brunelleschi studied architecture, Donatello studied sculpture. Back in Florence, Donatello became the first Renaissance sculptor whose works were as good as anything the ancient Romans carved.

Brunelleschi finished the Duomo in 1436, about 16 years after he started. This was 140 years after its foundations were laid, and 42 years before the Pazzi Conspiracy (Chapter 26).

About four million bricks went into the dome. Brunelleschi chose bricks because they were lighter than stone.

Donatello
(1386? – 1466)

Donatello was also a close friend to Cosimo de Medici. Cosimo admired Donatello's sculpting skills so much that he didn't want him doing anything else. If the great artist had to waste time doing other things— say, selling his art to earn a living— then there would be fewer great sculptures for Cosimo to enjoy.

To keep that from happening, Cosimo gave Donatello more money than he could ever need or use. Donatello grew so used to having money that he never worried about it. If Donatello's other friends needed money, then they simply borrowed it from an open basket in his studio. He trusted his friends so much that they didn't even need to ask.

The next great Renaissance artist, **Fra Filippo Lippi**, was a bit less trustworthy than Donatello. Cosimo de Medici never worried about wasting money on Donatello; for Donatello was always hard at work. But Cosimo worried a lot about wasting money on Fra Lippi. Even though Fra Lippi was supposed to be a priest, he was always falling in love with some young woman. And whenever he fell in love, he forgot all about his painting.

Cosimo once grew so frustrated with Fra Lippi that he actually locked him inside his house, hoping to get more work out of him. But Lippi simply tied some bedsheets together, and then used them to climb out a window. Even the richest man in Italy couldn't keep Fra Lippi away from his women— not if he wanted the fine paintings that only Fra Lippi could create.

Donatello's statue of the prophet Habakkuk. This statue is also called *Zuccone*, Italian for "Pumpkin" or "Bald Man."

Fra Filippo Lippi
(1406? – 1469)

While working in a church one day, Fra Lippi happened to meet a beautiful young woman called Lucrezia Buti. Lucretia's parents had sent her to live with some nuns— probably thinking that she would surely be safe with nuns! But Lippi was working on his latest masterpiece, "Madonna and Child with Two Angels"; and he needed a model for the Virgin Mary. So he pleaded with the nuns until they let him use Lucrezia.

Lucrezia never went back to the nuns, as Fra Lippi had promised she would. But she did give Fra Lippi a son: Filippino Lippi, who turned out to be as talented an artist as his father!

"Madonna and Child with Two Angels" by Fra Lippi

The next great Renaissance artist, **Sandro Botticelli**, came along a bit later. Lorenzo de Medici, grandson to Cosimo, paid for some of Botticelli's great works.

By this time, artists had started to branch out. Besides Christian art, Botticelli also painted Roman gods and goddesses. Botticelli's "Birth of Venus" is one of the best-known paintings of all time.

The beautiful face of Venus from Botticelli's "Birth of Venus"

Botticelli would live to regret painting non-Christian art. Like Lorenzo de Medici, Botticelli lived in the time of Girolamo Savonarola (Chapter 26). When Savonarola preached that non-Christian art was wrong, Botticelli believed him. Some say that Botticelli gave up painting for good. He may even have burned some of his best paintings in Savonarola's Bonfire of the Vanities.

The next great Renaissance artist was much more than just an artist. **Leonardo da Vinci** was a true Renaissance Man, a genius in both art and science.

Leonardo started as an apprentice to an artist called **Andrea del Verrocchio.** Like other master artists, Verrocchio sometimes let his apprentices paint backgrounds for him. That way, the master could spend more time on his main subject.

But when Leonardo painted backgrounds, Verrocchio wished he hadn't.

This Botticelli painting, "The Temptation of Christ," comes from the Sistine Chapel in Vatican City, Rome. The background shows three temptations from Matthew 4:1-11. At top left, Satan tempts a starving Jesus to turn stones into bread. At top center, Satan tempts Jesus to throw Himself down from the top of the Temple— knowing that angels will save Him. And at top right, Satan offers Jesus the whole world— if He will only bow to Satan.

Leonardo painted so beautifully that Verrocchio grew ashamed of his own paintings. In fact, Verrocchio finally gave up painting, and switched to a different form of art: casting big statues in bronze. This was good news for Leonardo; for he could now learn sculpture as well as painting.

Some of the best Leonardo stories tell of art that fell apart, or that he never finished in the first place. For

An **equestrian statue** is a sculpture of a horse and rider.

example, the Duke of Milan, Italy once hired Leonardo to cast a huge **equestrian statue** of the duke's war hero father. Leonardo spent ten years on the project, working on it off and on.

Finally, Leonardo finished a clay version of the horse part of his statue, which he called the **Great Mare**. From there, he had only to create the molds, and he would be ready to cast the Great Mare in bronze. So the Duke of Milan set aside 70 tons of bronze, thinking that the biggest equestrian statue in the world would soon be his.

That was before the Italian Wars. In 1494, King Charles VIII of France passed through Milan on his way to invade southern Italy (Chapter 26). With a war starting up, the duke decided that he needed cannon more than he needed statues! So he took back Leonardo's 70 tons of bronze, and used them for cannon.

A few years later, a French army used Leonardo's huge clay horse as a target for cannon practice. They smashed it to bits, ending all hope that Leonardo would ever finish his Great Mare.

"The Last Supper" by Leonardo da Vinci. This huge, beautiful mural filled the end wall of a monastery dining room, making it look as if the monks were sharing a meal with Christ and His apostles. Unfortunately, Leonardo's paint started flaking off the wall soon after he finished it. Later, someone cut a doorway through the wall where Jesus' feet would have been.

Fortunately, not all Leonardo stories end badly. One of them ends with the **Mona Lisa**, which may be the most famous painting in the world.

In 1503, a rich trader from Florence hired Leonardo to paint a portrait of his wife, Elisabetta del Giocondo. Ever since Leonardo painted the Mona Lisa, art lovers have wondered: What is the story behind that little smile on Elisabetta's face? Is she feeling pleased with herself? Or is she perhaps feeling irritated with someone else? She may have felt like laughing; for it is said that Leonardo hired clowns and jesters to keep Elisabetta smiling through all the long hours it took to paint her.

If Elisabetta's husband was expecting a nice portrait to hang in his home, then he was disappointed. Leonardo liked his Mona Lisa so much that he kept her with him for the rest of his life. Because Leonardo died in France, the Mona Lisa now hangs at the Louvre Museum in Paris, France.

"Mona Lisa" by Leonardo da Vinci

The next great Renaissance artist may have been the greatest of all. **Michelangelo Buonarroti** was born and raised near Florence, where Lorenzo de Medici was still training great artists. He was still quite young when Lorenzo recognized his breathtaking talent. With money and training provided by Lorenzo, young Michelangelo learned to chisel and polish sculptures of astonishing beauty.

Michelangelo was not yet 25 years old, and living in Rome, when he carved one of the finest statues ever: his **Pieta**. This was Michelangelo's vision of Mary grieving over the crucified Jesus. The heart-touching Pieta now stands in St. Peter's Basilica at Vatican City, Rome.

Oddly enough, the Pieta is the only sculpture Michelangelo ever signed. This is because the Pieta taught the great artist a lesson about pride.

When the Pieta was first finished, everyone in Rome crowded around to see it. Michelangelo joined the crowds, but didn't introduce himself. He wanted to hear what people would say about his work when they didn't know that he could hear them.

"Pieta" by Michelangelo in St. Peter's Basilica

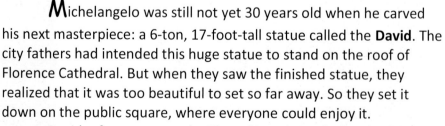

Michelangelo
Buonarroti
(1475? – 1564)

Michelangelo expected to be pleased by what he heard; but instead, he was infuriated. When someone asked what great artist had carved this magnificent statue, the man who answered named the wrong artist!

Michelangelo didn't want some other artist taking credit for his best work. So he decided to sign the Pieta. On a thin sash across Mary's robe, he chiseled in Latin, "Made by Michelangelo Buonarroti of Florence."

Later, Michelangelo was ashamed of himself. As a Christian artist, he was supposed to be working for the glory of God. But in signing the Pieta, he had proved that he was really working for his own glory. This is why Michelangelo vowed never to sign another work.

The head of Michelangelo's "David"

Michelangelo was still not yet 30 years old when he carved his next masterpiece: a 6-ton, 17-foot-tall statue called the **David**. The city fathers had intended this huge statue to stand on the roof of Florence Cathedral. But when they saw the finished statue, they realized that it was too beautiful to set so far away. So they set it down on the public square, where everyone could enjoy it.

David, of course, was the King of Israel. But before he was king, David killed a giant called Goliath (1 Samuel 17). Michelangelo's David is looking at Goliath with disdain, furious that he has defied the armies of the living God. David's sling rests on his shoulder, ready to strike.

In 1508, the Warrior Pope Julius II needed a great artist to paint the huge, arched ceiling of the **Sistine Chapel**. His first thought was to hire the greatest of all, Michelangelo. But Michelangelo was more sculptor than painter. He felt too unsure of his painting skills to take on such a big project. So he asked the pope to find someone else.

That might have been that— if not for jealousy. Some other artists wanted very much for Michelangelo to paint the Sistine Chapel Ceiling. They expected him to ruin it, which would also ruin his reputation. So they pestered the pope, who pestered Michelangelo until he finally took the job.

Betting against Michelangelo would turn out to be a mistake. Far from ruining the Sistine Chapel Ceiling, Michelangelo made it his greatest masterpiece yet.

Michelangelo spent four uncomfortable years plastering and painting the huge Sistine Chapel ceiling. With his neck stretched back and his arms overhead, he thoughtfully recreated dozens of scenes from the Old Testament. The only people who helped him were the workmen who built scaffold, or who mixed and carried plaster.

Inside the Sistine Chapel

A *sacra conversazione*, or "holy conversation," was a special kind of painting that showed the Virgin Mary speaking with other saints. Although the baby Jesus was always with Mary, the *sacra conversazione* focused on Mary, rather than Jesus. Catholics believed that if they prayed to Mary, then Mary would pray to Jesus for them.

"God Divides Light from Darkness," one of many Michelangelo paintings on the Sistine Chapel Ceiling

"Altarpiece of San Marco," a *sacra conversazione* by Renaissance artist Fra Angelico

The Radical Reformation

In Chapter 27, we read how Martin Luther nailed his **Ninety-five Theses** to the door of All Saints' Church in Wittenberg, Germany. This happened on October 31, 1517, the first day of the Protestant Reformation.

Three and a half years later, Luther appeared before a special government meeting called the **Diet of Worms**. The Holy Roman Emperor wanted Luther to take back all the ugly things he had written about the Catholic Church. But Luther refused, saying:

> "Here I stand; I can do no other. God help me."

From then on, Martin Luther was a wanted man. Although the emperor had promised not to arrest Luther at the Diet of Worms, he made no such promise after the diet. In fact, the emperor now offered a big reward to anyone who would arrest Luther for him.

Which is just what happened to Luther on his way home: he was arrested. While Luther was riding through a forest, a band of masked men leapt from behind some trees and seized him!

Fortunately, all was not as it seemed. These masked men didn't work for the emperor. Instead, they worked for Luther's friend **Frederick the Wise, Duke of Saxony**. Frederick seized Luther to keep him safe, not to kill him. Luther spent most of the next year hiding at Wartburg Castle in Eisenach, Germany— the same castle where Princess Elizabeth of Hungary had once lived (Chapter 11).

WARTBURG CASTLE

Meanwhile, back at Luther's home in Wittenberg, big changes were brewing.

What a strange, exciting time this was for Germany! For hundreds of years, every Christian church had followed the Sacred Tradition taught by the Catholic Church. But now, Luther's churches didn't believe in Sacred Tradition anymore. Instead, Lutherans believed that the Bible alone was inspired by God.

This meant that from now on, Lutherans could forget about Sacred Tradition. They could throw out all those old traditions, and build a completely new church— one based on the Bible alone.

The problem, Luther thought, was that some people wanted to change things too fast. While Luther hid at Wartburg Castle, a former priest called **Andreas Carlstadt** led his churches for him. Carlstadt turned out to be a **radical**— the kind of believer who wanted big change, and fast!

Luther agreed with some of the changes Carlstadt wanted to make. For example, he agreed that there were no monks and nuns in the Bible. So the Lutheran church had neither monks nor nuns. Every

> Remember what *Sola Scriptura* meant: that the Bible alone was inspired by God, and that Sacred Tradition wasn't inspired at all.

> A **conservative** is someone who wants to continue old traditions.
>
> A **radical** is someone who wants to throw out old traditions.
>
> The **Radical Reformation** was part of the Protestant Reformation. Some of Martin Luther's friends were radicals who wanted to throw out old church traditions, and build a brand new German church.

monastery and nunnery in Wittenberg closed, setting all monks and nuns free from their vows.

One of those vows was the **vow of chastity**— the one which said that monks and priests could never be involved with women. Neither Luther nor Carlstadt believed that this vow should continue. Carlstadt married in early 1522, before Luther even came home from the Wartburg. Luther, of course, married Katharina von Bora in 1525 (Chapter 27).

But Luther disagreed with some other changes Carlstadt wanted to make. For example, Carlstadt wanted to tear all artwork out of every church! He wanted none of the fine art that the Renaissance popes loved so much; for he believed that it broke the Second Commandment. But Luther wanted to keep some art; for he believed that Christians are saved by faith in Jesus Christ, not by strictly following the Ten Commandments.

The biggest question was how to celebrate Holy Communion. Here again, Luther disagreed with some of his friends. See Chapter 30 for more on communion.

〰〰

Currents and Columbus

The world's oceans are never still. Strong currents are always on the move, driven by strong forces like heat from the sun and the rotation of the Earth.

During the Age of Discovery, smart sailors like Christopher Columbus used these currents to speed them on their journeys.

Between the continents, ocean currents move in giant swirls called **gyres**. The gyres north of the equator all swirl clockwise; while the gyres south of the equator all swirl counter-clockwise. For example, the South Atlantic has the **South Atlantic Gyre**, which swirls counter-clockwise. And the North Atlantic has the **North Atlantic Gyre**, which swirls clockwise.

Without the North Atlantic Gyre, Christopher Columbus might never have made it to the West Indies and back. Columbus' first voyage was a clockwise journey around the North Atlantic. When Columbus set out from Spain, the gyre carried him down to the Canary Islands. When he set out from the Canaries, the gyre carried him across to the West Indies. And when he set out from the West Indies, he sailed north for a while— far enough for the gyre to pick him up and carry him back to Spain.

The farther south one sails, the less land stands in the way of ocean currents. Without continents to block them, the currents of the far south swirl swift and strong! This explains why sailors have a funny nickname for the southern seas: they call them the **"Washing Machine."**

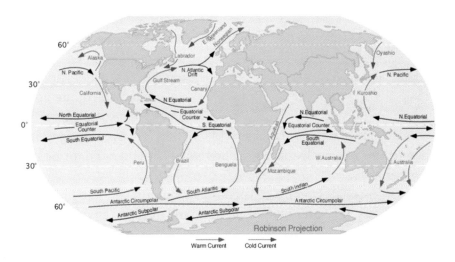

A map of major ocean currents

CHAPTER 29:   The Renaissance in Science

The Renaissance Man

The Renaissance was a time of new ideas. Explorers like Christopher Columbus taught new ideas about the globe. Reformers like Martin Luther taught new ideas about the Church. And artists like Michelangelo taught new ideas about all kinds of things, from the Bible to building science.

New ideas were part of what made Renaissance artists so special. To be truly great, an artist needed more than just paintbrushes and chisels. The best artists were the ones whose paintings and sculptures taught people new ways of thinking. To do that, an artist needed great ideas of his own.

In other words, a great artist had to be a Renaissance Man. What was a Renaissance Man? Basically, he was someone who knew everything! Renaissance men studied all subjects— not only art, but also religion, philosophy, science, engineering and more.

A **Renaissance Man** was someone who knew a lot about all fields of study, not just art.

The best example of the Renaissance man was probably Leonardo da Vinci. Leonardo knew just about everything that any man of his time could be expected to know.

Leonardo's learning started with his art. To paint better animals, Leonardo needed to know more about how animals were made. So he **dissected** animals, and then drew pictures of what he learned. He filled notebook after notebook with sketches of the bones, muscles and tendons that lay hidden beneath animal hides.

To **dissect** something is to cut it open and see what's inside.

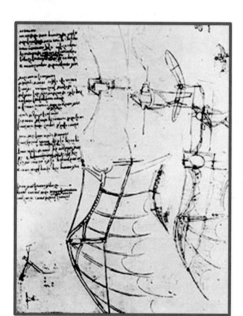

Leonardo's sketch of a glider wing, which he modeled after a bat's wing. Leonardo had a strange habit of writing notes from right to left across the page— possibly because he was left-handed.

From studying how animals were designed, Leonardo learned to design other things. For example, Leonardo designed parachutes, gliders and helicopters, all modeled after birds. He also designed movable walls to defend the city of Milan, Italy. He even designed a bridge to carry heavy loads over wide rivers, with no need for posts in the water.

Unfortunately, most of Leonardo's ideas never made it out of his notebooks. He never built his bridge. And as far as anyone knows, Leonardo never built any of his flying machines— although he did build and test a parachute.

A possible self-portrait of Leonardo da Vinci

The Copernican Revolution

An **astronomer** is a scientist who studies stars, planets and other heavenly bodies, as well as space itself.

The Renaissance was a scary time for one kind of Renaissance Man: the **astronomer**.

Astronomy and religion have always gone hand-in-hand. Why? Because both seek answers to some of the same deep questions. How did this world come to be? Are there other worlds like this one? How might this world end someday? From ancient times down through modern times, people have always looked to heaven for answers to questions like these.

The Catholic Church believed that it knew the right answers to all of these questions. Some of those answers came from the Bible; but most of them came from the science of the ancient Greeks.

An **element** is a basic building block of matter.

Greek science started with five **elements**. The first four were the worldly elements: **earth**, **water**, **air** and **fire**. The Greeks believed that every substance in the world was some mixture of these four basic elements.

The fifth element was out of this world. According to **Aristotle**, all heaven was made of a curious element called ether. The first four elements were for humans; but the fifth element, ether, was for the gods.

Remember who **Aristotle** was— the great ancient Greek professor who personally taught Alexander the Great.

Ether took many forms. The planets were one form of ether, and the stars another form. A third form of ether filled the space between the stars and planets. In Greek eyes, ether formed the ground the gods walked on, the lights in their skies and the air they breathed.

Two properties of ether are especially important to remember. One is that ether was perfect; and the other is that ether never changed. The stuff of Earth might be broken, dirty and imperfect; but the stuff of heaven was smooth, clean and perfect. The stuff of Earth might be here today, gone tomorrow; but the stuff of heaven was forever— as unchanging as the immortal gods. If Aristotle was right about ether, then nothing in the heavens could ever change.

Claudius Ptolemy (100? – 170?) using a quadrant to measure the positions of the stars

If the heavens never changed, then why did the stars and planets move? The answer came from the most important Greek astronomer of all: **Claudius Ptolemy** of Alexandria, Egypt.

According to Ptolemy, the whole universe is divided into huge spheres of different sizes. The smaller spheres are nested inside the larger ones.

The center sphere is the material world, home of the four material elements. Earth is lowest. Water floats over earth; air floats over water; and fire floats over air.

Next come the heavenly spheres— all made of ether, which floats over all. The first heavenly sphere contains the moon. Then come the spheres of Mercury, Venus and the Sun, followed by Mars and the other planets. Beyond all these, and much larger than the rest, lies the sphere that contains the stars.

The heavenly spheres all turn around the Earth, like some giant, invisible set of gears. It is the turning of the spheres that causes the planets and stars to move through Earth's sky!

But what causes the spheres to move? The answer lies beyond. Beyond the sphere of the stars lies one last sphere, larger than all others: the **Prime Mover**. And beyond the Prime Mover lies the highest heaven, which Greeks called **Empyrean**. The Greeks believed that some powerful force in the Empyrean must move the Prime Mover. In turn, the Prime Mover moves all the other spheres.

One illustration of the heavenly spheres. The Latin words outside the Prime Mover read "The Heavenly Empyrean, Home of God and all the Elect."

The Catholic Church liked most of these ideas. Of course, no Christian could believe in the many gods of the Greeks. But Christians could easily believe that God the Father lived in the highest heaven, moving the Prime Mover.

The Church especially liked the idea that Earth stood at the center of the heavenly spheres. If Earth was the center, then mankind must be the center of Creation— the main reason why God created everything else. The idea that the Earth stood still, and that the sun moved around it, also seemed to agree with Bible passages like these:

> "[God] set the earth on its foundations; it can never be moved."
>
> —Psalm 104:5
>
> "The sun rises and the sun sets, and hurries back to where it rises."
>
> —Ecclesiastes 1:5

The idea that the Earth is the center of the universe, and that the sun, planets and stars all revolve around the Earth, is called the **geocentric model of the heavens**. Almost everyone used the geocentric model. Few astronomers saw any reason to believe that the geocentric model might be wrong.

> The prefix **geo-** means "Earth." **Geocentric** means "Earth-centered."

That is, until Nicolaus Copernicus came along. Copernicus was a Renaissance Man who studied astronomy, mathematics and more at the University of Krakow, Poland. Unlike other astronomers of his day, Copernicus saw many reasons why the geocentric model might be wrong.

Some of Copernicus' reasons came from the orbit of Mars. One problem Copernicus noticed was that Mars seemed to move forward across the sky sometimes, and backward at other times. How could this be, if Mars was attached to a smooth-turning heavenly sphere?

Nicolaus Copernicus
(1473 - 1543)

Another problem Copernicus noticed was that Mars appeared brighter sometimes, and dimmer at other times. This probably meant that Mars was sometimes closer to Earth, and sometimes farther away. How could this be, if Mars was attached to a perfectly round heavenly sphere?

A more detailed view of Ptolemy's system

Ptolemy had clever answers for both of these questions. In Ptolemy's model of the universe, the planets weren't actually attached to their planetary spheres. Instead, they were attached to smaller spheres which turned inside the planetary spheres. Like ink pens on a Spirograph, the planets moved forward, backward and then forward again— just as Mars appeared to do. They also moved closer, and then farther away— again, just like Mars.

To Copernicus, though, Ptolemy's answers seemed terribly complicated. The math that went with all these spheres was endless. And even when the math was done, Ptolemy's answers still weren't very good. Rarely were the planets exactly where Ptolemy's model said they would be.

So Copernicus offered different answers. Around 1514, Copernicus wrote a short book that described a new model of the heavens. He called his book ***Commentariolus***, or ***Little Commentary***.

Copernicus' *Little Commentary* asked: what if the geocentric model of the heavens is wrong? What if a **heliocentric model** is closer to the truth?

> The prefix **helio-** means "sun." **Heliocentric** means "sun-centered."

In other words, what if Earth isn't the center of the heavens? Instead, what if the sun is the center— and what if Earth, Mars and all the other planets really orbit the sun? Then Copernicus' problems with Mars would be easy to explain. If Mars stood farther from the sun than Earth did, then Mars might take longer to orbit the sun. Over time, Earth would catch up to Mars, and then pass it by— making it appear that Mars was moving backward. And of course, Mars would appear brighter when it was closer to Earth, and dimmer when farther away.

But then, why did the sun appear to rise and set? According to *Little Commentary*, it wasn't because the sun revolved around Earth. Instead, it was because Earth rotated on its axis once each day.

The rotation of the Earth also explained why the stars appeared to move. As Earth rotated on its axis, different stars came into view.

Copernicus was very careful with his *Little Commentary*. His book was only for a few astronomer friends— people he knew he could trust. For Copernicus knew very well that astronomy and religion go hand in hand. And he didn't want to offend the Catholic Church.

With a lot of help from his astronomer friends, Copernicus finally worked out the math to back up his new model of the heavens. His last book, which he called *On the Revolutions of the Celestial Spheres*, was published in 1543— almost 30 years after his *Little Commentary*. According to legend, a printer showed Copernicus the first copy of his finished book on the day he died.

"Astronomer Copernicus" by artist Jan Matejko

model of the heavens was far from perfect. In placing the sun at the center,
[...] aside one bad old rule of Greek science: the geocentric rule. But he had kept another
[...] idea that the planets move in perfect circles. Since the planets don't move in perfect
[...]cus' math turned out to be as complicated as Ptolemy's— and almost as wrong.

The next great Renaissance astronomer, **Tycho Brahe**, was born 3 years after Copernicus died. Tycho started out as a bright young student at the University of Copenhagen, Denmark.

What drew Tycho to astronomy was a heavenly happening called a **total solar eclipse**. One day in 1559, when Tycho was 13 years old, the moon happened to pass directly in front of the sun. At the time, the moon was as close to Earth as it ever gets— which meant that the moon looked as big as it ever does. At that size, the moon completely blocked the sun, turning day as black as night. As birds plunged from the sky in fright, people ran for cover, terrified that the end of the world had come.

Tycho Brahe
(1546 - 1601)

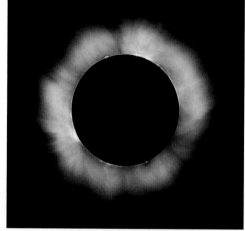

A total solar eclipse from 1999, photo courtesy Luc Viatour

But no Renaissance Man ran for cover. For by now, astronomers knew just when every eclipse would happen. In fact, almanacs had been publishing the correct dates and times of the next eclipse since before Christopher Columbus. This is what drew Tycho Brahe to astronomy— the fact that the science worked so well! Tycho longed to know this marvelous science that could predict heavenly happenings so perfectly.

This explains why Tycho was so disappointed a few years later. In 1563, Jupiter and Saturn were scheduled to appear close to one another in the night sky. Tycho checked two astronomical tables to see just when this would happen. One table was based on Ptolemy, and the other on Copernicus. To Tycho's horror, both tables were wrong! Ptolemy missed the date by a month, while Copernicus missed it by several days. These weren't the kind of perfect predictions Tycho was looking for!

Tycho had a good idea why both tables were wrong: because they were based on wrong measurements.

Both Ptolemy and Copernicus based their math on measurements taken by astronomers over the years. To understand a planet's orbit, astronomers measured two angles: altitude and azimuth. **Altitude** was the angle between planet and horizon; while **azimuth** was the angle between planet and north. They recorded these angles night after night, year after year, whenever the skies were clear enough to see the planets.

Two pages from the Alfonsine Tables, old astronomical tables based on the geocentric model of the heavens

The problem was the way astronomers measured those angles. Before Tycho, most astronomers used hand-held sextants or quadrants. On small instruments like these, the distance from one degree to the next might be only about one millimeter. This meant that a millimeter's mistake could throw off a measurement by a whole degree. But in astronomy, every fraction of a degree counts! The tiniest error can be huge for an astronomer.

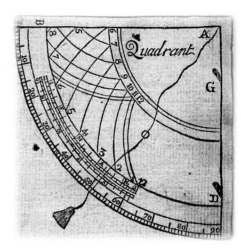

A hand-held quadrant for measuring altitude

Tycho knew how to fix this problem. Instead of using hand-held instruments, Tycho built instruments that filled whole rooms! On a room-sized quadrant like Tycho's, the distance from one degree to the next was more like 2 centimeters— which made it much easier to measure angles accurately. In fact, Tycho measured his angles to within one-sixtieth of one degree.

This was Tycho Brahe's greatest contribution to astronomy: accurate measurements. He spent his life recording the most complete and accurate astronomical charts the world had ever seen.

But charts weren't Tycho Brahe's only contribution to astronomy. Tycho also challenged another bad old idea from Greek science: the idea that ether never changed.

In 1572, astronomers noticed what looked like a bright new star in a constellation called Cassiopeia. Although none of them knew it at the time, they were actually watching a dying star called a **supernova**.

Since the ether was never supposed to change, most astronomers assumed that this new light couldn't be a new star. They thought that anything that changed must be in the same heavenly sphere as Earth.

But Tycho proved that this new light never moved— which meant that it must be in the same heavenly sphere as the stars. How could there be a new star, if heavenly ether never changed?

﷯﷯﷯﷯﷯﷯﷯﷯﷯﷯﷯﷯﷯﷯﷯﷯﷯﷯﷯﷯﷯﷯﷯﷯﷯﷯﷯﷯﷯﷯﷯﷯﷯﷯﷯

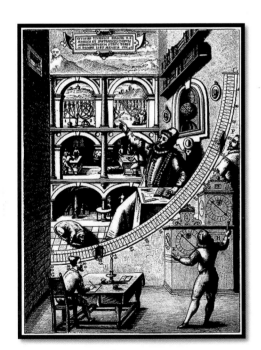

Tycho Brahe with a room-sized quadrant

In 1600, Tycho hired a brilliant German mathematician called **Johannes Kepler**. A year later, Tycho died, leaving his great astronomical charts in Kepler's hands.

It was Johannes Kepler who finally found what every astronomer had been seeking for years: a near-perfect way to predict the orbits of the planets.

ike Copernicus, Kepler was most interested in the orbit of Mars. Fortunately, Tycho had left him excellent measurements of Mars' orbit. Kepler filled book after book with long, complicated math, trying to find some formula that would fit Tycho's measurements.

Before he could find his formula, Kepler had to set aside one more bad old idea from Greek science. This was the idea that planets must always move in perfect circles.

The fun-loving Tycho Brahe kept two unusual helpers at his observatory. One was a dwarf called Jepp, whom Tycho believed could see the future. The other was a tame elk who entertained Tycho's rich friends at parties.

According to Tycho, his elk drank so much beer at a party one night that it got drunk, fell down a flight of stairs and died.

What Kepler learned is that the planets don't move in circles. In fact, they move in **ellipses**— which is what Kepler proved in **Kepler's Laws of Planetary Motion**.

> An **ellipse** is a special kind of oval.

- **Kepler's First Law** basically says that all planets revolve around the sun in ellipse-shaped orbits.

- **Kepler's Second Law** basically says that planets orbit faster when they are closer to the sun, and slower when they are farther away.

- **Kepler's Third Law** gave him a way to measure the solar system. If Kepler knew the size of one planet's orbit, then he could figure out the sizes of all the other planets' orbits.

Johannes Kepler
(1571 - 1630)

Johannes Kepler

Besides his three laws, Kepler also offered a better idea about what caused the planets to move. Kepler didn't believe in a Prime Mover out beyond the heavenly spheres. Instead, Kepler believed that the force that moved the planets must come from the sun.

In other words, Kepler came close to understanding the law of gravity! But Kepler didn't actually explain the law of gravity. The one who did was an English scientist called **Sir Isaac Newton**. Newton wouldn't be born until 1642— twelve years after Kepler died.

The Galileo Affair

START

Like many astronomers, Johannes Kepler had a lot of trouble with the Catholic Church along the way. But Kepler's troubles were nothing compared to the troubles of **Galileo Galilei**.

Galileo was a sharp-witted, sharp-tongued Italian born in Pisa. His father was a lute player who blended math with music. As a boy, Galileo watched his father experiment with his lute, trying to understand exactly how the length and tension of his strings affected their pitch. As a grown man, Galileo believed what his father believed: that the best way to understand the world was through experiments and measurements.

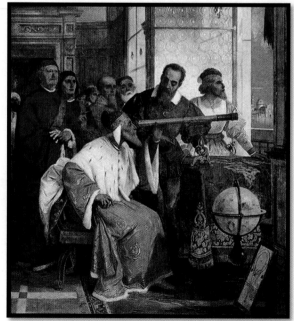

Galileo was known best for his telescopes. He didn't actually invent the telescope; for that was done in a Dutch eyeglass shop around 1608. However, Galileo immediately improved the telescope's design. And he was the first scientist anywhere to use telescopes for serious astronomy.

In 1610, when the telescope was still only about 2 years old, Galileo published an exciting new pamphlet called "The Starry Messenger." In it, Galileo shared news about the heavens that Ptolemy never would have believed. For example:

Galileo showing the leader of Venice how to use a telescope

> When Galileo turned his telescope on the moon, he saw that it wasn't smooth at all. Instead, it was dotted with craters and rocks. Clearly, the heavenly ether wasn't as perfect and unchanging as Ptolemy had believed.

> When Galileo turned this telescope toward Jupiter, he saw at least four moons revolving around the big planet. Clearly, Ptolemy had been wrong to say that everything revolved around the Earth.

GALILEO GALILEI

Maybe the Catholic Church shouldn't have been so surprised by "Starry Messenger." After all, some of Galileo's ideas were no different than Copernicus' ideas, or Kepler's; and some of those had already been around for almost 100 years.

But Galileo was different from Copernicus and Kepler. Unlike those two, Galileo didn't just suggest that the Earth might revolve around the sun. No, Galileo insisted that the Earth must revolve around the sun— and that anyone who didn't believe it was a stubborn old fool!

In the Church's eyes, Galileo seemed to be going against the Bible. For example, the Bible speaks of one special day when the Israelites needed more time to defeat the Amorites. To give them that extra time, the Lord stopped the sun and moon, as Joshua 10:13 says:

**Galileo Galilei
(1564 - 1642)**

"So the sun stood still, and the moon stopped, till the nation avenged itself on its enemies."

How could the sun stand still, the Church asked, if it wasn't moving in the first place? So Galileo must be wrong! No matter what Galileo's telescope showed, the sun must really revolve around the Earth.

When Galileo didn't change his mind, the Church sent the **Roman Inquisition** to deal with him. This was another powerful Church court— something like the Spanish Inquisition (Chapter 23), but for a different purpose. Galileo faced the Inquisition twice, once in 1616 and again in 1632.

Like other Church courts, the Roman Inquisition didn't waste time arguing with the accused. It simply announced that the accused was wrong, and then ordered him to change his beliefs.

The first time Galileo faced the Inquisition, the court ordered him to shut his mouth and stop his pen. He was to neither speak nor write one more word about the Earth revolving around the sun. As a Catholic who lived in Italy, and hoped to live there for many more years, Galileo had no choice but to obey.

Years later, Galileo felt too old, sick and tired to waste time arguing with the stubborn Catholic Church. So he published the book that would finally land him in prison. This was Galileo's ***Dialogue Concerning the Two Chief World Systems, Ptolemaic and Copernican***.

The *Dialogue* was a made-up talk between three made-up men. The first man was a learned scientist who proved beyond doubt that the Earth really did revolve around the sun. The second man believed the first. But the third man was a stubborn old fool who refused to believe, no matter how great the proof.

Now the Church was furious with Galileo. For when churchmen read the *Dialogue*, it seemed pretty clear that the stubborn old fool was really a churchman— maybe even the pope himself!

**Drawing from the frontispiece
of Galileo's "Dialogue"**

"Galileo facing the Roman Inquisition" by Cristiano Banti

This time, the Inquisition punished Galileo harshly. All of his books were banned, which meant that all Christians were forbidden to read them. As for Galileo himself, he became a prisoner. He would live under house arrest until the court decided to let him out.

There was also a third punishment. Before ordering Galileo out of its sight for the last time, the court commanded him to speak aloud these words: "The Earth does not move."

Under threat of torture and death, Galileo had no choice but to obey. So he said it: "The Earth does not move." But the stubborn scientist added this under his breath, too soft for the court to hear: "And yet it moves."

Galileo lived under house arrest for 10 years, until he died in 1642. During those 10 years, he gradually went both deaf and blind. Even so, Galileo did some of his best science in his last 10 years.

〰〰

In modern times, scientists look back on Galileo as an honored father of the **scientific method**. Why? Because Galileo taught a new approach to science.

Greek scientists started with philosophy, and worked from there. The reason Ptolemy believed in perfect heavenly spheres was because he believed that the heavens must be as perfect as the gods.

But Galileo was different. Instead of starting with philosophy, he started with experiments and measurements. He wanted to know the heavens as they actually were, not as he believed they should be.

More about Diets

In Chapters 27 and 28, we learned how Martin Luther faced the **Diet of Worms** in 1521. This chapter tells of more such diets, and how they changed the Reformation in Germany.

All of these diets were ordered by the same man: **Holy Roman Emperor Charles V**, who was also **King Charles I of Spain**. As a loyal Catholic, Charles tried to stop the Reformation before it could grow.

The next diets after Worms were the **Diets of Nuremberg**, held in 1522 – 1524. The emperor's orders at Nuremberg were clear: he wanted Martin Luther arrested,

Holy Roman Emperor
Charles V

and all of his books burned. The same was true for every Lutheran preacher in Germany: the emperor wanted them all arrested. Without powerful friends, Luther certainly would have been arrested— and probably burned to death, just like John Hus.

The situation changed before the next diet. After the Diets of Nuremberg, the Ottoman Empire invaded Eastern Europe! All of a sudden, Germany was threatened by the most powerful sultan of all time: Suleiman the Magnificent. To stand against Suleiman, the emperor would need every German soldier he could find— including Lutheran soldiers.

> Remember what a **diet** was— a meeting of the German government.

The emperor knew that if he wanted Lutheran soldiers, then he would have to give the Lutherans at least part of what they wanted. So he decided to compromise.

At the **First Diet of Speyer**, held in 1526, Catholics and Lutherans reached an agreement called *cuius regio, eius religio*. This meant that each part of the Holy Roman Empire would follow the religion of the noble who led that part. If a leader was Catholic, then his part of the empire would be Catholic. But if a leader was Lutheran, then his part would be Lutheran.

> *Cuius regio, eius religio* is Latin for "whoever's region, his religion."

Then, the emperor tried to take it all back. Between 1526 and 1529, the emperor won a big victory in the Italian Wars. Although Suleiman still threatened, the emperor felt stronger than before. So he changed his mind again.

At the **Second Diet of Speyer**, held in 1529, the emperor took away *cuius regio, eius religio*. In other words, he tried to force all Lutherans back into the Catholic Church!

Needless to say, the Lutherans were most upset. As the Second Diet of Speyer drew to a close, 21 German nobles wrote a letter of protest to the emperor. Part of this letter read:

> "We are determined by God's grace and aid to abide by God's Word alone… as it is contained in the Scriptures of the Old and New Testaments, without anything added to it. This Word alone should be preached, and nothing that is contrary to it. It is the only truth."

In other words, Lutherans would follow the Bible alone. No matter what the emperor might do to them, they would never go back to the Sacred Tradition of the Catholic Church.

The Memorial Church of the Protestation, built in Speyer, Germany as a memorial to the Protestation at Speyer

The name **Protestant** comes from the **Protestation at Speyer**, the formal letter of protest written by 21 German nobles at the end of the Second Diet of Speyer.

Different Kinds of Maps

Every map has a different purpose. The world is a big place, and there is much to know about it. To tell all there is to know on one map would be impossible. So instead, mapmakers create specialized maps that tell part of what there is to know.

One common kind of map is the **physical map**. Physical maps focus on a region's physical features— things like coastlines, rivers, mountains and valleys.

Some physical maps focus on more specific features. For example:

➢ A **topographic map** shows different elevations in different colors. Lower ground often appears in shades of green, with higher ground in shades of brown.

➢ A **climate map** focuses on weather patterns. One climate map might show a region's average temperature. Another might show average yearly rainfall, or the directions of prevailing winds.

CHAPTER 30:

The Reformation beyond Germany

As we read in Chapter 27, the Protestant Reformation started in Germany.

If the Catholic Church had had its way, then the Reformation also would have ended in Germany! The pope tried his best to stop the Reformation before it began. And when the pope failed, the Holy Roman Emperor tried as well.

Nothing worked. Despite everything Catholics tried, the Reformation spread— first to Switzerland, then to France, the Netherlands, England and beyond.

The Swiss Reformation

Down in Switzerland, the story of the Reformation started with a strong-willed Swiss called Ulrich Zwingli.

Like all early leaders of the Reformation, Zwingli started out Catholic. On his 35th birthday, Zwingli became the chief priest of the biggest church in the biggest city in Switzerland: **Zurich**. The date was January 1, 1519. Fourteen months had passed since Martin Luther nailed his Ninety-five Theses to a church door in Wittenberg. The Diet of Worms was still more than 2 years ahead.

From his first day as chief priest, Zwingli didn't preach the way other Catholics preached. Most priests preached simple moral lessons called homilies. But Zwingli preached straight from the Bible.

In some ways, Zwingli was a lot like Luther. For example, both Zwingli and Luther believed in *Sola Scriptura*— the idea that the Bible alone is inspired by God.

In other ways, Zwingli was quite different from Luther.

Zwingli wanted to change the church faster than Luther did, and in bigger ways. In Zwingli's eyes, Luther's Reformation didn't go far enough.

> **Switzerland** is a mountainous country in Central Europe. Its neighbors are Germany to the north, Austria to the east, Italy to the south and France to the west.

> Remember what *Sola Scriptura* was: the idea that the Bible alone was inspired by God, and that the Sacred Tradition of the Catholic Church wasn't inspired at all.

Although Luther wanted change, he was careful not to change his churches too quickly. As we read in Chapter 28, radicals like Andreas Carlstadt wanted to toss out all Sacred Tradition right away. But Luther preferred to keep some traditions. The Lutheran rule was that traditions were fine, as long as they didn't go against the Bible.

Zwingli was more like Carlstadt. Zwingli's rule was that traditions were automatically wrong, unless they came straight out of the Bible. Zwingli wanted to build a whole new church, basing everything he did on the Bible alone.

Ulrich Zwingli (1484 – 1531)

The first tradition Zwingli tossed out was a food law. The Catholic Church forbade Christians to eat meat during **Lent**. As Easter drew near, all Christians were supposed to give up the luxury of eating meat. This was to remind them how Christ had given up everything for them on the cross.

The season of **Lent** falls in the 40 days leading up to Easter.

Zwingli's teaching on food came from I Corinthians 8. The Apostle Paul's letter to the Corinthians included a long discussion about Christians and food. According to Paul, Christians were free to eat whatever food they liked, even food that had been sacrificed to idols. The only reason to avoid eating certain foods was if eating them might weaken someone else's faith.

This is just what Zwingli taught his followers. He didn't teach them to eat meat during Lent; nor did he teach them not to eat meat. Instead, he taught that Christians were free to choose.

Zwingli's teaching led to a strange happening called the **Affair of the Sausages**.

A Swiss printer called Christoph Froschauer took Zwingli's teaching to heart. When the season of Lent came around in 1522, Froschauer hosted a friendly meal for workers in his print shop. On the menu that day was a food that no good Christian was supposed to eat during Lent: sausage.

Nowadays, gnawing a bit of sausage might not seem like a big deal. But in Zwingli's day, it was a very big deal. Froschauer was deliberately breaking a food law set forth by the Church.

As for Zwingli himself, he didn't actually eat Froschauer's sausages. But he did preach that Froschauer had every right to eat them. Since Zwingli was still a priest at the time, he was as guilty of breaking Church law as Froschauer was.

ﭏﭏﭏ

The Affair of the Sausages marked the beginning of the **Swiss Reformation**— the first time Ulrich Zwingli deliberately broke with the Catholic Church. He would soon break many other Church laws.

To Zwingli, the Catholic Church seemed nothing like the early churches described in the New Testament. The Catholic Church was rich and fancy, full of fine art and grand ceremonies. But Biblical churches were poor and plain.

Zwingli's first step toward a more Biblical church was plain church buildings. He tore out all of the finery left over from Catholic days. Sculptures came down. Stained glass windows were replaced with clear glass. The murals on the walls were all covered over with clean white paint. Even Zwingli's expensive pipe organ came out— which was especially hard for Zwingli, who loved music. But he was willing to make the sacrifice; for he wanted no idols to tempt his people away from simple, Biblical worship.

The next step was to change his order of worship— especially the way he celebrated Holy Communion.

To Catholics, communion was often the main point of worship. The Catholic Church taught an idea called **transubstantiation**. This meant that during communion, the bread and wine actually transformed into the body and blood of Jesus Christ. Priests said that by taking communion, believers were taking part in Christ's sacrifice on the cross.

The *Grossmunster*, Zwingli's main church in Zurich

Zwingli taught a different idea: **memorialism**. In Zwingli's eyes, the bread and the wine didn't transform at all. Instead, they were symbols to remind believers of Christ's sacrifice. The idea of memorialism came from Luke 22:19, where Christ said:

"This is my body given for you; do this in remembrance of me."

Communion with Zwingli was nothing like communion with a Catholic priest. Where priests rang bells and burned incense, Zwingli spoke plain words from the Bible. And where priests used fancy plates and cups made of gold, Zwingli used plain wooden ones. Zwingli also held communion less often— only a few times a year, instead of one or more times per week. Zwingli wanted his people learning from the Bible, not watching priests put on fancy rituals.

Strangely enough, Zwingli's ideas about communion caused a big argument with someone who should have been his friend: Martin Luther.

In an age when few Christians could read, stained glass windows were one way to illustrate stories from the Bible. Some Christians called stained glass windows the **"Poor Man's Bible"**— the only kind of Bible that most poor men would ever read.

A stained glass angel holding the elements of Holy Communion

In Chapter 29, we read what happened at the Second Diet of Speyer— how Holy Roman Emperor Charles V ordered all Lutherans back into the Catholic Church. We also read how Lutherans refused.

After the Second Diet of Speyer, Lutherans knew that the emperor would attack them someday. Sooner or later, he would surely try to force them back into the Catholic Church. When that happened, the Lutherans would need help. And who better to help the Lutherans than their fellow Protestants down in Switzerland?

Unfortunately, Swiss Protestants and Lutherans disagreed about certain things— which meant that the Swiss might not come when the Lutherans needed them.

A German noble called **Philip of Hesse** was eager for Swiss help. So he arranged a meeting between Luther and Zwingli. Philip hoped that if these two could work out their differences, then their two churches could help each other. This special meeting is called the **Marburg Colloquy**, and it happened in late 1529.

The Marburg Colloquy pointed out a big difference between Protestants and Catholics. Unlike Catholics, Protestants didn't have to agree with each other— for there was no Protestant pope who could force them to agree.

Instead of a pope, Protestants looked to the Bible to answer important questions. All Protestants agreed that the Bible was inspired by God. However, they didn't necessarily agree about what the

Luther, Zwingli and others at the Marburg Colloquy

Bible said— or at least, how to interpret what the Bible said. And when they didn't agree, they often decided that they couldn't worship together.

Which is what happened at the Marburg Colloquy.

Martin Luther didn't like Catholic communion any more than Zwingli did. But he also didn't like memorialism, Zwingli's idea about communion. To Luther, the bread and wine were more than just symbols. Luther didn't believe that the bread and wine transformed, as Catholics believed. Even so, he insisted that Christ was somehow present in the bread and wine. Some Christians use the word **consubtantiation** to explain what Luther believed. Consubstantiation meant that Christ was "in, with and under" the elements of Holy Communion.

Back and forth the two men argued. Luther brought up Mark 14:22, where Christ said "Take [this bread]; this is my body." To Luther, Christ's meaning was clear: the bread really was Christ's body. But to Zwingli, the bread was still a symbol. Zwingli brought up John 15:5, where Christ said "I am the vine." Did Luther think that Christ was really a vine? Or was the vine a symbol— just as the bread was a symbol?

Of course, Luther and Zwingli agreed on many other things. But this one thing was enough to wreck their meeting. The two men never agreed about communion, and never became friends.

Zwingli could have used more friends. That same year, a civil war broke out between two kinds of Swiss: Swiss Protestants who followed Zwingli, and Swiss Catholics who stuck with the Catholic Church. Without Lutheran allies, Swiss Protestants were outnumbered. The great Ulrich Zwingli died in battle against Swiss Catholics in 1531.

"The Murder of Ulrich Zwingli" by artist Karl Jauslin

The Reformed Church

Our next great figure from the Reformation also lived in Switzerland. But **John Calvin** was born in France, not Switzerland. Calvin started as a **Huguenot**— in other words, a French Protestant. He only moved to Switzerland because French Catholics were so cruel to Huguenots.

When the Reformation started in 1517, **King Francis I** sat on the throne of France. Like Holy Roman Emperor Charles V, King Francis I was a strong Catholic. But unlike Charles, Francis didn't try to drive all Protestants back into the Catholic Church— at least, not at first.

A **Huguenot** was a French Protestant.

Why was Francis so easy on Huguenots? Partly because Francis and Charles were bitter enemies. Francis knew that the more trouble Protestants gave Charles, the less trouble Charles could give Francis. So Francis left Protestants alone, hoping that they'd give Charles as much trouble as possible.

What changed Francis' mind about the Huguenots was a happening called the **Affair of the Placards**.

A **placard** is a poster or sign.

King Francis I of France

HUGUENOT CROSS

The Affair of the Placards started with the **Catholic Mass**. No Protestant liked the Mass. Sometimes, the Huguenots disliked the Mass so much that they just had to say something.

One night in 1534, the Huguenots quietly spread out over five big French cities, hanging posters wherever they went. When Catholics arose the next morning, they read this at the top of the Huguenot posters: "True Articles on the Horrible, Great and Intolerable Abuses of the Popish Mass." Down below, they read why the Huguenots hated the Mass so much. To the Huguenots, the Mass seemed more like a pagan sacrifice than a Christian worship service.

> Remember what the **Mass** is— the Catholic celebration of Holy Communion.

Naturally, Catholics were furious. Even so, the Huguenots might have gotten away with the Affair of the Placards— if they hadn't hung one of their posters right outside King Francis' bedroom.

Whoever hung this poster probably hoped that Francis would read it, and maybe believe it. Instead, Francis was terrified! He shuddered to think how close the Huguenots had been to his bedroom, and how easily they might have assassinated him.

So the posters did just the opposite of what the Huguenots had hoped. Instead of reading and believing, King Francis started rounding up Huguenots.

What a terrible time to be a Huguenot! Three months after the posters went up, the Catholic Church put on a special parade in Paris. As King Francis looked on in approval, the Church tortured and burned many Huguenots to death.

Meanwhile, thousands of Huguenots fled France in terror. Many fled to Swiss cities like Geneva and Basel, which lay just across the border from France. One who fled to Basel was John Calvin.

"Portrait of Young John Calvin" on display at the University of Geneva

John Calvin
(1509 - 1564)

Calvin was still on the run, and still living in Basel, when he published the first edition of his greatest work. This was *Institutes of the Christian Religion*, better known as the *Institutes*. The Institutes spelled out John Calvin's **theology**— everything he believed about God and the Bible.

What made the *Institutes* so special was Calvin's brilliant mind. To Calvin's followers, the *Institutes* were the

> **Theology** is the study of God.

best explanation of Christian theology ever written. Through the *Institutes*, John Calvin became the father of a whole new family of Protestant churches: **Reformed churches**.

Reformed churches stress three main ideas.

➤ First, Reformed churches stress **sola scriptura**— the idea that the Bible alone is the inspired Word of God.

➤ Second, Reformed churches stress the **sovereignty** of God. Sovereignty means that all power and authority belong to God! He may do whatever He chooses to do, and save whomever he chooses to save.

➤ Third, Reformed churches stress the **grace** of God.

What is grace? In theology, "grace" means a gift from God that isn't earned or deserved.

Reformed churches teach that no one deserves to be saved. John Calvin believed in **original sin**— the idea that all people are born into the sin of Adam (Chapter 3). They are all so wrapped up in sin that they cannot possibly earn God's forgiveness.

This is why sinners need grace. Since no one can save himself, God saves some— not because they deserve to be saved, but because a sovereign God chooses to save them. It is all up to God, from beginning to end.

෴෴෴෴෴෴෴෴෴෴෴෴෴෴෴෴෴෴෴෴෴෴෴෴

Within a year after Calvin first published the *Institutes*, a fellow Huguenot called **William Farel** invited him to Geneva, Switzerland. Except for a 3-year break, Calvin stayed in Geneva for the rest of his life.

The longer Calvin stayed in Geneva, the more powerful he became. In fact, Calvin practically ran Geneva— much like Girolamo Savonarola ran Florence in the 1490s (Chapter 26).

Some Bible students use the word **TULIP** to remember the ideas in Calvin's *Institutes*. Each letter stands for a different point of Calvin's theology:

T is for <u>T</u>otal Depravity
U is for <u>U</u>nconditional Election
L is for <u>L</u>imited Atonement
I is for <u>I</u>rresistible Grace
P is for <u>P</u>erseverance of the Saints

Like Savonarola, Calvin frowned on any sin that drew his people's attention away from God. Of course, Calvin frowned on obvious sins like theft and murder. But he also frowned on less obvious sins. For example, Genevans were not to eat too much. They were not to wear too much makeup; too-fancy hairstyles; or too-lavish clothing. They were to sing no non-Christian songs, only Christian ones; and they were not to dance. Nor were they to play any game that involved rolling dice.

Most of all, Genevans were to go to church! By law, every Genevan was required to attend church every Sunday. All were to sit quietly and respectfully in church, and pay close attention to the sermon.

The punishments for breaking these laws were severe. For singing non-Christian songs, one's tongue might be pierced with an awl. For laughing in church, one might go to jail.

But the worst punishments were for crimes against God. Any **blasphemer** who cursed God, or any **heretic** who deliberately taught wrong ideas about God, might be put to death. Sad to say, the Church of Geneva sometimes burned heretics to death, just as the Catholic Church did.

Burning was the fate of poor Michael Servetus.

The Reformation Wall in Geneva depicts four figures from the Reformation. The first is William Farel, who first invited Calvin to Geneva. Next comes Calvin himself, followed by Theodore Beza of Geneva and John Knox of Scotland.

Servetus was a brilliant Renaissance Man who dreamed up new ideas on all kinds of subjects. His greatest gifts probably lay in medicine. Of all the doctors in Europe, Servetus was the first to understand **pulmonary circulation**.

Like most brilliant men of his day, Servetus was also interested in religion. As a boy, he served the Catholic Church. But as a young man, he grew disgusted by the many sins of the Renaissance popes; so he became a Protestant.

The Protestant Reformation excited Servetus. To a man filled with new ideas, the Reformation seemed like a great time to throw out all the bad old ideas that had led the Catholic Church astray.

Unfortunately, Servetus chose the wrong idea to throw out. In 1531, when he was only 20 years old, Servetus published a book called *On the Errors of the Trinity*. Servetus was convinced that the **Holy Trinity** was one of the bad old ideas that had led the Catholic Church astray.

> "Pulmonary" means "having to do with the lungs." **Pulmonary circulation** means that blood flows from the heart to the lungs, where it picks up oxygen. Oxygen-filled blood then flows back to the heart to be pumped out to the rest of the body.

Almost no one agreed with Servetus. Of course, Protestants had already thrown out a lot of Catholic ideas. But they had only thrown out ideas that they believed went against the Bible. And no Protestant believed that the Holy Trinity went against the Bible. On the Holy Trinity, there was no difference between Protestants and Catholics. All Christians believed in God the Father, God the Son and God the Holy Spirit.

> Remember what **Holy Trinity** means. God exists in three persons: God the Father, God the Son and God the Holy Spirit (Chapter 2).

Which made Michael Servetus an enemy to all Christians, Protestant or Catholic.

In the 1540s, when John Calvin took charge of Geneva, Servetus started writing letters to Calvin— trying to convince him that the Holy Trinity was wrong. At first, Calvin wrote friendly letters back, showing Servetus how to find the Trinity in the Bible.

Michael Servetus (1511 – 1553)

With one of his friendly letters, Calvin sent along a copy of his own best work, the *Institutes*. To Calvin's dismay, Servetus sent the *Institutes* back— all marked up with negative comments. Not even Calvin's best work could convince Servetus that the Trinity was true!

After several years of this, Calvin finally decided that nothing would ever change Servetus' mind. Calvin now considered Servetus a dangerous man— a heretic who was determined to tear down the Reformed church. In a letter to a friend, Calvin wrote this about Servetus:

"…if he comes here, if my authority is worth anything, I will never permit him to depart alive."

Much to Calvin's surprise, Servetus really did come to Geneva. In 1553, Servetus was arrested on charges of heresy— not in a Protestant city, but in a Catholic one. Somehow, Servetus managed to escape from jail and flee that city. But instead of going somewhere safe, Servetus went to

Geneva. One Sunday, he turned up in the pews of John Calvin's own church!

True to his word, Calvin ordered Servetus arrested on charges of heresy.

Since Servetus wasn't a citizen of Geneva, the city had no legal right to execute him. The court could have banished Servetus. Or it could have sent him back where he came from, where he probably would have been executed.

Instead, the court insisted on burning poor Michael Servetus to death— along with the pile of books he'd written against the Trinity.

Why? Because to John Calvin, Servetus was like a wolf in his pasture, tearing at his helpless sheep. Calvin wanted his people to hear Biblical truth, not lies intended to tear down the church.

To some people, though, the execution of Michael Servetus marked John Calvin as a **hypocrite**. After all, why had Calvin fled France? Wasn't it because French Catholics were killing Protestants for preaching what Catholics considered heresy? Now Calvin had killed Servetus for preaching what Calvin considered heresy. So how were Protestants any better than Catholics?

> In 1559, John Calvin established the **University of Geneva** as a school for Protestant ideas. Protestant students came from all over Europe to learn at Calvin's feet.
>
> The University of Geneva helped make this Swiss city the greatest Protestant city of its day. Some thought of Geneva as the **Protestant Rome**— the leading city of the Protestant Church, just as Rome was the leading city of the Catholic Church.

> A **hypocrite** is someone who doesn't live by the religion he claims to believe.

The French Wars of Religion

John Calvin was wise to leave France. As we've read, times were already bad for the Huguenots in 1534, when Calvin fled. Later, though, times got much worse.

This time, the trouble started with a horrible happening called the **Massacre of Vassy**. One day in 1562, a Catholic duke happened to be leading an army through the town of Vassy, France. Since it was Sunday, the Huguenots of Vassy were holding a church service. And since they were Huguenots, they were holding their service in a barn— for Huguenots weren't allowed to use Catholic church buildings.

Exactly what happened that day, no one now knows for sure. According to one version of the story, the duke tried to stop the service, which led to a fight. The fight ended when the duke set fire to the barn— burning the defenseless Huguenots inside to death.

This was the start of the **French Wars of Religion**. These were long, horrible wars between Catholics and Huguenots that lasted more than thirty years, all the way from 1562 – 1598.

In all those years, the Huguenots never came close to winning. For the Huguenots were always badly outnumbered. Only one King of France was ever a Huguenot; and even that one had to turn Catholic to keep his throne.

For Huguenots, the hardest time of the French Wars of Religion was the **St. Bartholomew's Day Massacre**. One night in August 1572, the Catholics launched a surprise attack, trying to hunt down and kill every Huguenot in Paris. Exactly who arranged this attack, no one now knows for sure. But the attacks soon spread to other cities. Before they were over, as many as 10,000 Huguenots lay dead, in key cities all over France.

Even then, the Huguenots weren't defeated; for they still held key cities of their own. The most important Huguenot city was **La Rochelle**, a port on the west coast.

St. Bartholomew's Day Massacre

Since they weren't wanted in France, some Huguenots sailed out of La Rochelle in search of new places to live. This made the Huguenots some of the first explorers from France.

Huguenots actually built two colonies in North America. One was Charlesfort, which stood on what is now Parris Island, South Carolina. The other was Fort Caroline, which stood in what is now Jacksonville, Florida. Sadly, neither colony lasted very long.

The French Wars of Religion ended, sort of, with a new law called the Edict of Nantes. For the sake of peace, the Catholics finally gave the Huguenots part of the freedom they wanted. From 1598 forward, the Huguenots were free to worship in any French city where they already worshiped. But no Huguenot could worship in Paris; for the Catholics of Paris still hated Huguenots as much as ever.

〰〰〰

The Huguenots weren't the only Frenchmen who explored the New World. In the mid-1500s, King Francis I of France— the same Francis who gave John Calvin so much trouble— sent an explorer to North America. The three expeditions of Jacques Cartier are a big reason why the French were the first Europeans to settle in what is now Canada.

Jacques Cartier

Like other early explorers, Cartier started out looking for a new route to the Far East. Later, though, Cartier went looking for something else: gold and diamonds. On his second trip to Canada, some natives told him of a place farther north where he could find these treasures.

On his third trip to Canada, Cartier thought he had struck it rich. Before heading home, he loaded his ships with what he thought were gold and diamond ores.

But Cartier didn't know his minerals. When he got back to France, his "gold" turned out to be worthless iron pyrite— also called "fool's gold." And his "diamonds" turned out to be worthless quartz! See Year Three for more on Jacques Cartier.

A man-shaped inuksuk in northern Quebec Province, Canada

An **inuksuk** is a landmark made of stacked stones. In the vast, frozen tundra of northern Canada, one stretch of ground looks much like another. So the Inuit people build inuksuk landmarks to guide them in their travels.

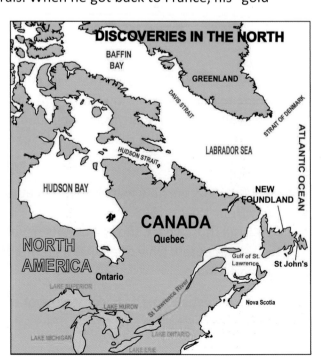

CHAPTER 31:

King Henry VIII; the English Reformation

The English Reformation

The Protestant Reformation came to different countries in different ways.

In Germany and Switzerland, the Reformation started with arguments over theology. Protestant leaders like Martin Luther, Ulrich Zwingli and John Calvin believed that the Catholic Church taught wrong ideas about God and the Bible.

The English Reformation started differently. Instead of arguing over theology, the English argued over Church law and politics. Basically, the English Reformation started because King Henry VIII of England wanted to divorce his wife, and the Catholic Church wouldn't let him!

ⁿⁿ

Back in Chapter 15, we read how Henry Tudor won the Wars of the Roses. At the Battle of Bosworth Field, fought in 1485, Henry defeated and killed King Richard III. Thus Richard was the last king from the royal House of York. Right there on the battlefield, Henry Tudor became **King Henry VII**, the first king from the new royal House of Tudor.

If the House of Tudor was to last, then Henry VII needed sons to take place when he was gone. Fortunately, Henry had what the English call "an heir and a spare." Henry's eldest son **Arthur, Prince of Wales** was the official heir to the throne. And his second son **Henry, Duke of York** was there to take Arthur's place if anything should happen to him.

As a future King of England, Prince Arthur attracted a powerful bride. In 1501, when he was just 15 years old, Arthur married **Catherine of Aragon**. Catherine was a daughter to two of the most powerful people in the world: **King Ferdinand of Aragon** and **Queen Isabella of Castile**.

Arthur Tudor, elder brother to the future King Henry VIII

Kings and Queens from the Royal House of Tudor

1. King Henry VII
(Reigned 1485 - 1509)

2. King Henry VIII
(Reigned 1509 - 1547)

3. King Edward VI
(Reigned 1547 - 1553)

4. Lady Jane Grey
(Reigned for 9 days in 1553)

5. Queen Mary I
(Reigned 1553 - 1558)

6. Queen Elizabeth I
(Reigned 1558 - 1603)

Remember who **Ferdinand of Aragon** and **Isabella of Castile** were: the Catholic Monarchs who ruled what would soon become Spain. Ferdinand and Isabella were the ones who sponsored Christopher Columbus' first voyage of exploration in 1492.

Then tragedy struck. Less than six months after the wedding, both Arthur and Catherine came down with a mysterious fever called **sweating sickness**. Catherine got over her fever. But Arthur died, leaving Catherine a widow at age 16.

Having lost its first heir, England called up its spare heir. In 1502, the 11-year-old Henry, Duke of York became the new Prince of Wales, official heir to King Henry VII.

As for Catherine, no one was quite sure what do with her. The same strengths that had made Catherine a good match for Arthur also made her a good match for Henry. But the Catholic Church forbade brothers to marry their brothers' wives. This Church law was partly based on Leviticus 21:20, which reads:

"If a man marries his brother's wife, it is an act of impurity; he has dishonored his brother. They will be childless [underline added]."

However, the Church was sometimes willing to bend its rules. Since Arthur and Catherine had had no children, the Church gave Henry special permission to marry his brother's widow. The wedding came in 1509— two months after Henry VII died, and the 17-year-old **King Henry VIII** inherited his throne.

Catherine's first job as queen was to give Henry sons. Like his father before him, Henry wanted at least two strong sons to carry on the House of Tudor after he was gone.

Sadly, Catherine couldn't seem to bear a healthy child. She was pregnant many times; but each time, the poor child died.

The couple had been married almost 7 years before Catherine finally gave birth to a healthy child. Much to Henry's disappointment, this child was a daughter: **Mary Tudor**.

After one more failed pregnancy, Catherine stopped getting pregnant. It looked as if Catherine would never give Henry the sons he wanted so desperately.

Catherine of Aragon, 1st wife to Henry VIII. Catherine gave birth to Mary Tudor, the future Queen Mary I.

The King's Great Matter

As King of England, Henry VIII was used to getting what he wanted. Since Catherine couldn't give him sons, Henry decided to divorce Catherine and marry someone who could.

The problem was, how to get a divorce? The Church didn't usually allow divorce— especially not for couples with children. So if Henry wanted a divorce, then he would have to give the Church an excellent excuse.

To find the excuse he needed, Henry looked back to his dead brother Arthur.

One day on 1527, an English **ambassador** rode into Rome with an urgent message for the pope. The King of England was troubled by a bad conscience, the ambassador said.

Henry knew now that he should never have married his brother's widow. After all, didn't Leviticus 20:21 spell out what would happen to a man who married his brother's widow? The Bible said "they will be childless." Surely this explained why Catherine couldn't give Henry sons?

An **ambassador** is an officer who speaks to a foreign government for his king.

Fortunately, the ambassador said, the pope had the power to save Henry. If the pope **annulled** Henry's marriage, then it would be as if he had never married his brother's widow!

Portrait of King Henry VIII from the studio of artist Hans Holbein the Younger

At any other time, the pope probably would have done as Henry asked. For Henry had always been a loyal Catholic.

> An **annulment** is a special kind of divorce. The Church dissolves the marriage, making it as if the couple never married.

In fact, Henry had even defended the Catholic Church against Martin Luther. Back in 1521, Henry had criticized Luther in a long paper called "Defense of the Seven Sacraments." For this, the grateful pope had given Henry the title *Fidei Defensor*— Latin for "Defender of the Faith."

At this particular time, though, the pope couldn't do as Henry asked. For the Papal States were at war with Holy Roman Emperor Charles V; and the pope had just lost a big battle to Charles. After that, the pope had to do as Charles told him. And Charles was against Henry's divorce— partly because Charles was Catherine of Aragon's nephew!

Catherine could have given Henry his divorce, if she had wanted to. If Catherine had taken nun's vows, then she would have become a bride of Christ, and Henry would have been free. But Catherine didn't want to take nun's vows. For if she did, then her daughter Mary would no longer be a princess. Instead, Mary would be an **illegitimate child**!

> An **illegitimate child** is one who is born while his or her parents aren't married.

When both Catherine and the pope turned him down, Henry turned to his home church. In 1529, the leaders of the English church held a special court to hear Henry's case for divorce.

Catherine of Aragon on her knees before Henry VIII in an English church court, begging her husband not to divorce her

But Catherine was too clever for Henry. When Catherine came to court, she threw herself on her knees before Henry, begging him not to divorce her. Any churchman with a heart couldn't help feeling sorry for Catherine.

Next, Catherine asked that the trial be moved to Rome. Now the leaders of the English church had a hard choice to make— whether to obey their pope, or obey their king.

To Henry's dismay, they chose the pope! Instead of granting Henry's divorce, the leaders of the English church moved the case to Rome— where they knew Henry would never win.

This was the last straw. In Henry's mind, no foreign court had any right to boss around a King of England! So he decided to make some big changes in the English church.

First, Henry got rid of old churchmen who were still loyal to the pope. In their places, Henry set new churchmen who were loyal to their king. That way, Henry would be sure to win his next case in church court.

Second, Henry wrote a new law called the **Statute in Restraint of Appeals**. This law made it illegal to do what Catherine had done: **appeal** to the pope. From now on, the pope would have no authority over English church courts. Whatever English courts decided would be final.

> To **appeal** a court's decision is to ask a higher court to change the first court's decision.

But the biggest change Henry made was a new law called the **Act of Supremacy**. Basically, this law created a whole new English church, completely separate from the Catholic Church. This was the **Church of England**, also called the **Anglican Church**.

The King of England was to be the supreme head of the Church of England, just as he was the head of government. In other words, the king would have all authority over the Church of England; while the pope would have no authority at all.

Now Henry had everything he needed to divorce Catherine of Aragon. In May 1533, the Church of England held a new court to hear Henry's case for divorce. In no time, the court agreed that Henry never should have married his brother's widow in the first place. The court annulled the marriage, just as Henry had hoped.

The heartbroken Catherine of Aragon lived for less than three years after her divorce. She died alone, forbidden even to see her daughter Mary.

As for Henry, he got a new wife. For years now, Henry had been planning to marry a smart, beautiful young woman called **Anne Boleyn**. With his first marriage at an end, Henry was finally free to start his second.

Anne Boleyn, 2nd wife to King Henry VIII. Anne gave birth to Elizabeth Tudor, the future Queen Elizabeth I.

More Reasons for the English Reformation

The king's divorce was only the first reason for the English Reformation. There were also many other reasons. In time, English Christians found as many reasons to complain against the Catholic Church as German and Swiss Christians found!

One complaint was that priests had gotten greedy. They now charged fees for their services. Every ceremony came with a price tag, from baptism to marriage to burial. Poor Christians had no choice but to pay these fees— for priests warned that if they didn't, then they wouldn't go to heaven when they died.

Another complaint was that English monasteries had gone bad. By this time, English monks lived nothing like Anthony of Thebes (Chapter 3). Instead of seeking God, they chased after pleasure. Instead of eating little, they grew fat. And instead of working hard to support themselves, they lived off donations.

Over the years, those donations had made monasteries fabulously rich. Just before the English Reformation, monasteries owned about one-third of all English farmland— plus a fortune in gold, silver and precious gems.

Those riches were very tempting to Henry, who always needed more money for the royal treasury. So he decided to kill two birds with one stone. Henry fixed England's monastery problem, and filled his treasury at the same time.

It all started with something called the **visitations of the monasteries**. As supreme head of the Church of England, the king was also head of England's monasteries. If those monasteries had gone bad, Henry said, then it was his job to fix them. So he sent inspectors to <u>visit</u> every monastery in England. If the inspectors found problems, then they closed down the monastery.

Needless to say, Henry's inspectors found plenty of problems. Over the next few years, King Henry VIII closed down almost every monastery in England— about 800 in all! The

Dissolution of the Monasteries took about 5 years, from 1536 – 1541.

As for the monasteries' money and property, those were all swallowed up by the king's treasury. As head of the Church, the king decided what happened to Church property.

Part of Reading Abbey, one of many monasteries that fell into ruins after the Dissolution of the Monasteries

If a local church wanted to use a monastery's buildings, then it could buy them from the treasury. If not, then the buildings might be left to rot.

The biggest treasure Henry swallowed came from the **Shrine of St. Thomas Becket** inside Canterbury Cathedral.

> A **shrine** is a memorial to an honored Catholic saint.

Do you remember Thomas Becket, Archbishop of Canterbury? Back in Chapter 13, we read how Thomas argued with King Henry II over common law. We also read what happened to Thomas in the end— how four of the king's knights burst in and killed him, right on the altar of Canterbury Cathedral.

Thomas Becket and the knights

Since then, the Catholic Church had named Thomas a saint, and built a shrine in his memory. Now when Christians confessed sin, their priests often sent them on pilgrimages to the Shrine of St. Thomas Becket. Part of every pilgrimage was making a donation to the shrine. With that many donations, Thomas' shrine was now the richest in England.

But Henry VIII didn't like Thomas Becket. In fact, Henry despised Thomas' memory! For Thomas had defied a King of England, while defending the Catholic Church. And the whole point of the English Reformation was that the Catholic Church had no authority over the King of England.

So in 1538, Henry VIII asked the Church of England to re-try the old case between King Henry II and Thomas Becket. As Henry wished, his court soon decided that the Catholic Church had been wrong, and that Thomas Becket was no saint.

Once the court ruled his way, Henry was free to tear down Becket's shrine. According to legend, the riches Henry carted away from the Shrine of St. Thomas Becket filled more than 20 wagons.

〰〰〰〰〰〰〰〰〰〰〰〰〰〰〰〰〰〰〰〰〰〰〰〰〰〰〰〰〰〰〰〰〰〰〰〰〰〰〰

In splitting the Church of England from the Catholic Church, the English Reformation almost split England itself. Some Englishmen were happy to become Protestant; but others wanted to stay loyal to the Catholic Church.

If **William Tyndale** had had his way, then the Church of England would have been as Protestant as any German or Swiss church.

Tyndale was an English Protestant with a gift for languages. According to legend, Tyndale knew eight different languages so well that he could speak or write any one of them just as well as he could English. Two of them were Biblical languages, Hebrew and Greek.

William Tyndale (1492? – 1536)

In the early 1520s, when the Protestant Reformation was just getting started, Tyndale set out to translate the whole Bible into English. Before the Reformation, all Bibles were in Latin— a language only priests and scholars could read. Tyndale believed that this was wrong. Like Martin Luther, William Tyndale wanted all Christians to read the Bible for themselves, in their own languages.

As we've already read, the Catholic Church didn't like Tyndale's idea. One priest warned that translating the Bible would be a big mistake— adding that it would be better for Christians to forget God's law than to forget the pope's. Tyndale answered:

> "I defy the pope, and all his laws; and if God spares my life, in a few years, I will cause the boy that drives the plow to know more of the Scriptures than you do!"

Tyndale soon moved to Protestant Germany, where he could work on his translation in peace. He published his New Testament in 1526, and worked on the Old Testament for the rest of his life.

The **Tyndale Bible** was the first English Bible that was translated directly from the three ancient tongues of the Bible: Greek, Hebrew and Aramaic.

Tyndale's translation work was so good that every English Bible since has been based partly on the Tyndale Bible.

Unfortunately, Tyndale got on the wrong side of the bad-tempered King Henry VIII. When Henry asked the Church for a divorce, Tyndale criticized him, insisting that divorce went against the Bible.

This was a mistake. In those dangerous days, one did not dare criticize Henry VIII— not if one wanted to live. When Henry's men finally caught up with Tyndale in 1536, they put him to death.

Sir Thomas More was another Englishman who paid a high price for criticizing the king's divorce. But More was different from Tyndale. Where Tyndale wanted England to go Protestant, More wanted it to stay Catholic.

More was the author of a much-read book titled ***Utopia***. He was also a high officer of the government, and a close adviser to Henry VIII.

At first, More and Henry got along quite well. When Martin Luther criticized the Catholic Church, both More and Henry criticized Luther right back.

This picture from *Foxe's Book of Martyrs* shows William Tyndale set to burn at the stake, saying "Lord, open the King of England's eyes."

But then Henry changed his mind, and started pulling away from the Catholic Church. This made More most uncomfortable. More knew very well that the Church had its problems. But he wanted to fix those problems, not tear apart the Church.

The farther Henry pulled away from the Catholic Church, the farther More pulled away from Henry. When Henry asked for his divorce from Catherine, More went along— even though he hated the idea. But when Henry split from the Catholic Church, More felt that he had no choice but to resign from the government.

Sir Thomas More
(1478 - 1535)

In the end, Thomas More wound up a lot like Thomas Becket. As friends of their kings, both Thomases should have been safe. But even close friends didn't dare disagree with the King of England.

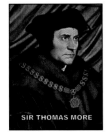

SIR THOMAS MORE

Henry's new wife, Anne Boleyn, never forgave Thomas More for criticizing the king's divorce. It was partly to please Anne that Henry charged his old friend with treason. Sir Thomas More went to the Tower of London, where he was put to death in 1535.

Divorced, Beheaded, Died...

William Tyndale and Thomas More were only two of many people put to death by Henry VIII. No King of England executed more people than Henry VIII.

In fact, not even Henry's own wives were safe from the executioner— as poor Anne Boleyn found out.

As Henry's second wife, Anne's job was to do what his first wife could not: give Henry sons. Fortunately, Anne got pregnant right away; and the pregnancy went well. After all the trouble Henry had been through, he felt sure that he would soon have the boy he had been wanting for so long.

Once again, Henry was disappointed. In 1533, Anne Boleyn gave birth to Henry's second healthy daughter: **Elizabeth Tudor**.

A second daughter might not have been so bad, if not for what came next. After Elizabeth, Anne's babies started dying, just as Catherine's had died.

After two lost babies, Henry lost patience with Anne. So he decided to get rid of her— but not in the long, drawn-out way he had gotten rid of Catherine.

Sir Thomas More was a special kind of scholar called a **Renaissance humanist**.

Humanists believed the opposite of what Protestant leaders like Luther, Zwingli and Calvin believed. Protestants taught original sin— the idea that all people were born into sin. But humanists taught that people were born good, and could become even better.

In other words, humanists believed in human progress. Thomas More believed that with good government, people could build a much better world— maybe even a heaven on earth.

The goal of More's best-known book, *Utopia*, was to explain these humanist ideas. Utopia was a made-up island where good government had already solved all of society's problems.

Since most of society's problems started with greed, the government of Utopia removed the reasons for greed. For example, there was no private property on Utopia. Instead, everyone shared everything.

An illustration from Sir Thomas More's *Utopia*

Instead, Henry had Anne arrested. In 1536, not quite 3 years into her marriage, Anne Boleyn went from a great palace to a tiny cell in the Tower of London. The charge against her was that she had carried on with other men. Under English law, that was a kind of **treason**— a crime that carried the death penalty.

On the one hand, the evidence against Anne was terribly weak. On the other hand, everyone knew that the king wanted Anne dead. Since Henry VIII always got what he wanted, the court soon sentenced Anne to death.

> To commit **treason** is to betray one's country.

The whole ugly business took less than three weeks. The only mercy Henry showed Anne was this: instead of his usual axman, Henry hired an expert swordsman from France. That way, he could be sure that his wife's head would come off in one clean stroke.

Anne had been dead less than two weeks when her heartless husband married one of her **ladies-in-waiting**. Henry's third wife, **Jane Seymour**, was just what Henry was looking for: quiet, respectful and able to have sons. In October 1537, Jane finally gave Henry the son he had been wanting for so long: **Edward Tudor**.

> A **lady-in-waiting** was a helper who waited on a queen.

Sadly, the stress of delivery wrecked Jane's health. Just 12 days after giving birth to Edward, Jane Seymour died.

Around this time, Henry VIII started having health problems of his own. One problem was that Henry was getting on towards 50 years old. Another problem was that in 1536, when Anne Boleyn was still alive, Henry suffered a bad fall in a jousting tournament. From that day forward, the king was never quite well. Before his fall, Henry was strong, athletic and handsome. After his fall, Henry grew lazy, fat— and rather hideous.

Jane Seymour, 3rd wife to Henry VIII. Jane gave birth to Edward Tudor, the future King Edward VI.

Henry's next marriage was to be a political one. With the Protestant Reformation going on, there was danger of a war between Protestant countries and Catholic ones. Since England was now Protestant, and so were parts of Germany, Henry's advisers wanted him to marry a German princess. That way, England would be sure to have German allies if war broke out.

Despite all the politics, Henry still wanted a pretty young bride. So he hired one of the best artists in Europe— a portrait painter called **Hans Holbein the Younger**. Holbein's job was to trek around Europe, painting portraits of princesses for Henry to approve.

Henry finally settled on a portrait he liked. His next wife would be **Anne of Cleves**, daughter of the Duke of Cleves. Cleves was a good-sized German duchy on the Rhine River, near the Netherlands.

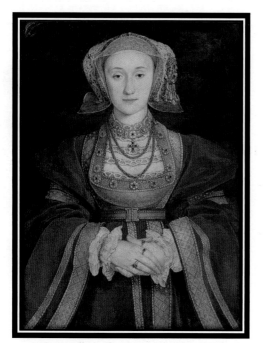

Hans Holbein the Younger's portrait of Anne of Cleves, 4th wife to King Henry VIII.

Between painting portraits and arranging the marriage, a long time passed before Anne finally came to England. By the time she did, the politics had changed, and England didn't need German allies as much. Henry also complained that Anne wasn't as pretty in real life as she was in her portrait.

Henry still married Anne; for the Germans would have been furious with him if he hadn't. After the wedding, though, he immediately looked for a way out of his unwanted marriage.

He soon found one. A few months into the marriage, Anne admitted that she had once been betrothed to a German prince. She also admitted she had never broken that betrothal properly — which meant that she never should have married Henry.

True or not, this excuse was good enough for Henry. The marriage was quickly annulled. To save Anne embarrassment, Henry gave her a comforting title: "The King's Beloved Sister." He also gave her a comfortable income.

After Anne of Cleves, Henry went back to English brides. His fifth wife, **Catherine Howard**, was a lively young woman who had served as a lady-in-waiting to Anne of Cleves. Henry married Catherine less than three weeks after he divorced Anne.

By this time, Henry was far too old and fat to make a good husband for a lively young woman. Less than two years into her marriage, Catherine Howard was beheaded for the same crime Anne Boleyn was accused of: carrying on with other men. She was not yet 20 years old when she died.

Catherine Howard, 5th wife to King Henry VIII

Henry's sixth and last wife, **Catherine Parr**, was the opposite of Catherine Howard. Where Catherine Howard was young and silly, Catherine Parr was older and more thoughtful. Even so, Catherine Parr almost didn't survive the murderous Henry VIII.

For Catherine Parr was a strong Protestant; while Henry still loved Catholic tradition. The year before Henry died, his Catholic friends almost talked him into arresting Catherine. If Catherine hadn't managed to talk Henry out of it, then she might have wound up just like Anne Boleyn and Catherine Howard.

Catherine Parr, 6th and last wife to King Henry VIII

The Six Wives of King Henry VIII

1. **Catherine of Aragon** (married 1509 - 1533)
2. **Anne Boleyn** (married 1533 - 1536)
3. **Jane Seymour** (married 1536 - 1537)
4. **Anne of Cleves** (married 1540)
5. **Catherine Howard** (married 1540 - 1541)
6. **Catherine Parr** (married 1543 - 1547)

Both Catherine Parr and Anne of Cleves outlived Henry VIII.

One way to remember the names of Henry's six wives is through this saying: "Henry married three Catherines and two Annes, but only one Jane."

One way to remember their fates is through this verse: "Divorced, beheaded, died; divorced, beheaded, survived."

The Church of England, a.k.a. the Anglican Church, never gave up some of its old Catholic traditions. For example, both Catholics and Anglicans still fast during **Lent**, the 40-day season leading up to Easter.

Lent begins on a special day called **Ash Wednesday**. The last Tuesday before Lent is called **Shrove Tuesday**— for this is the day when Anglicans are shriven of their sins. To be **shriven** is to confess and receive forgiveness.

Every Shrove Tuesday, Anglicans eat a big meal to prepare themselves for all the fasting ahead. Since eggs, butter and fat are all forbidden during Lent, most Anglicans eat pancakes on Shrove Tuesday. That way, they can use up all the eggs, butter and fat that might otherwise go to waste.

In France, Shrove Tuesday is called *Mardi Gras*, or "Fat Tuesday."

Like many kings of his day, Henry VIII made silver-colored coins with his face on them. To save money on these coins, Henry's mint first struck them out of cheap copper, and then coated them with a thin layer of precious silver.

After passing from purse to purse for a while, the silver started to wear off, showing the copper underneath— especially on Henry's nose. This explains how Henry got his unflattering nickname: "**Old Coppernose**."

Old Henry VIII coin, photo courtesy Classical Numismatic Group, Inc.

Bodies of Water around the British Isles

Many bodies of water surround the British Isles. The biggest, of course, is the **Atlantic Ocean** to the west. The next biggest is the **North Sea**, which lies to the east. Besides these, there are also:

➢ The **Irish Sea**, which lies between Ireland and northern England.

➢ The **Celtic Sea**, which lies between Ireland and southern England.

➢ **St. George's Channel**, which connects the Irish Sea to the Celtic Sea.

➢ **Bristol Channel**, a big inlet that cuts into Great Britain between Wales and southwestern England. The **Severn River**, the biggest in the British Isles, empties into Bristol Channel.

➢ The **English Channel**, which lies between England and France. The narrowest section of the English Channel, the **Strait of Dover**, is where most travelers go to cross over from England to France and back.

The Protestant Josiah

As we read in Chapter 31, King Henry VIII had three children. The oldest, **Mary Tudor**, was born to Henry's first wife: Catherine of Aragon. The middle child, **Elizabeth Tudor**, was born to Henry's second wife: Anne Boleyn. And the youngest, **Edward Tudor**, was born to Henry's third wife: Jane Seymour.

Between the three of them, the children of Henry VIII decided which the Church of England would be: Catholic or Protestant.

Mary, of course, was Catholic. For Mary was raised by Catherine of Aragon. And Catherine was a daughter to Ferdinand and Isabella, the "Catholic Monarchs" of Spain. Coming from family like that, Mary could never be anything but Catholic.

Elizabeth and Edward were different. Since both of their mothers were dead, Elizabeth and Edward were raised by Henry's 6th wife: Catherine Parr. And Catherine Parr was as strongly Protestant as Catherine of Aragon was Catholic.

⛨⛨⛨⛨⛨⛨⛨⛨⛨⛨⛨⛨⛨⛨⛨⛨⛨⛨⛨⛨⛨⛨⛨

The relationship between Mary and Elizabeth got off to a rough start. The 17-year-old Mary had many reasons to resent baby Elizabeth. Mary's father had not only divorced her beloved mother, but also split with her beloved Catholic Church— all so that he could marry Elizabeth's mother. Even worse, the divorce had made Mary an illegitimate child. Instead of having a palace and servants of her own, Mary became a servant to Elizabeth.

Three years later, Elizabeth suffered something even worse than what Mary had suffered. Elizabeth was still a toddler when her father beheaded her mother, Anne Boleyn! The disgrace of her mother left Elizabeth an illegitimate child, just like Mary.

It was in 1537, the year after Elizabeth lost her mother, that Edward came along. As the only boy, Edward was sure to be the next monarch. There was nothing Henry VIII would not do for Edward Tudor, his "whole realm's most priceless jewel."

The Old Palace at Hatfield House in Hertfordshire, just north of London. Elizabeth and Edward Tudor grew up at Hatfield House.

Kings and Queens from the Royal House of Tudor

3. King Edward VI
(Reigned 1547 - 1553)

4. Lady Jane Grey
(Reigned for 9 days in 1553)

5. Queen Mary I
(Reigned 1553 - 1558)

6. Queen Elizabeth I
(Reigned 1558 - 1603)

In fact, Henry even fought a war for Edward. From 1543 – 1551, England battled Scotland in a war with a funny name: the **War of the Rough Wooing**.

The person being **wooed** was a little girl called **Mary, Queen of Scots**. Mary was the only child of King James V of Scotland. Sadly, Mary was only six days old when James died, leaving his baby daughter on the throne of Scotland.

> To **wed** is to marry.
> To be **wooed** is to be courted for marriage.

From the moment Mary was born, Henry VIII wanted her to wed his son. By now, English kings had been trying to take over Scotland for more than 200 years. If Edward Tudor wedded Mary, Queen of Scots, then an English king might finally succeed— without firing a shot!

Of course, the Scots knew just what Henry was trying to do; and they didn't want him taking over Scotland. So instead of handing over their queen, the Scots asked the French to help them fight off the English.

In the end, the War of the Rough Wooing was all for nothing. Henry VIII never took over Scotland. And instead of wedding Edward Tudor, Mary went to live in France, where she wedded a French prince. See Year Three for more on Mary, Queen of Scots.

The mean, murderous old King Henry VIII finally died in 1547. Edward Tudor was just 9 years old when he took his father's place, becoming **King Edward VI of England**.

Since Edward was too young to run the country himself, his father had appointed a **Council of Regents** to run it for him. The leader of this council was the **Lord Protector of England**. While his job lasted, the Lord Protector

Edward Tudor in 1547, around the time his father Henry VIII died

As a young prince, Edward Tudor was probably assigned a **whipping boy** to take punishments for him. In those days, teachers didn't hesitate to whip students who misbehaved. But no one dared whip Edward Tudor— for all were terrified of Edward's father, King Henry VIII. So instead of whipping Edward himself, Edward's teachers whipped his whipping boy.

Teachers often chose a prince's best friend to be his whipping boy. That way, the prince would try harder to behave, if only to save his friend from suffering.

> Remember what a **regent** is— an officer who runs the government for a king who is too young, or too sick, to run it for himself.

would be the most powerful man in England— far more powerful than the boy king.

These were dangerous times for the Tudor family. With Henry VIII gone, the Tudors were down to just three people: a little boy, an unmarried woman and a teenage girl. And no woman had ever ruled England before— at least, not in her own name. So if anything should happen to Edward VI, then the Lord Protector might easily take his place— especially if that Lord Protector wedded Mary or Elizabeth.

An English noble called **Thomas Seymour** tried to do just that.

The king's mother, Jane Seymour, had two older brothers: **Edward Seymour** and **Thomas Seymour**. As uncles of the king, both Seymours won seats on the Council of Regents. And as the elder uncle, Edward Seymour won the top job: Lord Protector.

Like many younger brothers, Thomas was terribly jealous of his older brother. Thomas Seymour would do almost anything to take Edward Seymour's place.

It so happened that Thomas Seymour was a close friend of Henry VIII's 6th wife, Catherine Parr. In fact, Thomas and Catherine had almost married back in 1543. But then Henry decided to marry Catherine; so he sent Thomas overseas to get him out of the way.

Thomas returned to England after Henry VIII died in 1547. Later that year, Thomas took his first steps toward taking his brother's place. Unfortunately, Thomas took some crazy missteps along the way.

1. Just four months after Henry VIII died, Thomas married his old friend Catherine Parr. Loyal Englishmen saw this quick wedding as an insult to the king's memory.

2. After the wedding, Thomas moved in with Catherine. Since Elizabeth was still living with Catherine at the time, Thomas also moved in with Elizabeth. Even though Thomas had just married Catherine, he flirted shamelessly with the 14-year-old Elizabeth. Thomas may have offered to marry Elizabeth, and her sister Mary as well— even though he was already married to Catherine! To keep her husband away from Elizabeth, Catherine finally sent her away.

3. Thomas also tried to get closer to the king. As a member of the Council of Regents, Thomas knew that the king wanted more money than Edward Seymour would let him have. So Thomas secretly gave the king extra money— lots of it.

4. To get that extra money, Thomas made secret deals with pirates. This Thomas could easily do; for he was not only a regent, but also Lord High Admiral of the Royal Navy.

Thomas Seymour (1508? – 1549),
uncle to King Edward VI

5. When Thomas' brother found out about these secret pirate deals, he decided to arrest Thomas. This led to Thomas' craziest misstep yet. Late one night, Thomas tried to sneak into the king's bedroom with a loaded pistol. Just what Thomas planned to do there, no one now knows for sure. Whatever his plan was, it didn't work out— for as he tried to sneak in, he accidentally woke one of the king's dogs. To keep the dog off him, Thomas had to pull out his pistol and shoot the king's dog!

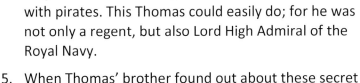

Imagine trying to explain why you have just shot the king's dog outside the king's bedroom, in the middle of the night! Nothing Thomas could say made any difference. Thomas Seymour went straight to the Tower of London, where he was beheaded for treason in March 1549.

♏♏♏

Remember what the **English Reformation** was— the long process of splitting the Church of England from the Catholic Church.

The fact that King Edward VI was only a boy didn't stop him from playing a huge part in the **English Reformation**. It was King Henry VIII who split the Church of England from the Catholic Church. But it was King Edward VI who made the Church of England Protestant— with help from his friend **Thomas Cranmer, Archbishop of Canterbury**.

Cranmer won the archbishop's job in 1532, when Henry VIII was still king. Cranmer's first job as archbishop was to give Henry his divorce from Catherine of Aragon (Chapter 31).

But Cranmer also had a more important job: guiding the Church of England through the Protestant Reformation. After Henry's split with Rome, the Church of England had a chance to become a whole new kind of church. Thomas Cranmer helped decide what that new church would be.

Like Luther and Zwingli, Cranmer wanted his new church to be more like the churches in the Bible. But Cranmer had to be careful; for he knew that Henry wouldn't hesitate to behead him if he made a mistake.

Henry was happy to make certain changes. For example, Henry shut down all of England's monasteries— partly because he wanted their money for his royal treasury (Chapter 31).

Henry also brought English-language Bibles to the Church of England. The year 1539 saw the first printing of the **Great Bible**— the first English Bible ever authorized by a King of England. The Great Bible was mostly the work of William Tyndale, the great translator whom Henry had executed in 1536 (Chapter 31).

But the biggest changes to the Church of England came under King Edward VI. Unlike Henry, Edward was a strong Protestant who wanted nothing to do with Catholic tradition. To Edward, Catholic traditions were more than just wrong. They were the very opposite of what God wanted.

The tradition Edward hated most was the **Catholic Mass**— in other words, the Catholic celebration of Holy Communion. To Protestants, all of the bells and incense that went into a Catholic Mass made it seem more pagan than Christian. And no Protestant believed in **transubstantiation**— the idea that the bread and wine actually transformed into the body and blood of Jesus Christ (Chapter 30).

So Edward outlawed the Catholic Mass.

In 1549, Parliament passed the first of several laws called the **Act of Uniformity**. From then on, no English church was to hold a Catholic Mass. Instead, all English churches were to follow the Protestant communion service in the new book Thomas Cranmer had just finished: the **Book of Common Prayer**.

Remember who the **Archbishop of Canterbury** was— the head bishop of all English churches.

Archbishop Thomas Cranmer (1489 – 1556)

The **Book of Common Prayer** was a worship book written for the Church of England by Archbishop Thomas Cranmer. Besides the communion service, the Book of Common Prayer also offered services for baptisms, weddings, funerals and more— all written out word-for-word, exactly as Cranmer wanted them spoken.

Although the Book of Common Prayer has changed over the years, the Church of England still uses parts of Cranmer's work. So do two churches that sprang from the Church of England: the Episcopal Church and the Methodist Church.

Banning the Mass was only one of many things Edward did to make the Church of England more Protestant. He also declared that all Church of England services were to be spoken in English, not Latin. And unlike Catholic priests, English priests were free to marry and have children— just like all other Christians.

ⅡⅡⅡⅡⅡⅡⅡⅡⅡⅡⅡⅡⅡⅡⅡⅡⅡⅡⅡⅡⅡⅡⅡⅡⅡⅡⅡⅡⅡⅡⅡⅡⅡ

Alas, the story of King Edward VI ended sadly— for Edward, and for all English Protestants.

In early 1553, when he was still just 15 years old, Edward came down with a bad cough. Instead of getting better, Edward got worse. By May, Edward's doctors had to admit the awful truth: that the young King of England would soon die.

After months of miserable health, Edward didn't mind dying. But he minded very much what might happen to the Church of England after he died.

Since Edward had no children, the law left the throne to his oldest sister Mary. And since Mary was a Catholic, the Church of England would be Catholic again— after everything Edward had done to make it Protestant!

Edward couldn't let that happen. So before he died, Edward tried to change the law. Instead of leaving the throne to his Catholic sister, Edward tried to leave it to a Protestant: a 16-year-old girl called the **Lady Jane Grey**.

Who on Earth was Jane Grey, and how could she possibly claim the throne of England?

The first answer is that on her mother's side, Jane was a granddaughter to the youngest sister of King Henry VIII. In other words, Jane was Edward's first cousin, one generation removed— which did give her some small claim to the throne.

The second answer may be more important. Besides being a cousin to the king, Jane Grey was the wife of **Guildford Dudley**— son of **John Dudley**, head of the Council of Regents.

By now, Lord Protector Edward Seymour had been beheaded for treason, just like his brother Thomas Seymour (above). The new head of the Council of Regents was John Dudley, Duke of Northumberland. Since the king was so sick, John Dudley had a lot to say about the king's decisions.

Like Edward VI, John Dudley wanted the next ruler of England to be a Protestant. But Dudley also wanted the next ruler to be his son's wife. That way, Dudley's son might become King of England through his wife. At the very least, Dudley's grandson would be king. Then the dying House of Tudor would give way to a new royal house: the House of Dudley!

Unfortunately for Dudley, things didn't work out that way.

House of Tudor Rose

Archbishop Thomas Cranmer gave King Edward VI a Biblical nickname: the **"Protestant Josiah."**

The first Josiah was a young king of Judah, the southern kingdom of the Israelites. Josiah's grandfather, King Manasseh of Judah, was a wicked king who turned his people away from God, teaching them to worship idols instead. When the good King Josiah came along, he led his people back to God.

This was Thomas Cranmer's hope for the boy King Edward VI: that he would lead his people back to God, just as Josiah had.

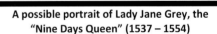

A possible portrait of Lady Jane Grey, the "Nine Days Queen" (1537 – 1554)

Bloody Mary

Dudley's troubles started on July 9, 1553— three days after King Edward VI died at age 15. That was the day when Dudley finally told Jane Grey that she was the new Queen of England. Before then, Jane hadn't even known that Edward was dead.

Dudley had been keeping Edward's death secret. For these were dangerous days. Most people expected Edward's sister, Mary Tudor, to be queen. If Jane was to be queen instead, then Dudley would have to do something about Mary— and fast.

John Dudley, Duke of Northumberland (1504? – 1553)

He was already working on it. Dudley had sent for Mary days before, asking her to come see her brother one last time before he died. Once Mary reached London, she would be at Dudley's mercy. If Mary tried to claim the throne, then Dudley could simply lock Mary in the Tower of London until the trouble blew over.

But Mary had more friends than Dudley new. Before Mary reached London, a friend warned her that she was walking into a trap— that Edward was already dead, that Jane Grey was already queen, and that Dudley meant to lock her up the moment she reached London.

So Mary changed her plans. Instead of going to London, Mary went to the east coast, where she could do one of two things. If possible, she would raise an army to overthrow Jane. If that failed, then she could still flee across the North Sea, where her Spanish relatives would protect her.

As it turned out, Mary had no trouble at all raising an army. All Englishmen knew Mary's story; and most of them felt sorry for the rough way her father had treated her. On the other hand, few Englishmen had even heard of Jane Grey.

When news of Mary's growing army reached London, the Council of Regents turned its back on Jane Grey. The next day, John Dudley gave up without a fight. He was beheaded for treason a month later.

As for poor Jane Grey, she went from a royal palace to a tiny cell in the Tower of London. She had been queen, sort of, for just about 9 days— from July 10 – 19, 1553.

Meanwhile, Mary Tudor became **Queen Mary I of England**— the first woman in history to rule England in her own name.

Queen Mary I entering London with her sister Elizabeth Tudor

Mary's reign was a terrible time to be an English Protestant. Before Mary, many Englishmen weren't sure whether they wanted to be Catholic or Protestant. But after Mary, most Englishmen were quite sure that they didn't want to be Catholic.

First of all, Mary undid everything Henry VIII and Edward VI had done. After almost 20 years of independence, the Church of England went back under the Catholic Church. The Catholic Mass was restored, and the Book of Common Prayer set aside.

If changing the church was all Mary had done, then she might have had less trouble than she did. But changing the church was only the beginning.

As a good Catholic, Mary wanted a Catholic husband to give her Catholic sons. That way, a Catholic would be sure to inherit her throne when she was gone.

The husband Mary chose was one of the most powerful Catholics alive: **Philip of Spain**. Philip was the son of **King Charles I of Spain** (who was also Holy Roman Emperor Charles V). Since Charles and Mary were first cousins, Philip and Mary were first cousins once removed. By this time, Charles was getting ready to retire, leaving Philip to take over as King of Spain.

Queen Mary I, a.k.a. "Bloody Mary"

Most Englishmen wished that Mary would find some other husband. Even Catholics feared what might happen to England if Philip became king. The Spanish Empire was already huge, and getting huger. Poor England might be swallowed up by the Spanish Empire, losing its independence forever!

As for Protestants, they were all dead set against the marriage— which is why they started Wyatt's Rebellion.

Sir **Thomas Wyatt** was a well-known military man and Member of Parliament. Like most Englishmen of his day, Wyatt had been born and raised Catholic. But Wyatt had also been to Spain, where he had seen the **Spanish Inquisition** first-hand (Chapter 23). After that dreadful experience, the last thing Wyatt wanted was a Spanish King of

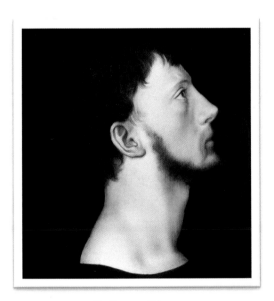
Sir Thomas Wyatt

England— least of all Philip of Spain, whose family had started the Inquisition.

The plan for Wyatt's Rebellion was to replace Mary with her younger sister: Elizabeth Tudor. For Elizabeth was a Protestant; and no Protestant would ever marry Philip of Spain. With Elizabeth as queen, Protestants' troubles would be over.

> Remember what the **Spanish Inquisition** was— a cruel church court established by Ferdinand and Isabella to hunt down heretics. The Inquisition was famous for two things: torturing people until they confessed to heresy, and then burning them to death.

But Wyatt never got the chance. Wyatt's Rebellion had hardly started when Mary discovered it, and put a stop to it. On his way to replace Mary, Wyatt was captured and beheaded. Mary wedded Philip later that same year, 1554.

The year after that, Wyatt's worst fears came true. With Philip of Spain at her side, Mary brought her own version of the Spanish Inquisition to England. This is when Queen Mary I of England earned the nickname she would carry into history:

Bloody Mary.

Starting in 1555, Mary ordered English church courts to place Protestants on trial for heresy. To save themselves, the accused had to admit two main things: that the Catholic Church was the one true Church of God; and that the Catholic Mass was the right way to celebrate communion.

As in Roman times, Christians faced a terrible choice. They could either lie to save themselves, or suffer one of the worst punishments imaginable: being burned alive.

One of the sadder results of Wyatt's Rebellion was what happened to Jane Grey. Although Jane had nothing to do with the rebellion, her father Henry Grey did. Poor Jane Grey was not yet 18 years old when Bloody Mary beheaded her for her father's part in Wyatt's Rebellion. Jane's husband Guildford Dudley was beheaded earlier that same day.

"The Execution of Lady Jane Grey" by artist Paul Delaroche. The helpful man at Jane's side is guiding her to the executioner's block, which poor Jane can't see through her blindfold.

Exactly how many Protestants Bloody Mary burned alive, no one now knows for sure. Some say no more than about 300; while others say far more. Either way, the years from 1555 – 1558 were deadly years for English Protestants.

The **Marian martyrs** were English Protestants who were tortured and killed during Bloody Mary's reign.

The **Marian exiles** were English Protestants who fled overseas to escape Bloody Mary.

The stories of the Marian martyrs were told by a Marian exile. In 1563, author John Foxe published the first edition of one of the best-known books of all time: *Foxe's Book of Martyrs.* This long book is packed with details about the great faith of the Marian martyrs, and how they suffered and died for that faith.

Sometimes, lying wasn't enough to save Protestants— as poor Thomas Cranmer found out.

As we read above, Thomas Cranmer was the Protestant Archbishop of Canterbury who served under Henry VIII and Edward VI. Mary had always hated Cranmer— mostly because Cranmer had helped Mary's father divorce her mother. But in 1553, Cranmer committed his last, worst offence against Mary: he supported Jane Grey as queen. Thus Cranmer was marked for death from the moment Bloody Mary became queen.

The Catholics who handled Cranmer's trial lied to him. They promised that all would be forgiven, if Cranmer would only take back all the ugly things he'd said about Catholics. After two torturous years in prison, Cranmer finally did what they asked. With his right hand, he signed a confession saying just what Catholics wanted him to say.

If the Catholic Church had followed its own law, then Cranmer's confession would have saved his life. Instead, the Church decided to kill him anyway.

This woodblock illustration from *Foxe's Book of Martyrs* shows Thomas Cranmer thrusting his right hand into one of Bloody Mary's fires

The new Archbishop of Canterbury wanted to make an example of Cranmer. He wanted him to admit, out loud and in public, just how wrong Protestants were. So before Cranmer faced the flames, the archbishop let him preach one last sermon.

The archbishop thought he knew what was coming. Before the day of the sermon, Cranmer wrote out every word he planned to say— all about how wrong Protestants were.

But when the day arrived, Cranmer didn't preach the sermon he'd written. Instead, he said that he'd only signed that Catholic confession to save his life. Now that he was about to die anyway, he could tell the world what he truly believed: that Catholics were wrong, and Protestants were right!

Naturally, the archbishop was furious. Cranmer was burned alive that same day. As the flames rose in front of him, Cranmer bravely thrust his right hand into them, and left it there— to punish that hand for signing a Catholic confession that he didn't believe.

⛧⛧⛧

Bloody Mary kept right on torturing and burning Protestants for as long as she lived. Fortunately for Protestants, Bloody Mary didn't live very long.

One day in November 1558, a horseman raced into Smithfield, London with big news. Smithfield was the section of London where many Protestants went to die in Mary's fires. In fact, several Protestants were tied to stakes in Smithfield that very day, waiting for executioners to set fire to them.

But the horseman told the executioners to stop— for Bloody Mary had just died, which meant that Protestants could stop dying.

Queen Elizabeth I in a coronation robe lined with ermine fur

An **ermine** is a big weasel with a special kind of fur. Ermine fur is brown in summer. But in winter, ermine fur turns white to blend into the snow. The only part that isn't white is the tip of the tail, which stays black year-round.

White fur was so rare, and so valuable, that ermine fur became a symbol of royalty. In cold countries like England, royals wore beautiful coronation robes lined with warm, white ermine fur. The short black lines in these robes' linings were the ermines' black tails, stitched in right alongside their white fur.

CHURCH HISTORY

The Anabaptist Movement

Sadly, Bloody Mary wasn't the only one who burned Protestants alive. Both Protestants and Catholics burned **Anabaptists**.

As we've read, the Reformation started with the Bible. Before the Reformation, most Christians never read the Bible, nor even heard very much of it. But things were different now. Between the Reformation and that all-important invention, the printing press, more people were reading the Bible than ever before. The problem was, not everyone who read the Bible understood it the same way.

Anabaptist means "to baptize again." Instead of baptizing people as infants, Anabaptists only baptized people who were old enough to understand the gospel. Since most of the people they baptized had already been baptized as infants, their enemies called them "re-baptizers."

The Anabaptist movement started with a new understanding of the **Sermon on the Mount**, which appears in Matthew 5 – 7. For example, Jesus says in Matthew 5:33-34:

"… you have heard that it was said to the people long ago, 'Do not break your oath, but fulfill to the Lord the vows you have made.' But I tell you, do not swear an oath at all…"

Most Christians didn't take Jesus' words literally. They assumed that some oaths were necessary— especially the oath of fealty to one's king or queen. To Anabaptists, though, Jesus meant exactly what He said: that true Christians must never swear any oath for any reason.

Another example comes from Matthew 5:38-39, where Jesus says:

"You have heard that it was said, 'Eye for eye, and tooth for tooth.' But I tell you, do not resist an evil person. If anyone slaps you on the right cheek, turn to them the other cheek also."

Again, most Christians didn't take Jesus' words literally. They assumed that some fighting was necessary. If criminals attacked Christians, then surely Christian police must protect those Christians? And if an enemy attacked a Christian kingdom, then surely Christian soldiers must defend that kingdom?

The Anabaptists saw things differently. Once again, they thought that Jesus meant exactly what he said: that true Christians must never fight for any reason.

**"Sermon on the Mount"
by Carl Bloch**

Why? Because to Anabaptists, there was no such thing as a Christian kingdom— at least, not an earthly one. In Anabaptist eyes, all true Christians belonged to just one kingdom: the Kingdom of Heaven. Since no one can serve two masters (Matthew 6:24), Anabaptists chose to serve their heavenly king, and ignore their earthly kings.

Being citizens of heaven meant cutting ties with all earthly kingdoms. Since Anabaptists wouldn't swear oaths, they couldn't swear in court like everyone else. And since Anabaptists wouldn't fight, they couldn't be policemen, nor serve in armies like everyone else.

In the eyes of most Christians, this made all Anabaptists traitors! Anabaptists who refused to fight for their countries were tortured and killed wherever they lived. Many, many Anabaptists died horrible deaths for their faith.

Just as *Foxe's Book of Martyrs* tells stories of the Marian martyrs, so a long book called *Martyrs' Mirror* tells stories of the many Anabaptist martyrs who died for their faith.

The best-known Anabaptists of modern times are the **Mennonites**, named for an Anabaptist leader called <u>Menno</u> Simons (1496 – 1561).

CHAPTER 33:

Queen Elizabeth I; William Shakespeare

The Last of the Tudors

In Chapter 32, we read part of what happened when King Edward VI died. Lord John Dudley, head of the Council of Regents, laid a trap for Edward's sister Mary— hoping to make Jane Grey queen instead of Mary.

What we didn't read is that Dudley also laid a trap for Mary's sister Elizabeth. Dudley sent the same message to Elizabeth that he sent to Mary. He asked both to come to London so that they could see their brother one last time before he died.

Like Mary, Elizabeth was too clever to fall into Dudley's trap. When Dudley's messenger showed up at her door, Elizabeth pretended that she was too sick to travel.

A few days later, Dudley surrendered without a fight. And a few weeks after that, Mary Tudor rode into London as the new Queen of England.

Mary didn't ride alone. Elizabeth rode into London with Mary that day, showing all the world that she supported her sister. She wanted everyone to know that she had no intention of going against Mary.

But was that really true?

As we read in Chapter 32, English Protestants soon rebelled against Mary. The first goal of **Wyatt's Rebellion** was to stop Mary's wedding to Philip of Spain.

One day, Mary's spies intercepted a letter written by the leader of Wyatt's Rebellion. Sir Thomas Wyatt's letter revealed another goal of the rebellion. After getting rid of the Catholic Mary, Wyatt hoped to set her Protestant sister Elizabeth on the throne!

Of all the details in Wyatt's letter, the one Mary's spies found most interesting was the name on the envelope. It was addressed to Elizabeth!

This time, pretending to be sick did Elizabeth no good. Thanks to Wyatt's letter, Elizabeth was soon locked up in the Tower of London.

The trip to the Tower must have terrified Elizabeth. For one thing, the Tower was where her poor mother Anne Boleyn had been beheaded. Like her mother, Elizabeth entered the Tower by the **Traitors' Gate**— a water gate that opened on the Thames River. When the royal guards arrested a noble, they usually brought him in through the Traitor's Gate. That way, they could avoid trouble with the crowds on the streets.

To reach the Traitors' Gate, Elizabeth had to pass under the famous **London Bridge**. In those days, London Bridge was a wide stone bridge lined with wooden shops. With Wyatt's Rebellion going on, London Bridge was also lined with something else: the

The Tower of London with the Traitors' Gate opening on the Thames River. London Bridge stands in the background.

~~~ 337 ~~~

heads of beheaded rebels! Mary's spies set the heads there as a reminder of the gruesome fate that awaited rebels. In passing by, Elizabeth might have recognized the heads of some nobles she had known.

Fortunately for Elizabeth, nothing in Wyatt's letter proved that she was actually involved in Wyatt's Rebellion. All the letter proved was that Wyatt had wanted Elizabeth to be queen.

Mary's spies questioned Elizabeth for hours on end, desperate to prove that she had ordered the rebellion. If they had found any proof, then Mary would have beheaded her right away. But they never did.

Some of Mary's Catholic friends wanted her to behead Elizabeth anyway. For Elizabeth was the last of the Protestant Tudors. With Elizabeth out of the way, there would be no more Protestants left to claim the throne of England.

Fortunately for Elizabeth, Philip of Spain didn't want Elizabeth beheaded. Philip feared that the English people might have blamed him for Elizabeth's death— which would make it even harder for Philip and Mary to wed.

One of many portraits of Queen Elizabeth I, a.k.a. "Good Queen Bess"

Thus Elizabeth was saved, by the skin of her teeth. After two months in the Tower of London, Elizabeth spent a year under house arrest. After that, she and Mary got along fairly well. Even so, there was always the chance that "Bloody Mary" might change her mind and kill her Protestant sister.

That chance ended in 1558, when Mary died. Since Mary had no children, her sister took her place. The 25-year-old Elizabeth Tudor became **Queen Elizabeth I of England**— the last monarch from the royal House of Tudor.

> The coronation of Queen Elizabeth marked the beginning of an important time in English history called the **Elizabethan Era.**

Kings and Queens from the Royal House of Tudor

3. King Edward VI
(Reigned 1547 - 1553)

4. Lady Jane Grey
(Reigned for 9 days in 1553)

5. Queen Mary I
(Reigned 1553 - 1558)

6. Queen Elizabeth I
(Reigned 1558 - 1603)

The Elizabethan Religious Settlement

Elizabeth's first job as queen was to answer an important question. Was England to be Catholic, or Protestant?

This question had been tearing England apart for Elizabeth's whole life. First, Henry VIII had broken with the Catholic Church— mostly because he wanted a divorce, and the pope wouldn't give it to him. Then, the Church of England had gone strictly Protestant under Edward VI— only to turn strictly Catholic again under Mary I.

Worst of all, "Bloody Mary" had just spent the last three years burning Protestants to death. After that, Protestants and

Catholics hated each other more than ever. If Englishmen were ever going to trust each other again, then Elizabeth had to decide: would England be Catholic, Protestant or somewhere in between?

Fortunately, Elizabeth was the perfect person to decide. For Elizabeth was less fussy about religion than Edward and Mary had been. She knew that if Protestants and Catholics were going to get along, then they would have to do something neither wanted to do: they would have to **compromise**.

Elizabeth wanted two main things from her compromise. First, she wanted all Englishmen to worship together in **state churches**. She believed that England could never be strong without a strong state church. Second, Elizabeth wanted all Englishmen to be loyal to queen and country.

> To **compromise** is to give away part of what one wants to gain another part.
> A **state church** is one that goes hand-in-hand with the state government.

As always, the biggest problem was Holy Communion. How could Catholics and Protestants possibly celebrate communion together? To Protestants, all of the bells and incense that went into a Catholic Mass made it seem more pagan than Christian. And no Protestant believed in **transubstantiation**— the idea that the bread and wine actually transformed into the body and blood of Jesus Christ (Chapter 30). But to Catholics, transubstantiation was the whole point of communion.

Elizabeth's answer was a small change to the **Book of Common Prayer**. In 1559, the year after Elizabeth became queen, the Church of England wrote a new Book of Common Prayer. The new communion service said:

> Remember what the **Book of Common Prayer** was— a worship book that was first written for the Church of England by Archbishop Thomas Cranmer in the days of King Edward VI.

"The body of our Lord Jesus Christ, which was given for thee, preserve thy body and soul… Take and eat this in remembrance that Christ died for thee, and feed on Him in thy heart by faith with thanksgiving."

Catholics who read this service could focus on the words "feed on Him." This sounded like the bread and wine really were the body and blood of Christ. Protestants who read it could focus on the words "in remembrance" and "by faith"— which sounded more Protestant. If both sides behaved themselves, then Catholics and Protestants could worship together in peace.

But there was one compromise Elizabeth wouldn't make.

Like her father before her, Elizabeth wrote a law called the Act of Supremacy (Chapter 31). After five Catholic years under Bloody Mary, the Church of England became independent again— completely separate from the Catholic Church. All Englishmen were to forget the pope, and obey their queen.

This means that in the end, the Church of England was much more Protestant than Catholic. For a key part of being Catholic was to obey the pope, which England no longer did.

Canterbury Cathedral, home church to the Archbishop of Canterbury

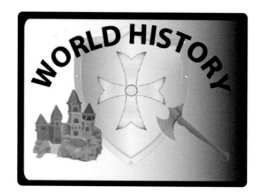

England versus Spain in the New World

Like Spain, England sent its first ships to the New World in the late 1400s. But unlike the Spanish, the English waited almost 100 years to build their first colonies in the New World. And even then, those first colonies didn't last.

The first explorer England sent wasn't even an

Englishman. In 1496, King Henry VII hired an Italian sea captain called John Cabot to do for England what Columbus had already done for Spain: discover new lands and new riches.

At the time, no one knew that Columbus had discovered a whole New World. Like Columbus, Cabot was trying to reach the Far East by sailing westward around the globe. He didn't know that the Americas stood in his way.

But Cabot added a twist of his own to Columbus' ideas. Columbus tried to circle the globe near the equator; but Cabot wanted to circle it in the north. He knew that the distance around the globe must be shorter in the north— which should mean a shorter trip to the Far East.

John Cabot sailed due west from Bristol, England in May 1497. After passing Iceland, then Greenland on his right, Cabot struck land somewhere in northeastern North America— probably in what is now Newfoundland, Canada.

Wherever he may have landed, Cabot claimed the whole east coast of North America for England. Years later, England would base its claim to North America on the fact that John Cabot got there before any other explorer.

〰〰〰〰〰〰〰〰〰〰〰〰〰〰〰〰〰〰〰〰〰〰〰〰〰〰〰〰〰〰〰〰〰

Meanwhile, the Spanish had already settled their first colonies in the West Indies, and were already starting to get rich.

Back in Chapter 25, we read how Christopher Columbus took over the gold mines on Hispaniola. He did it by winning the strange **Battle of Santo Cerro**. That battle fell in 1495, two years before John Cabot found Newfoundland. The Spanish were already mining gold and shipping it home before the English even made it to Newfoundland.

From an Italian mural featuring Giovanni Caboto, a.k.a. John Cabot (1450? – 1499?)

Hispaniola was only the beginning. Over the next 30 years or so, the **Spanish conquistadors** conquered all the main islands of the West Indies. In 1521, Hernan Cortes conquered the Aztec Empire of Middle America, winning a huge fortune. Then in 1532, Francisco Pizarro conquered the Inca Empire of South America, winning an even huger fortune.

Later, the Spanish turned from conquering to mining. Around 1546, in what is now Bolivia, South America, the Spanish discovered one of the richest silver

Remember who the **Spanish conquistadors** were— the soldiers who conquered the West Indies, Middle America and part of South America for the Spanish Empire.

mines ever: a mountain called **Cerro de Potosi**. This mountain was so full of silver that it almost seemed to be made of the stuff. From the 1550s on, Spanish ships carried tons of silver and gold from the New World to Spain every year.

Naturally, any ship filled with silver and gold made a tempting target for pirates. So the Spanish didn't send ships alone. Instead, they assigned fast, well-armed warships to protect slow cargo ships as they sailed to the New World and back.

These combinations of cargo ships and warships were called the **Spanish treasure fleets**. By Queen Elizabeth's day, the Spanish were running one or two treasure fleets to and from the New World every year.

> Remember what the *Quinto Real* was— Spanish for "King's Fifth." Under Spanish law, one-fifth of all precious metals from the New World automatically went to the King of Spain. The Quinto Real helped make Spain the richest country in Europe.

> The **Spanish treasure fleets** were groups of ships that carried silver, gold and other treasures from the New World to Spain. Anywhere from about 20 – 50 ships traveled together, protecting each other from pirates.

The richer Spain grew, the more Elizabeth worried. Catholic Spain was an enemy to all Protestants. The new King of Spain was Mary's old husband: Philip of Spain, who was now called King Philip II. Philip II had turned out to be just like his father Charles I— just as determined to make all countries Catholic again. The Spanish were already fighting Protestants in the nearby Netherlands. Elizabeth feared that they might do the same in England— unless she did something to stop the Spanish treasure fleets.

The problem was, what to do? How could England possibly stop the Spanish treasure fleets without going to war with Spain— which was the very thing Elizabeth was trying to avoid?

The answer lay in something called a **privateer**.

A **privateer** was the captain of a privately-owned ship with a special mission: to attack enemy trade ships. Instead of sending her Royal Navy to attack the Spanish treasure fleets, Elizabeth sent privateers.

Spanish ships at the port of Nombre de Dios, Panama

Privateers were a lot like pirates, and a lot like navy captains. Like pirates, they stole cargoes from other ships— sometimes killing sailors in the process. And like navy captains, they attacked their country's enemies on orders from their government.

The difference was that privateers helped Elizabeth shift the blame. Each time privateers attacked, Spain sent ambassadors to complain. But Elizabeth never admitted that her privateers were acting on her orders. Instead, she pretended not to know her privateers. "Whoever attacked you doesn't work for me," she would tell the ambassadors. "He must be a lawless pirate. How very unfortunate for you."

The greatest of all English privateers was **Sir Francis Drake**, captain of a powerful warship called *Golden Hind*. Drake was a patriotic Protestant who hated Catholics, and especially Spanish Catholics, all his life.

One reason Drake hated the Spanish was because of something that happened in 1568. In that year, Drake was aboard one of several English trade ships that showed up in Veracruz, Mexico— a port of the Spanish Empire. Drake and his friends had brought cargo to sell. That cargo probably included slaves from Africa.

If the cargo did include slaves, then that would explain why the Spanish attacked. In those days, all slave traders needed special permission from the Crown of Spain. Since no Englishman had permission, the Spanish let fly with their cannon.

If Drake hadn't known how to swim, then he would have gone down with his ship then and there! As it was, Drake swam to safety, escaping on one of the two English

Portrait of Sir Francis Drake (1540? – 1596)

ships the Spanish didn't sink. From that day forward, Drake was a deadly enemy to all Spaniards.

A few years later, Drake returned to the New World to take his revenge. One day in 1573, Drake left his ships at anchor while he led an attack inland. His target: a Spanish mule train carrying treasure from mines like Cerro de Potosi to the port of Nombre de Dios, Panama.

The attack was a huge success. When it was over, Drake and his men made off with 20 – 30 tons of treasure— so much that they couldn't possibly carry it all! So they buried most of it. Later, they went back to dig up their buried pirate treasure. Since England didn't have treasure fleets like Spain's, Queen Elizabeth was quite pleased with her share of the huge treasure from Nombre de Dios.

Drake's greatest mission came a few years later. By this time, the Spanish were getting used to attacks in the Atlantic Ocean. But no one had ever attacked them in the Pacific Ocean before. So in 1578, Drake sailed around the southern tip of South America, hoping to take the Spanish by surprise.

Since the Spanish had never needed defenses in the Pacific before, they were all but defenseless there. In a few months, *Golden Hind* was completely stuffed with stolen treasure.

Drake's next problem was how to get all that treasure home.

With *Golden Hind* getting leaky, Drake needed to stop for repairs. But he also needed to avoid the Spanish. So he sailed far to the north, beyond where the Spanish usually sailed.

At some hidden spot on the west coast of North America, Drake built a temporary base called *Nova Albion*— Latin for "New Britain." Nova Albion may have lain on what is now Drakes Bay, California, just north of San Francisco Bay.

Wherever it was, Nova Albion was the first English base on the west coast of North America!

Golden Hind **off the coast of what is now California**

Once he finished his repairs, Drake needed a safe route home. After all he'd stolen from the Spanish, he wanted to keep well away from all the Spanish ports in South America. So instead of sailing south, this incredible seaman sailed west, all the way around the world.

Drake finally made it back to England in 1580, three years after he'd left. The amount of treasure he brought home was astonishing. Queen Elizabeth's share alone was a huge fortune— about the same as the amount of tax money her government collected from all of England that year!

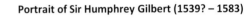

As far as anyone knows, Francis Drake left no colonists behind at Nova Albion. If he had, then Nova Albion might have been the first English colony in North America. Instead, Nova Albion was a temporary base.

But the first colony wasn't far behind. In August 1583, **Sir Humphrey Gilbert** built the first English colony on Newfoundland— the island John Cabot had discovered back in 1497.

One thing John Cabot had noticed about Newfoundland was the huge number of fish there. In places, the codfish were so thick that catching them was ridiculously easy. All a fisherman had to do was lower a basket into the water, and it came up full of cod!

Portrait of Sir Humphrey Gilbert (1539? – 1583)

From then on, fishing ships sailed to Newfoundland every summer— not just English ships, but also French and Dutch ones. But no one stayed at Newfoundland year-round, for a simple reason: because Newfoundland winters were too cold! Some Newfoundland harbors froze solid every winter, especially on the north side of the island. So Europeans built no colonies on Newfoundland, even though they visited every year.

Until Sir Humphrey Gilbert came along. In 1578, Queen Elizabeth issued a **royal charter** with Gilbert's name on it. Gilbert now had the queen's permission to settle an English colony in any "heathen and barbarous lands not... inhabited by Christian people." This charter was to last six years.

> A **royal charter** was a paper granting a certain person permission to do a certain thing in the queen's name.

DISCOVERIES IN THE NORTH

BAFFIN BAY · GREENLAND · Iceland · Norwegian Sea · DAVIS STRAIT · HUDSON STRAIT · STRAIT OF DENMARK · HUDSON BAY · LABRADOR SEA · Scotland · North Sea · Ireland · England · Quebec · Ontario · NEW FOUNDLAND · Gulf of St. Lawrence · St John's · LAKE SUPERIOR · LAKE HURON · LAKE ONTARIO · English Channel · France · LAKE MICHIGAN · Nova Scotia · LAKE ERIE · ATLANTIC OCEAN · Portugal · Spain · NORTH AMERICA · ROANOKE ISLAND · AFRICA · SPAIN

Gilbert's six years were almost up before he finally scraped together enough money to go to Newfoundland. Upon reaching Newfoundland in August 1583, Gilbert officially took possession of the big island in the name of the queen. From now on, Gilbert said, Newfoundland belonged to England alone.

Unfortunately, Gilbert couldn't stay in Newfoundland. Like everyone else, Gilbert was completely unprepared for the bitter cold of a Newfoundland winter. So Gilbert tried to go home.

But on the way, storms overtook Gilbert's small vessel, and he was lost at sea. Without Sir Humphrey Gilbert, the first English colony in the New World disappeared for good.

𝕎𝕎𝕎𝕎𝕎𝕎𝕎𝕎𝕎𝕎𝕎𝕎𝕎𝕎𝕎𝕎𝕎𝕎𝕎𝕎𝕎𝕎𝕎𝕎𝕎

With Gilbert gone and his charter expired, Queen Elizabeth issued a new charter for a new colony. This charter went to a charming friend of the queen, **Sir Walter Raleigh**.

Unlike Humphrey Gilbert, Walter Raleigh didn't go to the New World himself— at least, not at first. Instead, he paid ship's captains and governors to build his colony.

Raleigh chose a risky place for his first colony. **Roanoke Island** lay just off the coast of what is now North Carolina— dangerously close to the West Indies, where the Spanish Empire ruled.

Raleigh had two good reasons for choosing Roanoke Island. The first was so that English privateers could use his colony as a base for attacking the Spanish. The second reason was copper. The natives of Roanoke Island had already found copper, and Raleigh hoped to find more. Although copper wasn't as pricey as gold or silver, it was still a valuable resource— something the colony might use to pay for itself.

Portrait of Sir Walter Raleigh (1554? – 1618)

NATIVE COPPER

Roanoke Colony got off to a rocky start.

The first group of colonists reached Roanoke Island in July 1585. After exploring a bit, they built a small wooden fort near the northern end of the island.

Since the island was only about 2 miles wide and 8 miles long, the natives were never far away. Fortunately, most of them were friendly enough at first.

That is, until a silver cup that belonged to the colony went missing. The saddest thing about Roanoke Colony is how many people had to suffer and die over this one silver cup!

Although they didn't know for sure, the colonists believed that a native from a certain village must have stolen the cup. So they marched into this village and commanded the thief to step forward. When no one did, they burned the whole village to the ground— along with all of the food the villagers had stored for winter!

Obviously, the natives were a lot less friendly after that. When the ships that had brought the colonists left, the natives attacked the fort!

After that, the colonists were afraid to stay on Roanoke any longer. When Francis Drake happened to drop by with a small fleet, they begged him to take them home— which Drake did. Roanoke Colony was abandoned.

The Roanoke colonists who returned to England with Sir Francis Drake in 1586 carried three important plants with them: **tobacco**, **potatoes** and **maize** (also called **Indian corn**). All of these plants were well-known in the Americas, but completely unknown in England.

The first time Sir Walter Raleigh smoked a bit of tobacco from Roanoke, a servant doused him with water— thinking that his lord's head must have somehow caught fire.

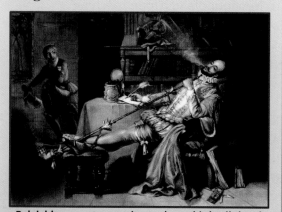

Raleigh's servant preparing to douse his lord's head

A week later, the ships that had brought the colonists to Roanoke returned to find an empty fort. To keep the fort out of enemy hands, 15 brave soldiers stayed on Roanoke. Everyone else sailed off again.

Raleigh's next expedition reached Roanoke the following year, 1587. By now, Raleigh had given up on Roanoke Island, and was planning a new colony farther north. The only reason the new colonists stopped at Roanoke was to pick up the 15 soldiers from the fort.

Except that there were no soldiers to pick up! By the time the new colonists reached Roanoke, all that remained of those 15 soldiers was one human skeleton. At the sight of that skeleton, the new colonists were gladder than ever that they wouldn't have to stay in that dreadful place.

Then came a nasty shock: all of a sudden, the captain of the ships that had brought the colonists announced that they would have to stay after all! When the colonists tried to board ship again, the captain refused to let them. Just what the captain was thinking, no one knows for sure. What is sure is that this cruel captain abandoned 150+ colonists and their governor, John White, on Roanoke Island.

Of course, the trouble between English and native soon started up again. The natives hadn't forgotten their hatred of the English. Even so, things weren't all bad. The day of August 18, 1587 brought good news of the first English child born in America: Governor White's granddaughter, baby **Virginia Dare**.

Roanoke's troubles soon grew bad enough for Governor White to take a bold risk. The colony happened to have a small fishing ship— so small that most people wouldn't dare cross the Atlantic in it. But John White dared. In late 1587, White and a few others set out across the Atlantic in that tiny fishing ship. Somehow, they made it home to England, where White begged Raleigh to send more help to his troubled colony.

Baby Virginia Dare being baptized at Roanoke Colony

Unfortunately, this was a terrible time to beg any Englishman for help. By now, war had broken out between England and Spain. See Chapter 34 for more on the terrifying **Anglo-Spanish War**.

Thanks to the Anglo-Spanish War, White didn't make it back to Roanoke in 1588, nor in 1589. In fact, almost 3 whole years passed before he made it back. Governor John White finally returned to Roanoke Island on August 18, 1590— which just happened to be the 3rd birthday of little Virginia Dare.

Governor John White of Roanoke Colony at the empty fort

If White was hoping to walk in on his granddaughter's birthday party, then he was badly disappointed. When he came to the fort, there was no one there! Not one of the 115+ colonists he'd left behind was anywhere to be seen.

The first place White searched was the fort itself. He noticed that its walls had been strengthened, and its plank houses taken down. Other than that, the only clue White could find was a single word carved on a post: "Croatoan," the name of a nearby island.

Naturally, White wanted to search Croatoan Island as well. But when he tried, bad weather drove him off. And that was the end of it. Neither White nor any other Englishman ever saw any of the Roanoke colonists again.

1590 map of Roanoke Island

So began one of the great mysteries of colonial times: what on Earth happened to the **Lost Colony of Roanoke**?

After all the trouble between English and native, it would be no surprise if the natives killed the colonists. It is also possible that the Spanish killed them, or maybe dragged them off in chains.

But then, why were the houses taken down? The natives had never built anything out of planks before. So why would they bother taking down plank houses?

The answer is only another guess. It may be that the Roanoke colonists took their houses down themselves, to turn the planks into ships. If they did build ships and sail for home, then they might have been lost at sea, just like Sir Humphrey Gilbert. Without new evidence, the world will never know.

The Bard of Avon

The Elizabethan Era was a fun time to be English. Besides all the fascinating news about Francis Drake and Walter Raleigh, there were also the plays of William Shakespeare to enjoy.

William Shakespeare grew up in Stratford-upon-Avon, a town about 100 miles northwest of London. He married a Stratford woman called Anne Hathaway when he was 18 years old. The couple had three children together; but William spent little time with them. The family stayed in Stratford, while William moved to London to work in theater.

Like most theater men, Shakespeare did a little bit of everything, from acting, singing and dancing to putting together costumes. But what he did best was writing plays. In 24 years, from about 1590 – 1613, Shakespeare wrote 37 or more long plays. Most were performed by a theater company which Shakespeare partly owned: the **Lord Chamberlain's Men**, which often played for the queen herself.

Besides plays, Shakespeare also wrote beautiful poetry. Many English teachers consider the works of William Shakespeare to be some of the best ever written in English.

Some Shakespeare plays tell dramatic stories from English history. For example, "The Tragedy of King Richard III" tells how Richard, Duke of Gloucester killed the Princes in the Tower— and how Henry Tudor later killed Richard at the Battle of Bosworth Field (Chapter 15). But historians are careful not to trust Shakespeare too far. Since real life was often too dull for the stage, Shakespeare made up juicy details to add to his history plays.

William Shakespeare (1564 – 1616)

One mark of Shakespeare's greatness is that he left the English language better than he found it. If he needed words that he couldn't find in English, then he simply made them up. In 37 plays, Shakespeare added more than 1700 words to the English language. He also added many well-known English phrases— including "All's well that ends well"; "One fell swoop"; "Brevity is the soul of wit"; "Parting is such sweet sorrow"; "Dead as a doornail"; "For goodness' sake"; "Wild-goose chase"; "Love is blind"; and more.

CHAPTER 34:

The Spanish Armada; the Counter-reformation

The Schmalkaldic War

The last time we read about the Reformation in Germany was in Chapter 29. The **Lutherans** were fighting for freedom of religion; while **Holy Roman Emperor Charles V** was fighting to make all Lutherans Catholic again.

For a while, it looked like Lutherans might win. At the First **Diet** of Speyer, held in 1526, Catholics and Lutherans reached a compromise. Each part of the Holy Roman Empire would follow the religion of the noble who led that part. If a leader was Catholic, then his part of the empire would be Catholic. But if a leader was **Lutheran**, then his part would be Lutheran.

All of that changed three years later. At the Second Diet of Speyer, held in 1529, Charles V took back his compromise. By order of the emperor, all Lutherans must now return to the one true church: the Catholic Church. As for the heretic Martin Luther, all loyal Catholics must hunt him down, arrest him and burn every copy of his books!

Once again, what saved Lutherans from Charles was an attack by Muslims. In that same year of 1529, Sultan Suleiman the Magnificent of the Ottoman Empire laid siege to one of Charles V's most prized possessions: Vienna, Austria (Chapter 20).

Although Suleiman failed to take Vienna, he succeeded in making Charles V nervous. After the **Siege of Vienna**, Charles V wanted every soldier he could get— even Lutheran ones.

Charles knew that if he wanted Lutheran soldiers, then he might have to compromise with the Lutherans again. So he called yet another diet: the **Diet of Augsburg**, held in 1530. Charles didn't want to hear what Lutherans had to say. He only wanted to reach some kind of deal that would make Lutherans willing to fight for him again.

But Lutherans wanted much more from the Diet of Augsburg. They wanted the emperor to hear what they believed, and why they could never go back to the Catholic Church.

> Remember what a **Lutheran** was— any Christian who followed Martin Luther, the first leader of the Protestant Reformation.
> Remember that **Holy Roman Emperor Charles V** was also **King Charles I of Spain**— father to **Philip of Spain**, who married Queen Mary I of England.
> Remember what a **diet** was— a meeting of the leaders of the Holy Roman Empire.

An engraving of Holy Roman Emperor Charles V. This portrait shows signs of the "Habsburg Jaw," a jutting jaw that ran in Charles' family.

Before the Diet of Augsburg, the Lutherans wrote a new statement of faith for Charles to hear. The **Augsburg Confession** listed all the key points of the Lutheran faith, along with all the places where Lutherans thought Catholics were wrong.

Even today, almost 500 years after the Diet of Augsburg, the **Augsburg Confession** is still the main statement of faith for the Lutheran Church.

Most of the Lutherans' complaints were ones we've already read. Lutherans didn't like the Renaissance popes. They also didn't like the Catholic Mass; nor the fact that Catholic priests couldn't marry. Nor did they like monks, nuns, monasteries or nunneries.

Most of all, Lutherans didn't like any church that taught salvation by works. Lutherans believed in salvation by faith, not by works of the Law (Chapter 27).

As always, the Lutherans' ideas came straight from the Bible. For Lutherans also believed in *Sola Scriptura*. They believed that the Bible alone is inspired by God, and that the Sacred Tradition of the Catholic Church isn't inspired at all.

Engraving of a scene from the Diet of Augsburg

Charles V didn't care how much Lutherans loved the Bible. What Charles mainly cared about was authority. He wanted all Germans united under a strong state church, the Catholic Church. Since the Lutherans refused to obey, and Charles refused to compromise, the Diet of Augsburg ended in failure.

Now the Lutherans were in even worse trouble than before. After the Diet of Augsburg, they all knew that Charles V would try to force them back into the Catholic Church someday.

So they tried to protect themselves. In 1531, the Lutherans formed an alliance called the **Schmalkaldic League**. The Lutheran parts of the empire all agreed that if Charles V attacked one of them, then the others would defend that one.

Coat of Arms of Charles I of Spain, Charles V as Holy Roman Emperor

The name **Schmalkaldic League** comes from the town in central Germany where the league was first formed: Schmalkalden.

It took 15 years, but it finally happened. In 1546, Charles V sent a huge army against the Schmalkaldic League. And if arguments about faith could be settled on the battlefield, then the **Schmalkaldic War** would have stamped out the Lutheran faith forever!

The worst battle of this war was the last one: the **Battle of Muhlberg**, fought in April 1547. When this awful battle was over, about half of the Schmalkaldic League's army lay dead. With losses that bad, the league was powerless to resist the emperor any longer. The war was over, and the Lutherans had lost.

Coat of Arms of Charles, Emperor of the Spains, Archduke of Austria, Duke of Burgundy

Unfortunately for Charles V, his big win came too late. By this time, the Lutheran faith had grown far too strong to tear out of German hearts. No matter how Charles tried, the Lutheran parts of the Holy Roman Empire simply wouldn't go back to the Catholic Church. In the end, Charles had to do what he had refused to do back in 1530: he had to compromise with the Lutherans.

Charles' last compromise was the **Peace of Augsburg**, signed in 1555. After 30 years of suffering, the Holy Roman Empire went back to what it had had in 1526. If a leader was Catholic, then his part of the Holy Roman Empire would be Catholic. But if a leader was Lutheran, then his part would be Lutheran— with a few exceptions.

Charles was tired after the Peace of Augsburg. He had good reason to be. After all, he had led two huge empires ever since he was a teenager.

So Charles retired. His German empire went to his brother, who became **Holy Roman Emperor Ferdinand I**. And his Spanish Empire went to his son, who became **King Philip II of Spain**.

> After settling his affairs, Holy Roman Emperor Charles V retired to a clock-filled apartment at a monastery in Yuste, Spain. Bad health ended his life about two years after he retired.
>
> Why clocks? Because Charles had been fascinated with clocks all his life. He loved to take clocks apart, study their mechanisms and then put them back together.
>
> Of course, clocks have changed quite a bit over the years. For example, most clocks of Charles' day didn't have minute hands. Instead, they had one dial to mark the hour, and another to mark the quarter hour. Charles' favorite clocks also had dials to mark the movements of the moon and stars.

> If only the Peace of Augsburg could have ended all the trouble between Catholics and Protestants! Alas, it didn't. From 1618 – 1648, the Holy Roman Empire was torn by one of the ugliest wars ever fought: the Thirty Years' War. See Year Three for more on the terrible Thirty Years' War.

The Anglo-Spanish War

> **"The Low Countries"** is an old name for the low-lying part of Europe that now belongs to three countries: the Netherlands, Belgium and Luxembourg. The Netherlands and Belgium lie just across the North Sea from England.
>
> The people of the Low Countries speak three main languages. **Dutch** is most common in the north, in what is now the Netherlands. **Flemish** is most common in the center, in what is now northern Belgium. And **French** is most common in the south, in what is now southern Belgium.

The Spanish Empire wasn't the only thing King Philip II inherited from his father. He also inherited his father's homeland: the **Low Countries**, also known as the Netherlands.

As we've already read, Philip II was another strong Catholic like his father. Both Charles and Philip were determined to make all countries Catholic again.

By this time, though, the Reformation had taken off in the Low Countries— especially in the north. The Lutheran faith had spread over from Germany; and the Reformed faith of John Calvin had spread over from Switzerland (Chapter 30). Even the Anabaptist faith was fairly strong in the Low Countries. The best-known Anabaptist leader, Menno Simons, came from the Netherlands (Chapter 32).

All these different kinds of Protestants had one thing in common: none of them wanted to be Catholic ever again.

Which is why they started the **Dutch Revolt**. In 1566, the Dutch Protestants of the Low Countries rebelled against King Philip II of Spain. Their brave rebellion would last 80 years, all the way to 1648.

As neighbors to the Dutch, the English couldn't help being dragged into the Dutch Revolt. Whenever Dutch ships got in trouble with the Spanish, they fled to English ports. Each time an English port welcomed a Dutch ship, England drew a little bit closer to war with Spain.

The Dutch Revolt was one of the biggest reasons behind the big war that broke out between England and Spain in 1585: the Anglo-Spanish War.

But the Dutch Revolt wasn't the only reason. Another reason was because English privateers had been robbing the Spanish treasure fleets. As we read in Chapter 33, Elizabeth lied to the Spanish, pretending that her privateers were only pirates. But the Spanish soon stopped believing Elizabeth, if they ever really believed her at all.

Another reason for the Anglo-Spanish War was that Philip II wanted to make England Catholic again. Remember that Philip had once been King of England! As husband to Elizabeth's sister Mary, Philip had done all he could to

Portrait of King Philip II of Spain by Titian

make England Catholic. To Philip's dismay, England had turned Protestant again the moment Mary died. As a Catholic king, Philip considered it his duty to force England back into the Catholic Church.

For her part, Elizabeth considered it her duty to stop Philip. Spain had already conquered much of the New World, and was now trying to conquer the Low Countries. Elizabeth feared that if she did nothing, then Spain might soon conquer England as well.

The main event of the Anglo-Spanish War came in 1588, when Philip launched the Spanish Armada against England.

The Spanish Armada was a huge invasion force. Philip assembled about 130 ships, including 20 or more brand-new warships built just for the occasion. He then

> An **armada** is a fleet of warships.

Portrait of Queen Elizabeth I

loaded his armada with about 8,000 sailors, plus another 18,000 **marines**— sea soldiers who specialized in boarding enemy ships and killing their crews.

"The Spanish Armada Leaving the port of Ferrol" by Oswald Brierly

But that wasn't all. Another 30,000 troops stood waiting for the armada in the Spanish Netherlands. This was the southern section of the Low Countries held by Spain.

These 30,000 troops were the real key to Philip's plans. All the Spanish Armada had to do was hold off the English navy long enough to carry these troops across the English Channel. Once they landed in England, these troops could crush Elizabeth's army and drag down her government. Or so Philip hoped.

Thanks to her spies, Elizabeth knew what Philip had planned, and was ready and waiting for the Spanish Armada. She had closed all her ports— which is why Governor John White couldn't make it back to Roanoke in 1588 (Chapter 33). The Queen of England wanted all English ships to defend their homeland, whether they belonged to the navy or not!

Elizabeth had also built a chain of signal towers along the English Channel, each within sight of the next. The first signalman lit his tower the moment he spotted the Spanish Armada. Then the next tower lit, and the next, until all of England knew that the Spanish had arrived.

After that, all Elizabeth had to do was fight off the Spanish Armada. And it all came down to one sea battle: the **Battle of Gravelines**, fought in late July 1588.

Gravelines was a port in the Spanish Netherlands, just across the North Sea from England. Since the launch back in May, the ships of the armada had been separated by storms. The Spanish admiral was waiting near Gravelines for the slower ships to catch up.

While the Spanish waited, the English attacked. Late one night, the English navy launched several **fire ships** against the Spanish Armada near Gravelines.

A fire ship was an old ship that was loaded with dry wood, set on fire and then aimed at an enemy fleet. Some fire ships were splashed with flammable liquids, such as tar and pitch, to make them burn hotter. Any ship that got rammed by a fire ship was in terrible danger of catching fire itself.

England's fire ships didn't burn many Spanish ships that night. But they did something just as important: they scattered the Spanish Armada.

The next morning, the English navy attacked the scattered armada with everything it had. Once again, the English didn't destroy many ships. But they did destroy several— enough to win the Battle of Gravelines. They also drove the armada north, beyond the Spanish Netherlands.

The army that awaited the Spanish Armada in the Spanish Netherlands was divided into powerful units called *tercios.* Each tercio held up to 3,000 soldiers, including pike-men, swordsmen and musketeers.

The Spanish tercio was the terror of its day, crushing enemy armies from one end of Europe to the other. The English shuddered to think of 10 Spanish tercios on the loose in their homeland.

OFFICERS OF A TERCIO

The English didn't know it yet, but they had just driven the Spanish Armada out of the war.

After the Battle of Gravelines, the Spanish admiral faced a tough choice. By now, his ships were running low on fresh water and food. Ordinarily, he would have stopped at some friendly port for supplies. But now he couldn't. For the English had driven him north of the Spanish Netherlands, where there were no friendly ports. So it was either tackle the English navy again, or head for home.

The admiral chose to head home.

"Defeat of the Spanish Armada" by artist Philip James de Loutherbourg

For the moment, though, the English didn't know the admiral's choice. As far as the English knew, the Spanish Armada might still attack at any moment.

Soon after the Battle of Gravelines, brave Queen Elizabeth delivered the best-known speech of her whole reign. It happened at Tilbury, a port near the mouth of the Thames River. Thousands of English troops stood waiting at Tilbury, still thinking that the Spanish might attack at any moment.

Elizabeth rode out to talk to her troops in person. She wanted them to know that she was with them all the way, no matter what happened. So she said:

> "I am come amongst you… being resolved, in the midst and heat of battle, to live or die amongst you all— to lay down for my God, and for my kingdoms, and for my people, my honor and my blood, even in the dust. I know I have the body of a weak and feeble woman; but I have the heart and stomach of a king— and of a King of England, too!— and think foul scorn that… any prince of Europe should dare to invade the borders of my realm."

Meanwhile, the Spanish Armada was facing a far deadlier enemy than the English navy had turned out to be.

Since the armada couldn't sail south without tackling the English navy, it sailed north. The admiral planned to sail all the way around the British Isles. Only after sailing around Scotland would he turn south, back toward Spain. The armada would pass down the west coast of Ireland, far from the English navy.

The admiral's plan would have worked, if not for the storms.

It so happened that 1588 was one of the stormiest years ever around the British Isles. As the Spanish Armada sailed down the west coast of Ireland, high winds and waves sent ship after ship crashing into the rocks.

The wreck of a Spanish warship off the west coast of Ireland

In the end, only about half of the Spanish Armada ever made it back to Spain! Storms wrecked far more ships, and drowned far more sailors and marines, than the English navy did.

The end of the Spanish Armada didn't mean the end of the Anglo-Spanish War. The Spanish still had the biggest, richest, most powerful empire in all of Europe. No one loss could change that, not even one as big as the armada.

Even so, the defeat of the Spanish Armada was a huge victory for England. Little England had shown that it could stand up to any country in Europe, even mighty Spain. After the armada, the power of England continued to grow; while the power of Spain started to shrink.

The defeat of the Spanish Armada was also a huge victory for Protestants.

To Catholics, the invasion of England had been another crusade— another holy war against the enemies of the Catholic Church. The pope himself had blessed this new crusade. In fact, the pope had promised that all who died fighting it would go straight to heaven. This was the same promise Pope Urban II had made before the First Crusade (Chapter 12). With a promise like that, Catholics felt sure that God would take their side.

Instead, God seemed to have taken the Protestant side! Winds and waves had destroyed far more ships than the English navy had, as King Philip II admitted:

After the defeat of the Spanish Armada, the English struck medals in honor of the **Protestant Wind** that had helped them so much. One Armada medal read *FLAVIT YAHWEH ET DISSIPATI SUNT*— Latin for "God blew with His wind, and they were scattered." "They," of course, were the ships of the Spanish Armada.

"I sent the Armada against men, not God's winds and waves."

The Virgin Queen

By the time England fought off the Spanish Armada, Elizabeth had been queen for 30 years— ever since her sister Mary died back in 1558. In 30 years, many nobles had lined up for their chance to marry Elizabeth. So why had she never married?

One reason was her family history. After all, Elizabeth's own father— King Henry VIII— had beheaded her own mother, Anne Boleyn. Who could trust marriage after something as awful as that?

Even so, Parliament pushed Elizabeth to marry— mainly so that she could have children. The reason was simple. If Elizabeth had children, then all would know who was to be the next king or queen. If she didn't have children, then there might be wars and rebellions to decide. No one wanted any more wars like the Wars of the Roses.

For Parliament's sake, and England's, Elizabeth tried to find a husband. But she could never seem to find the right man.

One of her problems was all the anger between Catholics and Protestants. Too many of the nobles Elizabeth might have chosen were Catholic. For example, she might have chosen some French noble; for both France and England were enemies to Spain. But most French nobles were Catholic— and English Protestants would have been furious if Elizabeth had married a Catholic.

**Portrait of Queen Elizabeth
by Nicholas Hilliard**

Another problem was that whoever married Elizabeth would automatically become King of England. This had already happened to Elizabeth's sister Mary, with terrible results. Few Englishmen wanted another bossy foreign king like Philip of Spain!

These problems explain why Elizabeth decided the way she did. After toying with the idea of marriage for 25 years, Elizabeth finally decided that she would never marry. In a way, Elizabeth said, she was already married— to England and its people! The only way England could stay strong and independent was for the queen to go unmarried all her life. All of the love and service that other women gave to their husbands, Elizabeth gave to her country.

Sir Walter Raleigh named the whole east coast of North America "Virginia" after Elizabeth, England's unwed "Virgin Queen."

Since Elizabeth never married, she left behind no children to take her place. But she did leave behind a cousin.

King James VI of Scotland was the son of Elizabeth's cousin Mary, Queen of Scots (Chapter 32). When Elizabeth died in 1603, cousin James became King of England as well. James held these two titles, among others: **King James VI of Scotland**, and **King James I of England**.

An English **knot garden** is a formal garden with hedges that have been carefully planted, trimmed and colored to look like knotted strands of rope.

The Counter-reformation

We already know what the Reformation was. In 1517, Martin Luther and his friends started complaining that the Catholic Church had gotten away from the Bible. At first, Luther tried to <u>reform</u> the Catholic Church— which is how the <u>Reform</u>ation got its name.

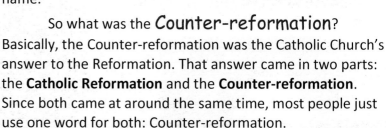

So what was the **Counter-reformation**? Basically, the Counter-reformation was the Catholic Church's answer to the Reformation. That answer came in two parts: the **Catholic Reformation** and the **Counter-reformation**. Since both came at around the same time, most people just use one word for both: Counter-reformation.

Oddly enough, one of the biggest heroes of the Counter-reformation was an author who had helped start the Reformation.

Back in Chapter 27, we read how a Dutch scholar called **Desiderius Erasmus** complained about the Catholic Church. In "Julius Excluded from Heaven," Erasmus criticized

Desiderius Erasmus (1466 – 1536)

the greedy Renaissance popes. And in "In Praise of Folly," Erasmus criticized every kind of churchman, from top to bottom.

But none of that meant that Erasmus wanted to tear down the Catholic Church.

After Luther decided to leave the Catholic Church, he wrote letter after letter to Erasmus— trying to convince the great author that Protestants were right. But Erasmus wrote back:

"Would a stable mind depart from the [Sacred Tradition] handed down by so many men famous for holiness and miracles, depart from the decisions of the Church, and commit our souls to the faith of someone like you who has sprung up just now with a few followers— even though the leading men of your flock do not agree, either with you or among themselves?"

In other words, Erasmus thought that Luther was crazy for leaving the Catholic Church. No loyal Catholic could ever set aside Sacred Tradition, the way Luther had. To do so would be to mock the whole history of the Church— as if all the saints had been liars, and none of their miracles had ever really happened. No one who believed in the saints could ever leave the Catholic Church, no matter how bad it got.

Instead of leaving, people like Erasmus worked to make the Catholic Church better. This was the goal of the **Catholic Reformation**: to fix some problems that had crept into the Catholic Church over the years.

Some reformers worked to fix the schools that trained Catholic priests. Before the Catholic Reformation, a lot of priests knew very little about the Bible. The preaching of some priests sounded more like superstition than Christian faith. Reformers wanted better Bible training for priests.

Other reformers worked to fix the way the Church handed out important jobs. The Renaissance popes had a bad habit of handing out all the best Church jobs to their nephews, or to the highest bidder. Reformers wanted Church jobs to go to the people who were best for those jobs.

Still other reformers worked to fix monasteries. Some monks had grown just as greedy as the Renaissance popes. Reformers wanted monks to live more like Anthony of Thebes lived (Chapter 3).

The **Counter-reformation** was something else again. Some Catholics felt that the Church's problems had nothing to do with the Catholic Church. The real problem was Protestant heretics like Martin Luther! Loyal Catholics would never believe what Luther said— that Sacred Tradition went against the Bible. When Luther criticized Sacred Tradition, loyal Catholics only believed in it all the more.

This is part of what the Council of Trent decided.

In 1545, Pope Paul III called a Catholic council to answer all the questions raised by the Protestant Reformation. Some Protestants had high hopes for the Council of Trent. After all Protestants had said and written about the Bible, they expected the council to admit that at least a little bit of Sacred Tradition might be wrong.

A meeting of the Council of Trent (1545 – 1563)

Ignatius of Loyola, founder of the Jesuits

JESUIT EMBLEM: IESUS HUMILIS SOCIETAS - Humble Society of Jesus

Instead, the council said that Sacred Tradition was never wrong! In fact, the council said, Sacred Tradition was just as inspired as the Bible— just as much a part of what God wanted all Christians to believe.

Furthermore, the council said, Protestants had no right to use the Bible against the Catholic Church. As the one true Church of God, the Catholic Church alone had the right to decide how the Bible should be interpreted.

The **Society of Jesus**, also called the **Jesuits**, had the same attitude as the Council of Trent.

The Society of Jesus was a Catholic organization founded by **Ignatius of Loyola** in 1534. The Jesuits were the Catholic knights of the Counter-reformation. They fought to defend the Catholic faith, and to spread that faith around the world.

The Jesuits became the leading Catholic missionaries of colonial times. Whenever a Catholic empire moved into a new country, the Jesuits were some of the first ones there. Jesuits built missions in the Americas, India, the Far East— wherever Catholics went.

Catholic Bibles contain a section that Protestant Bibles do not. The **Apocrypha** is a set of books that fall between the Old Testament and the New. Some books of the Apocrypha add to Old Testament stories; while others tell different stories of their own.

The main reason Protestant Bibles don't include the Apocrypha is because these books come from different sources than the Old Testament. The books of the Apocrypha seem to be much newer than the books of the Old Testament. This may mean that other writers added them to the Old Testament long after the ancient books were first written.

A scene from the Book of Maccabees, part of the Apocrypha

The little round cap that so many Catholic clergymen wear is called a **zucchetto.**

The first zucchettos were probably designed to warm their wearers' heads. Many monks wore their hair in the **tonsure**, which meant that they shaved the tops of their heads. For tonsured monks who spent their days in cold monasteries, the zucchetto added a welcome bit of warmth.

Map Helps

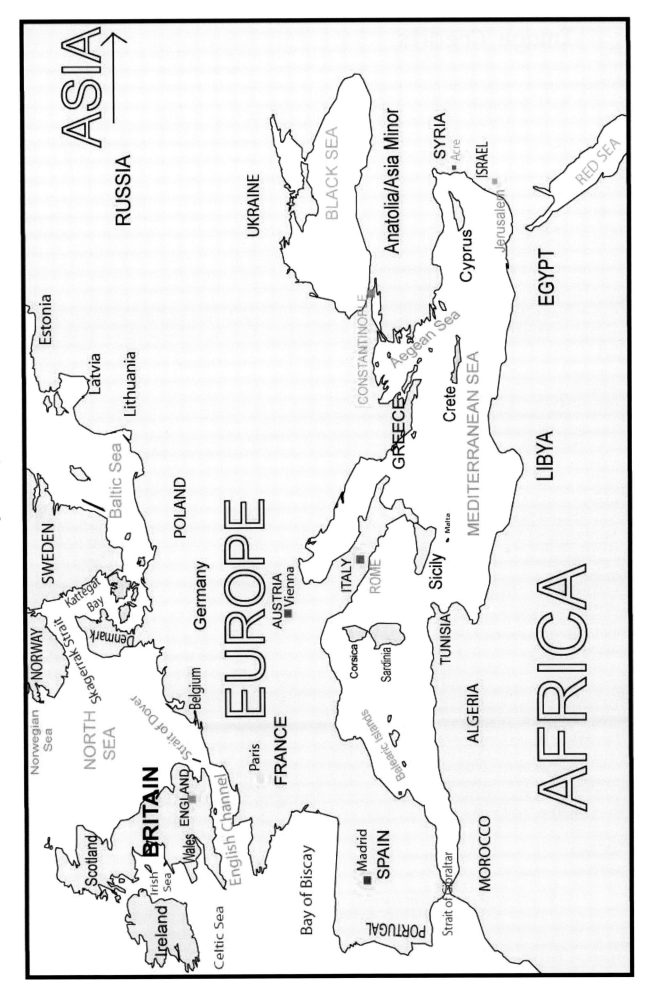

Image Credits

All images are in the public domain, except as
follows.

Prologue
1.   Medieval scene: Creative Commons by unknown

Chapter 1
1.   Galea: Creative Commons by unknown
2.   Pugio: Creative Commons by unknown
3.   Gladius: Creative Commons by unknown
4.   Pilum: Creative Commons by unknown
5.   Scutum: Creative Commons by unknown
6.   Papal coat of arms: Creative Commons by Odejea

Chapter 2
1.   Hauberk: Creative Commons by Urban
2.   Council of Nicaea: Creative Commons by Jjensen

Chapter 3
1.   Europe Map: Creative Commons by unknown
2.   Shroud of Turin: Creative Commons by unknown
3.   Peter's chains: Creative Commons by Raja Patnaik
4.   Thomas Becket casket: Creative Commons by unknown
5.   Catacomb: Creative Commons by Dnalor 01
6.   St. Catherine's Monastery: Creative Commons by Berthold
     Werner

Chapter 4
1.   Black Sea: Creative Commons by NormanEinstein
2.   Balkans: Creative Commons by ArnoldPlaton
3.   Justinian: Creative Commons by Petar Milosevic
4.   Justinian Coin: Creative Commons by Uploadalt
5.   Hagia Sophia exterior: Creative Commons by Andrey
     Nikolaev
6.   Hagia Sophia interior: Creative Commons by Steve Evans
7.   Mosaic: Creative Commons by Casalmaggiore Provincia
8.   Byzantine Empire map: Creative Commons by unknown
9.   Iron Crown of Lombardy: Creative Commons by James
     Steakley
10. Coptic Cross: Creative Commons by Sagredo

Chapter 5
1.   Arabian Peninsula map: Creative Commons by unknown
2.   Kaaba: Creative Commons by Tab59
3.   Quba Mosque: Creative Commons by Abdelrhman 1990
4.   Dome of the Rock: Creative Commons by David Baum
5.   Khamsa: Creative Commons by Bluewind
6.   Quran: Creative Commons by Hooperag
7.   Iconostasis: Creative Commons by Fingalo
8.   Icon wall: Creative Commons by unknown

Chapter 6
1.   Rhine River: Creative Commons by Felix Koenig
2.   King Chlodio: Creative Commons by Rinaldum
3.   Notre Dame: Creative Commons by DXR
4.   Gargoyles on Notre Dame: Creative Commons by Milvus
5.   Gargoyle atop Notre Dame: Creative Commons by Cornellier

Chapter 7
1.   Map Islamic Empire: Creative Commons by Mohammad adil

2.   Umayyad Mosque: Creative Commons by Roberta F.
3.   Strait of Gibraltar: Creative Commons by Xemenendura
4.   Rock of Gibraltar: Creative Commons by Joe Vinent
5.   Clothar coin: Creative Commons by unknown
6.   Chocolate fish: Creative Commons by D. O'Neil

Chapter 8
1.   Seax: Creative Commons by Bullenwachter
2.   Longhouse: Creative Commons by unknown
3.   Eric the Red Statue: Creative Commons by Aleph78

Chapter 9
1.   White Cliffs of Dover: Creative Commons by Immanuel Giel
2.   King Alfred's Tower: Creative Commons by Jurgen Matern
3.   Westminster Abbey: Creative Commons by unknown

Chapter 10
1.   New Forest: Creative Commons by Jim Champion

Chapter 11
1.   Baltic Sea Map: Creative Commons by NormanEinstein
2.   Germania map: Creative Commons by Jani Niemenmaa
3.   Adelaide stained glass: Creative Commons by Kaho Mitsuki
4.   Otto and Adelaide: Creative Commons by Kolossos
5.   Otto statue: Creative Commons by Ajepbah
6.   Khokhloma: Creative Commons by Dmfff
7.   St. Basil's Cathedral: Creative Commons by Paramecium

Chapter 12
1.   Middle East map: Creative Commons by Cacahuate
2.   Richard the Lionheart Coat of Arms: Creative Commons by
     Sodacan

Chapter 13
1.   Chateau Gaillard: Creative Commons by Urban
2.   King John seal: Creative Commons by W.C. Prime

Chapter 14
1.   Caernarvon Castle: Creative Commons by unknown
2.   King Edward's Chair: Creative Commons by Kjetil Bjornsrud
3.   Wallace Monument: Creative Commons by Finlay McWalter
4.   Black Death in Florence: Creative Commons by
     wellcomeimages.org
5.   Royal arms of Lancaster: Creative Commons by Sodacan
6.   Joan of Arc coat of arms: Creative Commons by Darkbob
7.   Joan of Arc statue: Creative Commons by Intersofia
8.   Solstice: Creative Commons by Blueshade

Chapter 15
1.   Coat of arms of Richard of York: Creative Commons by
     Sodacan
2.   Red Rose of Lancaster: Creative Commons by Sodacan
3.   White Rose of York: Creative Commons by Sodacan
4.   Tudor Rose: Creative Commons by Sodacan
5.   Tower of London: Creative Commons by Bernard Gagnon
6.   Gargoyle: Art Libre by Raminagrobis

Chapter 16
1.   Indo-Gangetic Plain Map: Art Creative Commons by Jeroen
2.   Hindu trinity: Creative Commons by Calvinkrishy
3.   Snakes and Ladders: Creative Commons by Nomu420
4.   Gupta coin: Creative Commons by PHGCOM
5.   Ajanta Caves: Creative Commons by Soman
6.   Buddha and bodhisattvas: Creative Commons by
     Karthikeyan.pandian

Index